Understanding the Modern Russian Police

Understanding the Modern Russian Police

Olga B. Semukhina
K. Michael Reynolds

CRC Press
Taylor & Francis Group
Boca Raton London New York

CRC Press is an imprint of the
Taylor & Francis Group, an **informa** business

CRC Press
Taylor & Francis Group
6000 Broken Sound Parkway NW, Suite 300
Boca Raton, FL 33487-2742

First issued in paperback 2019

ISBN-13: 978-1-4398-0348-6 (hbk)
ISBN-13: 978-0-367-87879-5 (pbk)

Library of Congress Cataloging-in-Publication Data

Semukhina, Olga B. B.
Understanding the modern Russian police / Olga B.B. Semukhina and Kenneth Michael Reynolds.
pages cm
Includes bibliographical references and index.
ISBN 978-1-4398-0348-6
1. Police--Russia (Federation)--History. 2. Police--Russia--History. I. Reynolds, Kenneth Michael. II. Title.

HV8227.2.A2S46 2013
363.20947--dc23 2012043466

Visit the Taylor & Francis Web site at
http://www.taylorandfrancis.com

and the CRC Press Web site at
http://www.crcpress.com

Contents

Preface

Understanding the Modern Russian Police represents the culmination of 10 years of research focused on the Russian police. It is a product of an ongoing and fruitful partnership with the Volgograd Academy of Russian Internal Affairs Ministry (VA MVD) and the Volgograd branch of the Russian Presidential Academy of National Economy and Public Administration (VAPA). The research would not have been possible without the support of leadership from the Volgograd Academy: Generals Dr. Boris Smagorinskyi and Dr. Vladimir Tretyakov as well as Dr. Oleg Tyumentsev of VAPA.

The book encompasses the efforts of many great researchers from Russia such as Nicolai Demidov and Anatoly Nickonov. The field research of this study was generously supported by grants from the Soros Foundation, the Fulbright Program, Marquette University, the University of Central Florida, and the U.S. Department of State. Also, the authors of this book are extremely grateful to Ann Roberston, Vladimir Sergevnin, and Mark Lanier for their valuable comments and reviews.

Introduction

The purpose of this book is to provide a timely and comprehensive analysis of the historical development, functions, and contemporary challenges faced by the modern Russian police, who are part of the Ministry of Internal Affairs of the Russian Federation (MVD). Although there is substantial historical information about the Russian police related to its history, sociological factors, and legal structure, there is no current single body of work that serves to integrate and compile the organization's historical and developmental origins, organizational dynamics, and current conditions.* The most recent comprehensive work in this area was published in 1996 and primarily focuses on the Soviet and early post-Soviet police development (Shelley,

* See Beck and Robertson, 2009a, 2009b; Berman, 1950, 1966; Butler, 2003; Clarke, 1993; Conquest, 1968b; Curfman, 1997; Daly, 1998; Favarel-Garrigues, 2011; Gilinskiy, 2000, 2007; Handelman, 1995; Hingley, 1971; Knight, 1988; Kucherov, 1970; Lapenna, 1968; Lavroff, 1963; Matthews, 1993; Orlovsky, 1981; Robertson, 2004; Shelley, 1992, 1995, 2000; Solomon, 1987, 1992, 1996, 2005b; Squire, 1968; Terrill, 1989; Uidriks and Reenen, 2003, 2005; Volkov, 2002; Waller, 2004; Waxmonsky, 1982; Weiler, 2004; Weissman, 1985; Wolin and Slusser, 1957; Zuckerman, 1996.

1996). Perhaps as important, most of the materials about the modern Russian police are only available in the Russian language. One intention of this book is that, with the inclusion of a large body of literature in Russian, the English-speaking reader will have access to a richer and more timely understanding of the historical, political, and organizational dynamics that have impacted the police for the past two centuries.

In addition to providing substantial new information from original Russian language sources, it became clear, during the decade of our research related to the Russian police, that to fully understand the modern police, it was necessary to have a contextual understanding of the institution's origins. The current police organization has interesting linkages to early nineteenth-century Russian empire characteristics and, of course, was substantially impacted by the 1917 October Revolution and the subsequent USSR (Union of Soviet Socialist Republics) period. Until there is a basic understanding of this history and context, it is challenging to fully appreciate the contemporary challenges faced by the police. Also, because the police are a major component of the broader society, without a basic framework to understand the public reaction to the police, it is difficult to appreciate the influences and interactions that result.

Two main areas are examined in this book. First, the institutional development of the MVD is examined. Arguably, it is one of the most important executive agencies of Russia. The book traces major institutional changes that have occurred within the MVD during the past 200 years. The changes reflect responses to major social change in the context of both the socioeconomic and political conditions in Russia. The second area of concentration is the development of complex public–police relationships during the past 200 years. Because the MVD is one of the most powerful government institutions, the evolution of public–police relations during the periods of change is an important topic and one that exemplifies the general public attitude of Russian citizens about their government.

Understanding the Modern Russian Police is based on the well-documented notion of the state police nexus. In the classical theory of the Weberian State, the police are understood as one of the main government instruments that has a virtual monopoly of legitimate coercion (Loader and Walker, 2001; Weber, 1948). Theories of police studies consistently agree that the nature of police institutions inherently depends on the development of the prevailing government political system (Hinton and Newburn, 2009; Pino and Wiatrowski, 2006; Ryan, 2011).

Many police systems evolved from the personal guard of the country's ruler, the king or other politicians (Haberfeld and Cerrah, 2008). The primary goal of the early police was never to protect the public, but instead the safety and security of the ruler and to maintain the status quo of the extant political system (Haberfeld, 2002). This is especially true for the continental model of policing; Russia is a part of this system. The continental police model developed in the context of a centralized monarchical system of government within the traditions of "benevolent paternalism" (Mawby, 1990). The majority of continental police systems (e.g., France, Germany) slowly evolved into democratic institutions as the societies transformed into democracies. This process was facilitated by the maturation of civil society that demanded police accountability and transparency (Mawby, 1990).

The modern systems of democratic police are far from ideal. As the agency of social control, they continue to be inherently coercive and militaristic (Haberfeld, 2002). This creates a continuous tension between the values of a democratic society and effective crime control (Haberfeld and Cerrah, 2008). The relationships between modern police systems and the state became complex as new private agents entered the security market and the development of new service-oriented policing (Jones, Newburn, and Smith, 1996; Loader and Walker, 2001; Morgan and Newburn, 1997).

The case of the Russian police is unique since its development from an early continental system was interrupted by the emergence of a Soviet regime (Mawby, 1990). It is clear that understanding the modern Russian police can be done only through the careful analysis of its government's development from monarchy to the Soviet regime followed by the post-Soviet (emerging democracy) form.

That is why a major portion of this book is devoted to the historical development of the Russian police beginning in 1802. The overview is intended to provide the contextual framework that is necessary and helpful in order to fully understand the contemporary issues and challenges that face the modern Russian police. Most of the current issues stem from this historical development and subsequent evolution. Despite major differences in the historical political systems, Tsarist, Soviet, and the post-Soviet police share unprecedented similarities in structure, function, and major problems. Historic parallels also are apparent in the public policy responses to increasing crime rates and various institutional reforms aimed at improving police performance.

The first chapter examines the Tsarist police evolution that witnessed the creation of the MVD in the year 1802 and concludes with the 1917 October Revolution. The historical review demonstrates that the MVD was initially a bureaucratic centralized hierarchal institution that possessed omnipotent authority in the spheres of law enforcement and administrative regulation. As the societal demands for effective policing escalated, the Tsarist government often conducted MVD "reforms." However, the reforms primarily focused on increasing the number of personnel, the creation of new MVD agencies, and the expansion of administrative control authority. The public–police relationships in Tsarist Russia were complex. Whereas the overwhelming control by the police was often criticized, it also was accepted as a societal norm when the monarchical ideology was strong and socioeconomic conditions were stable.

In Chapter 2, the Soviet era is examined from the 1917 October Revolution until Stalin's death in 1953. This Soviet period was one the most violent periods in the country's history that involved the Russian police. Because the regular police were subservient to the political police, they frequently participated in violent government-led repressions against different population groups. In this chapter, it is clear that despite drastic changes in both the ideology and socioeconomic conditions, the Soviet police (abbreviated as the NKVD, MVD, or MGB at different time periods) maintained a surprising resemblance to the Tsarist police. During most of this period, the early Soviet police were organized in a hierarchical centralized form with various responsibilities and with a wide range of almost limitless power. Unlike the Tsarist police structure, Soviet police enforcement was proactive. The police were used not only to solve crime, but also to control the homeless, delinquents, drunkenness, and other antisocial behaviors. The police were feared by the peasants, and other groups, for their reputation and participation in the political repressions; however, the factory workers and other active members of the new Socialist society supported the organization.

Chapter 3 examines the Khrushchev and Brezhnev periods. It is during this time that the Soviet police matured into a professionally educated and well-equipped law enforcement system. It continued the proactive tradition of fighting hooligans, delinquents, and "social parasites." However, nepotism emerged during this period along with corruption and the practice of altering the statistical performance reports to meet, or exceed, required levels. Most historians agree that, during this period, the Soviet police were effective in maintaining public order and solving routine crimes, but much less successful with white collar crimes, such as embezzlements, committed by state property managers. The high-ranking members of the Communist Party (*nomenklatura*) frequently interfered with investigations of corruption due to the fact that members of the *nomenklatura* and their families committed many of these crimes. Information related to serious offenses and white-collar crimes was concealed by the state-controlled media to maintain a positive image of the Soviet police. Consequently, during this period, the Soviet police enjoyed significant public support from all societal groups.

Chapter 4 examines the transformational period of police development that begins with Gorbachev's *perestroika* and concludes with the first term of President Putin in 2008. This period of transformation had mixed results for the police. On one hand, the police were freed from Communist indoctrination while being restructured to address the modern issues of an emerging post-Soviet society. On the other hand, during this period of transformation, organized crime became deeply intertwined with the police, causing unprecedented levels of corruption, police violence, and abuse of power. The crime rates continued to rise and the rate of solved crimes remained low. The hierarchal, militarized structure inherited from the Soviet period remained unchanged, and no effective control mechanism or public accountability was created to replace the Party's control. The cases of nepotism and police corruption that were concealed during Brezhnev's era became highly visible during *perestroika*. The media was no longer government controlled and depicted a new image of the post-Soviet police. Officers were often shown as dishonest, corrupt, violent, unable to solve crimes, and concerned primarily with personal gain. As a result, public support for the police declined drastically.

In Chapter 5, a detailed analysis is provided about the structure, authority, and workforce of the modern Russian police. During the Soviet Union era, detailed information about the police was considered a state secret. Even though this is no longer the case, it is still very difficult to obtain specific details on the structure and authority of the police. This is especially true in literature in English. The information is scattered among various laws and regulations and many of these are only available in specialized databases. To examine the detailed structure of the modern Russian police, more than 200 federal laws and decrees issued by the president were analyzed along with other bodies of government and the Minister of Internal Affairs. Seventy-five websites of specific police units were examined in order to explore the presence of regional differences. The findings of this analysis are presented in eight diagrams in this chapter. They include four major levels of the Russian police (central, district, regional, and circuit) and two special subunits of police (traffic and interior troops).

A significant part of Chapter 5 is devoted to the broad authorities of the contemporary police. Following the traditional division of authority, nine major areas of police responsibilities are examined:

1. Operative-search authorities (undercover police work)
2. Investigative authority (investigation of serious crimes)
3. Inquiry authority (investigation of minor crimes and first responses at the crime scene)
4. Authority related to administrative violations
5. Authorities to protect public order
6. Authorities in the area of juvenile delinquency
7. Agencies with traffic control authority
8. Authorities in the area of licensing (firearms and private detectives)
9. Activities of the interior affairs agencies (agencies of federal migration service) in the areas of passport control and registration of citizens' movement

As with the organizational structure, information concerning the considerable authority of the police is only available in a multitude of legal documents. Another serious obstacle that is addressed in this chapter is the inherent confusion of the relevant terminology. Many terms used in the legal documents (e.g., *operative search activities*) have unique meanings and are difficult to understand. Here, it is intended to define and clarify the meaning for the English-speaking reader and provide an explanation in lay terms. The scope of the authority of law enforcement also is discussed as related to the police structure that is presented in the diagrams earlier in the chapter.

In Chapter 5, problems associated with the contemporary police workforce are discussed including training, recruitment, job assessment, and gender issues. The information was obtained from the analysis of legal documentation, a review of existing Russian police university website curricula, and statistical information from the Ministry of Internal Affairs website.

The modern Russian police remain extremely centralized and are a hierarchically structured agency. The structure is highly formalized with a large management bureaucracy consisting of numerous personnel. The agency's authorities are vast and include functions that in many countries are performed by other government agencies or private businesses. The system of recruitment and job assessment is inadequate because the agency is unable to retain many of the qualified MVD staff. The police educational institutions are often used by applicants to obtain a free legal education without any intention of serving in the system. The reliance on quantitative job assessment indices does not promote effective performance and facilitates the altering of statistics and abuse of power at the officer level.

Chapter 6 examines the public–police relationships that exist today in Russia, including the areas of public trust, and satisfaction with police, and public–police cooperation. Until *perestroika*, public attitudes about the police were considered a state secret, but now this information is publicly available. This chapter's analysis is based on empirical data obtained by several leading Russian survey organizations, such as WCIOM (All-Russian Center for Research of Public Opinion), FOM (Fund of Public Opinion), Levada Center (named after the famous sociologist Yuri Levada), and ROMIR (Russian Public Opinion and Research of Market). Most of these organizations conduct national representative studies, but the results are only available in Russian and are located on their websites. In this chapter, the official statistical crime data that are provided by the Russian State Committee on Statistics, along with information extracted from the Ministry of Internal Affairs related to police performance, are discussed. Data that have been reported (published and unpublished) and collected by various Russian researchers from the Volgograd region during the period from 1997 to 2010 also is discussed here. The variety of data sources is intended to provide a comprehensive and timely analysis of public–police relations in Russia. The relationship between the media and police is discussed here as well. The discussion evolves from four major case studies and the examination of more than 100 articles published by the leading Russian newspapers.

Chapter 6 reinforces the findings most related to the strained public–police relationship that exists in Russia today. Since the Soviet Union's collapse, citizens have demonstrated high levels of public distrust and dissatisfaction with police. Despite the continuous reforms attempted by Yeltsin, Putin, and Medvedev, a majority of Russians do not see improvements in police work. The continued trend of pervasive public distrust and dissatisfaction with the police is consistent with statistics about the fear of crime, public concerns with safety, and levels of victimization in the past 20 years. The distrust and dissatisfaction are the main causes of poor public–police cooperation in Russia. Many Russians prefer to avoid the police even after becoming a crime victim. Law-abiding citizens fear the police. Officers themselves are often dissatisfied with their own performance, but assign blame to poor funding. Respondents identify the lack of accountability and corruption as the leading reasons for distrusting the police. The media remains one of the main sources of public information on police; however, the law enforcement bodies do not have an effective method of dealing with the media. Police often prefer to simply suppress the information instead of building a constructive dialog with the media. The results are that the media often uses unsupported and mostly unfavorable rumors related to the coverage of crime events and police performance. The process has intensified recently due to social media access.

Corruption and abuse of power are leading issues of the modern Russian police; therefore, Chapter 7 is focused primarily in these areas. The chapter is built from a combination of sources including various attitude surveys examining the experiences and views of corruption. Reports by Amnesty International and Human Rights Watch (among others) are discussed along with a legal analysis of practices by the European Court of Human Rights (ECHR). Then an analysis of recently implemented Russian anticorruption legislation is presented. As in Chapter 6, the survey data are obtained from leading Russian organizations, such as FOM, WCIOM, ROMIR, and the Levada Center; the Russian literature; and unpublished original data collected in the Volgograd region of Russia. Information from several leading human rights advocacy groups, such as The Committee against Torture, the Public Verdict, Memorial, and the Moscow Helsinki Group also were utilized in our analysis. The chapter includes information from the Russian Supreme Court related to cases of bribery, physical abuse, and pretrial detention.

Most Russians consider the police extremely corrupt and prone to abuse of power. Yet these views are not necessarily based on personal experience with corruption. Chapter 7 addresses the major forms of police corruption that include physical abuse, torture, bribery, and other "illegal income activities," and abuse of discretionary powers. Torture and physical abuse are often combined with arbitrary detention and are used to solicit forced confessions or misappropriation of valuables. The ECHR has stated that Russian legal remedies for torture and abuse victims are mainly ineffective. A significant amount of money is circulated through the bribery markets. There are estimates that the total amount from bribes is equivalent to the entire annual budget of the MVD. The most dangerous form of police corruption involves high-order corruption where high-ranking police officials are entangled with organized crime groups. In Russia, this practice is known as "roofing" or providing a set of services by police to cover up criminal activities of certain crime groups.

The recent anticorruption police reforms are detailed here as well. These reforms include the disclosure of all income for high-ranked police officers, new detailed regulations for police service delivery, increased liability for bribery, and changes in crime reporting and performance statistics. It appears the reforms have been more or less ineffective and most citizens agree. To effectively address the systemic corruption, more transparency related to major police decisions is needed along with the uniform prosecution of all known abuse and bribery cases. An overall increase in public accountability is necessary.

The conclusion of this book is focused on the 2011 police system reforms known as the "2011 Police Reform of Medvedev." The potential for the new reforms to improve all the elements of the police system is discussed. Alternative policies are explored that could be beneficial and improve police performance and the public image. The book concludes with some predictions on the future of the Russian police and its potential reforms.

About the Authors

Olga B. Semukhina is an assistant professor of criminology and law studies at Marquette University. Dr. Semukhina holds a law degree from Tomsk State University and Master of Science degree in criminal justice from the University of Central Florida (UCF). She defended her SJD dissertation on international standards and comparative criminal procedure at Tomsk State University in 2002. In 2007, Dr. Semukhina defended her PhD dissertation on the rule of law and comparative court process at UCF. Dr. Semukhina is also a former defense attorney in Russia and a former assistant professor of criminal law and procedure at Tomsk State University. Dr. Semukhina received multiple grants from Ford and the Soros Foundation, the Open Society Institute, the Civil Education Project, the IREX and the Bureau of Democracy, Human Rights and Labor (U.S. State Department) to conduct research and sustain the development of legal services in Russia. Together with Dr. Reynolds, Olga Semukhina participated in a number of projects examining police corruption and misconduct in Russia.

K. Michael Reynolds joined the faculty at the University of Central Florida in 1997. He was a law enforcement practitioner for twelve years prior to entering academia. For more than a decade, he has enjoyed productive partnerships with numerous Russian colleagues in Volgograd (formerly Stalingrad) and Moscow. He also participated in educational programs on several occasions in Tbilisi, Georgia, at the International Black Sea University. Dr. Reynolds received a long-term Fulbright award in 2007 and was hosted by the Volgograd Academy of the MVD of the Russian Federation where he was in-residence for six months. There he taught crime analysis courses utilizing GIS for crime analysis and conducted empirical research along with Dr. Semukhina. They focused on Russian police satisfaction and issues related to professional integrity. This decade-long partnership with numerous Russian collaborators provided a framework to secure a U.S. Department of State grant to promote civil society and address human rights issues in Southern Russia. Throughout their work in Russia, they received continual assistance from their dedicated foreign colleagues and also developed enduring friendships and sustainable research projects. Dr. Reynolds had the opportunity to invite numerous Russian scholars, practitioners and students to visit UCF in Orlando. Numerous research articles concerning the various challenges faced by the Russian police have been published in collaboration with Dr.

Semukhina, Dr. Reynolds was also a cofounder of a state-wide law enforcement information sharing system in Florida that has expanded to accommodate more than 4,000 users per day. The information sharing project has produced substantial results and removed barriers to the intelligence-led policing model.

List of Figures

List of Tables

I

Evolution of the Russian Police: From the Imperial Russian police to a post-Soviet Russian militia

There is probably no country in the world
where the police power occupies a wilder field,
plays a more important part or touches the private personal life
of the citizen at more points than it does in Russia

(KENNAN, 1889)

Russian Police Prior to the October Revolution of 1917

1

1.1 Creation of the Ministry of Interior Affairs and Subsequent Emergence of a Police Bureaucracy during the Reign of Alexander I and Nicolas I: 1801–1855

1.1.1 Early Development of the Ministry of Interior Affairs under the Reign of Alexander I

On September 8, 1802, the Russian Emperor Alexander I issued a Manifesto that established eight central ministries of executive power, including the Ministry of Internal Affairs (MVD) (Kaiser and Marker, 1994). Numerous historians noted this document instituted the Russian police bureaucracy and concurrent development of the Russian *politseistaat* (police state) (Fastov, 2005; Rybnikov and Aleksushin, 2008; Yaney, 1973). The new government institutional ministers were personally appointed by the emperor and ordered to consult with each other prior to reporting to him (Yaney, 1973). The result was the creation of an unofficial, and later official, "committee of ministers" (later known as the "state council") that met regularly and was the only consultative agency to the emperor other than the Senate. Both played an important role in the political life of the Russian Empire throughout the entire nineteenth century.

Initially, the creation of the eight ministries in 1802 was aimed at simply streamlining the executive apparatus and providing auxiliary functional offices for government operations. The ministries were created to enforce personal responsibility and executive discipline in the Empire's government (Gordon et al., 1911). However, it became known as a newly created form of administration in Russia. The professional bureaucratic government was no longer organized by the regional principle, but instead used a division of labor based on functionality. This is especially true when talking about the function of the local Russian police.[1]

The MVD replaced the collegial structure of the police organization created by Peter the Great, which was developed in part by Catherine the Great and Paul I during the eighteenth century. During his reign, Peter the Great created nine colleges that were modeled after the Swedish administration of government (Fastov, 2005). These government institutions were planned as collegial offices of executive power organized by the main government areas.

Police function was not listed as a separate area of public administration, but instead was included in the Justice College. Despite their centralization and functional division, colleges did not have any local institutions and their main goal was to assist the tsar in administration of his power and policy development (Yaney, 1973). The only local police agency created by Peter the Great was the Police Chancery of St. Petersburg. It was established in 1715 to maintain public order in the Russian capital and consisted of soldiers and other military personnel (Mulukaev, Malygin, and Epifanov, 2005).[2]

The major functions of local police prior to 1775 were relegated to the governors and their local agents (*voevody*). Their responsibilities regarding policing were extremely diffused, plus there was a lack of clearly defined lines of subordination. This allowed both the governor and the *voevody* to abuse their power as long as they complied with the fiscal demands of the tsar and avoided massive civil disturbances (Le Donne, 1970). Policing functions were often performed by military personnel (garrison troop subdivisions) due to the lack of manpower. The lack of manpower was especially problematic in the remote borderline provinces of the Russian Empire (Gonyukhov and Gorobtsov, 2002).

Catherine the Great reformed the local administration and, for the first time, provided local police with some structure and articulated authority. In 1775, she created a two-tier system of local administration: the entire territory of the country was split into 26 provinces consisting of the districts (*uezd*) and towns. The organization of (*uezd)* police was very simple. It was comprised of one land captain (*kapitan-ispravnik*), two elected noble assessors, and two peasant assessors.[3] Together they constituted the lower land court (*nizhnii zemskii sud*). Despite its name, the lower land court was mainly a police institution at the district level that also performed some minor judicial functions (Yaney, 1973).

Local police administration in the towns and cities was more complex and varied by city size. The policies were outlined in the Decree (*Ustav*) of Public Order and Police adopted by Catherine the Great in 1782 in reaction to the Pugachev riot.[4] The smallest administrative unit within the city was a ward administered by the supervisor (*nadziratel*) and his assistant (*poruchik*) (Le Donne, 1970). Wards were grouped into the city districts led by the inspectors (*pristav*) and served by two assistants (*gradskie serzhanty*) who were required to reside within the district's territory (Rybnikov and Aleksushin, 2008).

The highest police officer (*gorodnichii)* was aided by the city police board (*uprava*) together with the inspectors from the city districts and other staff (Sichinskii, 2002). The police officers in both rural districts (*uezds)* and cities were mainly appointed with the consent or the advice of the governor (Yaney,

1973). Land captains were elected by the assembly of local gentry (landlords) with the consent of the governor.

The level of police organizational complexity between cities and rural areas initially appears surprising. However, there is a simple answer. While the cities in the Russian Empire were inhabited by a number of different social groups, many of whom were free and with the ability to own private property,[5] the countryside was primarily populated by privately owned serfs that were not free and were bonded to their assigned estate (Mulukaev, Malygin, and Epifanov, 2005). The serfs could not own property, participate in contractual relations, marry, or be a party in court. The landlord (*pomeschik)* (the noblemen or the appointed manager) had the full control and the legal authority to maintain public order within the boundaries of each estate and performed both judicial and policing functions for offenses against the landlord (Waldron, 2007). To maintain daily order, the community of peasants or serfs provided elected or appointed elders for each 100 (*sotskie*) and 1,000 (*tysyachnye*) serfs. They would supervise the daily life of the community that was governed by the customary law (Confino, 1985).

Because the peasant community had mutual responsibility for all members, the police officials would usually rely on the communities to police themselves. When the land captain had to investigate a serious crime, he would expect the community and the elders to search for and give up the person who committed the wrongdoing (Sichinskii, 2002). The self-policing and the landlord's absolute power kept the rural police mostly free of the daily public order maintenance. Police officials were used primarily to investigate serious crimes against the tsar and to protect the landlords in cases of peasant disturbances and riots (Yaney, 1973).

The creation of the MVD in 1802 changed the organization of police administration in Russia, but the change was rather gradual (Torke, 1971). From the moment of its creation in 1802, the MVD was charged with an enormous array of poorly defined tasks. Overall, the MVD was responsible for national well being, maintaining peace, and "the good order in the countryside." In order to perform these functions, the minister of the MVD had an administrative power over all fields of industry except mining. He was responsible for the maintenance of all public buildings, and for providing citizens resources that would be required to sustain them in case of famine or a similar public emergency.

The Manifesto by Alexander I of 1802 did not provide any departmental structures for the MVD to fulfill these various administrative functions. The only new structure that was originally identified by the Manifesto was the position of the deputy minister (*tovarishch ministra*) who should assist the minister in his functions (Mulukaev, Malygin, and Epifanov, 2005). Instead, the MVD of 1802 inherited a conflicting mix of departments and colleges created by the previous tsars, and was charged with an overwhelming array of ill-defined duties (Orlovsky, 1981). The Manifesto also did not provide clear instructions about the relationships between the Senate, the MVD, and the governors of the local provinces in Russia. To support the overwhelming functions and react to the developing complexity of social and economic conditions in Russia during the first 30 years of the nineteenth century, the MVD had to develop numerous structures and a vast administrative apparatus.

On January 19, 1803, the MVD's Central Department was established along with its four "expeditions" (subdivisions): first (1) expedition responsible for living supplies and the salt industry; second (2) expedition responsible for "good order"; third (3) expedition responsible for industries; and fourth (4) expedition responsible for public institutions, such as hospitals, prisons, orphan houses, and shelters (Fastov, 2005). The second expedition, which was performing the true policing functions, was traditionally divided between the rural and urban police departments.

The MVD also inherited responsibility for passport control and registration that was required for peasants, merchants, and even some gentry. Without a passport or registration (*vid na zhitel'stvo*), these groups of citizens could only reside at their main place of residence as predetermined by law. Even a temporary move to a different location required a registration or a passport. As a result, the MVD created "address expeditions" in both St. Petersburg (in 1807) and Moscow (in 1816) to register, control, and issue the passports for new residents (Rybnikov and Aleksushin, 2008). The passport system used to control citizen movement would become one of the major future activities of the Russian Imperial police (Matthews, 1993).

The "public medical expedition" was established within the MVD in 1804 to oversee the work of public healthcare institutions. This tradition continued through the decades thus allowing the MVD to oversee public medical institutions that included mental and juvenile agencies.

In 1806, the Main Postal department was transferred from the Senate to the MVD, thereby enabling the notorious censorship activities conducted by the MVD during the late nineteenth century. These functions became especially evident after 1865 when the Censorship Department was transferred from the Ministry of Education to the MVD apparatus.

In 1819, a new "economic" department joined the numerous structures of the MVD. It was charged with the organization of urban life, providing the population with needed supplies, improving the agricultural practices in the countryside, and organizing settlements in the newly acquired territories. In 1823, the department of foreign religious affairs was created to protect the existing Orthodox Christianity and to supervise the activities of other religions throughout the Russian Empire. One of the major functions of this department was to control the Jewish population and limit their intracountry movements. The police were involved in the deportation of Jews from the western provinces to the restricted areas in central Russia, where the government allowed Jewish settlements (Baron, 1976).

At the same time the MVD, slowly but consistently, eliminated local police independence and the ability for governors to exert any control, while also transforming local land courts and city councils (*uprava)* into their own agents. The result was that the local police became representatives of MVD. In 1837, a new Statute on County (*zemskaya*) Police and the Instructions to the Governors were issued,[6] which directed the governors and the land captains to follow the instructions of the MVD and its head (Orlovsky, 1981).[7] Prior to the creation of ministries, governors (and later governor-generals) were considered absolute monarchs ("viceroys") of the territories that they ruled and local police institutions functioned as their personal security agents for both protection and maintaining order.

During the early years of the MVD, provincial governors continued to enjoy independence and resented any direct MVD orders (Yaney, 1973). They considered themselves, and their police agencies, to be directly responsible only to the tsar (Waldron, 2007). However, by the mid-1830s, the official power of the MVD bureaucracy grew significantly (Kaiser and Marker, 1994). The MVD took over the local police institutions and the governors, and established a vertical hierarchy of the Russian police. Local police agencies were no longer security forces and personal agents of the governors. The local agencies became a part of the police bureaucracy; a nationwide, uniform, formal, and professionalized structure.

> The ministers exercised the direct control over their subordinate agents in each province, and every sector of public activity had to be integrated into the jurisdiction of a ministry. The governor's office became gradually integrated into the linear organization of the MVD (Le Donne, 1974, p. 103).

The Instructions to the Governors of 1837 eliminated some elected positions in the county police and created a new network of lower police officials called *stanovoi pristav*. This police officer was directly subordinate to the land captain of a rural district (*uezd)* and was responsible for the territory of *stan* (a subdivision of the *uezd*) (Yaney, 1973).

The land captain reported directly to the governor and the gentry's assembly, who were controlled by the MVD minister. Despite these changes, the rural police remained undeveloped and archaic compared to the city police departments and especially those in the capitals. This was due to the fact that a majority of the country's rural population remained serfs and, consequently, attached to private or public estates. The government's power stopped at an estate's threshold (Le Donne, 1974).

1.1.2 Development of the MVD after the 1825 Decembrist Uprising: Establishment of the Third Department and Corps of Gendarmes

The unsuccessful 1825 uprising of the Decembrist prompted Nicolas I to create the "supreme police" known as the Third Department. The Third Department was the first permanent political police established in the Russian Empire, and that was done by the Decree of Emperor issued on July 3, 1826. The purpose was to protect the monarchy and the political regime.[8] It replaced temporary agencies of the political police created during the reign of Alexander I (the committee of supreme police, and Special Chancellery) (Mulukaev, Malygin, and Epifanov, 2005). The Third Department was structurally separated from the MVD and belonged to the Majesty's Own Imperial Chancellery. Moreover, according to the Decree (*Ukaz*) of 1826, the Third Department had a duty to oversee the work of MVD agents, with the result of making the Third Department the most influential office in Russia (Squire, 1968). This subordination of the regular police to the political police endured throughout the entire history of the Russian Empire, which included the period when the two police agencies would be united in the MVD structure.

One of the most unique features of the Third Department was the Corps of Gendarmes created in 1827. They were "personal agents of the tsar, explicitly charged to act according to their conscience rather than formal law" (Yaney, 1973, p. 224). Ideally, the gendarmes were created to be moral agents for the Russian Empire and by their personal example should inspire confidence and loyalty to the throne, the emperor, and the monarchy (Lemke, 1909). To carry out these functions, gendarmes were placed in every province and district (*uezd*) (Yaney, 1973). The entire country was divided between five (later eight) gendarme circuits headed by the gendarme-general. The local gendarme surveillance network grew significantly by 1850.[9] It consisted of 126 gendarme commands located through the entire country, whose main duty was to report on the local political environment, views of the local nobility, and other groups of the free population (Rybnikov and Aleksushin, 2008).

Though the Third Department was always functioning under the original Decree of 1826, its authority and influence over the administration of regular police continued to expand, and some researchers deemed the entity a superior and "supralegal" institution of police power in the Russian Empire (Squire, 1968). Because gendarmes were frequently performing functions of the regular police, the public perceived the Third Department and MVD as the same (Lemke, 1909).

Notwithstanding the phenomenal development of the police administration in the first half of nineteenth century, local offices of both urban and rural Russian police were heavily criticized for being ineffective, corrupted, and slow. Paradoxically, despite the centralization and almost omnipotent jurisdiction, the central MVD office had few mechanisms to control the implementation of their decrees by the local offices. The hierarchical linear structure assumed full compliance and provided no feedback mechanism for public response or performance assessment for local police officials. This created the potential for an enormous abuse of power and corruption. The more remote the province was from the capital cities of St. Petersburg and Moscow, the less police presence could be found there (Starr, 1972).

The lack of control mechanisms was not the sole issue contributing to the police availability problem. Since its creation, the MVD's jurisdiction was ill defined. The central administrative apparatus and MVD local offices were created sporadically and often irrationally (Mulukaev, Malygin, and Epifanov, 2005). Sometimes these had overlapping jurisdictions and were given conflicting instructions. Concurrently, they were provided with almost omnipotent authority in executing these functions. This alone created the opportunity for unlimited power abuse and corruption. Corruption was often a mechanism for the local authorities to filter duties that needed to be performed and discretionary duties ignored. The establishment of the Corps of Gendarmes was an entity that was known to be above the law and frequently performed duties of the regular police, which exacerbated abuse and corruption. The gendarmes were notoriously known to be both abusive and violent. The Third Department did little to prevent the abuse (Monas, 1961).

The broad functions of the MVD and its local agents also were responsible for the numerous problems (Le Donne, 1974). The MVD was charged with controlling almost every aspect of daily life in the Russian Empire ranging from the maintenance of public order and crime prevention to control over the public buildings and living supplies for emergency situations (Waldron, 2007). However, the local offices did not possess adequate manpower to perform the overwhelming duties. With an expansion of the MVD's central administrative apparatus in the capital, the amount of decrees and other directive paperwork grew exponentially. However, the expansion of the local MVD manpower occurred mostly at the provincial level and not at the rural district level (*uezd*) and their subdivisions (*stans*) (Starr, 1972).

On a monthly basis, local police officers received a tremendous amount of instructions, some of which were conflicting and some simply unrealistic to implement (Yaney, 1973).[10] In order to survive, the local police officials had to choose which instructions and decrees to follow and which to ignore. These decisions were often made under the influence of local power stakeholders: the governor-general, the governor, and the local gentry participating in the government of the city or county. The influence was executed by political means as well as bribery.

The other serious obstacle to proper police administration in Russia was the quality of the lower police personnel. Local police officials were underpaid and provided with little benefits in comparison to the other public servants. For this reason, soldiers that were no longer suitable for military service were frequently appointed as ward supervisors and their assistants in city police agencies. Many were either illiterate or semiilliterate, and attempted to use measures of military discipline to maintain public order in their wards. During criminal investigations, torture was frequently used to obtain confessions (Sichinskii, 2002). In the rural communities, peasants were electing (or the landlords were appointing) the elders for each 100 or 1,000 peasants (*sotskye* or *tysyachnye)* from a pool of handicapped peasants incapable of working in the fields. These men were either too old or disabled to work as police representatives in the local peasant communities (Gonyukhov and Gorobtsov, 2002). Nicolas I, during the period from 1832 to 1837, attempted to increase city police officials' salaries and urged the county gentry to provide suitable peasants for work as *sotskye* and *tysyachnye*. These measures proved inefficient.

1.2 Police Administration during the Reform Era: 1856–1881

1.2.1 Self-Governance Reform and Police Administration

Tsar Alexander II, historically known as the "liberator," conducted several important reforms of the Russian Imperial government. Two were directly related to police administration: (1) the self-governance reform of 1862, and (2) the judicial reform of 1864. The loss of the Crimean war of 1853–1855 revealed serious internal problems in Russian society associated with the archaic social structure of serfdom, the slow industrialization progress, and an extremely bureaucratic government apparatus. Therefore, it was not surprising that almost immediately after Alexander II's coronation in 1856 he announced plans for the emancipation of serf reform. It took another five years for the reform to be implemented while the question of emancipation was vigorously discussed by all societal groups. Alexander II relied upon the younger and more educated civil servicemen, so called "enlightened bureaucrats," who came into the government at the beginning of his reign to enact the reforms (Lincoln, 1994).[11]

Almost as soon as the question of serf emancipation was seriously considered, it became clear that the existing local administration would not be sufficient for the new social structure of society. Prior to the emancipation in 1861, Greater Russia consisted of 21 million private and 25 million state-owned serfs, of which the majority were illiterate and had never left the boundaries of their estate or their district (*uezd*) (Czap, 1967). The emancipation raised serious questions of whether the landlords could continue to maintain public order within communities of emancipated serfs (Frank,

1999). This also called to question the ability of the new police structure and its need to prevent civil disturbances and accommodate the new societal structure.[12] The rural police, on the eve of reforms, were modest in size and overwhelmed with an abundance of duties (Abbott, 1973).[13]

But, more importantly, the issue of local administration and the emancipation of serfs brought, perhaps for the first time, the questions of what are the police functions in the Russian Empire and, more generally, what is the nature of the police institution. The tsar approved an unprecedented freedom of public debates over the issues of local administration and emancipation of the serfs. In the early 1860s, not only the local governors and nobility were asked to report their opinions to the tsar, but also the new social groups of intelligentsia were allowed to publish their thoughts on this matter. In the turmoil of these debates, the government developed three alternative plans of local administration reform including police reform. To a certain degree, each of the plans represented a competing view of the functions of the police.

The first plan was proposed by Lanskoi, the MVD minister at the time, who called for decentralization of the local administration. This was to be accomplished by strengthening the existing governor's authority granting them with any residual administrative power that did not belong directly to the tsar and his ministries. The plan was apparently approved by most governors, but was strenuously opposed by other ministers. Because the MVD continued to execute a direct control over the governors according to this plan, the decentralization suggested by Lanskoi was simply strengthening the MVD over local ministry representatives. According to the plan, the local police administration was completely removed from the hands of the local nobility and landlords. Police administration became the sole function of the state bureaucracy with the main purpose of maintaining the existing autocratic regime.

The alternative plan proposed by the group of conservative ministers (the Ministry of State Domains, Ministry of Finances, Ministry of Justice, and others) was to reinstate the military governors-generals who would then have supreme authority in the countryside and report directly to the tsar and not to the MVD minister. On the district level (*uezd*), the governor-general would have a local representative named the "district governor" who would have authority to overrule any decisions by the local police. This scheme of complete administrative centralization reserved partial control of the local police agencies for the nobility and landlords. It also provided close administrative supervision over local police officers and streamlined the chain of command that was frequently broken within the MVD system. According to this conservative plan, the police continued to be a force serving the interests of local nobility, but also were closely controlled by state agents who were directly reporting to the autocratic tsar. This plan brought serious opposition among local governors because it undermined their authority and was subsequently abandoned despite the tsar's favorable opinion.

Finally, the third local administration plan included a new idea for the Empire that was a concept of self-governance. It was to function through elected provincial and district assemblies that included not only representatives of the nobility, but also representation of the other social classes within Russian society. These agencies (*zemstvo*) also would have an executive body (*uprava*) and would be responsible for the election of local police officials. These radical ideas of self-governance, surprisingly, came from the Zemskii section of the MVD, which evolved from the existing MVD Statistical Department. The original goal of the statistical department was to assist the tsar and ministers in the collection of local statistical data to support local administration reform.

Despite its limitations, the proposal creating the *zemstvo* had two important differences from the previous plans. First, it assumed for the first time that local police functions should be conducted in the name of the state and the autocratic Russian regime (tsar), as well as in the name of all other social groups represented through a local council. Though not all groups of Russian society were represented in the *zemstvo* due to the minimum property requirement in the proposal, it included social classes of merchants, clergy, and wealthy peasants that were previously disconnected from the local police administration. Secondly, it finally acknowledged that administrative functions that are not directly related to the public order and local security should be removed from the local police agencies and transferred to *upravas*, the executive agencies of *zemstvo*. This plan represented the most democratic option for the police organization. The police were to be charged with the duties to protect members of society, not just the tsar, and the police functions were to be limited by the self-governing agency (Anuchin, 1872).

On December 25, 1862, the "Temporary Rules on Organization of the police in provincial cities and districts governed by the General Rule"[14] were adopted to promote changes in the police structure. The rules did not exactly follow any of the three plans described above, but instead were a combination. A major disappointment of the policy was that the local police functions remained under MVD control and the *zemstvo* did not receive authority to elect local police officials.

Rural and city police were combined under the district police departments (*uezdnoe politseikoe upravlenie*) headed by the land captain (*uezdnyi ispravnik*). The new land captain was directly appointed by the governor predicated on the consent of the MVD and not elected by the assembly of local landlords and gentry.[15] The landlords and gentry, in essence, were removed from the direct administration of local police. Independent urban police organizations remained only in large cities, such as St. Petersburg and Moscow. The lowest rank of city police officer, *gorodovoi*, was mainly responsible for patrolling the streets, while his superior, *okolodochnyi nadziratel'*, was charged with informally supervising the ward residents (*okolodok)* and performing preliminary investigations (*doznanie*) (Anuchin, 1872).[16]

In 1864, when *zemstvos* were established as self-governing local offices, some basic functions of administration related to the maintenance of the local public buildings, roads, and structures were transferred from the local police to the *zemstvos.* However, a large group of controlling administrative functions (including passport control, liquor licensing, fire department administration, sanitary street norms, and fishing and hunting licenses, remained under the authority of the local police. Therefore, regardless of the changes, the new police of 1862 continued to be a function of the state bureaucracy and directly controlled by the autocratic tsar while most social groups were excluded from the process of police administration.

1.2.2 Judicial Reform of 1864 and Police Administration

The other important reform that was carried out by Alexander II was the judicial reform of 1864. While it was primarily conducted to improve the work of the court system, it did influence the police functions in the performance of criminal investigations. Prior to the reform, criminal investigations were usually conducted by a lower police officer called *stanovoi pristav* (*district subdivision inspector*) in the rural districts or by the *ugolovnyi uchastkovyi pristav* (*criminal circuit inspector*) in the city police departments (I.V. Gessen, 1905).

This first stage was called "preliminary investigation" and its purpose was to establish the corpus delicti (body of the crime) (Foinitskyi, 1912). A confession of the defendant was considered the best evidence and tempted many investigators to secure the admission of guilt at any cost. The next stage of the criminal process was termed the "official investigation," with the purpose to "establish with an absolute certainty the person or the property suffering from the crime, the criminal act, the method and the tool, when, where, and with which motive the crime was perpetrated" (p. 34). The prosecutor had a right to be present during the official investigation to ensure both the prosecution and the rights of the defendant were procedurally correct.

On some occasions, the lower land court (or its temporary subdivision) would participate in the official investigation, but for most of the cases it would simply review the results of investigation conducted by *stanovoi pristav* (I.V. Gessen, 1905). Cases that were resolved would be moved to the district (uezdnyi) court, whose purpose was not the fact-finding, but imposition of the sentence (Foinitskyi, 1912). In the district court, the law clerks first would create a written summary of the facts of the case accompanied by the relevant law. This summary, or parts, would be read to the judges by the clerk during the hearing and the judges made their decision based solely on the summary (I.V. Gessen, 1905). Public hearings were not conducted and the defendant was not provided with a defense counsel. Most court documents remained secret and defendants had no access to the materials before or after the verdict.

The rules of evidence were extremely formalized and prescribed to the judges related to the consideration and weighing of the evidence.[17] The social status of the witness was important when considering the reliability of testimony. When evidence was not strong enough, the court was allowed to issue a verdict of "remaining under suspicion," which basically allowed any weak case to avoid an acquittal. The person under suspicion could be prosecuted for the same crime if new evidence of his guilt was discovered later (Foinitskyi, 1912). It was clear that in such an environment the administration of justice and criminal procedure created very low expectations for criminal investigations and the quality of evidence collected by police.

The new system of criminal procedure and court organization adopted in 1864 was quite progressive for the time period. It allowed for most of the cases to have public court hearings, jury trials, and defense counsels during the trials (Rozin, 1913). The fact-finding process was no longer in the hands of the police. The verdicts of "remaining under suspicion" were abandoned for most crimes. New laws also called for judicial independence by making judges irremovable and increasing their salaries (I.V. Gessen, 1905).

Apparently, the new rules of criminal procedure required better quality investigations and evidence collected by police. To achieve this, the investigative function was removed from the police to the newly created institution of investigative magistrates (*sudebnye sledovateli*). This was done in 1860 as a precursor to the judicial reforms of 1864 (Kucherov, 1970). The investigative magistrates belonged to the Ministry of Justice, not the MVD, and had life appointments (Foinitskyi, 1912). They had legal training, practical experience, and were supposed to act as an independent inquirer into the facts of the case. The preliminary investigation (*doznaniye*) was still conducted by police, but the materials of *doznaniye* were not official until the investigative magistrate checked them. Under the Decree (Ustav) of Criminal Proceeding 1864, [18] the main document of judicial reform, police were allowed to perform only immediately required measures that were at the crime scene and transfer further investigation of the case to the investigative magistrate (Vladimirov, 1910).

The investigative magistrates were independent from both prosecutors and defense counsels. They were charged with issuing warrants for arrest, searches, and with deposing witness testimony for both sides. However, the new criminal law allowed for a warrantless arrest by police to prevent or suppress a crime (Szeftel, 1958). The removal of the investigative magistrates from the MVD system was a part of a larger judicial reform goal to separate the judicial and administrative functions (Kucherov, 1970). This was an important step in determining the role of the Russian police in the nineteenth century. The police were no longer viewed as an agency administering justice; it clearly became a law enforcement institution that nevertheless retained many controlling administrative functions.

Counter to the planned goals of self-governance and judicial reforms, the MVD continued to expand its omnipotent control over the different spheres of Russian life during the reign of Alexander II. On the eve of the liberal reforms, police functions in 1857 Russia reached staggering proportions and required 400 pages to describe the scope (Abbott, 1973). The growth of police duties became especially evident in the second half of Alexander's II reign (1865–1881) when the MVD extended its control functions over the press, freedom of movement, and public participation in Russian politics. "After the 1861 emancipation, the ministry [MVD] became an ever more visible symbol of static conservatism" (Orlovsky, 1981, p. 2).

1.2.3 Reform of Censorship and Police Administration

Between 1855 and 1863, the Russian press experienced a brief period of relative liberation along with the rampant development of independent media sources. It was partly due to the initial tsar's permission for the press to discuss government affairs, which included emancipation of the peasants and self-governance. The tsar's expectations were that the press would be a compliant assistant to government reforms. However, the press attacked the government with harsh criticism that made Alexander II believe that preliminary censorship was still necessary (Balmuth, 1979).

Prior to 1963, two ministries were sharing the responsibility of censorship. The Ministry of Education was in charge of the censorship process, while the MVD was only responsible for censors (Gusman, 2002). In 1863, the functions of censorship performed by the Committee on Foreign Censorship were transferred from the liberal Ministry of Education to the more conservative MVD and marked the end of open press policies during the reign of Alexander II.[19]

In 1865, the MVD established the Chief Administration for Press Affairs and Censorship (*Glavnoe upravlenie po delam pechati i tsenzury*) that concentrated all power of censorship with the MVD.[20] Valuev, the MVD minister, expressed the opinion that the majority in government did not believe in the value of open public discussions of government reforms. Moreover, he found the existence of independent writers and media outlets a threat to national security (Balmuth, 1979). In support of these ideals, the Chief Administration for Press Affairs and Censorship at the MVD actively interfered with the public discussions on land distribution for the peasants, representative government, authority of *zemstvos*, and other proposed changes that were a potential threat to the autocratic regime.

According to the new "Temporary Rules on Censorship and Press" adopted in 1865, the MVD Chief Administration for Press Affairs and

Censorship received the authority not only to issue press publication permissions (preliminary censorship), but also review books and articles after their publication (punitive censorship) (Rigberg, 1966). According to the new law, if the MVD would conclude after the review that the publication was leading in a "harmful direction," it had the right to reprimand the publisher, suspend his license for six months, or revoke the license. The MVD minister had the authority to decide which periodicals should be exempt from the preliminary censorship, and determine the amount of money that such periodicals should pay for an exemption (Rigberg, 1966).

By 1873, the MVD minister received absolute power to close any publishing agency using amendments to the "Temporary Rules on Censorship and Press" originally adopted June 7, 1872 (Gordon et al., 1911).[21] The Amendments also increased the time required for preliminary censorship (Balmuth, 1979). The MVD possessed an elaborate network of censors to perform these vast functions of censorship. The censorship network included local committees for the press (for large cities), inspectors of the press, and theater censors. This guaranteed close police attention to every local publication in press regarding government affairs.[22] The network of censors worked in cooperation with the local gendarmes of the Third Department and regular police.[23]

1.2.4 Further Police Development: 1860s–1870s

In 1866, the first Division for Preservation of Public Order was established in St. Petersburg in response to the unsuccessful attempt to assassinate the tsar. Later in 1882, this division would become a prototype for the newly fashioned political police in Russia. By the late 1860s, after several assassination attempts on the tsar, the failure of the Third Department to protect the existing political regime became more than apparent.

The Corps of Gendarmes (termed the "visible and repressive arm of autocracy") (Lemke, 1909) in Russian provinces and capitals was effective in controlling the daily lives of the ordinary citizens, but was unable to penetrate secret groups of ardent revolutionaries and terrorists. In 1867, the government made an attempt to improve the efficiency of the gendarmes by restructuring the eight gendarme districts and departments. The newly created Main Department consisted of 56 provincial departments, 50 district (*uezd*) departments, 22 departments of railroad safety, 13 mounted gendarme divisions, and 2 gendarme garrisons. This streamlined the structure and lines of command among the Corps of Gendarmes, but they did not drastically change the nature or methods of the political police (Mulukaev, Malygin, and Epifanov, 2005).

Moreover, the ineffective work of the political police was blamed again on the lack of the necessary authority available to the Corps of Gendarmes.

Thus, in 1871, the gendarmes received new powers to participate in the investigation of almost any criminal case and to subordinate both the governor and the regular police for their own purposes. Under the new rules, "about the order of activity of Corps of Gendarmes on the criminal investigation" (*O poryadke deisitvii chinov korpusa zhandarmov po rassledovaniyi prestuplenii)*, gendarmes also had exclusive authority to investigate political crimes without an investigative magistrate's participation.

In 1878, the government created a new lower police rank for the rural police (*Uriadnik)*, whose main duties were to assist the district subdivision inspector (*stannovoi pristav*) and to supervise the work of local peasant representatives (community elderly, *sotskye,* and *desytskie*).[24] According to the Instruction to the Police Uriadniks, 5,000 new police officers were employed in 46 provinces. *Uriadniks* were in charge of the *stan* and were instructed to reside within the controlled territory. They were responsible not only for public order maintenance, but also performed informal political surveillance of peasants and workers. *Uriadniks* were appointed and directly subordinated to the *stannovoi pristav*, who was directly responsible to the land captain. In the cities, the functions of *Uriadniks* were performed by *gorodovoi*, who not only resided in the controlled area, but also were present at stationary observation posts located on the streets, and patrolled on horseback.[25]

One of the major tasks for increasing numbers of lower rank police officials was to control the freedom of movement for recently emancipated peasants and the growing number of urban factory workers. The regulations related to registration, movement, and passports remained unchanged during the reign of Alexander II. Freedom of movement was governed by the policy called the "Collection of Statutes on Passports and Runaways" issued in 1833. This policy was published in 1857 under the Collection of Statutes of Russian Empire, which simply consolidated regulations dating from 1833 and thereafter. The document was comprised of 741 articles and was extremely complex, outdated, and contradictory (Matthews, 1993).

Contrary to some opinions, the 1861 emancipation of peasants did not deliver freedom of movement to the former serfs. It simply transferred authority to control their movement from the local landlords to the local police. Even after 1861, the law determined that the main place of residence for peasants was in the villages where they used to work prior to emancipation (*mesto pripiski*). The emancipation reform did not provide land to serfs owned by private landlords, but instead gave it to the village community and their membership in the communes remained mandatory. This also restricted the mobility of peasants (Matthews, 1993).

Further movement to the cities was regulated through passports, which were required for hunting trips of less than 30 *versts*,[26] short-term trips (less than 6 month) over 30 *versts*, and long-term trips over 30 *versts* provided by the local police (Mulukaev, Malygin, and Epifanov, 2005). The temporary workers in the cities were registered by police and were required to have a residence permission called address tickets (*vid na zhitel'stvo*) at any time. Urban residents who changed their location within the city also were required to get a new registration from the police. Each local police department had an "address department," the sole purpose of which was to control the movement of residents by means of registration and passports. The cities of Moscow and St. Petersburg were under special registration regimes that were even more restrictive than those of other Russian cities.[27] The lack of a valid passport or the proof of identity automatically resulted in arrest and criminal investigation. Ethnic and religious minorities (especially Jews) were under special quotas and their movements were regulated even more thoroughly.

Despite their manpower increase, the work of rural police found little respect among the emancipated Russian peasants. Abuse was facilitated through an abundance of police functions and authority coupled with the hierarchical MVD control structure (Frank, 1999).

> Apart from their inability to protect communities, the rural police lost what little credibility and trust they may have had through their arbitrariness, corruption, brutality, and their position as tools of the wealthy and agents of the state (especially in their role as tax collectors and enforcers of decrees) (Frank, 1987a, p. 206).

Peasants avoided rural police if possible. They often settled their disputes in the unofficial courts (known as peasant courts) and even lynched accused criminals in their community based on customary laws (Frank, 1987b; Worobec, 1985).[28] The city police also were criticized as being incompetent and unable to curb city crime rates (Abbott, 1977).[29]

There are several historical factors that explain the apparent contradiction between the policies of the liberal reforms conducted by Alexander II during 1855 through 1864, and the MVD expansion of the police-controlling functions observed during 1865 through 1881. In part, the measures of strengthening police during the 1870s were justified due to the rising danger of a revolution and terrorist organizations that were creating a threat to national security and public order. However, the changes in the public policy of Alexander II during 1866–1881 were mainly caused by the conflict that new democratic court institutions and self-governance encountered when they were incorporated into the existing autocratic administrative apparatus of the Russian Empire.

Already in 1914, Koni, a well-known Russian defense counsel, proclaimed that "the new establishment of the court institutions contradicted the existing mode of the government administration" (Koni, 1914, p. 2 back matter section). When some of the reform outcomes became inconvenient for the existing administrative apparatus and the tsar, the decision was quickly made to abandon the changes and return to the old state of governance. The most dramatic changes undermining the ideals of judicial reform included the exclusion of political crimes from jury trials, discretionary limitation of open trials by the Minister of Justice, and replacing investigative magistrates by gendarmes during official investigation of political crimes (Koni, 1914).

1.3 Imperial Police during the Counterreforms of Alexander III and Nicolas II: 1881–March 1917

Alexander III began his reign in personal fear due to his father's assassination, and developed "Measures for Protection of State and Public Order" issued on September 8, 1881.[30] This document started a series of exceptional measures taken by the tsarist regime in an attempt to maintain political status quo and prevent revolutionary movements through further assassinations. The MVD, which already had combined both political and regular police under its jurisdiction, gained a new structure called the Special Council (*Osoboe Soveschanie*). The council had the unprecedented authority of extrajudicial administrative exile for up to five years of any harmful persons, which included those suspected of political crimes, instigating factory strikes, precipitating peasant riots, and organizing religious sects.[31]

The "Measures" provided for the declaration of two different types of emergencies in Russian provinces. The provincial governor could obtain an exception of authority to terminate public assemblies, liquidate organizations, or businesses, and create military tribunals for certain types of cases (Tarasov, 1910). In provinces under a state of emergency, both regular and political police were able to arrest suspects without a court order, conduct extra-judicial searches, and exile suspects of political crimes (*politicheski neblagonadezhnykh*). Additionally, the police could summarily seize individuals that were simply "harmful to the society" (*prosto-porochnykh*) (Gessen, 1908).[32] While originally these measures were deemed to be temporary, their actions were extended for the next 36 years.

In this atmosphere of fear and political instability, the MVD undertook an unopposed expansion of political police administration (Khoroshun, 2007). The Department of State Police, a successor of the Third Department, was established in 1880 and already had a superior position within the MVD structure. After 1881, the Department of State Police had grown substantially, creating new Secretariats in the central apparatus and new local structures in the provinces. Just four years after its creation, the Department of State Police grew from three to five Secretariats and, by 1917, it had 10 Secretariats within its central apparatus.[33] The "Decree on Public Police Supervision" and the confidential "Decree on Secret Police Supervision," issued in 1882, expanded police power substantially. It provided both the regular and political police with the authority to enter any private property, conduct warrantless searches, and review and seize written communication anywhere in the Russian Empire without the governor declaring a state of emergency (Mulukaev, Malygin, and Epifanov, 2005).

These measures significantly undermined the authority of investigative magistrates and the 1864 judicial reform ideals. The 1883 "Decree on the Establishment of Secret Police" used Divisions for Protection of Public Order previously operating only in St. Petersburg and Moscow as an example of new secret political police for the entire Russian Empire. The decree was issued not only for the central apparatus, but also for some local agencies (security departments or *Okrannye otdeleniya*) in large cities and critical areas of the country. The establishment of a Special Section (*Osoboe otdelenie*) leading the security departments within the MVD in 1896 was an important step in consolidating the power of secrete political police in tsarist Russia (Suchkov, 2008). The Special Section became a powerful intelligence and investigative agency for all political crimes in Russia. It had unprecedented extrajudicial authority and was considered superior within the MVD structure. In 1902, the Special Section expanded the number of local security departments to eight. By 1903, the number of local security departments had grown to 17 and, in 1907, there were 27 security departments placed throughout Russia.[34] In 1906, local security departments were combined within the superior district security departments, abbreviated as ROO (*rayonnye okhrannye otdeleniya*), that were created in eight major regions.[35] One of the major goals of the ROO was to establish a national comprehensive surveillance network (Khoroshun, 2007).[36]

The local secret police departments operated separately from the local gendarmes; their main responsibility was not the official investigation of political crimes, but intelligence gathering, surveillance, recruitment of informants, and undercover work to prevent the commission of political crimes and to examine the political loyalty (*politicheskaya blagonadezhnost'*) of individuals (Frolov and Tyshkovets, 2009).[37] In the capital, the local security departments were more elaborate, with separate subdepartments. One, called the "special department," was created in 1905. The main function of this structure was to supervise both foreigners and Russian citizens coming from abroad and gather intelligence about potential revolutionaries among those arriving in Russia from foreign countries.[38]

The role of the district gendarme departments for criminal investigation also was expanded. Starting in 1904, the district gendarme departments (GZhU), together with the governor and the prosecutor, constituted a local "Special Council" whose duties included investigation of political provincial crimes, with the discretion to determine which cases would be investigated.[39]

The regular police also were expanding both their manpower and authority. In 1889, the position of *zemskyi nachal'nik* was created, whose duties were to supervise the work of a special peasant institution of justice known as the township (*volostnoi*) court. According to the reform of 1864, judges of the *volostnoi* court were elected from the peasants to ensure that justice was proximate to the people and customary law.

After 1889, the *zemskyi nachal'nik* was in charge of appointing the judges. He enjoyed the right to discipline judges and to stay any decision by the *volostnoi* court (Czap, 1967). The new position belonged to the MVD, and the change restored the bureaucratic supervision of peasant justice in contradiction to the very thing the judicial reform of 1864 attempted to accomplish (Foinitskyi, 1912).

In 1903, the rural police were expanded by a new lower rank of officers known as the "rural district guards" (*uezdnaya sel'skaya strazha*). One guard was appointed per each 2,500 registered male "souls" (residents) of the districts (*uezd*). The previously created rank of *Uriadnik* was included in the structure of the district guards and he became responsible for their supervision. The main purpose of the guards, according to the "Instruction for the District Police Guards of the Provinces," was to patrol the villages and provincial towns (A.V. Petrov, 2004). However, the instructions also mentioned that the guards were to observe and supervise any suspicious peasant gatherings and to protect the large land estates from peasant riots (*pogrom*) (Mulukaev, Malygin, and Epifanov, 2005).

In most provinces, the guards were appointed to supersede the work of peasant elders who previously were charged with these duties. The guards were deemed more reliable, especially pertaining to the prevention and suppression of the peasant riots (A.V. Petrov, 2004). Like many other measures, the creation of guards was deemed temporary until the local administration could be established to take over this function. Needless to say, such an administration was never created and the provincial guards, like any other regular police force, continued to be vertically subordinate to MVD authority.

Moreover, in 1906, as part of the measures to strengthen political police, some divisions of the rural district guards were subordinated to the local gendarmes (A.V. Petrov, 2004). The growth of the manpower and apparatus of the regular police also was combined with a continual extension of power to "limit the personal liberty... for the sake of prevention and suppression of crimes... based on a few ill-defined provisions of law" (Szeftel, 1958, p. 8).

Regular police also maintained significant control over the movement of peasants and factory workers using the Law on Passports (*Ustav o passportakh*) issued in 1903 and amended in 1906 and 1909. According to this new law, peasants were finally allowed to choose their place of main residence (*mesto zhitel'stva*) somewhere other than their former villages (*mesto pripiski*). Nevertheless, long-term (over 6 months) and long-distance moves (over 50 *versts*) were still restricted and only allowed by special permission from the police.[40] Most of the factory workers were required to have registration even if the factory where they worked was located in the place of their main residence.[41] The owners of hotels, shelters, and rental apartments were instructed to check for registration or passports from the temporary residents arriving in St. Petersburg and Moscow (Sichinskii, 2002). The law of 1903 continued to discriminate against ethnic minorities, Jews, and persons under police supervision, which related to their freedom to move around the country.[42]

The MVD continued to execute a central function of censorship for the entire empire during this period of time. The new, more comprehensive Law on Censorship (*Ustav o Tsensure*)[43] was issued in 1890, but it was quickly amended in 1906 after the coup d'état of 1905. The amendments of 1906 finally eliminated the preliminary censorship, but the "punitive" (post facto publication) censorship remained in place (Walkin, 1954). The Law on Censorship, even after the amendments of 1906, maintained prohibition of any publication that could be construed as a "violation of inviolability of the tsarist autocracy or disrespect to the tsar."[44] With continuing growth of both books and periodicals published in Russia,[45] the changes did not free many government resources. With the growing number of publications, "punitive" censorship became a more and more complicated task for the MVD.[46]

In 1908, 89 new "detective" (*sysknoe*) bureaus were added to both district and city police departments.[47] The purpose of the new structure was to improve the quality of official criminal investigation by separating it from the time-consuming undercover detective work (Matienko, 2007). Detective bureaus in the regular police were created using the example of security departments of the political police. The size of "detective" bureaus depended on the population; however, close attention also was paid to the cities with "special conditions," such as the existence of large administrative agencies or factories. These areas were considered to attract potentially "disorderly elements," and, therefore, required larger "detective" bureaus. New departments consisted of official detectives and undercover agents who not only recruited informants to report on criminal organizations, but also had an opportunity to spy on ordinary citizens (Abdulmalikov, 2007). The instructions to the detective bureaus by the head of the MVD issued in 1910 directed the agents to survey restaurants, low-class hotels, pawn shops, and other places of potential concentration of criminal elements (Mulukaev, Malygin, and Epifanov, 2005).

Despite these changes, the work of the regular police on solving nonpolitical crimes was mostly unsuccessful. This often caused distrust and alienation of the police from the public (Weissman, 1985).[48] The result was public attacks on police and low levels of reported crime and lack of public cooperation especially during the period of 1906–1907 (Thurston, 1980). In part, this can be explained by the government's focus on political crimes, and neglecting prevailing petty offenses (Lavrik, 2008; Neuberger, 1993; Politov, 2007; Sichinskii, 2002).[49] The situation was worsened by low wages of the lower police ranks, inadequate levels of education, and the government's toleration of abuse of power (Dunaeva, 2009; Masalimov and Masalimov, 2008; Naumenko and Almukhametova, 2009; Weissman, 1985). This was especially true for rural police (Dunaeva, 2009; Kladov, 2007a, 2007b, 2007c). In very serious cases, the political police (gendarmes) were used to assist the rural police in solving crimes (Makurina, 2008).

Beginning 1906, the tsarist government undertook several attempts to reform the Russian police.[50] The MVD commission reviewed several drafts before the final version was presented to the legislative body (*Duma*) in 1912 (Rybnikov and Aleksushin, 2008). The final draft on police reform suggested the elimination of many administrative functions and provided disciplinary responsibility for the abuse of power. However, with the assassination of the current MVD minister, Stolypin, and increasing political instability, the project was recalled from the *Duma* for further improvements (Peregudova, 2000). The *Duma* committee continued to discuss the drafts, but was never able to agree on the final version.[51] Finally, on October 30, 1916, the law entitled "Strengthening the Imperial Police in 50 Provinces and Improving Its Professional and Material Position"[52] was adopted. The law simply called for the increase of department manpower in relation to the size of the local population and also increased officer salaries. No changes to the structure of police functions were provided by the new law.

1.4 Police Development between the Two Revolutions: March 1917–October 1917

The MVD's broad functions guaranteed high public visibility to both political and regular police in prerevolutionary Russia (Orlovsky, 1981). With the growth of political alienation from the tsarist regime, the police remained one of the few loyal supporters of autocracy in Russia on the eve of the revolution.[53] Therefore, it was not surprising that tsarist police in 1917 personified, to many underprivileged Russians, a repressive mechanism of power control and abuse that the monarchy attempted to use to remain in power (Abdurakhmanova, 2006).

During the civil disturbances following the 1917 February Revolution, the tsarist police and Corps of Gendarmes were one of the first victims of unruly crowds (Wilcox, 1917). The buildings of police departments were stormed, police archives were burned, and prisoners were released from jails. The Provisional government declared on March 3, 1917, the intent to create a true people's police with elected leadership that would be responsible to the local administration. The work of the State Police Department of the MVD and Corps of Gendarmes was terminated and their leaders arrested.[54]

On April 17, 1917, the new structure of people's militia was outlined by the special decree of Provisional government (Rybnikov and Aleksushin, 2008). The new police were created as a part of the self-governance system based on existing *zemstvos* and city administrations. According to the decree, the head of the city or district police was elected by the local city, or *zemstvo* council *(uprava),* and had to report to the *zemstvo* or city assembly on an annual basis (Chudakova, 2011). *Zemstvos* in rural districts and city assemblies in the urban areas were to determine the staff and funding for the new local police. The head of the local police departments were required to have at least a middle school education level. The recruitment of the new police was conducted on the basis of recommendations from the public nongovernment organizations (Romanov, 2008).

From the moment of its creation, the new Provisional government police experienced serious problems. It was understaffed or staffed with nonprofessionals (Chudakova, 2011; S.A. Ivanov, 2008). The old police cadres were replaced because many of them were suspected as being loyal to the monarchy. The newly recruited police officers did not have the education or experience or mentors for on-the-job training. The new police also were severely underfunded. The decree had relied on 30% of its support from the central government with the rest to be provided through the local budgets. However, both central and local budgets were exhausted by continuous military expenses for World War I and the new police had little funding for basic items, such as uniforms and ammunition (Gonyukhov and Gorobtsov, 2002).

The social situation in the country remained unstable. The 1917 February Revolution resulted in massive civil disturbances, which required new police to focus on public order maintenance. Amnesty was provided by the Provisional government in March of 1917 and thousands of former convicts were released from jails and prisons (Hasegawa, 1992). This in combination with civil disturbances caused a dramatic increase in crime rates throughout the country (Rybnikov and Aleksushin, 2008). Understandably, the underfunded and understaffed police were unable to successfully address the problems. The unsolved crimes and continued civil disturbances undermined the reputation of new police forces.

The legitimacy of the new police also was challenged by the existence of the Red Guards, which were self-organized groups of factory workers. Though the Red Guards were not accepted by the Provisional government as the legitimate police force, they represented a strong alternative to a weak and disorganized police organization (Gutman, 2007). The existence of the Red Guards reflected the situation of conflicting political authorities in Russia: the Provisional government and Soviets of Workers and Peasants (Hasegawa, 1973).

The new police also experienced serious problems with their central leadership. The function of central control over the police remained at the MVD level. The ministers of the MVD were now appointed by the Provisional government. However, the political instability and conflicts within the Provisional government made the central control of the MVD extremely weak and its orders were inconsistent. Between March and October of 1917, three ministers of MVD were appointed and terminated.

1.5 Concluding Remarks

The purpose of this historical overview was to outline the major steps in the development and collapse of Russian version of the police state (*politseistaat)* during the nineteenth and early twentieth centuries (Table 1.1).[55] Most historians agree that prior to 1856, the Russian government built a typical police (well-ordered) state where the primary police function was to promote the well being of society while simultaneously maintaining the existing autocratic regime that controlled all spheres of Russian society (Orlovsky, 1981; Walkin, 1962). This was not an unusual structural model for the absolute monarchies of Western Europe in the eighteenth century, which included the classic examples of Prussia's Frederick II, Joseph II of the Austrian Empire, and Joseph Fouchè in France during the time of Napoleon (Zuckerman, 1996).

The state's structure in these countries combined paternalism, autocracy, and enlightenment with the secret police and paid informers. Initially they created a systematic omnipotent control by the absolute monarch and his agents over the subjects of the monarchy, but in the end they "initiated a trend that not only brought about great material and cultural progress, but also stimulated and strengthened individual initiative, enterprise, and rational or critical constructivism features of intellectual life" (Raef, 1983, p. 250).

This was achieved through a clash with developing civil societies that challenged the authoritarian political system and successfully removed the paternalistic control, thus allowing society to develop productively on its own account (Engelstein, 1988). What was different in Russia's case was the lack of a comprehensively structured civil society in the early 1800s that would develop and restrict the absolute tsar and his MVD from controlling all spheres of Russian life (Raef, 1983). The only social group whose interests were represented in the Russian political system in the early 1800s was loyal to autocratic noblemen and landlords, and the police primarily existed for the maintenance of this political status quo (Zuckerman, 1996).[56]

The reforms of Alexander II, despite their liberal nature, were, in fact, paternalistic. They were initiated by the political will of the enlightened monarch and facilitated by the MVD,[57] and they also were abandoned when the autocracy failed to control the subsequent outcomes. Though the reforms were brief, their impact on Russian society was significant. Peasant emancipation and creation of the self-governing *zemstvos* in the decades of the 1850s and 1860s were a substantial social change development. The emancipation in combination with the massive peasant migration to the cities caused by industrialization[58] transformed the entire Russian society, broke the traditional lifestyle of peasants,[59] and created new social groups and social relations.

However, the political system of absolute monarchy was reluctant to accept this new social reality. Between the period of 1860 and 1905, the newly created class of nonnoble businessmen, factory managers, professionals, university faculty, factory workers, and emancipated peasants had little legitimate means to participate in the political life of Russia. Leading government branches, the State Council, and executive ministers were filled primarily with hereditary noble appointees of the tsar. [60] Moreover, even at this time, the ministers and government leaders were still viewed as personal servants of the tsar rather than public officials (Orlovsky, 1981). It was only in 1905 when the first elected legislative body, the Duma, was established and allowed that some political representation of nonnoble members of the Russian society took place.

Without legitimate means of political representation, the most radical members of new social groups turned to political violence. Starting in the 1860s, Russia experienced unprecedented increases of violence that resulted in the assassination of the tsar, several MVD ministers, and an unsuccessful coup d'état in 1905.

The reaction of the monarchic regime was to further expand existing police control and provide almost unlimited authorities that allowed direct interference with the daily life of Russian citizens.[61] An accurate description of the Russian state and police functions during this time was provided by George Kennan, who traveled to Siberia in 1886:

> The theory upon which the government of Russia proceeds is, that the citizen not only is incapable of taking part in the management of the affairs of his country... but incapable of manage [*sic*] even the affairs of his own household; and that from the time when he leaves the cradle... to the time when his... grey head is finally laid under the sod, he must be guided, directed, instructed, restrained, repressed, regulated, fenced in, fenced out, braced up, kept down and made to do what generally someone else thinks is best for him. The natural outcome of this... theory is concentration of all administrative authority in the hands of few high officials and enormous extension of police power (1889, p. 890).

The unprecedented powers given to the police between 1880 and 1905 seriously undermined freedoms and rights of ordinary citizens,[62] but failed to curb the violence of revolutionary movements. Political changes occurring in Western Europe during the 1850s through the early 1900s significantly damaged the idea of autocracy in Russia (Daly, 1998). Without the legitimacy of absolute monarchy, many subjects of the Russian Empire were no longer inclined to tolerate the total police control of a paternalistic tsar.[63] Social and political unrest, caused in part by overwhelming police control, resulted in the first revolutionary attempt in 1905.[64]

After the unsuccessful coup d'état in 1905, the tsarist government made some changes in the political system by establishing the Duma, which was intended to be a representative legislative body. Reforms conducted by Stolypin, the minister of the MVD, brought some resolution and modernization to the peasant communities. Some of the previous restrictions, such as passports and censorship control, were eased, but not completely eliminated.

As a result, between 1906 and 1912, Russian society experienced relative political and social stabilization and the revolutionary movement underwent a significant disintegration (Haimson, 1964).[65] However, after the assassination of Stolypin in 1911 and the massacre of the Lena Goldfield miners in 1912, the labor and revolutionary movements intensified again (McKean, 1990). The upsurge of the political movement, on the other hand, exacerbated the conservative attitudes in government circles.[66] Police reforms that were started in 1906 were postponed and resulted in a simple increase of personnel and funding for the MVD in 1916 (Peregudova, 2000).

However, it was the social unrest and economic devastation brought by World War I that exaggerated the growing clash between the reactionary policy of the police state and liberal expectations of society in tsarist Russia (Haimson, 1965). In the end, Okhranka, one of the most elaborate and powerful networks of secret police in Russia, failed to control the growing polarization of Russian society and consequent alienation of the tsarist regime resulting in the successful 1917 February Revolution (Daly, 2004; Lauchlan, 2005). The very efforts of police to protect the authoritarian government by any means and maintain political status quo contributed to the downfall of the tsarist government.[67]

The provisional government that was formed after the 1917 February Revolution had the intention of establishing public accountability and police with the main function of societal protection and maintenance of public order. The problem was that these measures were well overdue. The country was torn apart by tremendous social strain and political violence, and was financially bankrupted from participation in World War I. In the few months of its existence, the new police of the Provisional government had little chance to organize an effective police system. It was not surprising that it failed.

The relationship between the imperial police and the public was never quiescent. Soviet historians traditionally portray the Russian Empire's police as oppressive toward the peasants and workers, and protective toward the nobility and "other ruling classes" (Golunskyi et al., 1953). However, the historical literature suggests that it can only be partially true. The relationships were complex and multifaceted.[63] As an agent of paternalistic tsarist surveillance over the entire Russian population, the police were executing visible control, not only over the peasants and workers, but over all classes of society. When the idea of the monarchy was strong and the social and economic conditions in the country were stable, the overreaching police control was mostly accepted by all as a given condition of society (Lieven, 1989).

However, even during this stable time, the police were commonly perceived by the public as inefficient and bureaucratic. Charged with enormous functions, the police were usually overwhelmed with task requirements and required better systematization of institutions and funding. The reforms of police in the nineteenth and twentieth centuries were done sporadically and attempts of liberal changes[69] were retracted in the face of violence and political instability. This resulted in more conservative measures that were quickly taken under substantial pressures from peasant disturbances (Pugachev riot), noble riots (Decembrists), revolutionary assassinations, and the coup d'état (assassination of Alexander II and Revolution of 1905).

As a result, the funding was spent mostly on political police activities while regular crime investigations were deemed less important.[70] Thus, during the times when social transformation caused the crime rates to rise, the overall public dissatisfaction became more apparent. Despite some Soviet historians' claims that the police were serving only the interests of the nobility in Russia, noblemen who did not serve in the MVD, or wealthy merchants, had little control over the activities of the MVD and police.

The lack of police accountability and the strict vertical subordination contributed greatly to the inefficiency of local police agencies. Thus, corruption seems to be a natural outcome in these circumstances. It was triggered by the wide discretionary authority, poor funding, and lack of accountability. Corruption served not only as income substitution for the police officers, but also as a filtering mechanism in ranking the importance of their abundant tasks and cases. Corruption diminished the authority of the police among all societal groups. This was especially true among those underprivileged classes that did not have adequate resources or social status to convince the police to perform their functions efficiently in regard to their cases. Naturally, the underprivileged avoided the police and attempted to resolve their problems by other means. Despite these shortcomings, the historical literature suggests that Imperial Russian police, on average, were regarded with some level of respect and fear as agents of the tsarist authority. It was when the legitimacy of the monarchy was undermined and the social conditions rapidly deteriorated that many groups of Russian society, including some privileged citizens, became alienated with the notion of increased police surveillance and control. During these critical times, police (especially the secret police) were often viewed with contempt and defiance.

Table 1.1 Timetable of major events: 1802–1917

Year	Description
1802	Alexander I issued a Manifesto establishing MVD
1803	MVD's Central Department established, along with its four expeditions (subdivisions)
1804	Public medical expedition established within the MVD
1806	Main postal department transferred from the Senate to the MVD
1807	MVD created "address expeditions" in St. Petersburg
1816	MVD created "address expeditions" in Moscow
1819	New economic department established
1823	Department of foreign religious affairs created
1826	Third Department established by Nicolas I by the Decree of the Emperor
1827	Corps of Gendarmes created as a part of the Third Department
1833	The "collection of statutes on passports and runaways" policy issued
1837	The statute on County Police and the Instructions to the Governors issued, eliminating some positions in the county police and creating a new network of lower police officials
1857	Collection of Statutes of Russian Empire is established, consolidating regulations from 1833 and thereafter
1860	Investigative function removed from police to the newly created institution of investigative magistrates
1862	Alexander II issues a self-governance reform
1862	"Temporary Rules on Organization of police in provincial cities and districts governed by the General Rule" adopted to promote changes in police structure
1863	Functions of censorship performed by Committee on Foreign Censorship transferred from the Ministry of Education to MVD, marking the end of open press policies during the reign of Alexander II
1864	Alexander II issues a judicial reform
1864	*Zemstvos* established as self-governing local offices, and some basic functions of administrations transferred from the local police to the *zemstvos*
1864	Ustav of Criminal Proceeding established new criminal process
1865	All censorship functions are transferred from Ministry of Education to the MVD apparatus
1865	MVD established Chief Administration for Press Affairs and Censorship, concentrating all power of censorship with the MVD
1865	Temporary Rules and Censorship on Press adopted
1866	The first Division for Preservation of Public Order established in St. Petersburg
1867	Russian government restructures the eight gendarme districts and departments and creates the Main Department
1871	Gendarmes receive power to participate in the investigation of almost any criminal case and subordinate the governor and the regular police for their own purposes
1873	The Minister of the MVD receives an absolute power to close any publishing agency using amendments to the Temporary Rules on Censorship and Press
1878	The government creates *Uriadnik*, a new, lower police rank for rural police

(continued)

Table 1.1 Timetable of major events: 1802–1917 (continued)

Year	Description
1880	The Department of State Police is established
1881	Alexander III begins reign and develops "measures for protection of state and public order"
1882	The Decree on Secret Police Supervision issued
1883	The Decree on the Establishment of the Secret Police issued
1889	The position of *zemskyi nachal'nik* is created and was in charge of appointing judges
1890	The Law on Censorship issued
1896	Establishment of Special Section leading the security departments within the MVD
1902	Special Section expands number of local security departments to eight
1903	Special Section expands number of local security departments to 17
1903	Rural police expanded by new lower rank officers called "rural district guards"
1903	The Law on Passports issued
1904	The district gendarme departments, governor, and prosecutor constitutes a local "Special Council"
1905	A subdepartment of the local security department called the "special department" is created
1905	The first elected legislative body, the *Duma*, is established and allows some political representation of nonnoble members of Russian society
1906	Local security departments are combined within superior district security departments, abbreviated as ROO
1906	The Law on Censorship amended, eliminating preliminary censorship, but the "punitive" censorship remains
1907	Special section expands the number of local security departments to 27
1908	Eighty-nine new "detective" bureaus added to the district and city police departments
1912	The final draft of police reform issued by the tsarist government
1916	The law titled "Strengthening the Imperial Police in 50 Provinces and Improving Its Professional and Material Position" adopted
1917	The Department of State Police grows to 10 Secretariats within the central apparatus
1917	The February Revolution. The work of the State Police Department of the MVD and Corps of Gendarmes terminated and their leaders arrested
1917	An amnesty provided by the Provisional government and thousands of former convicts released from jails and prisons
1917	New structure of people's militia outlined by the special decree of the Provisional government

Endnotes

1. There is a difference of opinions among historians on the role of new ministries in Russian administration of government. Some believe that new ministries made government more hierarchical and farther removed from the voices of its subjects. Others maintained that ministries cultivated new attitudes among civil servants, who came to identify themselves as professionals overseeing the entire society, rather than representatives of the privileged group. Nevertheless, most

studies on the role of ministerial government in Russia agree that its creation reinforced the tendency for centralization and contributed to professionalism of the government service workers. For details, see Kaiser and Market (1994) and Lincoln (1994).

2. According to Mulukaev et al. (2005), the Police Chancery of St. Petersburg was few in numbers and consisted of only 67 people, of which 33 were privates. Cited by Mulukaev et al. from work of Kirillov, published in 1727.
3. Peasants assessors were elected only from so-called state peasants, who were serfs who belonged to the state or the Emperor and not to a private landlord.
4. Full Collection of Laws in Russian Empire. Volume 21 #15379. Hereafter cited as PSZ.
5. These groups included nonnoble gentry, merchants, free peasants, and clergy.
6. 2nd PSZ Volume 12 #10305.
7. 2nd PSZ Volume 12 #10303.
8. 2nd PSZ Volume 1 #449.
9. According to Mulukaev et al. (2005), the 1827, the Corps of Gendarmes included 4,138 officers. By 1850, the number of gendarmes reached 5,797.
10. According to Orlovsky (1981), the number of circulars issued by the MVD increased from 2 in 1810 to 16 in 1825. Between 1826 and 1853, the number of circulars grew significantly and consisted of approximately 180 per year (Orlovsky, 1981, p. 36).
11. On the increasing levels of education among the bureaucracy in the early nineteenth century, see the work by Pinter (1970).
12. According to Czap (1967), private and state serfs emancipated in 1861 and 1866 constituted about 65% of the Russian population at the time of reforms.
13. For example Abbot (1973) in his article reports that in 1857 in Yaroslavl province there were 244 policemen, of which 194 were concentrated in towns and cities.
14. 2nd PSZ Volume 37, part 2 #39087.
15. According to the explanation of Professor Foinitskyi (1912), these changes were done with the understanding that police function is incompatible with the idea of elected officials.
16. Par. 6 of temporary rules on organization of police in the cities and districts of the provinces governed by the General Rule. 2nd PSZ Volume 37, part 2 #39087.
17. For example, the witness testimony of a single witness was considered unreliable and should be dismissed, but the testimony of two witnesses that corroborate each other should be considered reliable.
18. Par. 257 and 258 of Decree of Criminal Proceedings (*Ustav Ugolvnago sudoporozvodstva*), full collection of Laws of Russian Empire (*Svod zakonov Rossiskoi Imperii*), Volume 16.
19. 2nd PSZ Volume 38 #39162.
20. 2nd PSZ Volume 40 #41988.
21. According to the article in People's Encyclopedia (Gordon et al., 1911), 26 periodicals were closed by the government between 1862 and 1904, and the work of periodicals was stopped 93 times without any explanation.
22. The magnitude of censorship work conducted by the MVD is outlined in the article by Rigberg (1966). According to the author, in 1861 the censorship offices approved 1,773 books and pamphlets, and in 1873 this number was 4,441.

23. According to Mulukaev et al. (2005), the network of censors that existed in 1882 was not very large. Only 44 censors total were responsible for the entire bulk of published titles.
24. According to work by Mulukaev et al. (2005), most peasant representatives played a small role in the conduction of preliminary investigations. They were often illiterate and had little knowledge of the criminal procedural rules. Therefore, when the crime was committed, they limited their function to reporting the crime and relevant information to *uriadniks* or *stannovoi pristav* and removed themselves from further investigations.
25. Capital cities of Moscow and St. Petersburg experienced a significant increase of crime rates during 1867–1978, which placed a substantial burden on the police (Abbott, 1977).
26. *Verst* is an old-fashioned Russian unit of length equal to 3,500 feet.
27. The amount of work conducted by "address sections" can be seen from statistics cited in the *Encyclopedic Dictionary* of Brockhaus and Efron (1890–1907). The *Encyclopedic Dictionary* reports that 17,100 rubles were spent annually for the budget of the address section in St. Petersburg in 1894–1896. The section annually processed 3 million "address tickets" (*vid na zhitels'tvo*) and issued 500,000 *spravkas* (registration certificates and others) to private citizens. In 1896 in St. Petersburg alone, police arrested 23,000 persons without passports.
28. Article by Kennan (1889) provides a number of accounts on how the rural police in Siberia were using their power to extort money from peasants.
29. According to Mulukaev et al. (2005), between 1858 and 1961, the crime rates grew by 2% annually, while the growth of population was less than 1%. In 1900, the crime rates grew by 48% compared to 1984, while the population growth was only 25%. According to Petrov (2004), the annual increase of crime between 1900 and 1909 was 7%. Petrov reports that the crime rates increased by 3.5% between 1850 and 1913.
30. Measures for protection of state and public order (*Mery k okhraneniyu gosudartvennago poryadka i obschestvennogo spokoistviya*). Collection of laws of Russian Empire (*Svod zakonov Rossiskoi Imperii*), Volume 14, Decree on prevention of crimes (*Ustav o preduprezhdenii i prisechenii prestubplenii), Appendix (Primechanie)* 2 to Paragraph 1.
31. According to Mulukaev et al. (2005), the Special Council met 153 times between 1881 and 1904 and tried 7,159 cases against 11,879 people.
32. The warrantless arrest could be done on the basis of "found suspicion" (*osnovatel'noe podozrenie*). Paragraph 21 of Measures for protection of state and public order (*Mery k okhraneniyu gosudartvennago poryadka i obschestvennogo spokoistviya*). Collection of laws of Russian Empire (*Svod zakonov Rossiskoi Imperii*), Volume 14, Decree on prevention of crimes (*Ustav o preduprezhdenii i prisechenii prestubplenii) Appendix (Primechanie)* 2 to Paragraph 1.
33. The growth of the MVD apparatus is confirmed by the budget allocations for this ministry. According to Orlovsky (1981), in 1855, the budget of MVD was 8.5 million rubles. In 1866, the MVD budget already exceeded 15 million rubles. According to Mulukaev et al. (2005), in 1887, the budget of MVD was equal to 73 million rubles, while the budget of other ministries were averaging 20 million rubles per year. In 1905, the budget of MVD grew by 40% and, in 1917, it consisted of more than 126 million rubles, according Rigberg (1966). It

should be noted, however, that despite this growth, the true police functions of MVD (including political police) were only performed by 4% of the ministries personnel in 1904 (Rowney, 1972). Most of the manpower in the MVD apparatus was concentrated at the different administrative departments (economic, *zemstvo*, communication, and migration) and technical departments (statistics, medicine, and veterinarian).

34. Article by Gamerman (2005) on the most remote province of the Russian Empire, the Far East, provides a good example of actual growth for both gendarmes and security departments networks. The author cites that, in 1880, the entire Far East region was under the supervision of the Siberian Gendarme district and few cities had a resident gendarme. In 1893, a special gendarme division of the *Ussuri* railroad was created and, in 1902, local Irkutsk Provincial Gendarme Department (GZhU) was established. In 1907, the Far East division of security department (RRO) was created, and in 1909, separate security "stations" were established in three major cities in the Far East (Khabarovsk, Blagoveshchensk, and Ussuriysk).
35. Paragraph 2 of Decree on district security departments (*Polozhenie o rayonnykh okhrannyh otdeleniyakh*), issued on December 14, 1906. The text is cited from the book by Peregudova (2000).
36. Paragraph 7 of Decree on district security departments. The text is cited from the book by Peregudova (2000).
37. Paragraph 24 of Decree on security departments (*Polozhenie ob okhrannykh otdeleniakh*) issued on February 9, 1907. The text is cited from the book by Peregudova (2000).
38. The importance of undercover work for the security departments and MVD can be exemplified by the fact that 3.5 millions rubles were spent annually, according to Mulukaev et al. (2005), for the compensation of the undercover agents/provocateurs working with political parties.
39. The level of political conservatism exhibited by the Imperial Police Department prior to 1917 can be shown in the excerpt from the book by the last head of the Police Department, Aleksei Vasil'ev. In his memoirs published originally in 1928, he strenuously denies any wrongdoings by the Secret Police and insists that "strictly legal measures" were taken only against "those adversaries of the Empire who were attentively but surely aiming at the diffusion in Russia of the poisonous gospel of Socialism" (Vasil'ev, 1933, p. 37). According to Zuckerman (1992, p. 269), political police of post-1905 Russia "isolated themselves within the fortress of [the] declining regime" in self-denial and complete disconnect from society.
40. Paragraph 4 of Law about Passports. (*Ustav o passportakh*). Collection of laws of the Russian Empire (*Svod zakonov Rossiskoi Imperii*), Volume 14.
41. Paragraph 3 of Law about Passports. (*Ustav o passportakh*). Collection of laws of the Russian Empire (*Svod zakonov Rossiskoi Imperii*), Volume 14.
42. Special chapter of Decree about Passports (paragraphs 67–75) regulated the movement and allowed places of residence by Jews. The movement and registration for Polish, Finish, and Northern Caucasus residents were also regulated by separate chapters. Collection of laws of Russian Empire (*Svod zakonov Rossiskoi Imperii*), Volume 14.

43. Law on Censorship (*Ustav o Tsensure*), 1890. Collection of laws of Russian Empire (*Svod zakonov Rossiskoi Imperii*), Volume 14.
44. Paragraph 4. Part 2. Law on Censorship (*Ustav o tsensure*), Collection of laws of Russian Empire (*Svod zakonov Rossiskoi Imperii*), Volume 14.
45. According to Rigberg (1966), between 1890 and 1914, the number of published periodicals in Russia increased sixfold (from 500 in 1891 to 3,111 in 1914). The number of books that underwent censorship in 1914 was 32,338. This is compared to 8,699 titles that were censored in 1895. According to Viktorskyi (1912), between 1906 and 1910, 1,270 periodicals were closed by the Censorship Department of MVD.
46. According to Rigberg (1969), the limits of censorship that MVD could impose on publications in the early 1900s were diffused. Many liberal journals published articles that would assume (not directly pronounce) to be radical for the time; ideas such as "partnership of the public and government in labor affairs" or "constitution limitations of the power." Publications often included serious criticism of the Duma, "exceptional measures" taken by Alexander III, or the enlargement of MVD power over time. Though many of these periodicals were reprimanded or closed, they frequently reappeared again under a new name. However, it should be noted that a double standard existed for censorship in these matters. Issues described above were published in the journals aimed at the "educated scholarly community" and not the populace. The information published in the newspapers and other accessible press had more severe restrictions from the censors.
47. The law on creation of detective bureaus issued on July 6, 1908 (*Zakon ob organizatsii sysknoi chasti*).
48. According to Mulukaev et al. (2005), in Moscow in 1907, only 10% of all registered crimes were solved.
49. Government priorities at this time can be exemplified by comparison of funding allocated to the regular and political police in Russia. According to Sichinskyi (2002), approximately 1.3 million rubles were allocated for the "detective bureaus" in 1909. The political police were allowed to spend up to 3.5 million rubles at the same time.
50. The attempts at reform also were undertaken during 1880–1885, when the commission of Kakhanov was developing a new police reform. The results of the commission calling for decentralization, control of local government over police, and unified legislation determining police function were dismissed by Alexander III. For details, see the work of V. M. Gessen (1905). In 1902, after the appointment of Lopukhin, the MVD also had intentions of liberal police reforms. However, the massive labor strikes in 1903 and Jewish pogroms in the same year undermined these liberal ideas and caused Lopukhin's resignation in 1905. For details, see the work by Ruud (1993).
51. On the differences in understanding the function of police and unsatisfactory state of police-related legislation at this time, please see V. M. Gessen (1908).
52. The Collection of decrees and decisions of the government. 1916, #307 Article 2426.
53. An interview of a Ukrainian male conducted in 1951 by the Harvard Project on Soviet Social System (Vol. 36, Case 492/(NY)1654) provides a good example of public feelings about tsarist police prior to the revolution in 1917. The father

of the respondent, who was "actively interested in public affairs" . . . and "was a deputy to the Duma and active in local government . . . was not satisfied with the tsarist regime" for two reasons: the unfair distribution of land among peasants and the abuse by tsarist police: "The police and gendarmes could act as they pleased, without taking account of the laws. If an ordinary man was treated unjustly by a policeman or official, he scarcely had any legal means of righting this in court" (p. 50).

54. *Sobranie Ukazov Vremennogo Pravitel'stva* (Collection of Decrees of Provisional government), 1917, #79, Article 453.
55. Many Russian researchers of that era had a clear understanding of the Russian police state. For details, see Dergileva (2011).
56. See the work by Pinter (1970) on the class characteristics of the civil government servants at the dawn of the eighteenth and beginning of the nineteenth century. Pinter reports that over a 75-year period, up to the mid-nineteenth century, the social structure of civil servants in Russia remained stable: 40% were nobles, 30% were junior military officers or civil servants, 20% were sons of churchmen, 5% were from all tax-paying classes (this includes peasants and servants), and 2% were sons of merchants and foreigners.
57. On the dual role of the MVD as the power for promoting the political tradition and the force of change, see Orlovsky (1981).
58. According to Burds (1996), by 1890 in the Central Industrial region (Moscow), more than a third of all adult peasant males were involved in some form of work that took them away from their villages for extended periods each year. According to Kantsev (2008), by 1890, the majority of southern regions in Russia (Kuban and Stavropol) consisted of the former peasants relocated from central Russia.
59. On the impact of emancipation and industrialization on the customary law and lifestyle of Russian peasants after the reforms, see Lewin (1985).
60. Data supplied in the article by Rowney (1972) provides a good example of this social class disparity. The first Russian census conducted in 1897 revealed that 86% of all the European population of the Russian Empire consisted of peasants, merchants of all classes constituted 11%, while hereditary nobility (class 1 and 2 in the table of ranks) were 1% of the population. Yet, among MVD managers, there were no peasants present at any time, merchants were at 3% in 1905, and at 5% in 1916, and the hereditary nobility constituted a majority: 83% in 1905 and 75% of all MVD managers in 1916.
61. The understanding of police function existing in the early twentieth century in Russia is very well outlined in the book of Deriuzhinskii (1911), who described factory workers' relations, healthcare (drunkenness and prostitution), public education, censorship, and emergency situations as areas included in the function of police. Also see Tarasov (1910) and Gessen (1908) on what areas of administration were included in the police law.
62. For example, the contemporary critique of excessive police authorities infringing on the personal liberties of the Russian citizens was offered by Viktorskyi in his book on criminal procedure published originally in 1912 (Viktorskyi, 1912).
63. An interview of Ukrainian–Russian males conducted in 1951 by the Harvard Project on Soviet Social System (Schedule B, Vol. 20, Case 440 (interviewer R. F.) provides an interesting example of attitudes within the tsarist government

of the late Russian Empire: "A tsarist officer [in the army] would never stop to shake hands with gendarme because the officer regarded the gendarmerie with contempt" (p. 14).

64. One of the signs of economic and political strain in urban Russia was an increasing amount of beggars. On the scope and efforts of both MVD and local administrations to resolve the problem of beggars and the homeless, please see Lindenmeyr (1982).
65. Soviet historians provided a different account for this period of time. In most Soviet literature, the period between 1881 and 1917 is portrayed as a constant increase of tsarist government oppression and rise of revolutionary movements by factory workers and peasants, which concluded with the revolution of 1917. However, this ideological point of view is not fully supported by historic evidence. Instead, the documents on economic development of the country, factory strikes, and activities by Mensheviks and Bolsheviks show that measures taken by the government right after the coup d'état in 1905 significantly reduced social instability in the country between 1906 and 1912. For details on these competing historic interpretations, please see Haimson (1964, 1965) and Thurston (1980).
66. This should not be unusual considering the social background of MVD leadership. According to the data provided by Rowney (1971) , 83% of MVD managers in 1905 were hereditary nobility. This number decreased only by 4% in 1914.
67. There is a difference of opinion on the exact role that tsarist policies on law enforcement played in the revolutions that occurred in the Russian Empire. Soviet and some post-Soviet historic literature traditionally claims that the reactionary oppression through total police control was the major (or sometimes even the only) reason for both revolutions in 1917. The Western literature frequently suggests that revolutionary coups occurring in Russia in 1905 and 1917 were mainly caused by the social and economic strain resulting from inefficient economy, participation in wars, and government administration. However, historians from both groups do not deny that police control executed by the MVD in the Russian Empire was a factor contributing to the political instabilities that in the end resulted in the February revolution of 1917.
68. One ethnographic account of such relations is presented by Gorer and Rickman (1949).
69. For example, the commission of Khananov and Lopukhin's appointment.
70. For example, see Abbot (1977) on neglect of solving crimes in St. Petersburg.

Creation and Early Development of the Soviet Police: 1917–1953

2

2.1 Creation of the Soviet Militia of Peasants and Workers—Its Role during the Civil War of 1917–1919

The new Bolshevik government was formed immediately after the Bolshevik coup d'état known as the October Socialist Revolution of 1917. The new government included the Peoples Commissariat of Internal Affairs (NKVD), the successor of the vast functions of the Ministry of Internal Affairs (MVD). Traditionally, the function of policing became a part of the NKVD's jurisdiction. Along with the NKVD, 13 other People's Commissariats were established forming the core of the new government headed by the Council of People's Commissariats (*Sovnarkom* or SNK).

Officially, the "workers' militia" was created by the decree of the SNK on November 10, 1917, titled "About Workers' Militia."[1] However, it was not considered a government institution per se, but rather a self-organization of armed people. This notion was based on the idealistic premise that in the Communist society, with no private property and equal rights for working people, there would be no crimes and over time the state and its institutions would wither away and became obsolete (Conquest, 1968a). According to the early theories of state by Lenin, instead of having police during the transitioning period to Communism, the entire working population should be armed and form a militia (Collins, 1976). Thus, the decree simply prescribed that local Soviet workers and soldiers' deputies (local executive agencies) establish the militia. The decree instructed all civil and military authorities to cooperate with the workers' militia and supply it with both materials and ammunition. The decree did not provide details of how the workers' militia should be staffed and funded, nor did it describe what the exact functions of the militia were, and it was left to the local Soviets to decide. The militia also was viewed as a part of the local executive authorities consisting of the Soviet people rather than a centralized law enforcement agency. Not surprisingly, the process of its creation varied by province and was quite cumbersome.

In some areas, the local Soviets required all workers to serve in the militia (Mityukova, 2008).[2] In other provinces, especially the ones that did not have a significant factory population, the militia of the Provisional

Government remained in place. However, this was only permitted if the existing policemen were loyal to the new Bolshevik regime and were supplemented by members of the Communist Party. However, in most provinces, the police functions were performed by the Red Guards and sometimes by the Red Army.[3]

The Red Guards were created earlier in 1917 and played an important role in the October Revolution of 1917.[4] However, "... they considered themselves regular workers who volunteered to take arms and stations in times of crisis. They were neither free nor inclined to long-term continuous duty" (Wade, 1984, p. 317). Therefore, Red Guards were reluctant to perform various police duties on a permanent basis, which were required at the time of a crisis and government transition. These duties included patrol, the maintenance of street-level public order, performing searches and seizures, providing security for the newly created government agencies (People's commissariats or *narkoms*), preventing "hooliganism" and public disorder, investigating both regular crimes and counterrevolutionary activities, and enforcing decrees of the new government (Collins, 1976). Nonprofessional militarized units of the Red Guards and the New Workers' Militia were ill-suited for many diverse duties. The lack of professional policing served to aggravate existing issues of public disorder, growing crimes, counterrevolutionary attempts to overturn the Bolshevik regime, and national movements in the remote provinces of the former Russian Empire.[5]

To alleviate the problem of anti-Bolshevik movements, in December of 1917, the Bolshevik government (SNK) created the notoriously famous extralegal *Cheka* (The Extraordinary Commission for Combating Counterrevolution and Sabotage). Originally, the *Cheka* was seen as a temporary solution for the extraordinary situation known as the "war Communism" period. The agency was envisioned to be above the law and guided only by the circumstances of the case and the employee's revolutionary conscience (Berman, 1963).

In reality, *Cheka* (later *Vecheka*), became "an iron hand" of the proletariat against "the bourgeois state machinery" and the new political police of the Bolshevik government (Juviler, 1976; Lapenna, 1968). Unlike other government agencies created right after the October revolution, *Vecheka* was not responsible to the SNK; instead, it was controlled by the Bolshevik Party itself. Between 1917 and 1921, *Vecheka* ran the border control and created a net of undercover agents in all spheres of Russian society that acted as an investigative and punitive agency for political crimes and any counterrevolutionary activities (Hingley, 1971; Levytsky, 1972).[6] "No significant aspect of Soviet economy and administration escaped its scrutiny or was safe from extralegal methods or repression" (Wolin and Slusser, 1957, p. 8).

The *Vecheka* took away the functions of political police from the regular factory militia (Knight, 1988). However, in reality, the NKVD and militia often acted as an accomplice to the *Vecheka* in conducting massive arrests and repressions (Juviler, 1976).[7] Predictably, in the eyes of the regular citizens, the *Vecheka* and NKVD were viewed as one repressive mechanism of the new Bolshevik government (Knight, 1984).[8] This situation resembled the relationship that the tsarist political police (Third Department, Corps of Gendarmes, and *Ohkranka)* had with the regular police and tsarist MVD (Waxmonsky, 1982).

During the years 1917–1918, the NKVD was rebuilding its departments and subdepartments and creating a new centralized apparatus. The functions of new departments within the MVD strikingly resembled the functions of the tsarist MVD prior to the February revolution. This was an executive agency that combined tremendous controlling, policing, and administrative duties. By June of 1918, the NKVD created 11 departments and hired over 400 staff members, who were responsible for the local self-administration, statistics, finances, medical aid, veterinary affairs, agriculture, immigration, foreigners, and the press (Mulukaev Malygin, and Epifanov, 2005).[9]

However, the central apparatus was helpless without efficient local police, therefore, in October of 1918, the NKVD acting jointly with the People's Commissariat of Justice (*Narkomiust*) issued a decree on the creation of a professional militia.[10] The new police forces were considered the executive agency of the local Workers and Peasant authorities and were created as a temporary measure to protect the revolutionary law and order. Unlike the previous decree, the instruction "On Organization of the Soviet Militia of Workers and Peasants" provided detailed structure, staff, sources of funding, and duties to the newly created institution. The members of the militia were appointed by the executive committees of the local Soviets of workers and peasants. The decree emphasized the class nature of the new law enforcement agency as the clergy, individuals who were employed in a trade, those receiving their income from nonlabor sources, individuals who employed others, and former members of the tsarist police were excluded from the Soviet police service (Fastov, 2005).

The duties of the Soviet militia included numerous activities other than maintenance of public order and crime investigation. Their responsibilities included administrative functions, such as control over the distribution of food and other goods; issuance of identification documentation; control of the population's movement including immigrants, war deserters, and captives; audit of budgetary spending; enforcement of medical and public sanitary requirements; and public order maintenance and conditions at strategically important buildings and structures (railroad stations, bridges, squares, etc).

The Soviet militia also was charged with first response and initial preliminary inquiry at the scene of a crime even though preliminary investigation of crimes itself was delegated to the "investigative commissions" or judges who worked under the People's Commissariat of Justice (Zelitch, 1931). In practice, the investigative commissions or judges frequently relied on the preliminary inquiry of the militia for adjudication due to high caseloads and the lack of qualified personnel (Mityukova, 2008).

A careful comparison of the Soviet militia's duties with the those of the imperial tsarist police demonstrates an amazing resemblance despite ideological and class differences. Also, like the tsarist police, the Soviet militia was facing similar issues. The abundance of administrative and control duties left little resources to perform functions of protecting public order and investigating regular nonpolitical crimes. The emphasis on suppressing political anti-Bolshevik riots and the "class nature" of crime control often led to selective enforcement and arbitrary use of power. These issues were exacerbated by the lack of funding and continuous chaos of civil war.

In April of 1919, the SNK issued a new decree "On Soviet Militia of Workers and Peasants," which significantly militarized the existing professional police.[11] The police service was considered equal to military duty. One third of all policemen were instructed to be sent to active army duty and all policemen were to receive military training (Rybnikov and Aleksushin, 2008).[12] According to another decree issued in June of 1920,[13] all local police departments could be used in military operations when ordered by the Revolutionary Military Council (the central command of the Red Army). The militarization of the police somewhat streamlined the chain of command and discipline within the local police departments. At the same time, militarization created an erroneous perception of the police function as being just another auxiliary military unit.[14] The militarization of the militia is believed to be a direct response to the continuous challenges presented by the civil war and interventions of foreign armies.

During the period of 1918 through 1920, the militia ranks also were expanded as the law enforcement body assisted the army in suppressing political opposition to the Bolsheviks. This opposition often was well organized and controlled large territories in several Russian provinces. There were over 10 known "White" governments (organized political opposition of a democratic or monarchic nature fighting against the Soviet government) that existed during the period of 1917 to 1920 in Russia.[15]

They controlled remote territories of Russia in Southern, Siberian, and Far East regions for various periods of time. Oftentimes, these oppositional centers were directly or indirectly supported by foreign governments. During the creation of the typical White government, pro-White law enforcement agencies were often established from the old tsarist cadres and supporters of the monarchic or non-Bolshevik governments. So, when the Red Army defeated the troops of the White government, the most experienced militia workers within the body of the army would be left to destroy the existing White oppositionists' law enforcement agencies and create their own "Red" law enforcement agencies from the loyal local supporters (Gonyukhov and Gorobtsov, 2002).

Similar processes were happening in the remote provinces of the former Russian Empire inhabited by ethnic minorities. In the Ukraine, Belarus, Central Asia, and the North Caucasus, nationalistic governments, supported by various forces, were establishing sovereign countries and proclaiming independence from the former Russian Empire. Members of militia were often sent to these regions as a part of a "liberating" Red Army. After defeating the rebellious nationalistic governments, the militia remained to rebuild the law enforcement infrastructure to ensure loyalty to the Bolsheviks.[16] In this regard, the Soviet militia was no different than a tsarist police colonizing force used to shape the antagonistic regions to the will of the central state in Moscow (Shelley, 1996).

The overall quality of manpower in the Soviet militia during this period remained questionable.[17] The "class origin" was given a priority when recruiting the new cadres and very little training was offered to the newly hired staff (Shelley, 1996). With expanding demand for new policemen, the new recruits were mostly illiterate, inexperienced, and often were of questionable moral character.[18] Experienced professional policemen were often transferred to work at the *Vecheka* because struggles against political enemies continued to be a priority over the maintenance of public order and solving regular crimes.

Crimes continued to grow while industry and agriculture suffered a sharp decline due to a lack of manpower and the civil war.[19] These factors created thousands of unemployed, homeless individuals, soldiers deserting from the war, and abandoned children wandering the streets.[20] The Soviet militia, however, was mostly preoccupied with the "class struggle" against enemies of the Revolution and enforcement of the new state economy. The new state economy often resulted in the redistribution of goods from the wealthy to the poor (so-called "*prodrazverstka*"), arrest, execution of "class enemies," and enforcement of mandatory labor duties.[21]

The notoriously known decree, "On Red Terror," issued September 9, 1918, provided law enforcement officers with almost unlimited repressive authority to arrest, seize, and execute "the counterrevolutionary elements." Not surprisingly, the abuse of power among Soviet militiamen was unprecedented and created strenuous and sometimes hostile relationships between law enforcement agents and citizens (A.V. Petrov, 2006b). Wealthy peasants, servicemen, educated professionals, and other "nonworking classes" had little respect for the new law enforcement arrangement and often considered their activities criminal (A.V. Petrov, 2006a). Unfortunately, the existing alternatives were not much better. The law enforcement agencies of the White governments were often reported to act in a similar manner in controlled territories by terrorizing the local population, seizing goods, and executing political enemies with no justice or mercy (Gonyukhov and Gorobtsov, 2002).

2.2 Policing during the New Economic Policy (NEP) of 1921–1928

By 1921, the Red Army defeated the majority of political opposition in the central, western, and northern provinces of Russia. The foreign interveners were expelled and nationalistic governments in the Ukraine, White Russia (Belarus), and the Transcaucasia area[22] were liquidated. Some areas of political resistance still existed in Siberian and Far East provinces, but they no longer represented a significant threat to Soviet authority. In the aftermath of the civil war, it became clear that the Russian economy was devastated and that methods of "war Communism" (forceful expropriation of food from the peasants, liquidation of currency, and control over the distribution of goods by law enforcement) were not sufficient to restore the country's wealth (Zakhartsev, 2004). Rioting by hungry peasants and factory workers were frequent during 1920 as chaos continued to reign over the Russian territory (Juviler, 1976).[23]

Under these circumstances, the New Economic Policy (NEP) was announced by Lenin as a temporary measure of relative economic liberalization. Private trade (both wholesale and retail) was initially allowed and "cooperatives" of workers were organized to produce goods for sale. The food was no longer expropriated from the peasants by means of force, but instead wealthy peasants were taxed. Again, hired labor was allowed and skillful managers ("nepmen") were appointed to run state businesses that would be working independently without government subsidies (so-called *khozraschet*) (Zakhartsev, 2004). Yet this economic liberalization was limited and government administrative control placed restrictions on pricing, hiring conditions, profits, and other economic factors. Even new legal codes, adopted during the NEP period. included official restriction on the legal transactions that would preclude "prejudice against the state" and "unjust enrichment." The private rights were guaranteed as long as they did not contradict their "socioeconomic purpose" (Berman, 1950). These new economic conditions required a new government structure. Therefore, it was not surprising that the NKVD, as the largest controlling agency of the state, underwent some transformation during this period.

The new decree on the legal status of the NKVD was adopted on May 24, 1922, and prescribed that the NKVD should administer all "communal" business, supervise local administration, and enforce execution of all "administrative" decrees of central and local authorities.[24] Numerous documents that followed supplemented this ill-defined jurisdiction with various functions created by the new economic relationship.[25] The NKVD was responsible for registration of nonprofit organizations, unions,[26] and religious organizations; issuance of various licenses; building and maintaining local roads, power stations, municipal transportation, and bridges; collecting taxes from peasants; and enforcing military drafts (Mulukaev, Malygin, and Epifanov, 2005; Rybnikov and Aleksushin, 2008; Timofeev, 2006).[27] This was in addition to the preexisting duties of the NKVD that currently included registration of citizen's movement, issuance of all documents, administration of correctional institutions including labor camps, prevention and investigation of crimes, and the maintenance of public order.

With the abundance of administrative functions, recent political threats, and new complex relations based on a limited free market, the militia's attention to regular crimes and public order remained minimal. Moreover, the crime prevention idea was based on the premise that all crimes were committed by the "antisocial harmful elements" reflecting a residual of capitalist society (Kamalova, 2008). At the same time, crime rates continued to grow, streets were filled with homeless adults and abandoned children, and rates of solved crimes remained low.[28] The situation was exacerbated by the antialcohol campaign started by the Communist Party, tensions between political police and the NKVD, along with the creation of the USSR in 1922.

On December 14, 1922, following the instruction of the VtSIK[29] and SNK, the NKVD issued "The Instruction on Struggle against Drinking."[30] The instruction outlawed not only binge drinking and public drunkenness, but also distillery of alcohol, including domestic production for personal consumption. The new policy was adopted three weeks before Orthodox Christmas holidays, a traditional period of festivities in Russia. To execute the new policy, the militia made raids on villages where they seized and destroyed alcohol produced by wealthy peasants (*kulaks*) and to city restaurants where both customers and owners were arrested for serving or consuming alcohol publicly (Weissman, 1986).[31] Needless to say, the new policy diverted the already strained resources of the Soviet militia away from solving crimes and maintaining public order, which created opportunities for new abuse of power and public–police tensions (Shelley, 1996).[32]

Growing dissatisfaction with the methods of "Red Terror" among the members of the Communist Party resulted in the abolition of the notorious *Vecheka* on February 6, 1922.[33] It was a logical step because the *Vecheka* was declared to be a temporary office needed only "for protection of revolution," which by 1921 was no longer in danger. The abolition was also a measure to restore "the revolutionary legality" because the arbitrary visible terror tactics were no longer tolerated by both the Russian and international communities (Levytsky, 1972).[34]

The functions of the struggle against counterrevolutionaries and the protection of borders were traditionally transferred to the NKVD, which established the "State Political Department" (abbreviated GPU) to accomplish these purposes. The authorities of the newly created institution were significantly curtailed compared to the ones provided to the *Vecheka,* and the political police were officially subordinated to the NKVD and, thus, to the SNK. The GPU was created as a purely investigative agency without the power to impose death penalties in the absence of a judicial sentence. Regular crimes, such as speculation, malfeasance, and other offenses that were previously adjudicated by the *Vecheka* were transferred to the *Narkomiust* (People's Commissariat of Justice) and dealt with by the revolutionary tribunals, or people's courts (Gerson, 1976).[35] However, both the new limitations and subordination were a short-lived phenomenon. Already in August of 1922, the GPU regained the authority to exercise extrajudicial "administrative exile." This allowed three years of confinement for counterrevolutionaries to remove them from society (Conquest, 1968b).[36]

By July of 1923, the GPU was transformed into the OGPU (United State Political Department) after the USSR was established and reinstated as an independent permanent institution (Knight, 1988). According to Article 61 of the first USSR Constitution, the OGPU was charged with the duty to "unite the revolutionary efforts of all Union republics in the struggle against political and economic counterrevolution, espionage, and banditism"[37] (Richelson, 1985). Many historians believed that even during the years of 1922 and 1923, the subordination of the GPU was just a formality and no significant changes were made to the structure of the *Vecheka* since its transformation into the GPU (Dziak, 1988; Hingley, 1971; Wolin and Slusser, 1957). Like its predecessor, the GPU retained control over "special troop units" and special departments to combat a counterrevolution in the armed forces and railways (Gerson, 1976).

Moreover, in 1923, under the premise of a NKVD reform, the OGPU made an attempt to take away the law enforcement functions from the NKVD. However, the VtSIK rejected this proposition because this would create an unnecessary centralization of the law enforcement function. Centralization would have contradicted the agreement establishing the USSR and signed by Russia, the Ukraine, Belarus, and the Transcaucasian republics on December 12, 1922 (Mulukaev, Malygin, and Epifanov, 2005).[38] Tensions between the NKVD and OGPU continued during the NEP period with the OGPU regaining many of its extrajudicial powers.[39] There were ongoing attempts to subordinate the local militia to the needs of the political police and a centralization of the law enforcement functions.[40]

The function of law enforcement was considered to be the jurisdiction of the republics even before the establishment of the USSR. Since its creation in 1918, the professional militia had a dual subordination to both local executive authorities (soviets) and to the republic NKVD. Thus, when the union agreement was signed by the republics in 1922, there was no all-union or federal NKVD created. Each of the four republics continued to have their own autonomous NKVD, even though criminal law and procedure was considered a matter of federal jurisdiction. To coordinate the law enforcement policy within the country, the republican NKVDs conducted consulting conferences where they developed coordinated efforts for crime prevention and public order maintenance. Moreover, even before the USSR was created, the majority of NKVD funding was transferred to the local provincial budgets. This resulted in serious underfunding of the local militia in all four new USSR republics[41] (Holodny, 2010; Mulukaev, Malygin, and Epifanov, 2005). Local authorities (Soviets) did not always find the work of the local militia important when facing other serious demands for funding (Weissman, 1991). On the other hand, the funding of the OGPU, as a federal agency, continued to grow, which created a significant drain of personnel from local NKVD to local OGPU offices.[42]

The ill-defined abundance of functions, poor funding, lack of coordination among republican leadership, and continuing political intrigues between both the OGPU and NKVD resulted in further deterioration of police work and widespread abuse of power by policemen during the NEP period.[43] The situation with police was even worse in the countryside where Soviet authorities could not rely on the peasants to the same degree as they relied on the factory workers in the cities (Weissman, 1991). The Soviet government's solution to these issues was a combination of economic stimulus, grassroots initiatives, and some repressive measures.

In early 1922, the total number of policemen was reduced by 60%, which was justified by the end of the active military operations against counterrevolutionaries and serious deficits that had affected local budgets (Holodny, 2010). The republics became responsible for the funding of the law enforcement agencies.[44] The local authorities continued reduction of police manpower through the entire period of the NEP and, by 1929, the Soviet militia was only 40% of the total number of the tsarist police that existed in 1916 (Mulukaev, Malygin, and Epifanov, 2005). Significant disparity existed among different provinces in levels of militia salary and other funding.[45] Local factories and businesses were assigned to be "mentors" to the different militia units that sometimes resulted in a temporary improvement of the militia's funding, but these measures were unable to solve the problem in general. Monetary compensation was provided to the local NKVD's personnel, who achieved extraordinary results in solving crimes or other important activities.[46] Often percentages from administrative fines or seized property's value were used to fund the local Soviet militia.[47] These economic measures, however, produced additional abuse of power rather than improvement in the work of local militia.

The conferences of factory workers and administrative militia commissions conducted regular meetings during the years 1922 to 1927 where they provided feedback on the work of local policemen.[48] During these meetings, citizens recommended terminating or promoting certain militia members based on the overall assessment of their work. New candidates from the pool of workers, or peasants, were suggested to become the local militia members (so-called "*vydvizhenchestvo*"). Though these measures can be considered democratic, they were limited only to the discussion of lower-rank police officers, were mostly conducted in the urban areas, and did not influence the overall leadership or direction of the NKVD's policy. Moreover, *vydvizhenchestvo* supported the idea that police work can be done by anyone (former workers or peasants) with no prior training or education. Instead, the most important factor when selecting the new members from the pool of workers or peasants remained their "class origin" and the "revolutionary conscience" of the candidate.[49]

Finally, the quality of police work was sought to be improved by the "purges" in the ranks of the NKVD. Officially, Soviet historians admit that at least one major purge occurred in the 1922–1923 period among the NKVD members. Unlike repressive measures conducted during the "war Communism" period, this purge targeted not only the "class enemies" of the ruling proletariat, but also was focused on finding the "bad apples" among the militia's members, workers, and peasants themselves. The repressions were done by the OGPU as a part of continued tensions between the two major law enforcement agencies. The arrests were frequently based on denunciation from members of the NKVD themselves and resulted mostly in sentences to labor camps, exile, or sometimes executions. However, the scale of these repressions and level of violence were incomparable to the purges that occurred in the 1930s.[50] Thus, the repression's deterrence effects remained relatively low and the impact on the quality of police work was insignificant (Mulukaev, Malygin, and Epifanov, 2005).

2.3 Transformation of the Soviet Police under Stalin (1930s–1953)

During the period from 1924 to 1928, Joseph Stalin emerged as the sole leader of the Bolshevik Party by skillfully navigating the intraparty differences among the factions of the Bolshevik government. In the process of these long-lasting intrigues, Stalin used the existing extrajudicial powers of the OGPU to wipe out his political opponents within the party and government structures. This was a time when the political police became a tool of a one-man dictatorship rather than a vehicle of political party control. During this process, the NKVD became an unnecessary "alternative" to the OGPU's monopoly. Unlike the OGPU, by the late 1920s, the NKVD was still mainly a decentralized agency with regular police operating under the local executive power of Soviets. The leadership of the NKVD was among supporters of potential Stalin rivalries[51] and the overall performance of the NKVD in campaigns against religion and forceful collectivization of peasants was found unsatisfactory.[52]

Thus, in December of 1930, the NKVD was officially abolished and its functions dispersed among other agencies. Formally, an independent law enforcement agency (Main Directorate of Militia) was created at the level of the SNK for each republic to direct the work of the militia.[53] However, the secret instruction issued on the same day commanded the OGPU to take control over the militia in their law enforcement activities. To fulfill these duties, the OGPU created a "Main Inspection of Police and Detective Work" within its structure on December 30, 1930.[54]

By the end of 1932, the relationships between the OGPU and militia were no longer a secret. Both the SNK and VtSIK issued a decree on the "Establishment of the Main Directorate of Factory Peasant Police under the Structure of OGPU."[55] It was during this time in the early 1930s that the regular police were sought to be reformed by the "best practices" gathered through the experiences of the Vecheka, GPU, and OGPU. These novelties included expansion of "preventive policing," close public–police interaction, and promotion of self-policing, thereby making the process of policing more of a rationalized, automatic, and bureaucratic process (Hagenloh, 1999).

The "preventive policing" ideas developed in Soviet society during the NEP period were based on the understanding of criminal offenders as being "harmful, antisocial" elements that were "reminiscent of capitalism" (Gonyukhov and Gorobtsov, 2002). The proactive, rather than reactive policing, therefore, prescribed to isolate and incapacitate these elements before they could do any significant harm to the society. The criminal punishments, including exile and labor camps, were viewed, according to the Criminal Code of 1923, as the measures of social protection rather than deterrence or rehabilitation. The class origin and socialist danger of the offender's personality were key factors in determining the severity of "protective measures" while the nature of the offense itself played a much smaller role in the sentencing process (Berman, 1963). The policy of "preventive policing" was at the core of the GPU–OGPU work, but was only infrequently used by the regular police during the NEP period (Zakhartsev, 2004).

However, after the acquisition of the regular police by the OGPU, preventive policing became a pronounced technique used by the regular police during the 1930s. The category of "harmful elements" was expanded to include speculators, hooligans, "kulaks" (landowning peasants), violators of the passport regime, and, later, violators of state property. Other initiatives of the OGPU to reform regular police, the creation of undercover agents, and expansion of voluntary popular participation in the work of regular police had failed by the mid-1930s (Hagenloh, 1999).

On July 10, 1934, the NKVD was reinstated as the all-union agency of executive power.[56] The OGPU, worker-peasant militia, and detective departments ("*ugro*") all became parts of the new, large NKVD. However, it is hardly disputed that the OGPU continued to play a leading role within the structure of the NKVD during this time. According to the decree, the goals of the new agency included not only protection of the revolutionary law and order, and borders of the USSR, but also protection of the socialist "state" property and maintenance of "the records of act of citizen's conditions" (so-called ZAGS).[57]

The republics of the USSR were instructed to create subordinate NKVDs at their level, except for the RSFSR (Russian Soviet Federated Socialist Republic), for which the position of the representative of the NKVD of the USSR was established. Creation of the federal law enforcement agency was a direct violation of the all-union agreement signed by the republics in 1922 when the USSR was established (Mulukaev, Malygin, and Epifanov, 2005). Most historians agree that the establishment of an all-union NKVD signified further strengthening of political police and processes of centralization occurring in the 1930s under Stalin (Fastov, 2005; Shelley, 1996; Solomon, 1996).

With the existence of the all-union NKVD, the funding for local offices was centralized, which significantly reduced the connection of local militia offices with the local executive authorities. This tendency continued through the 1930s, effectively disallowing the local Soviets to nominate the members of the local militia or to remove them from their position (Hagenloh, 1999).[58] Instead, these functions were absorbed by the local OGPU officers and/or local party officials. The appointments were done through the superior officers of the NKVD, which transformed the NKVD into a hierarchical linear system directed from the center and controlled by the political police leadership.[59]

Even prior to the absorption of the regular police, the OGPU began waives of oppressive measures—purges—that were focused on finding "harmful" elements within the Soviet apparatus including the NKVD itself. In 1929, in connection with the Tolmachev case (head of the NKVD), over 15% of the existing NKVD apparatus was "cleansed" of the "bourgeois elements," "counterrevolutionaries," and other harmful individuals. Throughout the period from 1929 to 1931, purges continued among "old Bolsheviks" and "intelligentsia."[60] In the early 1930s, "dekulakized"[61] wealthy peasants also became main subjects of oppressions.

Up until the mid-1930s, purges were conducted among party members at all levels and especially after the assassination of Kirov in 1934.[62] The period from 1937 to 1938 is traditionally viewed as the culmination of the repressive purges. During this period, the local police were given quotas and required to arrest "harmful" elements. They were ordered to fill the quotas with suitable individuals (Levytsky, 1972).[63] The NKVD itself, including the political police, was under a constant cleansing with two heads of the NKVD (Yagoda and Ezhev) vanishing at the hands of their own subordinates.

During the late 1920s, the regular police remained relatively separated from the extrajudicial repressions conducted by the political police and were only viewed as auxiliary manpower needed for massive political operations. However, after the submission of the regular police to the OGPU in 1930, and the later creation of the all-union NKVD, which united political and regular police under the same name in 1934, the line between repressions of political police and activities of regular militia gradually disappeared.

The Special Board (*osoboe soveschanie,* abbreviated OS, of the NKVD) that was created as a part of the reinstated NKVD in 1934 became a new extrajudicial agency for repression (Rousset, 1953). The NKVD OS had authority to sentence "harmful elements" to "administrative exile" outside the Soviet Union or up to five years in a labor camp (Lavroff, 1963). In 1937, the term was extended to seven years and also became extendable "at the sole whim of the authorities of the NKVD to imprisonment of unlimited duration" (p. 31). Yet, at the time, this was considered a limitation of political police power because NKVD OS did not have the authority to carry out death sentences (Getty, 2002).

The panels of two or three (so-called "*dvoiki*" *and* "*troiki*") members of NKVD, Bolshevik Party members, and prosecutors were created to execute the authorities of the Special Board. Their decisions were made without any specific procedure, did not require the presence of defendants, and were impossible to appeal. Although, according to NKVD instructions, a *troika* should usually include members of the political police in the remote provinces, and under the extremely high case load, members of the regular police and other NKVD officials were also included in these repressive agencies (Getty, Rittensporn, and Zemskov, 1993).

During the process of forced collectivization, records maintained by the regular police officers, or even their personal recollections, were often used to identify wealthy individuals whose property was to be seized for use on the collective farms. Again, when special troops of the OGPU were unavailable, regular police were summoned to conduct the collectivization, to seize the property, and sentence to administrative exile the most dangerous kulaks from the villages.[64] The successful process of industrialization proclaimed by the Communist Party in the 1930s was mainly achieved by use of slave labor from those "harmful elements," kulaks, and other repressed categories.

The labor camps became a part of the reinstated NKVD in 1934 and remained one of the most important economic assets of Soviet industrialization for over 20 years.[65] Though the Main Department of Labor Camps (GULAG) was a separate subdivision of the NKVD unrelated to regular police and detective bureaus, the gradual involvement of regular police in the work of labor camps made this division of duties less clear. Members of the regular police were often charged with surveillance of exiled individuals in the remote provinces and were present in the areas of "special settlements as representatives of the state." [66]

A passport system was reinstated by Stalin in 1932 and became one of the most important ways in which regular police participated in the repressions. Even though some control of factory workers' movements had existed in the cities since the 1920s (through labor books and required registration in the urban areas), this control was neither total nor systematic (Matthews, 1993). The duties to maintain records of citizens' movement were transferred multiple times from militia to the local executive agencies, which resulted in a poor quality of record keeping (Goldman, 2003). However, starting from 1932, the internal passport became a universally required document for specified areas and the militia received a valuable tool to control the movement of undesired elements within certain territories (Benvenuti, 1997).[67]

The members of collective farms were denied passports, which precluded them from leaving rural areas and moving into the cities. Regular police also had the discretion to deny passports to other citizens categorized as being harmful elements by which they continued the policy of "preventive policing" (Waxmonsky, 1982).[68] Persons without passports, and those who were denied passports, were exiled to the remote provinces of Russia.[69] Records obtained as a result of passport applications allowed the police to maintain information on each citizen and became a basis for selecting victims of planned purges (Matthews, 1993).

Important changes also were made to the investigative functions of regular police in the late 1930s. Prior to 1928, the Soviet criminal justice system, at least formally, was loosely based on the judicial reforms of 1864. The official legal function to conduct a "preliminary investigation" was given to the investigator who was the judicial officer and belonged to the People's Commissariat of Justice.[70] This judicial officer was authorized to order arrests, searches and seizures of defendants, and to depose witnesses from both the prosecution and defense (Borisenko, 1925). He was neither a representative of the prosecution nor of the defense and was enjoying at least some level of independence (Gutsenko, 2005). The regular police were charged only with undercover and other nonlegal activities that focused on finding the perpetrator, solving the crime, and conducting the "preliminary inquiry" (Lyubimov, Pomerantsev, and Kiselev, 1928).

It was only for minor offenses that such a police inquiry was sufficient to transfer the case to the court. In other more serious offenses, the police inquiry was simply a predecessor of the investigation conducted by the judicial investigator.[71] After the creation of the State Attorney's office (*procuracy*) of the RSFSR in 1922, and later the Procuracy of USSR in 1924, the procurators received authority to supervise the courts and authorize arrests and seizures (Karnitskyi and Strogovitch, 1925).[72] In 1928, the investigators were transferred from the court to the *procuracy*, and, in 1933, the *procuracy* was removed from the court system and became an executive law enforcement agency (Vyshinskyi and Undrevitch, 1934). This transformation allowed the officers of the *procuracy* to conduct investigations completely independent from any judicial oversight.[73]

During 1930s, *procuracy* investigators were overburdened with the campaigns against political crimes, so they often unofficially allowed regular police to conduct investigations for all nonpolitical crimes (Solomon, 1996). By the late 1930s, this practice was legalized and the investigative function was officially provided to some agencies of regular police.[74] No judicial oversight for search, arrest, pretrial detention, and deposition of witnesses was required; the prosecutor's review alone was sufficient (Strogovitch, 1940).[75] By the late 1940s, the investigative departments were created in almost every regional department of the regular police (Chel'tsov, 1948). This expansion of authority created some confusion about the nature of police investigation and became one of the key issues in the reform of Russian police after the Soviet Union collapsed.

The overall relationship between the regular police and public remained difficult throughout the 1930s. The increasing participation of regular police in political repressions, policies of "preventive policing," and administrative control through the passport system resulted in public fear of the entire NKVD including regular police.[76] The wealthy strata of the Russian peasants remained hostile toward representatives of the police after the process of forced collectivization. However, the poorest members of peasant communities who benefited from collectivization were among police supporters. Regular police were mainly using the position of "rural executives" (*sel'skie ispolniteli*) to coordinate their daily activities in the villages.[77] Rural executives were established in 1924 as a semigovernment position to bridge the gap between the urban police and villages' population, but, by 1932, they were deeply involved in the forcible processes of dekulakization and collectivization (Govorov and Remneva, 2007).

The regular police continued to ignore "nonpolitical" crimes or those that did not threaten state security. Stalin's "political controls had no equal. But his social controls against ordinary crimes of everyday life turned out flaccid, spiritless, and bumbling" (Juviler, 1976, p. 67). However, the tremendous repressions of population resulted in some decline of all the crime rates from 1934 through 1935, which had remained high since the 1917 October Revolution.

The situation was somewhat different for the population of factory workers. In 1928, the clubs of factory workers in Nijnii Tagil (located about 1,250 miles northeast of Moscow) created the first voluntary society for police assistance (so-called *Osodmil*), which became a successful populace movement in public–police cooperation in Soviet Russia.[78] However, by 1932 the movement was institutionalized and subordinated to the control of the OGPU. As a result, the effectiveness of the volunteer organizations reportedly declined.[79]

In the period from 1939 to 1940, the USSR annexed the Baltic States, parts of the Western Ukraine, Belarus, and Finland, which resulted in the influx of new populations into the USSR (Hingley, 1971). The political police shifted their massive repressive operations to the newly acquired territories, while the regular police were charged with the task of building Soviet law enforcement systems in the new areas.[80]

Soviet historians traditionally portray the creation of the new law enforcement systems in these regions as a democratic process,[81] but accounts of witnesses and historic documents suggest otherwise. Prior to annexation, socialist parties in these regions were weak, small, and underdeveloped. After the annexation, representatives of the newly established political police were instructed to determine "socially harmful elements" in the new provinces (which in most cases contained individuals with higher education, the wealthy, economically independent, and unsupportive of socialist ideals) (Levytsky, 1972).

The surveillance of "anti-Soviet" elements usually resulted in deportations to the remote regions of Siberia and Kazakhstan (Rousset, 1953).[82] Political repressions were followed by the creation of a new law enforcement system that was formed on the basis of "class origin" and membership in the socialist parties. Members of regular police from the USSR often resided in the newly acquired areas to control and develop new police agencies. Many of these representatives were of "Slavic" origin and spoke Russian.[83] Thus, repressions and abuse of power by political and regular police were often viewed by locals as an assault on national identity and Russian occupation. "Verbal and physical attacks on the militia in the Gorbachev period were one legacy of this repressions" (Shelley, 1996, p. 35).

After the USSR entered World War II in June of 1941, all structures of the NKVD were mobilized for participation in the active military operations. Just in the first month of the war alone, 35% of regular police personnel were drafted into the Red Army. The special and interior troops of the NKVD were drafted as well to participate in the active military operations. Their main police functions were often focused on the operations of partisan groups in occupied territories, a search for spies within Red Army members, and so-called protective "*zagraditelnye*" activities in the army (when the troops were placed behind the infantry to prevent their retreat during critical battles) (Dziak, 1988; Mulukaev, Malygin, and Epifanov, 2005; Rybnikov and Aleksushin, 2008). [84] In the unoccupied territories of the USSR, the military subdivisions of the NKVD also protected strategic factories, food supplies, and ammunition for the Red Army.

Beginning in 1943, the NKVD special and interior troops were focused on restoring pubic law and order and enforcing Soviet authority on recently freed provinces (Levytsky, 1972). In doing so, troops were allowed to patrol the streets, create checkpoints on the main roads, and detain any "suspicious elements." A decree of the NKVD issued on July 1, 1943,[85] instructed interior troops to search for all suspicious individuals who should be detained and transferred for further investigation by the political police. The decree applied to those who were previously captured by German troops, those residing in areas surrounded by German troops, those who served in any government institution created during the German occupation (especially the agencies of German police), those who had collaborated with German authorities in any way, and, finally, those involved in counterrevolutionary activities (Hingley, 1971).[86] The situation was especially difficult for those in the recently acquired territories of Western Ukraine, Belarus, and the Baltic states.

The local residents had already suffered from the political repressions during the period of 1939 to 1940. Subsequently, these local residents of the annexed nations often saw collaboration with Nazi Germany authorities as the only way to restore their national sovereignty and separate from the USSR. Using the chaos and disorder of war, many nationalistic resistance groups were formed by Ukrainians, Belarusians, and residents of Baltic states (Dziak, 1988). German authorities often manipulated the nationalistic sentiments of locals by providing these groups with ammunition and supplies. The NKVD special and internal troops, as the most loyal members of Soviet authority, were sent to battle with the armed separatist resistance after 1943. As a result of these operations, most members of nationalistic resistance groups were killed while some were arrested and deported to labor camps or sentenced to death.[87]

The remaining regular police in unoccupied territories of the USSR were supplemented with women and retired militia officers to compensate for the loss of manpower that resulted from the war (Kalinin, 2007).[88] In addition to regular functions, their duties included street patrols to detect deserters and spies, enforcing universal labor duties, and protection of state property (Mayurov, 2005).[89] The war-time conditions exacerbated state-related property crimes, such as black marketing of food and theft from collective farms and factories. All of these offenses were treated as counterstate activities and punished harshly (Gusak, 2010).

The work of regular legal institutions was frequently suspended during the war and many cases were processed on the basis of summary justice or by extrajudicial institutions, such as the Special Board of NKVD (OS of NKVD) (Solomon, 1987). Preliminary investigations were done in a matter of days, no authorization for arrests and searches was needed by police, and verdicts were often subject to immediate execution with no right to appeal (Isaev, Karev, and Utevskyi, 1948). The authorities of extrajudicial agencies (OS of NKVD) also were expanded in 1941 under the martial laws of wartime and included the ability to sentence "counterrevolutionary elements" to the labor camps for 25 years or to death.[90] These authorities were often used when dealing with the citizens of the USSR who were captured by the German army and those who had any type of contact with German authorities. According to official statistics, OS of NKVD sentenced over 10,000 citizens to death for treason-related activities between 1942 and 1945 (Mulukaev, Malygin, and Epifanov, 2005). The opportunities of the OS also were used to continue the policy of "preventive policing." The territories declared under martial law were often swept by police to find individuals who will potentially cooperate with Nazi Germany if the territory will become occupied. The "pro-Nazi" elements were exiled to the remote territories of Siberia and Central Asia or placed in the labor camps.[91]

At the same time, the war period brought to life new forms of public–police cooperation. Starting in 1941, factory workers and other urban residents often organized themselves into popular resistance and extermination battalions (*voennoe opolchenie i istrebitel'nye batal'ony*). These groups consisted mainly of Bolshevik Party members and candidates who patrolled streets and factory territories to prevent diversions, theft, and to stop suspicious individuals. In doing so, the battalions of popular resistance and extermination coordinated their work with the regular police and other NKVD structures (Dziak, 1988). These forms of voluntary policing were especially effective in the areas adjacent to areas of active battles and near state borders. The other form of public–police cooperation reported during World War II was the participation of the *Komsomol*[92] members. The members searched for counterrevolutionary elements and profascist individuals and assisted the internal troops that were located in territories recently freed from German troops. The *Komsomol* youth members were local inhabitants who provided the NKVD troops with valuable information from the interior of the regions and on local residents.[93]

The regular and political police were again split into two agencies by the decree of April 14, 1943. The newly created NKGB (People's Commissariat of State Security) gradually assumed all security and law enforcement functions (Richelson, 1985). The special and border troops, transport police, and railroad troops became a part of the NKGB system during the late 1940s. In March of 1946, both agencies were renamed ministries and titled the MGB (Ministry of State Security) and MVD (Ministry of Internal Affairs), accordingly (Levytsky, 1972). Then in August of 1950, the function of the regular police was once again transferred from the MVD to the MGB (Knight, 1984). By 1950, the MVD was left mainly with administrative and economic functions including the management of forced labor camps.

In the postwar period, the political police in the USSR were preoccupied with screening repatriated prisoners and Soviet citizens who had been deported to Germany for forced labor (Wolin and Slusser, 1957). Most of these individuals were sent to labor camps and some were released (Levytsky, 1972). In this process, the political police heavily relied on the passport control system enforced by the regular police. Routine militia visits to private dwellings were conducted often to check the validity of passports, registration stamps, and unauthorized residents. Returnees from the labor camps were among the most frequent victims of such raids (Matthews, 1993). The other victims of regular police raids included homeless (*brodyagi*) and unattended children (*bezprizornye*). The populations of both groups increased after the chaos of war. In 1951, homelessness became a crime punishable by five years of imprisonment and police forces were focused on catching *brodyagi* and placing them into special institutions (A. P. Volkov and Berkutov, 2009).[94] The regular police continued to approach state-related property crimes as one of the most important issues of the crime prevention policy.[95] The lack of qualified cadres within regular police due to the casualties of war caused some problems of discipline and power abuse (Kalmykov, 2008; Mayurov, 2005).

2.4 Concluding Remarks

This historic overview of the Soviet police from its establishment in 1917 until the death of Stalin in 1953 provides a basis for several important conclusions. This basis will became crucial in fully understanding the police crisis that existed in the Soviet Union from the late 1980s through the early 1990s as well as subsequent problems faced by the modern Russian police.

First, it would be an oversimplification to say that the entire history of the Soviet police during the period of 1917 through 1953 can be viewed as an evolution of repressive law enforcement mechanisms focused on the subjugation of ideological enemies and for support of the Bolshevik political regime. To a larger extent, this statement is true when discussing the Soviet political police entities of the *Vecheka*, GPU, OGPU, NKVD, and the MGB. The regular Soviet police (militia) saw some truly democratic moments during its early development, albeit they were always contained within one social class of the proletariat.

The naïve idea of "popular armed resistance" maintained by Lenin in 1917 faced tremendous challenges during the time of the civil war, but, for the class of workers and peasants, it was truly a liberating proposition. The idea of police subordination to the local Soviets and an opportunity for public assessment of policemen by the factory workers that was practiced during the NEP period was also a drastic departure from the centralized and closed tsarist police system. However, these were isolated historic incidents restricted in time and within social classes, and they merely had an impact on the overall direction of police development in Soviet Union.

Second, similar to the tsarist police system, the Soviet regular police were always secondary to the political police. Even when the two structures were formally separated in the early stages of the Soviet state, political police took precedence over the practices of the regular police and were used as auxiliary forces for massive repressive operations. However, by the 1930s, regular police agencies were not simply subordinated to the political police but also were subjected to permanent surveillance and control. This, of course, also was true for the other government and societal institutions in the USSR during the 1930s when the political police power was raised to unprecedented levels. The subordinated role of the regular police will remain a prominent feature of the Soviet state and became important for understanding why the demise of socialism had such a devastating impact on the regular police during the 1990s.

Third, the crime prevention and crime control policies practiced by the militia were seriously politicized as well. Even during the liberation of the NEP period, the idea of crime control was based on the premises of social classes and their struggle with one another. Crime was viewed as an attribute of the capitalist past and sought to be eliminated with the isolation and liquidation of the "antisocial" social classes themselves. Logically, the main vehicle of the crime control policy for the Soviet police was penal repressions including the isolation of large groups of people or their physical elimination. At the time of the NEP, when economic relations were relaxed and criminal sentencing was mild, the regular police were incapable of effective crime control and prone to bribery and other forms of corruption. Though not entirely, this situation resonates with the conditions of economic liberation pursued during the Gorbachev era.

Fourth, unlike its predecessor in the Russian Empire, the Soviet militia was a tool of proactive social change, not a reactive law enforcement agency. Preventive policing, and other campaigns, in which the regular Soviet police routinely participated, were intended to mold the new social structure of society. Within this new structure, peasants and factory workers were to be united and governed through the collective entities, such as factories and farms. Private property was eliminated, or at least significantly diminished, and there would be no bourgeois classes that profit from hired labor and capital. In this proactive goal, the Soviet militia employed an administrative control over the society even greater than the one developed by the tsarist police. The proactive role of the Soviet militia provides some explanation and understanding of the last idea in this chapter: the contextual understanding of public–police relations in the new Soviet state.

Public–police relationships during the period from 1917 to 1953 can be described as complicated. In the early years of war Communism, the militia was often ruthless and violent. It fought against "class enemies" (merchants and the clergy) and expropriated food from the wealthy peasants. These groups of people all had substantial reasons to fear the Soviet militia. For factory workers, one of the most loyal Bolshevik social groups, participation in the factory militia was an unprecedented elevation in the social power structure. Many enthusiastically took this opportunity and cooperated with the new law enforcement or even became a part of it.

The complex economic relations during the NEP period demonstrated the police's inability to solve regular crimes. It also showed the bureaucratic nature of the militia's administrative control and demonstrated its level of corruption. Factory workers, and other urban supporters of the Bolsheviks, were appalled by these problems and, therefore, determined to solve them by putting new cadres into the militia. Peasants, who were heavily taxed, remained skeptical and less cooperative with the new law enforcement.

Repressions conducted in the late 1920s and early 1930s brought fear and hostility toward the entire law enforcement community, but also brought drastic social changes. Economically independent peasants (kulaks) almost disappeared as a social class by the late 1930s. This created a situation where the newly established communities of collective farms were much easier to control and presented a much friendlier environment for the militia. The urban population also changed. The old Bolsheviks who participated in the 1917 October Revolution were gone as well as the military elite and some of the NEP administrators. The intellectuals (*intelegentsia*) who were educated during the tsarist times were mainly purged and new intellectuals were produced using indoctrinated Soviet materials. Thus, in the 1940s and early 1950s, the militia found more favorable support among young and patriotic citizens of the USSR, even though fear from repressions and routine denunciations also were present (Table 2.1).

Table 2.1 Timetable of major events: 1917–1953

Year	Description
1917	February Revolution. The work of the State Police Department of MVD and Corps of Gendarmes was terminated and their leaders arrested
1917	An amnesty provided by the Provisional government and thousands of former convicts released from jails and prisons
1917	The Red Guards were created
1917	New structure of people's militia outlined by the special decree of Provisional government
1917	The October Socialist Revolution, also known as the Bolshevik coup d'état
1917	New Bolshevik government formed, including the People's Commissariat of Internal Affairs (NKVD) and 13 other People's Commissariats
1917	Worker's Militia created by a decree of the SNK titled "About Worker's Militia"
1917	*Cheka* (later known as *Vacheka)* created by the Bolshevik government
1918	NKVD had 11 departments and had hired over 400 staff members
1918	NKVD, along with the People's Commissariat of Justice, issued a decree on creation of professional militia
1918	The Decree "On Red Terror" issued and provided law enforcement with almost unlimited repressive authority
1919	SNK issued a Decree "On Soviet Militia of Workers and Peasants"

(continued)

Table 2.1 Timetable of major events: 1917–1953 (continued)

Year	Description
1920	The decree issued that all local police departments could be used in military operations in cases when ordered by the Revolutionary Military Council
1921	The Red Army defeated the majority of the political opposition in the central, western, and northern provinces
1922	The Decree on the Legal Status adopted, indicating that NKVD should administer all "communal" business, supervise local administration, and enforce execution of all "administrative" decrees of central and local authorities
1922	Establishment of the USSR
1922	All all-union agreement signed by republics
1922	Establishment of the *Procuracy* of RSFSR
1922	Abolition of the *Vecheka*
1922	The NKVD issued "The instruction on struggle against drinking," outlawing public drunkenness and distillery of alcohol
1922	The GPU regained the authority to exercise extrajudicial "administrative exile"
1923	The GPU transformed into the OGPU (United State Political Department) and reinstated as an independent permanent institution
1923	The OGPU attempted to take away law enforcement functions from the NKVD under premise of NKVD reform
1923	The Criminal Code established
1924	The establishment of the *Procuracy* of USSR
1924	The rural executives established as a semigovernment position to bridge the gap between the urban police and villages' population
1928	"Investigators" transferred from the courts to the *Procuracy*
1928	Clubs of factory workers in Nijnii Tagil created a first voluntary society for the assistance of police
1930	The NKVD officially abolished and its functions dispersed among other agencies
1930	The OGPU created the "Main Inspection of Police and Detective Work"
1932	Stalin reinstated the passport system
1932	The SNK and VtSIK issued a decree on "Establishment of the Main Directorate of factory-peasant police under the structure of OGPU"
1933	The *Procuracy* removed from the court system and became an executive law enforcement agency
1934	The NKVD reinstated as an all-union agency of executive power
1934	The Special Board (OS of NKVD) created as a part of reinstated NKVD and became a new extrajudicial agency for repressions
1934	Labor camps became a part of reinstated NKVD
1934	Kirov assassinated
1937	The term in labor camp extended to seven years and became extendable "at the sole whim of authorities of NKVD to imprisonment of unlimited duration"
1941	All structures of NKVD mobilized for participation in the active military operations
1941	Authorities of extrajudicial agencies (OS of NKVD) expanded under martial laws of war time

(continued)

Table 2.1 Timetable of major events: 1917–1953 (continued)

Year	Description
1943	A decree issued splitting the regular and political police into two agencies, and resulted in a creation of the NKGB, which gradually transferred all security and law enforcement functions from the NKVD
1946	The NKGB is renamed MGB (Ministry of State Security) and NKVD is renamed MVD (Ministry of Internal Affairs)
1950	The function of regular police transferred from the MVD to the MGB, leaving the MVD with mainly administrative and economic functions, including management of labor camps
1951	Homelessness became a crime punishable by five years imprisonment
1953	Stalin's death

Endnotes

1. Collection of decrees of RSFSR (*Sobranie Ukazov*). Heretofore cited as SU of RSFSR, 1917, #1, p. 15.
2. This was a case in Kronschtadt and other areas of St. Petersburg.
3. This was the case, for example, in Ufimskaya province currently known as Bashkortostan. See Emelin (2008) for details.
4. There is a difference of historical opinions as to what exactly was the role of the Red Guards in the October revolution. Collins (1972) suggests that the role of the Red Guards in the Bolshevik coup d'état in the capital was limited, but maintains that their role in provinces and establishment of public order immediately after the October revolution was much greater. Soviet historians traditionally report that the Red Guards played a crucial role in supporting the Bolsheviks during the October revolution (Gutman, 2007; MVD, 2008a).
5. According to Mulukaev, Malygin, and Epifanov (2005), the number of serious crimes increased 10-fold in 1918 compared to 1916.
6. One of the earliest descriptions of *Vecheka* was provided by Carter (1922) who reported in his article that Vecheka bears no resemblance to any Anglo-Saxon judicial agency and that it possesses tremendous power over the Soviet society.
7. There is a difference of opinion as to why the functions of political police were not included in the sphere of NKVD's original influence. Soviet historians traditionally maintain that NKVD was overburdened with economic and administrative duties and it was too slow and bureaucratic for measures of "red terror" (Fastov, 2005). Others suggest that if political police function had been given to the NKVD, the Bolsheviks would have been forced to provide access to it for the other members of socialist parties, which participated in formation of the first Soviet government (Gerson, 1976). Despite these differences, it is clear from historic documents that regular police (NKVD) were always subordinate to the political police represented by *Vecheka* during the period of "war Communism."
8. The official relationship between the *Vecheka* and militia was defined by the Resolution of deputies NKVD issued on June 4, 1919. According to this document, the head of the local *Vecheka* was included in the administration (collegiums) of the local militia, while the head of the local militia was included in

the administration (collegiums) of the local *Vecheka*. The other important way of *Vecheka* and NKVD interaction was a shared network of concentration labor camps introduced by decree in 1919 (Dziak, 1988).

9. According to Mulukaev, Malygin, and Epifanov (2005), the quality of the staff remained questionable. Because both tsarist and "bourgeois" professionals were deemed inappropriate for the new workers' government, positions at the ministry level were often filled with former students.
10. SU of RSFSR, 1918, #75, article 813.
11. SU of RSFSR, 1919, #13, article 133.
12. The process of militarization was happening gradually. In remote provinces of Siberia and the Far East, the militarization of police was achieved only by the end of 1920 to the beginning of 1921. Lack of resources, ammunition, and training, and slow communication impeded the process. For example, see Petrov (2006c) on the process of militarization in the Ural and Western Siberian provinces.
13. SU of RSFSR, 1921, #79, article 683.
14. For example, see work by Fedorenko (2009) on this issue in Stavropol province in the early 1920s.
15. Among the most famous White governments are the Greater Army of Don, the army of Denikin, Ufimskaya directory, Provisional Siberian government, government of Kolchak, Northern-Western government, Provisional government of Northern region, and Provisional government of Amur region.
16. For example, according to Mulukaev, Malygin, and Epifanov (2005), over 1,000 Soviet militia representatives were sent to Central Asian cities in January of 1918 when the Turkestan region's SNK made a decision to develop their new law enforcement agencies.
17. The situation also was exacerbated by the lack of legally trained personnel. Most law schools were closed by 1919 because students and professors were representatives of the bourgeoisie and not from "workers and peasant" classes. The new institutions for training both lawyers and law enforcement personnel were opened mostly during 1921–1924. See, for example, Oleinik (2008) for details.
18. For example, Ivanov and Sedunov (2005) reported on the manpower of northern provinces militia in the 1918. Their data suggest that only 1.7% had previous law enforcement experience and almost 75% were illiterate.
19. According to Mulukaev, Malygin, and Epifanov (2005), in 38 provinces of the RSFSR in 1919, there were 2,816 registered robberies; in 1920, this number tripled with 7,319 registered robberies.
20. The number of homeless children even prior to the October revolution of 1917 was already astonishing. According to Stolee (1988), there were at least 2 million homeless children by 1917 and this number grew exponentially during the 1920s. It was estimated that in 10 years (by 1927) it reached 7 million.
21. According to Petrov (2006b), the struggle against crime was often considered a continuation of the class struggle, therefore, the regular crimes were viewed as a result of capitalism, which would disappear as soon as the conditions of "true Communism" would be reached.
22. During this time, the Transcaucasian region traditionally included republics of Armenia, Georgia, and Azerbaijan. When the USSR was established in 1922, these three countries were united under the term "Transcaucasia republic."

23. In March of 1921, one of the most fervent pro-Bolshevik military units, Kronstadt garrison, staged an uprising, but was mercilessly crushed by the special troops of NKVD-GPU.
24. SU of RSFSR, 1922, #33, article 386.
25. See Waxmonsky (1982) on examples of "economic duties" carried out by the militia in 1922 to 1924 in Leningrad, North Caucuses, and Tver.
26. Decree of VtSIK and SNK issued on August 3, 1922. Cited from Morukov (2007).
27. Instruction of the head of the militia of Republic #269 issued on June 26, 1922. Cited from Morukov (2007).
28. Liberalization of economic conditions impacted the structure of crimes, increasing the number of white-collar crimes and state officials' corruption. According to the official data by Narkomyust, in 1923, 29% of all sentenced individuals were convicted of bribery, in 1924, 40% of all court sentences were bribery-related. The investigation of white-collar and other economic crimes required professional training of a different nature, which most members of the Soviet militia did not possess at the time. For example, Mamedova (2006) reports, that in Adygeya in 1923, only 33% of all crimes were solved by militia. Among the most-solved crimes were minor offenses like thefts, but serious felonies remained unsolved (only 7% of all murders and 16% of all robberies were solved).
29. VtSIK is an abbreviation of All-Russian Central Executive Committee.
30. Collection of Instructions by NKVD, pp. 218–219. Cited from Morukov (2007).
31. To understand the scale of this campaign, Mulukaev, Malygin, and Epifanov (2005) cited that just during a period of 45 days (November–December 1922), Moscow police conducted 5,807 searches of which over 3,000 resulted in seizure of alcohol or alcohol-producing equipment.
32. The new penal policy also overburdened the court system, where 29.7% of all sentences in 1924 were related to crimes of home brewing (Solomon, 1981).
33. On criticism of *Vecheka* by NKVD and other narkoms, see articles by Leggett (1975, 1980).
34. Some researchers also suggest that abolition of *Vecheka* and creation of GPU with more limited repressive functions was serving the purposes of the international community. The Soviet Russia and later USSR experienced international obstruction in the first years of its development, which was partially responsible for the devastated economy. *Vecheka* was a symbol of Red repressions and its abolition some viewed as a concession to the international community. See, for example, Hingley (1971) and Levytsky (1972) on this issue.
35. Even though GPU–OGPU was no longer able to adjudicate their victims, the justice provided during this period of time for political defendants remained questionable. For example, the first-hand experience in GPU interrogation techniques, trial, retrial, and imprisonment during the NEP period is provided by Brunovskii (1928), who published his memoirs as a political prisoner after he was sentenced to death, but was later extradited to Latvia. The value of the article by Brunovskii is not only in his first-hand experience with GPU–OGPU during this time, but also in his "research" (personal communication) that he conducted while awaiting the trial and sentencing. He communicated with numerous prisoners on the circumstances of their arrests and trials and pub-

lished specific information in his 80-page memoir. Even though these memoirs have to be taken critically, many facts reported by Brunovskii were later corroborated by other researchers, witnesses, and archival data.

36. Decree of VtSIK issued on August 10, 1922. SU of RSFSR, 1922, #51, article 646.
37. The inclusion of banditism as a political crime is one example of how the OGPU was attempting to take over the law enforcement function in the country from the regular police. Though during the period of civil war, banditism was often coupled with political opposition, at the NEP period it became mostly a regular crime with little political connections. Yet OGPU insisted on investigation of banditism even after 1922. For an example of banditism crimes and actions by OGPU in 1922–1929 in Irkutsk province, see Brjuhanov (2009).
38. For more details on proposed reform of NKVD in 1922–1924 and attempts of the OGPU to take over the law enforcement function in the country, see Waxmonsky (1982).
39. The key factor in the growing power of OGPU was enactments of the Criminal Code and the Criminal Procedural Code in 1922 and 1923, respectively. These documents provided both theoretical foundation and legal basis for the supremacy of political police in the USSR (Knight, 1988).
40. It has to be noted that, even though GPU–OGPU was officially a very powerful state institution during the NEP period, its factual record of repressions remained relatively low. For discussion of this phenomenon, see Hingley (1971).
41. For example, Erin and Bubnova (2008) report that Vladimir industrial police were staffed only by 40% of the required militiamen in 1920. Also Erin (2009) maintains that, in 1921, Petrograd urban police required 20,000 militiamen to maintain public order in the factories. However, the "industrial police" only had 13% of this number in staff. Also, see Shabel'nikova (2009) on the Far East police.
42. Using archival data, Slusser (1959) reported that OGPU's funding grew from 35 million rubles in 1923 to 50 million rubles in 1929. However, the NKVD's funding was decreased by 40% at the same time, according to Fastov (2005).
43. One of the striking statistics provided on the work of the NEP police was the total number of cases dismissedand acquittals. According to data by Solomon (1996), 64% of cases handled by police were dismissed by the *procuracy* in 1926 and the number grew to 74% in 1927.
44. The lack of funds also was responsible for the decrease in the funding of militia schools. In 1922, there were 50 schools for local militiamen, but, by 1923, there were only 13. The rest were closed due to underfunding issues. For details, see Oleinik (2008).
45. The situation was especially difficult in the remote provinces of Russia. For example, Pasechnik (2008) reports that in 1926 the territory of the Anadyrskyi region in Kamchatka (288,396 km^2, the equivalent of the territory of modern Germany) was staffed with 2 police officers serving 18 villages with over 6,000 residents.
46. For example, the so-called employees of "ugro" (detective departments) received 50% increase of salary in 1923. See Mulukaev, Malygin, and Epifanov (2005) for details.
47. For example, during the antialcohol campaign, "government promised individual policemen substantial rewards, amounting to half of all fines imposed ... with half balances available for payments to informants" (Weissman, 1986, p. 349).

48. For example, on the work of Leningrad's citizen's commission on improvement of police work in 1926, see Pavlov (2006).
49. Unsurprisingly, even police chiefs and heads of detective units in the late 1920s consisted mainly of peasants with elementary education alone (Solomon, 1996).
50. On the comparison of repressions between the Lenin's and Stalin's periods of OGPU, see Hingley (1971).
51. Beloborodov, the head of the NKVD from 1923 to 1927, was accused of Trotskyism, while the next head, Tolmachev, was accused of being a Rightist.
52. The regular police were ill-equipped for the campaign work on *dekulakization*. They were understaffed and underfunded, had high turnover rates, and burdened with administrative functions (Solomon, 1996).
53. The regulation of the SNK and VtSIK was issued on December 15, 1930. Collection of laws of USSR (hereinfore cited as CZ of USSR), 1930, #60, article 40.
54. Instruction of the OGPU #475/224, issued on December 30, 1930. Cited from Morukov (2007).
55. CZ USSR, 1932, #84, article 518.
56. CZ USSR, 1934, #36, article 283.
57. Paragraph 2 of the decree of SNK and VtSIK issued on July 10, 1934, CZ of USSR, 1934, #36, article 283.
58. Solomon (1985) argued that the tendency of centralization and reduced influence of local politicians was typical not only among militia, but was true for the entire criminal justice system of the 1930s.
59. The situation of political police supremacy over the NKVD remained even when the two agencies were separated in February of 1941. See, for example, Levytsky (1972) on reforms of NKVD–NKGB conducted by Beria.
60. For example, see article by Paneiakh (2003) on the purges conducted against academic historians during the early 1930s.
61. "Dekulakization" is a process of forcefully seizing the assets of the wealthy peasants into the collective farms.
62. Barnes (1939) cites official data available at this time on the party membership in the USSR. According to his report, just between 1932 and 1935, the party membership was reduced by 345,000 party members and 866,000 party candidates. Barnes concluded that one out of three party members or candidates were expelled from the Bolshevik party between 1932 and 1935.
63. According to data reported by Khlevnyuk (2003), between 1937 and 1939, the population of the GULAG rose from 1.2 to 1.7 million people. On the discussion of official statistics for purges, also see work by Getty, Rittersporn, and Zemskov (1993).
64. "Liquidation of kulaks" was indeed a massive extermination of the population that required tremendous manpower. Conquest (1968b) estimated that *kulaks* constituted of at least 6 million people prior to the process of forced collectivization.
65. Aside from political deterrence, many researchers believed that massive repressions in the 1930s had important economic goals. In the absence of significant foreign investments, the low wages of collective farm employees, and forced labor in the camps provided needed surplus for the country to support the rapid economic development of the USSR. For example, see Dallin and Nicolaevsky

(1947) on the economic significance of forced labor in the USSR. Also see Jasny (1951) on the type of economic activities that the NKVD was involved in when running the labor camps and other correctional institutions in 1940.

66. For example, on November 21, 1939, the position of regular police officers was established in all labor settlements of NKVD by Instruction # 0395. Cited from Morukov (2007).
67. The decree issued by SNK and VtSIK on December 27, 1932, CZ of USSR, 1932, #80, article 490.
68. The passports were issued in accordance with the Instruction issued on 04.28.1933. The secret section of this instruction directly maintained that individuals who were denied passports should be prosecuted by the "troiki" and directed that regular police should prepare the materials for such prosecution.
69. Residence in most urban cities without a passport became a crime.
70. According to a decree on "People's court" issued on October 21, 1920, the investigative sections were created within the structure of the Narkomiust. Paragraph 5, Article 23 of the Criminal Procedural Code (CPC) of RSFSR of 1923 listed three types of investigators: investigators for the peoples' and revolutionary courts, military investigators, and special investigators at the Narkomiust itself.
71. Article 97 and 108 of the CPC of RSFSR of 1923.
72. See Articles 97–107 of the CPC of RSFSR of 1923 for more details on detention.
73. The *procuracy* was charged with functions of both criminal prosecution and "supervision of socialist legality," which created so-called "accusatory bias" in the preliminary investigation of the Soviet criminal process. The problem is still discussed in relation to the changes introduced into the criminal process by the CPC of Russia in 2002.
74. First, "special investigators" were established at the specialized departments like departments of economic crimes (BkhSS) and, in 1941, the investigative groups were created at the Department of Struggle against Banditism.
75. During the time of the Great Terror, these legal remedies proved to be futile. Even though many defendants who were sentenced by OS of NKVD were arrested by the warrant of State procurator (attorney), these warrants were signed at large by scared procurators who routinely did not acquaint themselves with the reason for the arrest or nature of charges. For example, see Beck and Godin (2006) on details of their first-hand experience with the criminal justice system of the USSR in the late 1930s. According to Benvenuti (1997), the problem of weak and complacent procurators was even discussed by the Soviet officials during the 1930s.
76. There are no known quantitative data on public opinion about the NKVD in the 1930s. Numerous accounts of witnesses exist as qualitative data to support the idea of fear. However, some researchers suggested that work in the NKVD (the political police departments) was prestigious and desirable due to various privileges and the high salaries it provided. This statement can be substantiated by the fact that political police did not experience a lack of staff during the 1930s. For example, see Connor (1972b) on this issue.
77. It appears that work of "rural executives" at the beginning was not very efficient. They suffered from lack of communication and transportation, poor education, and lack of instructions from the local police (Kolemasov, 2011).

78. According to data reported by Govorov and Remneva (2007), in 1926, Osodmil consisted of 26,000 people and, by 1930, this number grew to 46,000. According to Pavlov (2006), members of Osodmil not only participated in auxiliary policing activities, but also were present at meetings conducted by regular police where they were able to take part in the discussion of local crime prevention policies.
79. Despite purges that were conducted even within the members of Osodmil, prior to 1932 these organizations were successful at least in the urban areas with a high factory population. They were organized on the basis of local executive agencies by the initiative of workers. However, by 1932, the OGPU decided to restructure Osodmil into brigades of cooperation of militia (so-called Brigadmil), which were organized by the militia and were headed by the representatives of political police. The candidates into Brigadmil had to obtain the recommendations from political police. Though there were over 400,000 registered members of Brigadmil in 1940, their efficiency was declining.
80. According to Shelley (1996), 23 million new citizens were acquired by the USSR in 1940 as a result of annexation.
81. For a traditional Soviet description of law enforcement development in Belarus, see, for example, Martinovitch and Pluta (1977).
82. According to official statistics reported by Vladimirtsev and Kokurin (2008), in May and June of 1940, NKVD exiled 11,000 residents from Western Ukraine, 21,000 residents from Western Belarus, 13,000 residents from Lithuania, 10,000 residents from Latvia, and 6,000 from Estonia. Also, 14,000 residents of the Baltic States were sentenced to forced labor in correctional camps. Among these individuals, many members of Jewish communities were deported as well. See Baron (1976) for more details.
83. For example, see Dallin and Nicolaevsky (1947) on the composition of the Lithuanian NKGB in 1940–1941.
84. The Special Diversions Brigade was created within the structure of the NKVD in October of 1941 to coordinate the work of partisan groups who penetrated occupied territories and committed acts of sabotage by destroying roads, communication, and infrastructure. Between 1942 and 1945, over 2,500 special NKVD officers infiltrated occupied territories and carried out acts of diversion.
85. Directive of the Main Department of the Interior Troops of NKVD issued on July 1, 1943. Cited from Mulukaev et al. (2005).
86. For example, according to Mulukaev et al. (2005), just in December of 1941 over 1,000 residents who allegedly cooperated with German authorities were arrested in Moscow, Tula, and Ryazan.
87. According to the official data provided by Vladimirtsev and Kokurin (2008), during 1943–1945, 44,000 members of nationalistic resistance groups were killed by interior troops of the NKVD in Western Ukraine and 17,000 were arrested. In Belarus, for the same period, 1,335 were killed and 2,701 were arrested.
88. According to official statistics, the number of female police officers increased 30-fold compared to the prewar period. Cited from Rybnikov and Aleksushin (2008).
89. According to Gusak (2010), at least 50% of all militia duties during this period were pertinent to the war and not law enforcement.

90. Decree of November 17, 1941 of State Committee of Defense (GKO). Cited from Mulukaev et al. (2005).
91. Using this premise, between 1943 and 1945, the entire ethnic groups of Kalmyk, Balkars, Tatars, Chechens, Armenians, Greeks, and other minorities were deported from Crimea, Stavropol, Krasnodar, and Astrakhan regions. See, for example, Conquest (1968b) for the list of deported ethnic minorities.
92. Communist Union of Youth. The organization was officially established in 1918 and was created as a precursor of membership into the Communist party.
93. Mulukaev et al. (2005) report that in the Leningrad region alone, there were 580 members of Komsomol who participated in searches conducted by NKVD troops during 1942.
94. According to official statistics, police annually detained between 150,000 and 200,000 people for being homeless.
95. For example, see Moore (1947) who describes the power abuse in collective farms, undue expansion of administrative apparatus in the industry, and other issues of postwar USSR.

Further Soviet Police Developments: 1953–1985

3

3.1 Development of the Soviet Police after Stalin's Death: 1953–1964

The death of Stalin on March 5, 1953, prompted an intensive political struggle for leadership among elite members of the Central Committee of the Communist Party of the Soviet Union (CC of the CPSU) (Dziak, 1988). Lavrenty Beria, who had extensive experience as the leader in NKVD/MVD under Stalin since 1938, assumed the position of the minister of the MVD. He was also appointed as a deputy chairman of the Council of Ministers of the USSR (the executive body within the USSR government at the time). Georgy Malenkov, another prominent Stalinist, was appointed the chairmen of the Council of Ministers, and Vyacheslav Molotov was renamed the Minister of Foreign Affairs. Nikita Khrushchev, a relatively new political figure, was given a less important position at the time within the Secretariat of the CPSU. There is consensus in the historic literature that between March and June of 1953, the USSR was under collective leadership of these three men: Beria, Malenkov, and Molotov (Shelley, 1996).[1]

During this time, Beria took a number of steps to strengthen his position within the Soviet government and the Communist Party (Fastov, 2005). Just 10 days after the death of Stalin, the MVD (Ministry of Internal Affairs) and MGB (Ministry of State Security) were again amalgamated into one organization under the formal leadership of Beria (Knight, 1988). As did his NKVD predecessors, Beria moved to replace a number of key personnel in both the MVD and MGB structures to ensure loyalty within the new law enforcement agency. Beria also championed the idea of "liberalization," which included amnesty for both political and ordinary prisoners. The new policy was announced on March 27, 1953 (Morukov, 2007).[2] He also transferred most of the MVD economic functions, including the administration of labor camps, to other ministries during his short period of leadership (Conquest, 1968b).[3] As the head of the MVD in early 1953, Beria suggested dismantling the forced labor economy and significantly reducing the number of labor camps (Khlevnyuk, 2003; Levytsky, 1972).[4] Beria was also among the first Soviet officials who admitted that mistakes were made during the so-called Doctor's plot and other Stalinist repressions (Rybnikov and Aleksushin, 2008).[5]

Most historians now believe that Beria's sudden reforms and manipulations of the political and regular police were efforts to simultaneously gain public popularity and predominance in the CPSU leadership (Fastov, 2005). Beria's actions to gain more power alarmed other leading members of the CPSU and provided the catalyst for building a united opposition against Beria. With the direct involvement of Khrushchev, Beria was dismissed as head of the MVD and deputy chairmen in June of 1953 and later that year was tried and executed for state crimes. Five other politically motivated trials were conducted among high-ranking police officials and Beria's followers during the period of 1953 to 1956 (Hingley, 1971).

This episode of political struggles has important implications for the history of Soviet policing. Stalin had elevated the institution of political police above the Party and used it to strengthen his personal power through the arbitrary prosecutions and repression of both Party elites and regular citizens. The regular police, with its vast administrative authority, was often a willing accomplice to most of these actions. Beria's dismissal was a direct result of fear from members of the CPSU. They were concerned that the omnipotent leader of both the regular and political police would once again use the same formula to gain personal control over the country (Shelley, 1992).

Thus, following Stalin's death, the Soviet political elite made every effort to ensure that a united political and regular police structure would not "reemerge as the dominant institution of the Soviet system" and remained under control of the Party (Knight, 1988, p. 48).

Though, in 1953, Khrushchev became the first secretary of the CPSU after Beria's demise, it was not until 1957 that he obtained absolute political power in the country. The period from 1953 to 1957 can be described as a continuous political struggle between Khrushchev and Malenkov. Malenkov continued as the chair of the Council of Ministers until 1957. This political competition is responsible, to some degree, for the inconsistency of policy development that would have furthered liberalization during this period.

The first order of business for Khrushchev was to reestablish the CPSU's control and to weaken the MVD as the most powerful government institution. He achieved this by once again separating the political and regular police by creating the Committee of State Security (KGB) in 1954. The split was critical in the depoliticization of the regular police system (Shelley, 1996). This separation remained in place until the Soviet Union collapsed in 1991.

During the USSR period in 1953, Beria had already stripped the MVD of its economic requirements to support elements of the infrastructure. So, with the departure of political police, the MVD became mainly an institution of vast administrative control and law enforcement and remained as such until the end of the Soviet Union (Shelley, 1992). Formally, the KGB regained the powers and authorities that previously belonged to the MGB shortly after it was reestablished in 1954 (Wolin and Slusser, 1957). The KGB continued to play an important role in the Soviet government, even though it was now subordinated to the full control of the CPSU.

Critical structural changes were made to decentralize the existing law enforcement apparatus and to increase the rights of Union Republics in their performance of policing functions. To make this change possible, the RSFSR (Russian Soviet Federated Socialist Republic) finally established a republican-level MVD office in 1955 (Mulukaev, Malygin, and Epifanov, 2005).[6] In 1956, local police departments also were transferred back to the "dual subordination" model where they were accountable not only to the republican MVD, but also to the local executive Soviets (Bescherevnykh, 1973).[7] The final act of decentralization was the termination of the USSR MVD's authority in 1960 and subsequent transfer of leading policing functions to the republic-level institutions (Kuritsyna, 2008).[8] In 1962, the MVD was also renamed the Ministry for Defense of Public Order (MOOP) (Bezlepkin, 2001).

Simultaneously, with the other structural changes, Khrushchev launched a campaign to improve the level of MVD–MOOP personnel and to ensure their loyalty to the CPSU (Knight, 1984). Under Khrushchev's leadership, a significant number of party members were mobilized and transferred to the various MVD–MOOP offices (Rybnikov and Aleksushin, 2008).[9] At the same time, the MVD–MOOP administrative apparatus was significantly reduced and over 35,000 people were fired from the MVD system by 1958 (Mulukaev, Malygin, and Epifanov, 2005).[10] The reshuffling of the central apparatus in conjunction with cutbacks also was intended to keep MVD–MOOP under control of the CPSU (Shelley, 1996).

Also, in order to increase levels of law enforcement professionalization during the late 1950s, the MVD–MOOP leadership undertook critical measures to build a network of police educational institutions.[11] Several decrees were adopted during the 1954–1955 period to improve social benefits and the salary of police officers and to encourage retention of experienced cadres.[12] The higher education requirements were imposed on newly hired police officers (Bondarenko and Dorokhov, 2006).[13] The new Criminal Codes were also amended in 1962 to include harsher penalties for crimes committed against police officers and members of auxiliary police (Bolotin and Godunov, 1977; Grzybowski, 1965).

Important steps toward the liberalization were taken during the "Khrushchev thaw" by the introduction of new criminal law and procedure legislation (Savitsky, 1979). As a precursor of these reforms in September of 1953, the Special Council (an extrajudicial agency of MVD–MOOP), responsible for numerous Stalinist repressions, was abolished (Mulukaev, Malygin, and Epifanov, 2005). "Basic principles of criminal legislation of USSR" were introduced in 1958, followed by a new Criminal Code of the RSFSR, and the Criminal Procedural Code of the RSFSR, which was enacted in 1960. These reforms provided a model for reforming codes for the other republics (Grzybowski, 1965). These policies raised the age of criminal liability, significantly restricted the use of analogy of law, and finally subjected both the political and regular police investigations to the same rules (Berman, 1966). The new criminal procedure prevented extrajudicial and investigative agencies from imposing criminal punishment, eliminated the indefinite pretrial detention, and provided the defendant with additional rights (Lapenna, 1961; Lavroff, 1963).

However, it was also during this period of time when the regular MVD police officially obtained additional powers to conduct a "preliminary investigation" that became an important instrument of MVD authority in later years (Kucherov, 1970; Lapenna, 1968). The new Criminal Procedural Code of the RSFSR was amended in 1963 to list regular police (MOOP) as one of the institutions authorized to conduct preliminary investigations (Conquest, 1968a).[14] Prior to 1963, only investigators of the prosecutor's (*Procuracy*) office and political police were officially authorized to conduct investigations, while MVD was left only with the functions of "inquiry."[15]

The power for regular police to conduct a preliminary investigation meant that police officers could arrest and detain (with the prosecutor's permission) defendants for up to nine months and compile an official criminal file dossier along with criminal charges, which included the right to initiate, terminate, or suspend criminal prosecution (Kucherov, 1970). The official criminal dossier was accepted by courts as admissible evidence for prosecution and typically was the only evidence collected in a criminal case (Osakwe, 1983). The power of the preliminary investigation also prompted the creation of investigative departments within police precincts that required additional resources and more qualified legal personnel (Morukov, 2007). In the early years of its creation, the investigators of the MOOP–MVD were systematically criticized for poor work and lack of required legal training[16] (Kucherov, 1970).

A number of measures were taken by Khrushchev to improve the public image of the regular police. The key element of these changes was the reintroduction of popular justice through institutions of the auxiliary police and Comrades' courts. The institutions of auxiliary police had existed in the USSR since the 1920s in the form of Societies and Brigades for police cooperation (Egoryshev and Linkevitch, 2008). However, starting in 1958, auxiliary police units were reestablished and termed *druzhinniki* and millions of citizens were mobilized to participate (Berman, 1963).[17] The units of auxiliary police were created on the basis of factories and other places of employment often through the initiative of Komsomol and Party leaders (Govorov and Remneva, 2007).

The 1960 Decree on Voluntary People's Patrols (DND) (*druzhinniki*) granted broader functions to these organizations and members than existed prior to the societies (brigades) for cooperation of police.[18] The voluntary members of auxiliary police were charged not only with the duty to patrol the streets and improve public order through a close public–police interaction, but also were responsible for neglected children. They had the right to send materials about administrative violations to the Comrades' courts and other justice agencies (Berman, 1963). As a part of their preventive functions, *druzhinniki* also participated in prosecution, took part in neighborhood public educational programs, and could make recommendations to the state organizations about certain offenders.

The liberalization of the Khrushchev period had only a mild effect on the passport control system (Matthews, 1993). The Council of Ministers of the USSR adopted a new passport law in October of 1953 (Morukov, 2007). The passports became more uniform, the period of validity for both passports and temporary certificates were extended while released ex-convicts were allowed to get passports under certain conditions (Matthews, 1993). Yet the movement of rural inhabitants from their villages was still significantly restricted and no changes were made to the registration requirements (*propiska*).

The regular police continued to control illegal migrations of Soviet citizens through enforcement of earlier regulations on vagrancy and homelessness (*brodyazhnichestvo*).[19] In 1955, new centers of detention (*spets-priemniki*) were included into the MVD system to enforce vagrancy laws. These centers were responsible for short-term detention of those arrested as vagrants or homelessness as well as their transfer to the various institutions for treatment and/or forced labor (A.P. Volkov and Berkutov, 2009).

Consistent with past ideas of proactive policing, Khrushchev initiated a number of campaigns aimed at molding and improving members of the Soviet society. These campaigns were intended to eradicate bourgeoisie signs: alcoholism, hooligans, speculation, and antisocial parasite lifestyle. The Decree of May 4, 1961, instructed police to find and investigate all cases of antisocial parasite behavior (which included cases of capable people avoiding work) and gave police a right to issue a warning and send violators to the people's courts or local administrations for further trials (Berman, 1963). The fight against black markets, currency speculations, and other prohibited economic practices also intensified during the Khrushchev period. The new Criminal Code of the RSFSR contained numerous provisions against such practices and prescribed lengthy prison terms, confiscation of property, and forced labor.[20] In the Decree of the Supreme Court issued on October 29, 1963, the people's court was instructed to impose more serious sentences on speculators and other antisocial elements.[21] There is some evidence to suggest that many of these defendants were Jewish and they received more serious sentences when compared to non-Jewish offenders (Baron, 1976).

During this period, the police also continued to work with homeless and unattended children *(beznadzornost')*, but the direction of this work changed compared to the postwar period. Immediately after the war, the primary concern of police was to find unattended children whose parents had died or were missing due to the war and send them to orphanages to prevent delinquency (Stolee, 1988).[22]

After 1953, so-called "children rooms" (special units within regular police),[23] had to deal not only with orphans, but also with children from problematic families who had committed or were at risk of committing a crime. The police were charged with finding parents or guardians responsible for delinquent children and imposing administrative punishment to ensure better parenting and care (Kuritsyna, 2009). Poor supervision was identified as the main cause of juvenile delinquency and the regular police had a duty to supplement parental supervision when needed (Golovizina, 2005). Often, auxiliary police members worked closely with children rooms to both detect and prevent juvenile delinquency (Connor, 1972a).

The "Khrushchev thaw" also encouraged some public criticism of the MVD–MOOP work, which was done mostly through newspapers and other public media (Shelley, 1996). The criticism was prompted by a series of CPSU documents where the MVD–MOOP system was condemned for both bad policing style and disconnects with the public.[24] During this time, the newspapers and other media outlets were allowed to draw connections between ineffective policing and crime rates[25] in the country. This was something that was unheard of previously and was not allowed afterwards (Bondarenko and Dorokhov, 2006). It was also the MVD–MOOP that was blamed in the press for the many atrocities of Stalinism, while the newly created KGB maintained a relatively clean reputation (Dziak, 1988). The newly created auxiliary police also was publicly criticized for unprofessional behavior and abuse of power (Levytsky, 1972).

Many changes in the Soviet police initiated by Khrushchev were short-lived and were quickly reversed after his dismissal from his leadership position. The demise of Khrushchev in 1964 is often explained in the post-Soviet literature by public outcry due to supply shortages in 1963. There also were massive antigovernment demonstrations as well as his inconsistent policies in agricultural and industrial areas of the economy (Rybnikov and Aleksushin, 2008). Yet, this can be hardly considered the main reason. Like his predecessor Beria, Khrushchev's demise was orchestrated by the elite members of the CPSU who felt threatened by his policy of regional party elite turnovers, reshuffling of the regional party offices, and limited office tenures (Clarke, 1993). Changes made by Khrushchev to the MVD–MOOP apparatus were deeply resented by organs of internal affairs (Knight, 1984). Khrushchev's policy of frequent Party members' rotation significantly undermined the influence of the CPSU members and without the threat of repressions, they were no longer inclined to tolerate encroachment into their authority (Boffa, 1990).

3.2 Counterreform of the Soviet Police during the Late 1960s and Stagnation during the mid 1980s (1964–1985)

In 1964, Leonid Brezhnev became the first secretary of the CPSU after the forceful dismissal of Khrushchev with direct support from several influential members of the CPSU (Shelley, 1996). Most historic literature also maintains that Brezhnev's rise to power would not have been possible without support from the leadership of both the political and regular police (Knight, 1988). Brezhnev's main policy regarding the regular police was the restoration of hierarchical subordination and centralization, which was significantly weakened during the Khrushchev period. In 1966, the All-Union Ministry for Defense of Public Order (MOOP) was reestablished and all republican MOOP offices were subordinated to it.

In 1968, the MOOP was renamed again as the Ministry of Internal Affairs (Bezlepkin, 2001). The local network of MVD offices was also restructured. MVD local departments became independent offices and were no longer a structural part of the local executive Soviets. Though, formally, the local MVD officers still had a dual subordination to the executive Soviets and the superior MVD officers (Bescherevnykh, 1973), the influence of local executive Soviets became rather insignificant (Shelley, 1994).

Several measures also were taken to reverse Khrushchev's cadre policy. The All-Union MVD restored most of its administrative staff that was cut during the Khrushchev period. Instead of one main department of militia, the MVD created six main departments responsible for administrative, investigative, and other functions of the regular police (Fastov, 2005).[26] The republican-level offices of the MVD also created corresponding departments within their structure, thus enlarging the administrative apparatus (Milton, 1976).

In 1965, each regional police office was supplemented by a deputy chair position responsible for the political ideological education of police officers. This position was occupied by members of the CPSU who were often affiliated with the KGB and whose main duties were to supervise police departments to ensure adherence to CPSU ideological guidance (Rybnikov and Aleksushin, 2008). This position existed previously during Stalin's period, but was temporary eliminated by Khrushchev in an attempt to depoliticize the regular police.

During the Brezhnev period, the political supervision of police was restored and expanded as the new position was superior to all local police officers except the chair of the local department.[27] In 1969, each regional MVD office was supplemented by the department of political and ideological education.[28] Centralization and politicization of the MVD system was coupled with the policy of cadre stability, which became a prominent feature of the Brezhnev era. Created as a reaction to Khrushchev's idea of staff reshuffling, the policy of cadre stability provided unlimited office terms for political elites of the CPSU and ensured Brezhnev's security as political leader.

Under Brezhnev, the minister of the MVD remained in office for 14 years (Clarke, 1993). The combination of extreme centralization and stability of cadres also resulted in a predominance of Russians (or Slavs) in many republican and regional MVD officers, which contributed to the growing ethnic tension between Russians and non-Russian ethnic political elite groups during the period from 1970 through the 1980s (Shelley, 1994).[29]

Unlike Khrushchev, who heavily relied on popular participation in both police and justice institutions, Brezhnev's approach was focused on further professionalization of police with some limited elements of popular participation (Knight, 1984). New educational institutions were created within the system of MVD and, by 1973, most police officers were required to get at least a secondary education from an MVD institution prior to employment. In 1974, the new law on auxiliary police (*druzhiny*) was adopted, which assigned new duties to the members of the *druzhiny*, integrating them further into the police departments. This legislation, for all purposes, "completed and ratified the conversion of the once independent *druzhiny*, into the agents of local Soviets and militia" (Milton, 1976, p. 200).[30] The executive local Soviets were charged with organization and supply of *druzhiny* patrols and the MVD agencies had responsibility for supervising the duties of the auxiliary police (Bakhanskaia, 1975).

During the late 1970s and early 1980s, a number of local educational training centers and schools were organized to educate members of the auxiliary police. While the measures to "professionalize" auxiliary police created a reduction of power abuse in comparison to the Khrushchev period, it also made auxiliary police units more of a professional service and diminished their role as representatives of popular justice (Govorov and Remneva, 2007). The work of the auxiliary police became more bureaucratic and formalistic, while the motivation to assist police was slowly transformed into the desire to obtain free days off and other privileges (Egoryshev and Linkevitch, 2008; Favarel-Garrigues, 2011).[31]

At least during the first 10 years of Brezhnev's period, proactive policing continued to be a priority of the MVD's work. Regulations previously adopted against "parasites," beggars, and vagrancy required police to patrol the streets, detect antisocial elements, detain them for a short period of time if needed, impose administrative fines, transfer violators to special institutions, or supervise their mandatory labor (Korenev, 1984).

Additionally, in 1966, new laws on hooliganism were adopted increasing both criminal and administrative measures taken against hooligans and also broadening the definition of hooliganism itself.[32] Some public behavior that was previously legal,[33] according to the new law, was considered an administrative offense of "petite hooliganism" and required police to investigate and impose a fine or transfer the case to the people's court.[34] The cases of "aggravated hooliganism" required an inquiry from the regular police and led to a criminal sentence by the people's court.[35]

To enforce new hooliganism laws, police were equipped with cars that were patrolling areas in search of new law violators. In 1967, police duties were supplemented by the organization of centers for detention (*spets-priemniki*) of petite hooligans who were sentenced to administrative arrest and forced labor at local factories and other organizations.

In 1967, the government started a new campaign against alcoholism by allowing simplified procedures for forceful institutionalization of alcoholics in special medical institutions. Prior to 1967, only defendants in a criminal trial who were alcoholics were subjected to such forceful treatment (Connor, 1972a).[36] The regular police again were charged with both the investigation of complaints about alcoholics and enforcement of institutionalization.

The medical labor institutions (LTP), termed *lechebno-trudovye profilaktorii,* were created within the MVD structure for addicts' institutionalization. These institutions provided some medical treatment, strict regimen, supervision, confinement, and mandatory labor for alcohol abusers (Connor, 1972a). In 1972, public consumption of alcohol was outlawed as well as public intoxication.[37] The police were once again charged with duties to enforce new laws by patrolling the streets, detecting drunken citizens, and placing them in "sobering up" stations (*vytrezviteli*) that were created as a new part of the police infrastructure. The police were allowed to impose fines for public drinking and intoxication, and to send materials to the Comrades' courts or employers for further measures. The new law also imposed administrative fines on individuals who illegally sold alcohol from stores or produced and stored alcohol at home. According to the new laws, chronic alcoholics could be found legally incompetent and subject to forceful institutionalization at medical labor institutions by the people's court.[38] In 1974, an escape from a medical labor institution became a criminally liable offense.[39]

Also in 1967, the government intensified efforts against juvenile delinquency. Previously established Commissions on Juvenile Affairs (*Komissii po delam nesovershennoletnikh*) were named the coordinating centers for prevention of juvenile delinquency. While commissions were not part of the MVD system, the regular police were charged with assisting the commissions in any way possible.[40] In 1977, special units, termed Inspections for Juvenile Affairs *(Inspektsii po delam nesovershennoletnikh)* (IDN), were created and staffed by MVD personnel to fulfill duties of cooperation and assistance with the Commissions on Juvenile Affairs.[41] The inspections had broad functions that allowed them to visit juveniles both at home and in school for interviews, detain juveniles for up to three hours, search them while detained, file motions with the court to terminate parental rights, and send requests for official criminal investigations.[42] The "children rooms" (*detskie komnaty*) also continued to function under the MVD structure to allow for short-term detention (up to 30 days) of unattended and runaway children, socially dangerous minors, and minors who were transferred to special needs schools.[43] Komsomol organizations and auxiliary police (*druzhiniki*) also were involved in the preventive and educational work of both Commissions on Juvenile Affairs and "children rooms" (Connor, 1972a).

The prevention of crimes, in general, became a clear priority during the early Brezhnev era (Milton, 1976).[44] During the Stalin period, crime prevention was denounced and criminological science was abandoned. During the "Khrushchev thaw," the goals of crime prevention were restored and new criminological research was encouraged. However, the preventive functions during the Khrushchev period were fulfilled sporadically by police, CPSU, local executive Soviets, and were mainly focused on the reintroduction of popular justice (auxiliary police and Comrades' courts). Though post-Stalin mainstream criminological research was still heavily influenced by the communist ideology, after 1953 crimes were no longer considered to be just characteristics of certain antisocialist classes who were reminiscent of Russia's tenacious presocialist past. It was thought that poor supervision of individuals by societal institutions, which included certain families and socialist employers, were responsible for criminality.[45] Social "diseases" of alcoholism and antisocial lifestyle were considered consequences of such failures and facilitators of crimes (Solomon, 1978).

During the pre-World War II period, crime prevention was primarily based on incapacitation and the destruction of antisocialist classes, such as wealthy peasants (*kulaks*) and successful entrepreneurs of the prewar NEP (New Economic Policy) period. During the Stalin period, forced labor and incapacitation in remote camps were seen as the principal method to eliminate criminality, and criminology was essentially dismissed as a science (Solomon, 1981). During the Khrushchev, and especially Brezhnev, eras Soviet crime prevention relied less on incapacitation and social class destruction, but instead involved more of a comprehensive plan that included fighting against social diseases, the close supervision of families and persons at risk, and education and mandatory labor treatment. During Brezhnev's regime, crime prevention was "gradually coming to mean a broad political, economic, social, and educational effort at engineered change in social behavior" (Juviler, 1974, p. 200).

In 1967, as a part of the crime prevention strategy, police duties were refined in relation to nonsecret administrative supervision of repeat offenders and released convicts (Fastov, 2005). Passportization and limitations on movement imposed by registration were among some of the main police tools to supervise ex-convicts and repeat offenders (Matthews, 1993). Passportization and registration (*propiska*) were effectively reducing crime rates in the large metropolitan areas of Moscow and Leningrad by banning ex-convicts from residing there. However, these policies led to the displacement of crimes to other less controlled territories, such as the new growing cities in the eastern section of the USSR (Shelley, 1980).

In 1974, a single, "prophylactic" service was created within the MVD to unite the efforts of criminal investigative departments, offices on the prevention of juvenile delinquency, and district police officers (*uchastkovyi*). Previously, the district police were charged with the supervision of citizens at predetermined geographic locations (districts) (Morukov, 2007). The duties of the preventive service included the detection of individuals at risk, conducting educational work with them, and creating a single plan of crime prevention in the police precinct (Fastov, 2005). Consistent with the ideas of crime prevention, many courts were charged with a duty to supplement regular sentencing with measures of "averting a particular crime" committed by the defendant (Connor, 1972a).

The 1974 law "On Passports" finally allowed rural residents to have passports. Residents still needed permission from the collective farm leadership to leave the village. However, rural residents were no longer dependent on the local Soviets for issuing their passports, which had become a mandatory document for citizens that were 16 and older. The new law continued to require registration (*propiska*) for both temporary and permanent relocations; however, the rules on registration were somewhat eased (Oda, 1989). The MVD continued to issue most of the passports for Soviet citizens and was able to have special rules on registration for specific areas (Moscow, St. Petersburg, areas close to the state border, military, and closed settlements). Special rules and limitations that applied to ex-convicts and other citizens under administrative police supervision were continued (Matthews, 1993). With minor changes, the rules remained in place until the fall of the Soviet Union in 1991.

During Brezhnev's period, the MVD continued to expand their investigative functions granted to them initially in 1963 by the Amendment to Article 125 of the Criminal Procedural Code of the RSFSR. Numerous additional crimes were added to the MVD's investigative jurisdiction. Only serious or politically motivated crimes were investigated by the *Procuracy* or KGB (Shelley, 1989).[46]

The growth of the investigative jurisdiction prompted a further expansion of the investigative departments and staff in the MVD system (Viktorov, 1974). The network of pretrial detention centers was already part of the MVD system (*sledstvenno-ispavitel'nye izolyatory*) (SIZO). However, prior to 1963, only investigators of the *Procuracy* and KGB were empowered to order long-term, pretrial detention of criminal defendants (Milton, 1976). After the MVD acquired the function of preliminary investigation, both the administration of detention centers and control over the process of pretrial detention became focused in the hands of one agency: the MVD. The MVD investigators now could detain both the suspects and defendants with the permission of the prosecutor as a part of their preventive measures during their preliminary investigation (Savitsky, 1979).[47]

The early Brezhnev years are considered, by some, the golden age of Soviet policing. In the late 1960s and early 1970s, the MVD system developed and matured, and the level of professionalism grew significantly as the educational institutions of the MVD were built in almost every region (Mulukaev, Malygin, and Epifanov, 2005). The morale of the law enforcement agency recovered from exposure to Stalinism atrocities and harsh public criticism of the early 1950s (Shelley, 1996). The extremes of populist policing and justice were adjusted while the overall public order remained stable. Pay raises, new militia days, a code of professional honor and disciplinary code,[48] and other measures taken during the late Khrushchev and early Brezhnev eras significantly improved the public image of the average police officer.

The late Brezhnev years (latter 1970s to 1982) marked the period of "stagnation" where both political and economic problems in Soviet society became more evident and, subsequently, contributed to the fall of the USSR in 1991. The economic problems were grounded in the growing inefficiencies of the planned economy, which resulted in a further development of black markets.

Official government stores with regulated prices experienced increasing shortages of primary public supplies, while black markets matured into a second "shadow" economy.[49] This economy was based on the system of "*blat*" (corruption), an exchange of personal favors among those individuals who had access to the scare resources or power. The members of the political elite responsible for approval of every key official in the state (the "*nomenklatura*") were at the top of the black markets and used their power and influence for personal gain (Simis, 1982). The law enforcement apparatus, controlled by the Party, did little to prosecute illegal businesses of the *nomenklatura* and the policy of cadres' stability allowed no newcomers into the system (Clarke, 1993).

During this period, nepotism developed and pervaded all levels of Soviet society, which further exacerbated growing economic and political issues. The Party *nomenklatura* became a clan with its own privileges and was untouchable by law enforcement and closed to outsiders (Luryi, 1986). Members of the *nomenklatura* promoted family members to positions that allowed access and control of the country's resources (Ra'anan and Lukes, 1990).[50] Outside the Party elites, nepotism also continued to flourish and allowed citizens with access to some basic resources (e.g., the director of the store or the head of the collective farm) to give personal favors to their family members and other privileged citizens (Simis, 1982).[51]

The growing status gap between the Party elites and ordinary citizens, coupled with the expanding system of *blat*, the black market, nepotism, and string-pulling significantly undermined the image of the CPSU and Party rule during the late Brezhnev era (Shelley, 1994). It also corrupted the regular police by legitimizing selective prosecution (Knight, 1984).[52] The MVD was an active participant in the growing corruption and concealed undesired investigations into the illegal activities of political elites (Favarel-Garrigues, 2002; Luryi, 1986; Shtromas, 1977).

The leadership of the MVD during the Brezhnev era had strong ties to the CPSU as well as the Brezhnev family.[53] This situation also inoculated the ministry from a careful scrutiny of rising corruption in the law enforcement apparatus itself (Shelley, 1992). During the Brezhnev period, members of the political elite enjoyed the right to influence the legal system including the outcome of MVD criminal investigations where the *nomenklatura* had particular interests in either increasing or decreasing the severity of any punishment (Shelley, 1986).

The increasing demands for proactive policing, the struggle with controlling alcoholism, parasite-life styles, juvenile delinquency, and the prevention of crime became more difficult to achieve in the late Brezhnev era. As the urban population continued to grow and more private one-family apartments were built to replace communal living, the heavy administrative control that was required from Soviet police became a difficult task. The slow disintegration of both ideology and public support for the police resulted in diminished public–police cooperation.

Yet the crime rates continued to grow steadily while political leadership demanded glowing reports on preventing and solving crime (Shelley, 1991; Shikhantsov, 2009).[54] As in other areas of the planned economy, policing in Soviet Union became somewhat of a planned activity (Fastov, 2005). The MVD leadership evaluated police performance based on specific quarterly quotas related to solved crimes as well as annual or five-year plans. Under these circumstances, MVD offices at all levels were routinely involved in a game of "numbers cooking" when statistical data used for reports were manipulated. The reports became an artificial formality rather than true criteria to assess police performance (Shtromas, 1977).[55] At the same time, public criticism of the MVD was limited and carefully censored. There were only a few "show cases" of government corruption and bad policing available for public scrutiny.[56] Any public criticism of the KGB was completely abandoned while public literature featured the glorified work of the security police (Knight, 1988).

In November of 1982, Iurii Andropov, the former head of the KGB, succeeded Brezhnev as the General Secretary of the CPSU. Andropov was not one of Brezhnev's supporters, thus both the KGB and MVD were instrumental in the succession of power (Knight, 1984). In 1983, Andropov launched a wide anticorruption campaign in both the trade organizations and the MVD system. The most well-known cases of *nomenklatura* corruption in the Soviet Union (e.g., the "cotton case" in Uzbekistan) were investigated and tried during this time (Kalinichenko, 1998). The anticorruption campaign in the MVD resulted in a purge of approximately 5% of the MVD personnel. The most visible victims were Brezhnev's cronies and included the minister of the MVD himself (Shelley, 1996). Konstantin Chernenko, one of Brezhnev's associates, became the leader of the Soviet Union in 1984. During his short-term leadership, reform of the MVD system was continued by streamlining the militia administration, but the drastic anticorruption scandals were slowly terminated (Shelley, 1996).

3.3 Concluding Remarks

The Khrushchev liberalization reforms of the MVD system share remarkable similarities with judicial reforms conducted by Tsar Alexander II in the 1860s. First, in both cases, the reforms were prompted by social and economic conditions that demanded the leadership launch government change. It was hardly the personal initiative of Khrushchev to start the de-Stalinization of the law enforcement apparatus. Beria, Malenkov, and other political leaders of the Soviet Union during that period were looking for ways to change the situation created by years of Stalin's repressions.

Second, both the tsarist reforms of the 1860s and Khrushchev's liberalization were reforms conducted from "above." It was not a reform shaped and developed through the interaction of civil society and an elected government as in many other countries. Instead, this was another policy change resulting from a top-down personal initiative and implemented by the hierarchical system. Thus, reforms were short-lived after the changes in leadership and did not create a quality and sustained change in the system itself. The decentralization and depoliticization of the MVD system was resented and reversed quickly after Khrushchev's dismissal and its bureaucratic apparatus only continued to grow despite Khrushchev's best intentions.

Third, both reforms were limited in their scope and application. The goals of new policy changes in both cases were to alleviate existing tensions in society and not to completely remodel the criminal justice system. As soon as changes became threatening to the political leadership of the country they were abandoned. In case of the MVD during the Khrushchev era, the Communist Party was willing to weaken the law enforcement apparatus to prevent another round of Stalinist repressions. They were not interested in a decentralized, more transparent, and less controlled system of regular police.

The regular police of the Brezhnev period are referred by some as the golden standard of Soviet policing. Then, the public perception was that police officers were effective, courteous, and incorruptible (Bondarenko, 2002).[57] At the same time, historians continue to point to the Brezhnev period of police development as a major source of problems in the modern Russian police (Fastov, 2005; Shelley, 1996). This paradox has its logical explanation in the dual nature of this historic period.

On one hand, especially during the early Brezhnev period, the Soviet regular police matured and developed into a professional, educated, and well-equipped system. The enhanced system has vast administrative capabilities and effective means of public–police interaction (Mulukaev, Malygin, and Epifanov, 2005). Even though crime rates continued to grow, much of the growth was attributable to everyday crimes often committed by intoxicated offenders (Shtromas, 1977). These crimes were easily and efficiently investigated by the regular police and were one of the most visible police activities that improved public–police interaction. Existing Party control in every precinct, and severe sentencing for bribery, prevented regular low-ranked police officers from soliciting or taking bribes when investigating everyday crimes.[58] Information related to organized and more vicious crimes (e.g., serial killers) were carefully concealed from public view and created a feeling of public safety and security (Luryi, 1986). At the same time, the fully controlled media were used to create an image of an honest, hard-working, and incorruptible police officer (Bondarenko, 2002; Bondarenko and Dorokhov, 2006). This mythology of effective and honest Soviet policemen is long-lived and can be easily traced in the modern public views of the police.

On the other hand, higher-level Soviet police officers during the Brezhnev period had to deal with a different reality. Then, criminal investigations, related to the elite members of the CPSU, were allowed only after receiving permission from a high-ranked Party official (Ra'anan and Lukes, 1990). Criminal investigations where elite members of the CPSU were either victims or witnesses were done with extreme care. Criminal law was sometimes used retroactively, or arbitrarily, to allow for harsher penalties than existed at the time (Luryi, 1986). Known facts of corruption by the political elite were gathered by high-ranking officers in the KGB and MVD and used only for sanctioned cases and mostly for the purposes of political advantage (Knight, 1988). The continuous demands of reporting and the growing bureaucratization resulted in altered criminal statistics and was also a part of the life of police leadership. The succession of power in the Soviet Union occurred under the direct leadership of both law enforcement agencies and made personal loyalty the most important virtue of a police leader (Shelley, 1996). This world of selective prosecution, arbitrary use of the law, doctored statistics, and participation in political intrigues was carefully concealed from public view. Yet these exact problems continue to be at the core of the modern Russian police problems and exacerbated by new issues brought by *perestroika* and the free market economy (Table 3.1).

Table 3.1 Timetable of major events: 1953–1984

Year	Description
1953	USSR under collective leadership of Beria, Malenkov, and Molotov
1953	Beria's policy of "liberalization," including amnesty for ordinary and political prisoners established
1953	Beria dismissed as a head of MVD and a deputy chairman, tried, and executed for state crimes
1953	Khrushchev became the first secretary of CPSU after Beria's death
1953	The Special Council was abolished
1954	Khrushchev separated political and regular police by creating the Committee of State Security (KGB)
1955	New centers of detention included into MVD system to enforce the vagrancy laws
1956	Local police departments transferred back to the "dual subordination" model and were accountable to the MVD and local executive Soviets
1958	"Basic principles of criminal legislation of USSR" introduced
1958	Auxiliary police units established in the form of brigades (*druzhinniki)* and millions of citizens mobilized to participate
1960	The new Criminal Code of RSFSR and the Criminal Procedural Code of RSFSR enacted
1960	The Decree on Voluntary People's Patrols (DND) issued
1961	The decree instructed police to find and investigate all cases of antisocial parasite behavior
1962	MVD renamed the Ministry of Defense of Public Order (MOOP)
1963	The Criminal Procedural Code of RSFSR amended to list the regular police (MOOP) as one of the institutions authorized to conduct preliminary investigations
1963	The Decree of the Supreme Court instructed people's court to impose more severe sentences on speculators and other antisocial elements
1963	The Amendment to Article 125 of Criminal Procedural Code of RSFSR, granting investigative functions to MVD
1964	Forceful dismissal of Khrushchev
1964	Brezhnev became the first secretary of CPSU
1965	Each regional police office supplemented by the deputy chair position responsible for political–ideological education of police officers
1966	MOOP reestablished
1966	New laws on hooliganism adopted
1967	Police duties supplemented by the organization of centers for detention (*spets-priemniki)*
1967	The government started a new campaign against alcoholism by allowing simplified procedures for forceful institutionalization of alcoholics in special medical institutions
1967	The government intensified efforts against the juvenile delinquency with Commissions on Juvenile Affairs
1967	As a part of crime prevention strategy, police duties refined in relation to the nonsecret administrative supervision of repeat offenders and released convicts
1968	MOOP renamed back to Ministry of Internal Affairs, and MVD was no longer a structural part of the local executive Soviets

(continued)

Table 3.1 Timetable of major events: 1953–1984 (continued)

Year	Description
1969	Each regional MVD office supplemented by the department of political and ideological education
1972	Public consumption of alcohol and public intoxication outlawed
1974	The Law on Auxiliary Police adopted and assigned new duties to members of *druzhiny* and integrated them further into the police departments
1974	An escape from the medical labor institution became criminally liable offense
1974	A single "prophylactic" service created within MVD to unite efforts of the criminal investigative departments, the offices on prevention of juvenile delinquency, and district police officers
1974	The Law on Passports allowed rural residents to have a passport
1977	Inspections for Juvenile Affairs *(Inspektsii po delam nesovershennoletnikh)* (IND) created and staffed by MVD personnel
1982	Uirii Andropov, former head of KGB, succeeded Brezhnev as General Secretary of CPSU
1983	Andropov launched a wide anticorruption campaign in trade organizations and MVD system
1984	Konstantin Chernenko became the leader of Soviet Union

Endnotes

1. In the post-Soviet historic literature, there is also an opinion that the triumvirate consisted of Beria, Malenkov, and Khrushchev. Molotov is deemed to be of lesser importance.
2. According to the official statistics, over 1,600,000 people were released during this amnesty (Fastov, 2005).
3. According to Fastov (2005), by Decree of the Council of Ministers issued on March 16, 1953, the functions of Glavpromstroi (Main Industrial Building Department) and Glavspetzstoi (Main Special Building Department) were transferred from MVD to the 1st Main Department. By Decree on March 18, 1953, other building and industrial departments mainly related to the use of forced labor were transferred to various economic ministries. Also, in March of 1953, the notorious GULAG was transferred from MVD to the Ministry of Justice.
4. These changes also were caused by mounting economic problems faced by the GULAG in the postwar period. With the development of heavy industry and continuous decreases in labor productivity, the economy of forced labor became economically inadequate by the early 1950s (Khlevnyuk, 2003).
5. According to Rybnikov and Aleksushin (2008), Beria was the first official who mentioned that the rights of citizens were violated in this country during his speech on March 9, 1953, at Stalin's funeral.
6. Prior to 1955, RSFSR was the only union republic that did not have its own republican MVD and policing was administrated in Russia through the central MVD USSR.

7. The heads of the local police were confirmed during the annual conferences of local executive Soviets.
8. This situation existed in the USSR until the late 1930s. According to the USSR agreement, "internal affairs" were considered a sole function of the republics. It was Stalin and his desire to concentrate all the law enforcement power that led to centralization of NKVD/MVD under one centralized agency.
9. According to Rybnikov and Aleksushin (2008), over 3,000 communist members and 30,0000 of Komsomol members were assigned to work in the MVD system in October of 1954. During 1962–1964, at least 300 members of the Communist Party with higher levels of education were transferred to leading positions in the MVD–MOOP system.
10. According to Bondarenko and Dorokhov (2006), between 1956 and 1960, over 65% of low ranking police officers and 75% of high ranking police officers were replaced by new cadres.
11. According to Rybnikov and Aleksushin (2008), the number of "militia schools," secondary educational facilities for the majority of police officers in USSR, grew from 12 in 1956 to 25 in 1958. According to Fastov (2005), by 1959, the police educational system in the USSR included 38 institutions, with only one higher education institution in Moscow.
12. For example, Decree of the Council of Ministers #8348 issued on December 15, 1955, provided free rides in the local transportation for police officers. The Decree of the Council of Ministers #1444 issued on October 25, 1956, provided a significant pay raise for police officers with experience of more than three and six years.
13. According to Bondarenko and Dorokhov (2006), several instructions by regional MVD offices were issued in 1954 and 1955, recommending that newly hired police officers should have at least seven years of secondary education. This was in comparison to the previously existing requirement of 1923, which allowed police officers to be hired with only four years of school education (elementary level).
14. Article 125 of the Criminal Code of RSFSR lists agencies authorized to conduct preliminary investigation and type of crimes for which each agency has jurisdiction.
15. Inquiry is a short-term investigation conducted for misdemeanor cases or prior to conducting the preliminary investigation for felony cases.
16. The levels of Soviet police education prior to the Khrushchev era were extremely low. For example, in 1940, only 11.2% of the police workforce had middle school degrees and 0.5% had a college degree. The rest of the workforce consisted of men with elementary school education (Gorbatenko, 2011).
17. According to Govorov & Remneva (2007), by 1960 the auxiliary police (DND) consisted of 2.5 million individuals serving in more than 80,000 auxiliary police units and, by 1967, there were 6.5 million citizens participating in auxiliary police units (*druzhiny*).
18. Decree by the Bureau of the Central Committee (CC) of CPSU of RSFSR and Council of Ministers of RSFSR issued on March 30, 1960, #435, "About confirmation of the decree on the Voluntary People's Patrols and protection of public order" (Morukov, 2007).

19. The Decree of the Presidium of the Supreme Council of USSR issued on July 23, 1951; "About measures of struggle against antisocial parasite elements" established criminal liability for vagrancy punishable by up to five years of imprisonment (Morukov, 2007).
20. See, for example, Article 154 of the Criminal Code of RSFSR. Retrieved from www.consultant.ru.
21. Plenum of the Supreme Court of RSFSR, Decree, "About court practices on speculation" #20/1, issued on October 29, 1963 (Morukov, 2007).
22. According to Kuritsyna (2009), the majority of juvenile crimes committed during 1945 to 1953 were related to theft of food and other items needed for survival of children on the streets. However, the nature of juvenile delinquency changed by the mid-1950s with a significant number of public disorder (hooliganism) crimes committed by juveniles at that time.
23. Decree of the Council of Ministers #171 issued on January 30, 1954, "About measures to improve the work of orphanages" (Morukov, 2007).
24. On March 12, 1954, the CC of CPSU issued a decree, "On the main goals of MVD," among which, the MVD was required to improve the work with the population and improve the situation with personnel. In January of 1956, the leadership of the MVD issued instructions to the police officers requiring them to inform the public about the results of their work in order to improve the public–police relationship. On March 2, 1959, CC of CPSU issued Decree #218 in which MVD was heavily criticized for poor work with the public. The auxiliary police (*druzhinniki*) were established by this decree to improve the situation (Morukov, 2007).
25. The official statistics of crime rates in the USSR were secret information and were not published between 1928 and 1956. Many foreign researchers, who attempted to reconstruct the data from secondary sources, were facing serious challenges. For example, see Chalidze (1977) and Berg (1985). Even Soviet and post-Soviet literature still have scarce information on the exact crime rate statistics of this period (Shikhantsov, 2009). However, taking into consideration all existing information, it is safe to assume that after 1953, the crime rates dropped significantly (mostly due to decrease in the war and postwar-related crimes) and remained somewhat stable until 1966 (with some increases and drops due to amnesties, new legislation, and antisocial elements campaigns). Unlike general crime rates, the literature and existing data suggest a significant increase in juvenile delinquency rates during this period.
26. The new decree on MVD USSR issued in 1972 (Decree of the Council of Ministers #452) outlined an elaborated structure for the MVD USSR including a special department to struggle against illegal economic activities (Morukov, 2007).
27. On November 19, 1968, the Central Committee of the CPSU and the Supreme Council of the USSR issued a letter in which the MOOP was criticized for its work. As a result of the criticism, the letter instructed it to establish a special school in Leningrad to educate political–ideological supervisors of police and correctional institutions. Cited from information on the history of the MVD from www.mvd.ru.
28. According to MVD decree issued on February 5, 1969. Cited from information on the history of the MVD from www.mvd.ru.

29. On measurement of some ethnic issues in the USSR during the 1970s, see, for example, Karklins (1987).
30. Decree of the presidium of the Supreme Council of the USSR issued on May 20, 1974 "On the basic duties and rights of the Volunteer People's Patrols for Protection of Public Order" and decree of the Central Committee of the CPSU and the Supreme Council of the USSR, "On further improvement of the activities of the Volunteer People's Patrols for Protection of Public Order" issued on the same day (Morukov, 2007).
31. Some indirect evidence on decreasing public motivation to participate in auxiliary police can be found in Zimmerman's work (1987), which surveyed immigrants leaving the Soviet Union. According to his study, slightly over 10% of all surveyed regularly participated in various aspects of public mobilization including auxiliary police. These findings should be taken carefully, because the sample of immigrants does not represent the entire Soviet Union population. However, after 1987, when the service in the auxiliary police no longer was rewarded through paid days off, the number of auxiliary policemen significantly dropped (Govorov and Remneva, 2007).
32. The presidium of the Supreme Council of the USSR issued a new decree on July 26, 1966, "About increasing the liability for hooliganism" (Morukov, 2007).
33. For example, public cursing, "unpleasant public stalking of other citizens," and other actions violating public order.
34. Article 3 of the decree issued on July 26, 1966, "About increasing the liability for hooliganism" (Morukov, 2007).
35. Articles 9 and 10 of the decree issued on July 26, 1966, "About increasing the liability for hooliganism" (Morukov, 2007).
36. The presidium of the Supreme Council of the RSFSR issued a decree on April 8, 1967 by which alcoholics were to be forcefully institutionalized in medical and labor institutions (Morukov, 2007).
37. The presidium of the Supreme Council of the RSFSR issued a decree on June 19, 1972 by which public drinking and intoxication was outlawed and the special commissions against alcoholism were created within the executive local Soviets (Morukov, 2007).
38. Articles 1–4, 8, 16, and 17 of the decree issued on June 19, 1972 by the presidium of Supreme Council of RSFSR, "About measures to strengthen struggle against drunkenness and alcoholism" (Morukov, 2007).
39. The decree of presidium of the Supreme Council of RSFSR issued on March 1, 1974, "About forceful and labor treatment of chronic alcoholics" (Morukov, 2007).
40. The new decree on "Commissions for juvenile affairs" was issued on July 3, 1967 by the presidium of the Supreme Council of the RSFSR. In compliance with this document, the new decree by MOOP was issued on August 10, 1967, which instructed police to assist commissions for juvenile affairs in any way possible in their struggle against prevention of juvenile delinquency and repeated offending (Morukov, 2007).
41. According to the decree of presidium of the Supreme Council of the USSR issued on February 15, 1977, the inspections for juvenile affairs were not officially a part of MVD system, but they were staffed with police personnel (Morukov, 2007).

42. Articles 6–7 of the decree of presidium of the Supreme Council of the USSR issued on February 15, 1977, "On main rights and duties of Inspections for juvenile offenders" (Morukov, 2007).
43. Articles 8–10 of the decree of presidium of the Supreme Council of the USSR issued on February 15, 1977, "On main rights and duties of Inspections for juvenile offenders" (Morukov, 2007).
44. According to the decree of the MVD issued in 1972, all possible prevention of the reasons causing crimes and other antisocial behavior was named one of the main goals of the MVD office (Morukov, 2007).
45. In this section, we refer to the mainstream official criminological opinions that were expressed by the scientists working in academic institutions affiliated with the MVD and *Procuracy*. It is true that some variety of opinions existed among Soviet criminologist on the causation of crime. Yet these outside mainstream course opinions rarely impacted the official policy.
46. Amendments to the Article 125 of the CPC of the RSFSR issued on May 21, 1970. Cited from consultant.ru
47. These amalgamations of power for pretrial detention contributed to the abuse of power exhibited by the MVD later. These centers (SIZO) will became notorious for human rights violations in the post-Soviet period of policing.
48. For details on the Disciplinary Code, see, for example, Gavrilenko (1975–1976).
49. On levels of material supplies in the Soviet Union in comparison to other countries during the 1970s and 1980s, see, for example, Matthews (1993).
50. An indirect reference to the privileged position of Party Elites can be found in a study of immigrants' perceptions conducted by Swafford (1987). In this study, members of the regional Party and KGB officers were ranked highest for their social status and the influence they had in society.
51. On details of illegal income-earning activities involving the support of Party officials, see, for example, Favarel-Garrigues (2011).
52. The data on public opinion of regular police during Brezhnev's era is scarce and difficult to interpret. Many researchers believe that available data about public views were doctored or that respondents were simply afraid to give any negative assessment of the Soviet government.
53. For more details on ties between the MVD leadership, CPSU, and Brezhnev, see, for example, Milton (1976).
54. This included a rise of economic crimes during the Brezhnev era (Favarel-Garrigues, 2011).
55. On the issue of "percentage-mania" and issues with Soviet crime statistics, see, for example, Chalidze (1977).
56. There is probably only one well-known case of government corruption that was investigated and tried during the Brezhnev period—the so-called "fish case." The defendant in this case was a deputy minister of the fish industry who was convicted on corruption charges and sentenced to death. For details, see Kalinichenko (1998), who investigated this case.
57. On the issue of general corruption paradox, see, for example, Krastev (2002).
58. Sometimes citizens bribed police officers with gifts for "improved" services, but such gifts were not solicited by the police and did not prevent them from doing their job without such a reward (Favarel-Garrigues, 2011).

Transformation of the Soviet and Post-Soviet Police from 1985 to 2008

4

4.1 Soviet Police under Gorbachev: 1985–1991

Mikhail Gorbachev's accession to power in March of 1985 was the same as that of his predecessors, Brezhnev and Andropov. Gorbachev used the support of certain political Party elite members and KGB leadership to take control of the office of General Secretary (Knight, 1988). Also, similar to Andropov, during his first year as a general secretary, Gorbachev launched an anticorruption campaign that was often used against his political opponents within the party and the MVD (Ministry of Internal Affairs).

The drive to "tighten the discipline" and improve the quality of MVD personnel resulted in significant turnovers (Galeotti, 1993). The head of the MVD was replaced, once again, by a loyal member of the Party elite ("apparatchik") with no law enforcement experience. In 1987, Gorbachev authorized an investigation of the former MVD deputy minister, Yuri Churbanov (Brezhnev's son-in-law), which resulted in a publicized trial and subsequent lengthy imprisonment for charges of abuse of power and corruption (Clarke, 1993). As with Andropov, in 1985, the MVD was again heavily criticized in the press for allowing crime rates and corruption to grow (Shelley, 1994). At the same time, the head of the KGB announced that his agency's role was to "cleanse society of all negative manifestations" (Knight, 1988).

Similar to previous Soviet leaders, just two months after his appointment, Gorbachev decided to launch another proactive policing campaign against excessive drinking.[1] The decree was prescribed to create commissions to fight drunkenness on the regional and republic levels. Local Soviets, together with local MVD offices, were responsible for not only controlling the public drunks by placing them in the special "sober-up stations," but also for raiding and seizing illegal distilleries. Unlike the previous antiparasites campaigns during the 1960s, the antialcohol campaign of 1985 was very unpopular and only alienated citizens from the police (Shelley, 1994). The campaign not only diverted police resources from critical crime control issues, but it also significantly reduced budget revenues of the state, which had profited for years from the production of inexpensive vodka (Sergeyev, 1998).

However, Gorbachev was faced with much more serious issues than just a problem of alcohol consumption. By 1985–1986, the number of political, social, and economic issues became apparent after a long period of neglect by the Soviet government. One of the most obvious problems was the stagnation and decline of living standards that had started slowly in the late 1970s and became apparent by the mid-1980s. The shortage of consumer goods, housing, and adequate healthcare, coupled with an ineffective system of distribution, a growing shadow economy, and loss of the motivation to effectively work when all salaries were regulated by the government became a visible and recognizable problem under Gorbachev (Field, 1991; Matthews, 1993).

The issue of steadily growing crime rates and the inability of police to solve cases became more apparent. Even according to the official statistics, the number of registered crimes in 1985 grew by 37.8% when compared to the crime rates in 1980 (NII_MVD, 1993). Starting in 1964, officially registered crime continued to grow annually, exceeding growth of the general population. The increase in crime during the mid-1980s was primarily from a spike of nonviolent crime, such as state property embezzlement and theft (MVD, 1990).

The fallen standard of living, and diminished political control, were often to blame for growing state property crimes; whereas the interference of Party elites with the investigations often prevented the apprehension of the main culprits responsible for embezzlement (Association for Criminology, 1996). Other crime trends were increasing at an alarming rate and included repeat offenders,[2] crimes committed by organized groups, and drug-related violations (Galeotti, 1993; Mulukaev, Malygin, and Epifanov, 2005).[3]

Drug abuse in the USSR was adamantly denied by the authorities until 1985 and any related studies were deemed secret (Kramer, 1991; Treml, 1991). As a result, low-ranking police officers often felt unprepared to deal with drug-related crimes (Gilinskiy and Zazulin, 2001). Following the implementation of *glasnost* (openness), crime statistics were published for the first time in 1987 and revealed climbing rates and declining numbers of apprehensions, which concerned the public (Shelley, 1994).

One of the major problems that Gorbachev faced during his early tenure was the diminished legitimacy of the Communist Party and Soviet regime, in general. The most profound manifestation of declining political power was a number of public disturbances and nationalistic movements that mushroomed in Soviet Union republics beginning in 1986 (Rybnikov and Aleksushin, 2008).[4] Detachments of MVD "internal troops" were sent to these areas for crowd control as the local police were incapable, or not trustworthy enough, to complete the task (Shelley, 1996).

In January of 1987, Gorbachev officially announced his "perestroika" policy at the Plenum of the Central Committee of the CPSU (Communist Party of the Soviet Union). The original idea of *perestroika* was rather a mild economic and political liberalization policy. The Communist Party would retain a leading political role and socialism would continue to be the major economic goal of the country (Terrill, 1989). Under these premises, perestroika of the MVD and police was viewed as the establishment of "a Socialist law-based state in which the Communist Party and its institutions would be subordinate by the law and individuals would enjoy greater legal protection vis-à-vis the state" (Shelley, 1994, p. 53). Two major laws were issued to allow for "individual private enterprise" in 1986[5] and the establishment of cooperatives in 1988.[6] These documents, for the first time since the NEP (New Economic Policy) in 1921 permitted private citizens to conduct some for-profit activities by either producing goods or offering services to the Soviet citizens (Matthews, 1993).

The law on cooperatives was much less restrictive than for individual private enterprise. Groups of at least three individuals were required to register a cooperative organization that would produce goods or services for sale. The law permitted the cooperatives to act independently from the administrative agencies of the state. These entities had their own budget and cash flows and were not a part of the administrative distributive economy of the state (Rybnikov and Aleksushin, 2008).[7]

Existing organized crime groups of "black marketers," working in connection with corrupted government officials and the Party *nomenklatura*, immediately took advantage of the economic liberalization offered via "individual private enterprises" and cooperatives (Glinkina, 1994). Many cooperatives in the late 1980s were operated by organized crime groups and used to launder money and materials embezzled by the government officials from the state enterprises (Sergeyev, 1998).

According to eyewitness accounts reported by Handelman (1995), even when the police and prosecutors opened investigations related to these cases, they were often stalled by the Party officials that were involved in covering up the embezzlement. Only low-level offenders were prosecuted while the organizers and facilitators of the crime remained mostly uncharged. As a result, the organized crime groups continued to grow, mature, and build closer ties with the new private businesses, administrative apparatus, and international crime groups (Finckenauer and Voronin, 2001).

The maturation of organized crime in the late 1980s created additional increases in registered crime, which grew rapidly by 32.7% in 1989, 13.6% in 1990, and 18.1% in 1991. The crime rate virtually doubled in two years between 1989 and 1991 (Association for Criminology, 1996). At the same time, the effectiveness of criminal investigations continued to decline sharply. This was especially true for theft of state and public property (Favarel-Garrigues, 2011). According to official statistics, in 1988, 51.3% of property-related crimes were solved by investigators as compared to only 36.2% in 1989 and 35% in 1990 (Serio, 1992).

Another negative factor attributed to the growth of organized crime during the period from 1989 to 1991 was an increase in the number of violent offenses. The number of registered person-related crimes (including homicides, assaults, and bodily injuries) increased by 28.8% in 1989 and by another 9.1% in 1990 (MVD, 1990). The steady growth of crime rates during 1964 through 1985 was mainly attributed to nonviolent property crimes that existed during the time of media censorship and was easily concealed from the public. The sharp growth of violent crimes during the period from 1989 to 1991, along with the policy of *glasnost,* made it difficult for the Soviet authorities to cover up growing crime rates. The result was that for the first time since the 1960s the public perception of a "safe" Soviet society[8] and public legitimacy of the police was challenged (Carton, 1992).

Both the MVD investigative and detective apparatus faced serious challenges during the period from 1989 to 1991. In addition to the problems of interfering Party officials, police departments were often understaffed and underequipped. As a result of sharply growing crime rates, most departments experienced an increase of case loads. Also, with development of private businesses, many skilled investigators decided to leave MVD jobs and move to more profitable enterprises, such as private law practices or security-related professions. In 1989 alone, the official shortage of general staff in the police rose from 2.6% to 3.1% (Serio, 1992). As a result of growing ethnic conflicts and organized crime rates, work in the police force during late 1980s became much less safe (Galeotti, 1993). This resulted in higher personnel losses and reduced the quality of MVD personnel during the period from 1989 to 1991 (Serio, 1992).

In 1988, almost 70% of all MVD investigators had a university-level legal education and over three years of experience. However, just two years later, qualified and experienced investigators constituted less than 50% of MVD personnel (Gavrilov, 2003b). Uncensored public coverage of police institutions, growing crime rates, and ineffective police work significantly undermined the public image of the police in the late 1980s (Curfman, 1997).

The Soviet government made some attempts to reform the law enforcement and criminal justice systems to comply with the policies of *perestroika* and *glasnost* during 1985 to 1991. However, these attempts were often insufficient, late, and did not result in more effective policing. The new department of Public Relations was created in 1986 to coordinate public–police interaction within MVD USSR (MVD, 2008b). In 1987, new performance criteria related to solving crime were introduced and eased the unrealistic demand that 95% of all crimes had to be solved (Shelley, 1996). In 1989, the growing problem of organized crime was acknowledged and a new organized crime department was established in the MVD USSR (Galeotti, 1993).

In order to diminish the over-centralization and power of the KGB, in October of 1991, Gorbachev ordered it to be dismantled into three separate agencies (Pustintsev, 1996). Democratic amendments were included in the criminal procedural law that provided each criminal defendant with the right to counsel during some pretrial stages of investigation (Huskey, 1986). Many offenses related to the planned economy and private entrepreneurship were decriminalized in the Criminal Code of the RSFSR (Solomon, 1992).

One of the most significant ideological shifts in Soviet law enforcement policy can be found in the new law "On Soviet Police" promulgated in March of 1991 and just a few months before the Soviet Union collapsed.[9] Unlike the previous decree on Soviet police issued in 1973, the new law did not describe the police as an organization that "under direction of the Communist Party was created to build Communism in the society."[10] Instead, the new law emphasized that the purpose of the police was to protect the personal security of citizens, protect property, and provide social assistance to the population. The law provided new principles for police work that included *glasnost*, rule of law, respect of persons, social fairness, democracy, humanism, interaction with the workers' organizations and the public, as well as consideration of public opinion.[11] This law was short lived as just one month later in April of 1991, during the drive for independence, the Russian Socialist Federated Socialist Republic (RSFSR) promulgated its own law "On Police" and declared the law "On Soviet Police" void (MVD, 2008b).

In order to respond to the continuous civil disturbances in republics of the Soviet Union, the new police detachments "for special purposes" (OMON) were created by USSR MVD decree in 1988 (Gonyukhov and Gorobtsov, 2002).[12] These units were better equipped and trained to react to the public civil disturbances and riots that were accompanying the nationalist and separatist movements from 1988 to 1991 (Curfman, 1997). However, when these units were deployed in Kazakhstan, Georgia, Moldova, and the Baltic states, "they did irreparable damage to the legitimacy of central government" and further exacerbated antagonistic feelings against "colonizing Russians" (Shelley, 1996, p. 55).[13]

In an attempt to curb nationalistic movements, the MVD of the USSR in 1988 announced a push for further decentralization of law enforcement functions by providing republics with more rights and autonomy (MVD, 2008b). As a part of this move, the RSFSR was provided with its own republican MVD office in 1989. This move was unsuccessful as republican law enforcement agencies became victims of a continuous struggle between nationalistic separatism and the federal government's desire to contain it (Galeotti, 1993). As time progressed, the leaders of Soviet republics, in pursuit of sovereignty, took progressive steps to assure control over the republican-level MVD offices while breaking away from the central government's hold over the administration of internal affairs (Shelley, 1996). These actions were first taken by Lithuania, Latvia, Estonia, Moldova, and several republics in the Caucasus regions and concluded with Russia in 1990.[14]

The measures taken by the MVD USSR during the late 1980s were unsuccessful because they were simply another internal "reform" dictated from central government and "the democratization of police in form but not substance" (Curfman, 1997, p. 64). As the result of Communist decades-long ideology indoctrination, conservative forces within the MVD agency were incapable of initiating reforms in accordance with the new social and political reality.[15] The participation of the MVD USSR minister in a coup in August of 1991 (together with the ministers of defense, KGB, and other prominent Party members) was one of the most discrediting acts of the MVD USSR that demonstrated the conservative nature of its leadership and resentment for change. In three days, the coup attempt failed and the minister of the MVD USSR committed suicide. Within a few months, the Soviet Union collapsed and functions of the MVD USSR were transferred to the MVD RSFSR.

4.2 Early Development of the Post-Soviet Police under Yeltsin: 1991–1999

Arguably, the most challenging stage of post-Soviet police development began in the early 1990s when the new Russian Federation was attempting to embrace both rapid economic and political liberalization under the leadership of Boris Yeltsin (Huerou, 2002). In 1992, the president officially ordered "liberalization of the price policy,"[16] which meant that government was no longer controlling prices of goods and services and the Russian Federation no longer followed the administrative command economy model practiced in the USSR. As a result, the severe shortages of consumer goods the country was experiencing in the late 1980s were replaced by skyrocketing price increases followed by hyperinflation of the currency in the early 1990s. The life savings of most Soviet citizens were lost through the significant depreciation of currency. As a result, over one third of the Russian population (33.5%) in 1992 was living below the poverty level. These numbers remained at an average of 25% through the entire period of the Yeltsin presidency.[17] Other problems included growing unemployment and deterioration of the healthcare system,[18] and continuous delays in salary payments.[19] The overall Russian Federation economy suffered from acute changes. The Russian gross domestic product (GDP) continued to fall through the period from 1992 through 1999 and reached record lows during the financial crisis of 1998.[20] The numbers of foreign investments and level of industrial development also declined through the entire period (Rutkevitch, 1998).

Whereas for the majority of Russians, the early 1990s reforms brought a significant decline in living conditions, for a smaller group of privileged individuals who substantially benefited from the introduction of a free market economy, it became a time of unprecedented enrichment. Many of these new businessmen were representatives of the shadow economy that was flourishing in the USSR through the mid- and late 1980s (Favarel-Garrigues, 2011; Handelman, 1995). The former members of Party *nomenklatura*, KGB representatives, and members of organized crime who embezzled or stole state funds during the turmoil of the USSR collapse were now investing illegal funds into the new economy (Waller, 1994; Waller and Yasmann, 1995).[21] They were creating joint Russian–foreign ventures and used these funds to purchase valuable assets of the Soviet economy through the processes of privatization and closed auctions (Shelley, 2000; Waller, 1995b).

The rapid deterioration of economic conditions together with the further development of organized crime caused new crime rate increases during the early 1990s. The number of registered crimes grew from 1,243 per 100,000 residents in 1990 to 1,886 per 100,000 residents in 1993[22] and then quadrupled between 1991 and 1996 (Association for Criminology, 1997). The increase of crime rates in the early 1990s was attributed mostly to the growth of felonies, violent crimes, and crimes committed by organized groups (NII MVD, 1993). According to official statistics, the number of serious crimes in Russia tripled from 513,910 in 1993 to 1,633,367 crimes in 1995.[23] The same upward trend could be observed for offenses committed by organized crime groups,[24] repeat offenders,[25] and drug-related crimes.[26] Other disturbing numbers include 550,000 fatal crime victims during the years from 1991 to 1996 in which 213,590 died in 1992 alone (Association for Criminology, 1997).

Russian criminologists suggest that official statistics do not accurately reflect the difficult crime situation that developed during the early 1990s. The true crime rate is thought to be least two times higher than officially reported by victims as a result of "number cooking" by police (Kolennikova, 2002). Public concern with safety mirrored the escalation of true crime rates and increased from 30% in 1991 to 69% in 1995 (Kolennikova, 2002).

During these difficult times of rapid economic transformation and growing crime rates, the Russian Ministry of Internal Affairs was attempting to implement reforms to address the new conditions. Officially, these changes were focused on the democratization of the post-Soviet police and the development of the modern law enforcement system. However, in reality, the reforms were sporadic, often contradictory, and lacked a conceptual framework (Shelley, 1999).

Large packages of legal documents were enacted during the 1990s to facilitate various reforms. The most important document, the law "On Police of RSFSR" was promulgated even before the USSR fell in April of 1991. This statute became key legislation governing post-Soviet policing until 2011 (Fastov, 2005; Marshunov, 2001). The law removed any mention of Communist ideology, duties of Soviet-style proactive policing, and emphasized respect for human rights as the goals of policing (Kondrashev, Solovei, and Chernikov,

2006; Pysh'ev, 2006). It also regulated, for the first time, the physical force, and firearms and special equipment used by police officers (Avrutin, 2006; Elizarov and Petryuk, 2006). However, the new law retained the old centralized hierarchical and militarized system of the MVD (Kolemasov et al., 2007). Experts from the European countries criticized the law for lack of clarity and enforceable mechanisms of public accountability, decision transparency, and protection against police abuse (Fadin, 2006; Pustintsev, 2000).

A number of documents were adopted in the early 1990s that reaffirmed previous functions of the MVD including the registration of vehicles,[27] registration of citizens' movements,[28] licensing of firearms,[29] detective activities,[30] and others. The purpose of these reforms was to modernize obsolete Soviet regulations, to replace secret Soviet regulations, or to create new regulations where none existed (Fastov, 2005). As the country's free market economy developed, the authority of the MVD continued to expand, which included new administrative functions to license private detectives[31] and to control emigration.[32] Despite previous declarations and intentions of reformers to strip the MVD of unnecessary administrative functions (Avrutin, 2006), only two major areas of responsibility were removed: (1) the emergency protection duties, which were moved to the newly established Ministry of Emergency Situations,[33] and (2) the correctional system administration, which was moved back to the Ministry of Justice[34] (Butler, 2003). The only new law enforcement agencies that were established during this period outside the MVD system were the tax and customs police (Gregory and Brooke, 2000; Mulukaev, Malygin, and Epifanov, 2005). Various documents also were adopted to regulate service within MVD,[35] which included updated benefits,[36] uniform,[37] and training[38] regulations.

The decade of the 1990s was a time of constant restructuring within the MVD system. New agencies were created, changed, renamed, and eliminated during this time (Mulukaev, Malygin, and Epifanov, 2005). The most notable changes included the creation of separate criminal and public order police that signified the division between federally funded and locally funded police units[39] (Butler, 2003), the creation of an internal investigation department[40] the renaming and revising of the passport service functions,[41] the juvenile delinquency service,[42] and the traffic police service[43] (Gonyukhov and Gorobtsov, 2002).

Regardless of the vast organizational restructuring, new authorities, and a variety of new regulations, the reform results during 1990s were troublesome (Shelley, 1999). The capability and efficiency for crime solving and prevention did not improve (Gavrilov, 2003b). Serious violent crimes committed by organized groups remained mainly unsolved and charges were often dropped due to lack of witnesses willing to testify (Association for Criminology, 1997).[44] The levels of public distrust and dissatisfaction with police work and public fear of crime remained high through the entire period. The levels of police satisfaction ranged from 3% to 25% during the period from 1992 through 1999 and the fear of crime remained at 60%.[45] Moreover, the public often became fearful of the police due to widespread cases of police corruption and abuse.[46] Several interrelated factors were responsible for this situation:

1. Most revisions introduced in the MVD system during the 1990s did not change the nature of the post-Soviet police system. The MVD remained closed to the public, hierarchical, militarized, and highly bureaucratic with vast administrative discretionary authority over citizens and proliferating private businesses. Even though new policing laws during the 1990s proclaimed the pursuit of democracy, openness, and protection of human rights, many were merely a declaration without enforceable mechanisms.
2. The new system did not create an effective internal self-control mechanism (Waller, 1997). The old Soviet system was controlled primarily through special Party officials as staff members in each police district. These officials were, to a certain degree, independent from the chief police officers and reported directly to the local division of the Communist Party (Shelley, 1996). Whereas the Party's supervision understandably failed to control the abuse of power by Party members (*nomenklatura*), it was somewhat effective in the control of daily police activities and restrained the levels of police corruption (Shelley, 2000). When the Party control was removed from the MVD system in an effort to depoliticize the police by President Yeltsin, a newly created internal security service was assumed to take its place. However, the new service was within the MVD system and hierarchically subordinated to the minister, and, thus, had reduced control over abuse of power and corruption.
3. The post-Soviet police in the early 1990s were in a difficult position created by a "legal vacuum and chaos" and fragmented legal reform (Favarel-Garrigues, 2011; Shelley, 2000). The Soviet laws on contracts and torts were obsolete because they were created for the administrative command economy. In the early 1990s, the new free market economy was developing with little legal guidance until new civil codes were adopted in 1994 and 1996. The Criminal code also was outdated and did not include new dangerous crimes, such as racketeering, blackmail, and organizing the criminal gangs (Serio, 2008). The new Criminal code encompassing socioeconomic changes was not promulgated until 1997 (Barber, 2000). In the environment of legal chaos, egregious and harmful actions were difficult to investigate and prosecute because some were simply not illegal at the time. This situation persisted until the new laws were put into effect (so-called "grey areas of law") (Sergeyev, 1998). The dramatic, rapid, and

sometimes contradictory changes in major laws during the 1994–1997 period required police officers to be retrained even though their Soviet legal education was outdated. However, due to high case loads, the MVD employees were forced to retrain themselves on the spot with little guidance from their leadership. This often led to poor investigative results (Rybnikov and Aleksushin, 2008).

4. During the 1990s, in the effort to democratize the criminal justice system, the government took steps to provide criminal defendants with additional rights. In 1992, all criminal defendants were provided with the right to counsel incident to arrest and the right to appeal an arrest in court (Barber, 2000).[47] The opportunity for some defendants to have a jury trial was also introduced in 1993.[48] Access to an attorney during the investigation, the opportunity to appeal, and the availability of a jury trial put additional requirements on the quality of investigations. Under conditions of continuously increasing case loads and drastically changing laws, MVD investigators often found themselves undertrained compared to defense lawyers and lacked the basic resources to complete an investigation successfully. It was not unusual that under these conditions many police officers resorted to abuse of power and falsification of evidence during investigations (Human Rights Watch, 1999; Pustintsev, 1996).
5. Stress created by the systematic delay of salary payments,[49] increasing caseloads, and growing safety concerns[50] in the MVD system created a demoralized staff and dramatic turnover rates among detectives, investigators, and other employees (Shelley, 2000; Williams, 1993).[51] Experienced cadres were leaving the MVD in search of higher pay and less stressful private sector jobs.[52] New hires were often poorly educated and trained (V. Volkov, 2002).
6. Organized crime, which developed through the 1980s, had already begun its penetration into the government and law enforcement. Organized crime continued to mature and prosper during the rapid economic reforms of the early 1990s. It also continued to penetrate the law enforcement system and form a mutually beneficial partnership, which was now even more vulnerable under the new conditions (Finckenauer and Voronin, 2001). "Despite the apparent progress in uncovering crime and confiscating weapons and valuables, it was believed by many that law enforcement didn't stand a chance . . . the crime groups, businessmen, and bureaucrats had become deeply entangled" (Serio, 2008, p. 255).

All of these factors were instrumental in the failure of democratic legal reforms of law enforcement and were a major contribution to the growing poor public image of the post-Soviet police during the 1990s.

Yet, arguably, the most important issue of successful MVD reforms during the 1990s was its "political subservience" and considerable participation in the redistribution of political power in the country (Gilinskiy, 2000; Waller, 1997). The tradition of using the MVD as one of the tools in the accession of power was born in the USSR and continued through the leadership of Khrushchev, Brezhnev, and others. Once the Russian Federation chose the path of liberal economic and political reforms, one would think that the role of major policing agencies related to the redistribution of political power in the country would be curtailed to ensure its impartiality and legitimacy. However, that was not the case during the 1990s (V. Volkov, 2002). One of the first decisions made by President Yeltsin in 1991 strikingly resembled the decision made by Beria in 1953. This was the merger of the KGB and MVD agencies under one superpowerful Ministry of Security and Internal Affairs (Waller, 1995a).[53] Fortunately, this decision was overturned by the Constitutional Court of the RSFSR and annulled just a month later on January 15, 1992 (Shelley, 1996). The juxtaposition of political powers between the Supreme Council of the RSFSR (parliament) and the president in 1993 also was accompanied by significant participation of the leadership of the MVD (Dormin, 2006). Prior to declaring the emergency situation that led to the dismissal of the Supreme Council, President Yeltsin met with leaders of the "power" (*silovye*) ministries that included the MVD minister to assure personal loyalty and support for actions that may be potentially unconstitutional. Public support at the time was almost evenly divided between the Supreme Council and the president. The support of the interior affairs troops played an instrumental role in the presidential victory over the parliament (Dormin, 2006). Shortly after that, President Yeltsin issued a decree that placed the MVD under direct control of the president.[54] Since 1994, neither the Russian *Duma* (parliament) nor any other government agency has had control over the MVD system and its regular police (Gilinskiy, 2000).

The MVD's political nature also is evident when examining the appointments, resignations, and major campaigns of its ministers during this period. There were four major ministers of the MVD appointed by Yeltsin. Yerin, the first minister, was appointed shortly after the dissolution of the Soviet Union and served for over three years. He was faced with tremendous challenges due to growing organized crime and his main purpose was to find "traitors within the ranks of police officers."[55] He was dismissed after the tragedy in Budennovsk, when Chechen separatists seized a local hospital, killing over 120 and wounding more than 400 civilians (Curtis, 1998). Even though the MVD was not a primary agency responsible for fighting terrorism, Minister Yerin was chosen, in the opinion of many, as a "political victim" to show a presidential determination to be tough on terrorism and punish agencies that fail to fight it.[56] He was fired in June of 1995. The new minister, Kulikov, had significant military experience and was previously the commander-in-chief of the MVD interior troops.

His appointment in 1995 was logical because the country was in the aftermath of the Chechen war and terrorist attacks.[57] Kulikov launched an anticorruption campaign named "Clean Hands," which mainly targeted the leadership of the MVD in Moscow.[58] Despite the initiative's high publicity and promises, the campaign ended with only a few convictions of low ranking police officers.[59] Kulikov's tenure ended in 1998 when the rumors of his own corruptive behavior and nepotism toward the professional military reached General Prosecutor Ustinov.[60]

The next minister, Stepashin, was a former Minister of Justice, whose tenure lasted only for a year and whose main personnel policy was the reversal of former Minister Kulikov's decisions[61] (Thomas, 1998). Stepashin launched an anticorruption campaign against the traffic police. A few publicized antibribery operations were conducted using questionable entrapment tactics; however, no criminal charges were filed.[62] One result was that the traffic police were renamed and restructured (from State Automobile Inspection (GAI) to State Inspection of Security of Road Movement (GIBDD)) and more thorough regulations were made regarding traffic stops.[63] These changes appeared to have almost no effect on the public perception of traffic police as being the most corrupt unit within an already corrupt MVD.[64] Stepashin promptly left the MVD after he was promoted to the position of Prime Minister in 1999.[65]

The last MVD minister appointed by Yeltsin was Vladimir Rushailo who established a network of independent detective bureaus at the regional level to fight organized crime (abbreviated RUOP).[66] Ironically, after Yeltsin's resignation, Minister Rushailo was dismissed on allegations that the RUOP system was corrupt and assisted organized crime groups in avoiding prosecution.[67] It also is important to note that, despite allegations of corruption or public criticism of their failure to adequately reduce crime, all four former ministers of the MVD were quickly reappointed to key state positions within the Yeltsin or Putin governments (Table 4.1).[68]

Regardless of the government's claims about democratic transitions, the 1990s post-Soviet police system continued to be involved in redistributing power in the country. The situation closely resembled the Soviet police (Timoshenko, 1997). While in the USSR, this participation was often invisible to the public, in the new post-Soviet Russia it took center stage in political life. The appointments and resignations of the MVD leadership in the 1990s were clearly politically motivated and directly dependent on presidential will and the person's political position at the time. The internal MVD reforms became political campaigns when allegations of corruption were used to score political gain for the president, or other authorities, and rarely resulted in any fundamental changes within the police system.

Table 4.1 Leadership of the Ministry of Interior Affairs from 1992 to 2012

Minister of the MVD	Term	Previous Position	Main Campaigns	Critique	Position Acquired after Leaving the MVD
Yerin Victor Fedorovitch	Jan. 1992–June 1995	Deputy Minister of MVD	Finding "traitors" within the MVD system who were connected to organized crime groups	Failure to prevent Budennovsk tragedy	Deputy director of Foreign Intelligence Agency
Kulikov, Anatoly Sergevitch	June 1995–Mar. 1998	Commander-in-Chief for the Interior Troops of the MVD	Anticorruption campaign "Clean Hands" against Moscow MVD leadership in 1994–1995	Failure to investigate corruption within Interior Troops, the allegations against Deputy Minister Shkirko and Commander-in-Chief Rovensky in 1997–1998	Member of "United Russia" Party and elected representative in the State *Duma* since 2003
Stepashin, Sergey Vadimovitch	Apr. 1998–May 1999	Minister of Justice	Reform of traffic police, antibribery campaign against traffic police, reducing numbers of Interior Troops, transferring public order police to the local authorities in 1998	President Yeltsin criticized him for "over-optimism" and sugar-coating the crime statistics in 1998	Prime Minister of the government, head of the Security Council
Rushailo, Vladimir Borisovitch	May 1999–Mar. 2001	Deputy Minister of MVD	Created an independent system of regional departments to fight organized crime (RUBOP) and independent from local authorities' Committee of Criminal Police in 1999	Was criticized for corruption within RUBOP and illegal methods of investigation in 2000	Secretary of the Security Council

(continued)

Table 4.1 Leadership of the Ministry of Interior Affairs from 1992 to 2012 (continued)

Minister of the MVD	Term	Previous Position	Main Campaigns	Critique	Position Acquired after Leaving the MVD
Gryzlov, Boris Vyacheslavovitch	Mar. 2001–Dec. 2003	Elected representative in the State *Duma*, leader of political faction "Unity"	Eliminated the system of RUBOP, and Committee of Criminal Police, created a new Agency of Criminal Police in 2001; conducted highly publicized anticorruption campaign against " werewolves in uniform"	General criticism on continuous growth of crime and corruption; criticism of "werewolves in uniform" campaign as PR action	The leader of the "United Russia" Party—the majority party in the State *Duma*
Nurgaliev, Rashid Gumarovitch	Mar. 2004–May 2012	Deputy Minister of FSB, Deputy Minister of MVD, head of the Agency of Criminal Police	Current reform of the MVD from the "militia" to the "police" in 2010–2011	General criticism of systemic corruption, torture scandals, and an inability to reform the MVD including major 2011 police reform	Deputy Secretary of the Security Council
Kolokoltsev, Vladimir Aleksandrovitch	May 2012–current	Head of the Moscow MVD office			

4.3 Development of the Modern Russian Police under Putin: 1999–2008

The period of President Vladimir Putin's leadership brought mixed results for development in Russia. It is often referred to as a time of the country's "stabilization" in comparison with the rapid changes brought by the presidency of Yeltsin. One of the major achievements during this period pertains to economic improvements in the country. Russia's unprecedented drop in the GDP ended by 1999, and GDP increased steadily through the entire period of Putin's presidency when it reached $2,100 billion (International Monetary Fund dollars) in 2007.[69] Following the improvement in the GDP, the number of people living below the level of poverty dropped from 41.6% in 1999 to 18.7% in 2007,[70] and male life expectancy grew from 59.9 to 61.4 years.[71] Critics suggest the Russian economic achievements during the 2000s were mostly a result of the increased crude oil prices and the development of large public corporations that controlled the natural resources.[72] The 2009 report by Freedom House (an independent watchdog organization based in Washington, D.C. that supports the expansion of freedom around the world) listed Russia among other authoritarian regimes that undermined democracy by building "selective capitalism and kleptocracy" (Freedom House, Radio Free Europe/Radio Liberty, and Radio Free Asia, 2009). The supporters of Putin argued that economic prosperity was a result of liberal reforms implemented during the 1990s along with the effective government management of resources.[73]

Putin's political reforms included changes to the membership of the Council of Federations (an upper chamber of Russian parliament),[74] substitution of the regional or republican elections by presidential appointment,[75] and the replacement of elections to the State *Duma* (lower chamber of Russian parliament) from single-mandate, nonparty candidates to Party membership only.[76] Most of these changes are thought to strengthen the centralization of federal power and provided the government-supported Party (United Russia) with a profound advantage during the 2007 elections to the State *Duma*. Even though Western observers often criticized President Putin for "curtailing the democracy" and freedoms of Russian citizens, he had significant public support among Russians in the 2000s.[77]

Together with economic achievements and political centralization, the first decade of the new century brought some improvement in crime rate statistics. Even though the registered crime rates continued to grow, the increase was not as dramatic as it was during the previous decade.[78] The number of registered serious felonies decreased by 40%,[79] and the number of crimes committed by repeat offenders dropped by 22% during the period from 1999 to 2007.[80] The data, however, have to be taken critically as they only reflect official statistics provided by the MVD. According to Inshakov, who conducted an analysis of unregistered crimes during the period from 2001 through 2007, the "true" crime rates in Russia were seven times higher than reported. He estimated that 24,900,000 crimes were committed in 2006 alone and, in 2007, this number reached 25,800,000 cases (Inshakov, 2008). Inshakov also suggested the "true" crime rates grew at least 5% annually, while official statistics reported only 23% over the eight-year period[81] (2007).

The law enforcement reforms conducted in the 1990s continued through the period of 2008 under President Putin. One of the major legislative changes of this period was an adoption of the new Code of Criminal Procedure (CPC) in 2001 that replaced the outdated Khrushchev Code of 1966 (Mizoulina, 2006a). The goal of the CPC was to continue the introduction of adversarial elements into criminal procedure and to ensure compliance with international standards (Carothers, 2006; Orland, 2002).

In the role of police, there were several important changes: the requirement to obtain approval of the procurator to initiate an investigation, the requirement to apply for a judicial warrant prior to an arrest or search, a ban on judicial remand of cases for additional investigation, and additional opportunities for the defense to collect exculpatory evidence during the preliminary investigation (Fillipov, 2003). Other various changes were introduced into the preliminary investigation providing new rights to the defendant and defense lawyer, and streamlining existing procedures (Solomon, 2005a). The drastic changes required new training for investigators and better quality evidence for adversarial proceedings (Gavrilov, 2006; Sheifer and Bobrov, 2006). Not surprisingly, the initial reaction to the CPC of 2001 from the law enforcement community was rather negative (Gavrilov, 2003a; Mizoulina, 2006b).[82] However, with time, more investigators entered the system that had received training related to the CPC reform and the changes introduced by the CPC were tolerated as a part of daily operations (Mizoulina, 2006c).

Other changes were introduced into the MVD system through additional reshuffling of its structure. The MVD central apparatus alone received at least one complete restructuring when the new decree "Issues of the Ministry of Internal Affairs" was issued on July 19, 2004, along with more than 10 other structural changes through the period of 2000–2008.[83] In 2000, 89 regions were united into several federal circuits and a new layer of MVD departments was created for each of the seven circuits, thereby increasing the tendency of centralization within the MVD system (Moskal'kova, 2006).[84] The new layer of administrative agencies hardly appeared to have any positive effect on the law enforcement system, according to police officer opinions (Studenikin, 2004).[85] In 2003, the tax police that seemed to be working effectively were abruptly eliminated as an independent agency. The function of investigating tax crimes was returned to MVD jurisdiction, which required the creation of new units within each level of the system (Easter, 2002).[86] In 2005, the MVD acquired the new functions of protecting witnesses and judges that again required new structures to be established at various levels.[87]

As a result of the nonstop restructuring, the number of MVD personnel continued to grow, which was especially apparent at the central apparatus level. In 1991, when the MVD USSR was eliminated and merged with the MVD RSFSR, the estimated central apparatus staff for MVD USSR was 2,400 and for the MVD RSFSR it was 1,500 personnel (Mulukaev, Malygin, and Epifanov, 2005). In 2004, the number of staff in the central apparatus of the MVD of Russia was 9,264 employees, excluding service personnel.

The continuous restructuring was accompanied by a further increase in the number of new documents regulating MVD work. New detailed instructions were issued in the various agencies of internal affairs, such as police service,[88] work of juvenile delinquency agencies,[89] work on the registration and review of citizens' complaints about crime,[90] the seizure of citizens and detention at the police precinct,[91] financial audit of businesses,[92] issuing licenses for private detectives,[93] and conducting internal investigations into the misbehavior of police officers.[94] While the intent of the instructions was to streamline the work and prevent discretionary abuse within the various MVD agencies, it often resulted in excessive bureaucracy and unnecessary formalization of police work (Beck and Robertson, 2005).

The continuous reforms of the MVD during Putin's first presidency can hardly be considered a success (Sweet, 2002). Despite the improvement in socioeconomic conditions, questionable declining crime rates, and increased budget allocations for law enforcement activities,[95] public respect for the police remained low. Police effectiveness related to solving crime did not improve significantly,[96] and the personnel situation within the MVD system continued to be troublesome (Shishkin, 2006; Solomon, 2005b).[97] Table 6.1 indicates that during the period 1999 through 2008, public satisfaction with police work ranged anywhere between 11% and 43% with no apparent improvement compared to the 1990s decade. The same is true for trust of police, which remained low through the entire period, as well as fear of crime, which did not improve despite the drop in official crime rates.[98] Even the official rates of solving crimes were decreasing from 2002 through 2006 and reached 49.5%. Considering the unreliable nature of official statistics and that only 12.5% of all crimes were estimated to be registered, criminologists suggest that, in 2006, police were resolving just a little over 6% of all crimes (Inshakov, 2007).

The major reason for the police ineffectiveness was that MVD reforms introduced during the period from 1999 to 2008 were not that different from the reforms of the previous decade and did not change the core issues involving post-Soviet policing. The MVD system remained highly centralized, closed to the public, and a militarized agency with hierarchical subordination and vast administrative functions (Beck and Robertson, 2005). No independent control mechanisms were created and public accountability of any employee within the MVD system remained highly questionable.

The structural instability and increased bureaucratization that were added during this period only exacerbated the situation. However, the major problem of the law enforcement system during this period continued with high levels of corruption and an entanglement with organized crime. The nature of organized crime in Russia changed during the past decade. The overt characteristics of organized crime appearances, which were easily recognized as part of the criminal underworld culture, became much more presentable and institutionalized through respectful-looking businesses (Webster et al., 2000). However, the mutually beneficial relationships between organized crime, government officials, and law enforcement established in the late 1980s and early 1990s did not change (Serio, 2008).

The government's commitment to political appointments of MVD ministers did not change, and the use of anticorruption and reform campaigns as political tools also continued (Beck and Robertson, 2005; Kolennikova, 2006). Similar to the 1990s period, during the early 2000s era, the MVD continued to play an important role in Russian Federation politics (Babanov, 2004). Minister Rushailo was relieved of his duties by President Putin in 2001. Rumors surfaced that the network of regional organizations to fight organized crime (RUOB) that Rushailo created was corrupt and infiltrated by organized crime.[99]

The new minister of the MVD, Boris Gryzlov, was the only minister with no previous law enforcement or military leadership experience. He was a professional politician and President Putin stated that it was "a political appointment."[100] Under Minister Gryzlov, the system of the RUOB was eliminated and a new service named the "criminal police" was created to encompass investigative and operative search (detective) services within the same agency.[101] More importantly, Gryzlov launched an increased and publicized anticorruption campaign within the ranks of the MVD, termed by the media as "a hunt on werewolves in uniform." The campaign was orchestrated with unusually high access of the media to report the initial moments of arrests among seven "werewolves." This included one general of the Ministry of Emergency Situations and six employees of the Moscow criminal search department (a detective department with the main purpose of solving crimes through informants, undercover work, wiretapping, surveillance, and other activities).

In connection with this case, over 700 detectives from the Moscow criminal search department (abbreviated MUR) were retested in order to cleanse the agency from the taint of corruption.[102] Many believed the campaign was staged to ensure the "United Russia" Party (Minister Gryzlov was the leader of United Russia) would win during the 2003 *Duma* elections.[103] Rashid Nurgaliev, who had significant law enforcement experience in both the KGB and MVD, replaced Gryzlov. His tenure lasted from 2004 until 2012. He was one of the few leaders with longevity within the agency even when he was a subject of harsh criticism at various points during his career. In May of 2012, Nurgaliev was replaced by Vladimir Kolokoltsev when the new government was formed under the leadership of Prime Minister Dmitry Medvedev. [104]

4.4 Concluding Remarks

The results of police reform that started with *perestroika* by President Gorbachev and were continued by Presidents Yeltsin and Putin are mixed. On one hand, the police were freed from the ideological indoctrination of the Communist Party. The institution of the police became much more open to the public than during the Soviet Union and was able to restructure the system to somewhat address the key issues of modern Russia. The new laws, promoting democratic principles of policing, were introduced and some economic benefits were provided to ensure better stability of cadres.

On the other hand, the MVD reform during the period of 1989 through 2008 failed to create a democratic police institution compliant with international standards. The major structural and functional obstacles that restricted reform were not removed during the 1990 decade or the following one. The highly hierarchical, centralized, and militarized nature of the MVD agency was never challenged. The vast administrative functions designed to control Russian citizens and businesses (which in other democratic states are either abolished, transferred to the various local authorities, or private companies), remained under MVD jurisdiction and prone to abuse of power. The lack of external independent controls and public accountability made such violations and abuse of power massive. The rhetoric directed to combat organized crime remained mostly a political tool used to score points and not to address the key problems. The same is true of anticorruption campaigns that were conducted to ensure redistribution of political power in the country. The failure to remove the MVD from political life made the new post-Soviet police a victim of political manipulation, subservient to the government, and illegitimate in the eyes of average citizens (Table 4.2).

Table 4.2 Timetable of major events: 1985–2012

Year	Description
1985	Gorbachev came into power
1985	Unpopular antialcohol campaign as a part of a decree issued to create commissions to fight drunkenness on regional and republic levels
1985	The number of registered crimes grew by 37.8% compared to 1980
1986	A major law issued to allow for the "individual private enterprise"
1986	New department created to coordinate the public–police interaction within the MVD USSR
1987	Gorbachev authorized an investigation against Yuri Churbanov, resulting in publicized trial and lengthy imprisonment for charges of abuse of power and corruption
1987	Crime statistics published for the first time that revealed climbing rates and declining numbers of apprehensions, which concerned the public
1987	Gorbachev officially announced his "*perestroika*" policy at the Plenum of the Central Committee of the CPSU
1987	New performance criteria related to solving crime introduced and eased an unrealistic demand that 95% of all crimes had to be solved
1988	A major law issued for the establishment of cooperatives
1988	Almost 70% of all MVD investigators had university-level legal education and over three years of experience
1988	New police detachments "for special purposes" (OMON) created by MVD USSR decree in order to respond to the continuous civil disturbances in republics of the Soviet Union
1988	MVD USSR announced a push for further decentralization of law enforcement functions by providing republics with more rights and autonomy
1989	RSFSR provided with its own republic MVD office
1989	The growing problem of organized crime acknowledged and a new organized crime department was established in the MVD
1990	Qualified and experienced investigators constituted less than 50% of MVD personnel
1991	Gorbachev ordered the KGB to be dismantled into three separate agencies in order to diminish the over-centralization of power
1991	The Law "On Soviet Police" promulgated, signifying a major ideological shift in Soviet law enforcement policy
1991	Russian Soviet Federated Socialist Republic (RSFSR) promulgated its own Law "On Police" and declared the Law "On Soviet Police" void
1991	The Minister of the MVD participated in a failed coup together with ministers of defense, KGB, and other prominent party members
1991	The Minister of the MVD committed suicide
1991	Collapse of the Soviet Union
1991	Functions of the MVD USSR transferred to the MVD RSFSR
1991	Yeltsin became the first president
1992	Yeltsin officially ordered the "liberalization of the price policy"
1998	Stepashin succeeded Kulikov as the minister of the MVD
1999	Stepashin promptly left the MVD after being promoted to the position of Prime Minister

(continued)

Table 4.2 Timetable of major events: 1985–2012 (continued)

Year	Description
1999	Yeltsin appointed Vladimir Rushailo as the minister of the MVD
1999	Yeltsin resigned as president
1999	Vladimir Putin became president
2001	Boris Gryzlov became the minister of the MVD, and became the only minister with no previous law enforcement or military leadership experience
2001	Adoption of new Code of Criminal Procedure (CPC), which replaced outdated Khrushchev Code of 1966
2003	Tax police abruptly eliminated as an independent agency
2004	New Decree "Issues of the Ministry of Interior Affairs" issued, completely restructuring the MVD central apparatus
2004	Rashid Nurgaliev replaced Gryzlov as the MVD minister
2012	Kolokoltsev replaced Nurgaliev as the new MVD minister

Endnotes

1. Decree of Presidium of Supreme Council of USSR issued on May 16, 1985. Cited from consultant.ru
2. According to Mulukaev, Malygin, and Epifanov (2005), repeated offenses grew by 44% from 1974 to 1984.
3. According to Mulukaev, Malygin, and Epifanov (2005), drug-related crimes and crimes committed by drug abusers grew by fivefold (from 6,978 to 35,862) from 1976 to 1985.
4. One of the early public disturbances occurred in the city of Alma-Ata, Republic of Kazakhstan, in December of 1986 (Morukov, 2007).
5. The Law on the Individual Labor Activity was promulgated on November 19, 1986. Cited from www.consultant.ru
6. The Law on Cooperation in the USSR was promulgated on May 26,1988. Cited from www.consultant.ru
7. Articles 6–12 of the Law on Cooperation in USSR. Cited from www.consultant.ru
8. According to Krivel'skaya (1990), 74.1% of Soviet citizens had a fear of crime, which she refers to as extremely high for Soviet society (1990).
9. Law on Soviet Police #2001-1 promulgated on March 6, 1991. Cited from www.consultant.ru
10. Preamble of the decree on Soviet police issued on March 8, 1973, Collection of Laws of USSR, Vol. 10. Cited from consultant.ru
11. Articles 2, 3, and 4 of the Law on Soviet Police #2001-1 promulgated on March 6, 1991. Cited from www.consultant.ru
12. Decree of MVD USSR #206 issued on October 1, 1988. Cited from www.consultant.ru
13. A detailed account of MVD efforts to curb ethnic conflict in Oshkaya oblast of Kyrgyzstan in 1990 is provided by Dzhakishev (2007). His article supplies detailed analysis of mistakes made by MVD authorities in the Soviet republic trying to prevent multinational public conflicts.

14. The first session of deputies of the RSFSR issued a declaration about the sovereignty of the RSFSR and instructed that the MVD RSFSR should be taken out of the control of the MVD USSR and placed under the direct control of the Council of Ministers of the RSFSR on June 12, 1990.
15. The coup itself became possible when, in 1990, the "reformist" minister of MVD USSR Bakatin was replaced with a "conservative" former leader of the KGB in Latvia, Minister Pugo.
16. Also known as a "shock therapy."
17. Data retrieved from http://www.gks.ru/free_doc/new_site/population/urov/urov_51g.htm, the Web site of the State Statistical Committee (GKS), an official statistical agency of the Russian Federation on June 20, 2011.
18. According to the data provided by GKS, the male life expectancy alone dropped from 63.7 years in 1990 to 57.4 years in 1994. Retrieved from http://www.gks.ru/dbscripts/Cbsd/DBInet.cgi?pl=2415003 (June 6, 2011).
19. According to data cited by Rimashevskaya (2002), over 72,000 policemen in the organization had significant delays in their salary payments in 1996.
20. According to the International Monetary Fund, gross domestic product based on purchasing power parity (PPP) valuation of the country's GDP in current international dollars constituted $900 billion in 1998, compared to almost $1,200,000 billion in 1992. Data retrieved on June 6, 2011 from World Economic Outlook Database, www.imf.org
21. On the process of penetration of the organized crime culture into the various levels of Russian society in the 1990s, see Oleinik (2003).
22. According to the data provided by GKS. Retrieved on June 20, 2011 from http://www.gks.ru/dbscripts/Cbsd/DBInet.cgi?pl=2318002
23. According to the data provided by GKS. Retrieved on June 20, 2011 from http://www.gks.ru/dbscripts/Cbsd/DBInet.cgi?pl=2318037
24. According to the data provided by GKS, the number of offenses doubled from 13,589 in 1993 to 26,433 in 1995. Retrieved on June 20, 2011 from http://www.gks.ru/dbscripts/Cbsd/DBInet.cgi?pl=2318015
25. According to the data provided by GKS, the number of offenses committed by repeat offenders grew more than 1.5 times from 274,339 in 1991 to 459,602 in 1995. Retrieved on June 20, 2011 from http://www.gks.ru/dbscripts/Cbsd/DBInet.cgi?pl=2318014
26. According to the data provided by GKS, the number of drug-related crimes almost doubled from 53,169 in 1993 to 96,762 crimes in 1995. Retrieved on June 20, 2011 from http://www.gks.ru/dbscripts/Cbsd/DBInet.cgi?pl=2318012
27. Decision of Cabinet of Ministers of Russia issued on May 28, 1992, promulgating the decree "On State Automobile Inspection of MVD of Russia," and decision of Cabinet of Ministers of Russia issued on August 12, 1994 promulgating the decree "On State Registration of vehicles on the territory of the Russian Federation." Retrieved on June 20, 2011 from www.consultant.ru
28. Law of Russian Federation #5242-1 "About freedom of movement and freedom to select place of residence within Russian Federation," and decree of Cabinet of Ministers of Russia issued on July 17, 1995 "On Promulgation Rules of registration and deregistration of Russian citizens at the places of residence within the territory of Russian Federation and the list of officials responsible for registration." Retrieved on June 6, 2011 from www.consultant.ru

29. Law of Russian Federation #4992-1 issued on May 20, 1993 "On weapon," Federal Law of Russian Federation #150-FZ issued on December 13, 1996 "On weapon," decree of Cabinet of Ministers of Russia #814 issued on July 21, 1998 "About measures to regulate transactions with civil and service firearms and bullets on the territory of Russian Federation." Retrieved on June 6, 2011 from www.consultant.ru
30. Law of Russian Federation #2506-1 issued on March 13, 1992 "About operative-search activity" and Federal Law #144-FZ issued on August 12, 1995 "About operative-search activity." Retrieved on June 6, 2011 from www.consultant.ru
31. Law of Russian Federation #2487-1 issued on March 11, 1992 "About private detective and protection activities in Russian Federation." Retrieved on June 6, 2011 from www.consultant.ru
32. Decree of Cabinet of Ministers #124 "On reorganization of departments of visas, registration, and passport work of militia into passport–visa services of agencies of interior affairs." Retrieved on June 6, 2011 from www.consultant.ru
33. Decree of the president of Russia #66 issued on January 10, 1994 on creation of the Ministry of Emergency Situations. Retrieved on June 6, 2011 from www.consultant.ru
34 Decree of the president of Russia #904 on transferring of criminal executive system from MVD to Ministry of Justice. Retrieved on June 6, 2011 from www.consultant.ru
35. Decree of Supreme Council of Russian Federation #4202-1 issued on December 23, 1992 "On promulgation of decree on service in police and oath of employee of the agencies of interior affairs." Retrieved on June 6, 2011 from www.consultant.ru
36. Law of Russian Federation #4468-1 issued on January 12, 1993 "On pensions to the persons serving in the agencies of interior affairs, state antifire services, agencies controlling the drug transactions, and criminal-executive system and their family members." Retrieved on June 6, 2011 from www.consultant.ru
37. Decree of MVD #371 issued on October 2, 1995 "On military uniform, signs according to the rank and rules of wearing it." Retrieved on June 6, 2011 from www.consultant.ru
38. Decree of MVD #467 issued on December 22, 1992 "On promulgation of decree on reattestation of employees of MVD Russia system." Retrieved on June 6, 2011 from www.consultant.ru
39. Decree of president of Russia #209 issued on January 12, 1993 "On promulgation of decree on militia of public security (local militia)." Retrieved on July 6, 2011 from www.consultant.ru
40. Decree of MVD #401 issued on October 30, 1994 "On promulgation of the structure and number of staff within the central apparatus of MVD of Russian Federation," and decree of MVD issued on May 26, 1996 "About measures to strengthen legality in the agencies of interior affairs and strengthening internal security." Retrieved on June 6, 2011 from www.consultant.ru
41. Decree of Cabinet of Ministers #124 "On reorganization of departments of visas, registration, and passport work of militia into passport–visa services of agencies of interior affairs." Retrieved on June 6, 2011 from www.consultant.ru

42. Decree of the president of Russia #1338 issued on September 6, 1993 "On prevention of truancy and juvenile delinquency and protection of their rights." Retrieved on June 6, 2011 from www.consultant.ru
43. Decree of MVD #329 issued on June 1, 1998 "On reforming the activities of the State Automobile Inspection MVD of Russia." Retrieved on June 6, 2011 from www.consultant.ru
44. For example, only 7% of all individuals suspected in banditism were convicted of this crime in 1996, compared to 12% in 1993, 18% in 1994, and 9% in 1995 (Association for Criminology, 1997).
45. For more details, see Chapter 6, Tables 6.1 and 6.2.
46. For example, the study conducted by FOM (Public Opinion Foundation) reported that 25% of respondents were afraid of police over any other public fears and that police abuse ranked sixth in the top 10 public fears of Russians (FOM, 1997).
47. Amendment to the Articles 47, 51, 60, 96, and 97 of the Criminal Procedure Code of RSFSR promulgated by Law #2825-1 issued on May 25, 1992. Retrieved on June 6, 2011 from www.consultant.ru
48. Law of Russian Federation #5451-1 issued on July 16, 1993 "On Amendments and revisions to the Law on court system and the Criminal Procedural Code of RSFSR and Code of Administrative Delinquent Acts."
49. According to Avrutin (2006), in 1993, the Ministry of Internal Affairs was funded at 38% of its required budget. According to Babanov (2004), in some regions, during 1997 to 1998, the delay of salary payments for police officers was up to 1.5 years. According to Burdin (1999), the salary delays in 1998 were so severe that it caused some police riots.
50. The police job became increasingly unsafe during the early 1990s. According to the study by Safronov (1997), between 1993 and 1994 alone the death and injury statistics among MVD employees increased by 45% and 60%, respectively. According to Artem'ev (2003), between 287 and 549 policemen died each year between 1991 and 1998 while performing their duties.
51. According to a study conducted by Kikot' (2002), only 40% of policemen in 1993–1997 said they did not regret their choice of profession compared to almost 60% in 1991. According to a study by Pukhno (2005), between 59 and 87% of policemen in 1995 felt they no longer fit in the new socioeconomic reality.
52. According to Pistor (1996), in 1996 there were over 8,000 registered private security companies that employed over 17,000 known former officers of MVD.
53. Decree of the president of RSFSR #289 issued on December 19, 1999. Retrieved on July 6, 2011 from www.consultant.ru
54. Decree of the president of RF #66 issued on January 10, 1994. Retrieved on June 6, 2011 from www.consultant.ru
55. For example, see the article "MVD is getting rid of traitors in their ranks" by "Kommersant" #22(490) published on February 9, 1994. Retrieved on June 8, 2011 from http://www.kommersant.ru
56. For example, see the article "Sacrifice" by "Kommersant" #121(839) published on July 1, 1995. Retrieved on June 8, 2011 from http://www.kommersant.ru
57. For example, see the article "Reshuffling the deck of cards" by "Kommersant" #126(844) published on July 8, 1995. Retrieved on June 8, 2011 from http://www.kommersant.ru

58. For example, see the article "The silence of the generals" by "Kommersant" #238(956) published on December 23, 1995. Retrieved on June 8, 2011 from http://www.kommersant.ru
59. For example, see the article "Tracing the 'Clean Hands' by Kommersant #62(1020), published on April 12, 1996. Retrieved on June 8, 2011 from http://www.kommersant.ru
60. For example, see the article "The end of 'Clean Hands' campaign" by "Kommersant" #54(1457) published on March 28, 1998. Retrieved on June 8, 2011 from http://www.kommersant.ru
61. For example, see the article "The military are thrown out of MVD" by "Kommersant" #82(1485) published on May 12, 1998. Retrieved on June 8, 2011 from http://www.kommersant.ru
62. For example, see the article "Raid on traffic police" by "Kommersant" #70(1473) issued on April 21, 1998. Retrieved on June 8, 2011 from http://www.kommersant.ru
63. For example, see the article "The traffic police lost their rights" by "Kommersant" #102(1505) published on June 9, 1998. Retrieved on June 8, 2011 from http://www.kommersant.ru
64. According to the study conducted by WCIOM (2010b) (All-Russian Public Opinion Research Center), GIBDD (traffic police) scored 2.8 out 5 on satisfaction of police. This value did not change when measured in 2006 and 2008. According to WCIOM, 50% of respondents did not see any improvements in the work of traffic police and 15% reported that its work only got worse.
65. For example, see the article "Stepashin ended the reforms" by "Kommersant" #173(1576) published on September 18, 1998. Retrieved on June 8, 2011 from http://www.kommersant.ru
66. For example, see the article "New reorganization in MVD" by "Kommersant" #187(1831) published on October 13, 1999. Retrieved on June 8, 2011 from http://www.kommersant.ru
67. For example, see an article "Eagle wings of Rushailo" by "Moscow Komsomolets" #21402 published on May 12, 2000. Retrieved on June 8, 2011 from http://www.mk.ru
68. For more details on MVD leadership, please see Table 4.1.
69. According to the International Monetary Fund, Gross Domestic Product based on purchasing power parity (PPP) valuation of country GDP in current international dollars constituted $2.1 billion in 2007, compared to only $1 billion in 1999. Data retrieved from World Economic Outlook Database, www.imf.org (retrieved on June 6, 2011).
70. According to the data provided by GKS (Federal State Statistic Services). Retrieved on June 20, 2011 from http://www.gks.ru/dbscripts/Cbsd/DBInet.cgi?pl=2415003
71. According to the data provided by GKS. Retrieved on June 20, 2011 from http://www.gks.ru/free_doc/new_site/population/urov/urov_51g.htm
72. In 1999, Russia exported 134,917,000 tons of crude oil estimated at $14,157,541,000; in 2008, this number grew to 243,114,367 tons of crude oil estimated at $121,502,874,000, according to the data provided by GKS. Retrieved on June 20, 2011 from http://www.gks.ru/dbscripts/Cbsd/DBInet.cgi?pl=2123011

73. On the nature of "putinism" and its differences from both autocratic and democratic regimes, see the article by Lev Gudkov (2009).
74. According to Federal Law #113-FZ issued on August 5, 2000, the Council of Federations now consists of two members who are appointed by the heads of the regions/republics and elected by the regional/republican legislative bodies. This is different from previous regulations when the heads of the regions/republics were themselves members of the Council of Federations. Cited from www.consultant.ru
75. Amendment to Article 18 of the Federal Law #184-FZ issued on December 29, 2004 "On the main principles of organization of legislative and executive power of government of the Russian Federation." The original law was promulgated on October 6, 1999. Cited from www.consultant.ru
76. Federal Law #51-FZ issued on May 18, 2005 "About elections of representatives of the State *Duma* of Federal Sobranie of Russian Federation." Retrieved on June 6, 2011 from www.consultant.ru
77. For example, according to WCIOM (2011a), the rating of President Putin remained at the 45 to 58% range through the entire period of his presidency.
78. In 1999, there were 2,039 registered crimes per 100,000 inhabitants, whereas in 2007, there were 2,521 registered crimes, which is a 23% increase in an eight-year period, according to the data provided by GKS. Retrieved on June 20, 2011 from http://www.gks.ru/dbscripts/Cbsd/DBInet.cgi?pl=2318002
79. In 1999, there were 1,847,835 serious felony crimes registered, whereas in 2007, this number was only 961,133 serious felony crimes registered, according to the data provided by GKS. Retrieved on June 20, 2011 from http://www.gks.ru/dbscripts/Cbsd/DBInet.cgi?pl=2318037
80. In 1999, there were 692,134 crimes committed by repeat offenders, whereas, in 2007, this number was 534,072 crimes, according to the data provided by GKS. Retrieved on June 20, 2011 from http://www.gks.ru/dbscripts/Cbsd/DBInet.cgi?pl=2318014
81. In 1999, Russia exported 134,917,000 tons of crude oil estimated at $14,157,541,000; in 2008, this number grew to 243,114,367 tons of crude oil estimated at $121,502,874,000, according to the data provided by GKS. Retrieved on June 20, 2011 from http://www.gks.ru/dbscripts/Cbsd/DBInet.cgi?pl=2123011
82. For example, according to the study by Berezina (2003), 86% of surveyed investigators were against new rules on the initiation of the criminal investigation and only 9% supported it. From the same study, 82% believed that new regulations would negatively impact their ability to initiate the investigation and fight the crimes.
83. Prior to 2004, the MVD structure was regulated by decree #1039 issued on July 18, 1996 "On promulgating the Regulation on the Ministry of Internal Affairs." This document sustained two revisions in 2001 and 2003. The new structure was determined by decree #927 issued on July 19, 2004. This document was revised eight times between 2004 and 2008. Retrieved on June 6, 2011 from www.consultant.ru
84. Decree of MVD #644 issued on June 4, 2001. Retrieved on June 6, 2011 from www.consultant.ru

85. According to Studenikin's research (2004), 72.6% of surveyed employees of MVD reported that a new federal district layer just made the system work even less effectively, whereas only 6.4% believed that it brought improvements to the administration of law enforcement.
86. Decree of president of Russia #306 issued on March 11, 2003 "On some questions to improve government administration." Retrieved on June 6, 2011 from www.consultant.ru
87. Federal Law #113-FZ issued on August 20, 2004 "On state protection of victims, witnesses, and other participants of the criminal procedure." Retrieved on June 6, 2011 from www.consultant.ru
88. Decree of MVD #1038 issued on December 14, 1999. Retrieved on June 6, 2011 from www.consultant.ru
89. Decree of MVD #569 issued on May 26, 2000. Retrieved on June 6, 2011 from www.consultant.ru
90. Decree of MVD #158 issued on March 13, 2003. Retrieved on June 6, 2011 from www.consultant.ru
91. Decree of MVD #438 issued on June 21, 2003. Retrieved on June 6, 2011 from www.consultant.ru
92. Decree of MVD #636 issued on August 2, 2005. Retrieved on June 6, 2011 from www.consultant.ru
93. Decree of MVD #447 issued on June 19, 2006. Retrieved on June 6, 2011 from www.consultant.ru
94. Decree of MVD #1140 issued on December 25, 2008. Retrieved on June 6, 2011 from www.consultant.ru
95. According to the Ministry of Finances of Russia, in 2001, 35,894,526,500 rubles were allocated for the agencies of internal affairs. In 2012, the MVD budget was estimated at 1,103,000,000,000 rubles, which is over 30 times more. Retrieved from http://www1.minfin.ru/ru/budget/federal_budget/08-10/ and an article at: http://top.rbc.ru/politics/23/10/2011/621606.shtml
96. According to Inshakov (2007), even the official statistics of MVD in solving crimes continued to drop from 62.5% of crimes solved in 2002 to 49.6% of crimes solved in 2006. See Chapter 6, Table 6.9 for more details.
97. According to data provided by Artem'ev (2003), the exodus of qualified cadres from MVD continued in 2002, whereas the number of employees with less than three years of experience grew from 21.5% in 2000 to 24.5% in 2002, and the number of employees with more than 10 years of experience decreased from 50.9% in 2000 to 50.6% in 2002. However, the educational level of employees grew from 36.4% in 2000 to 41.3% of employees with higher legal education in 2002 (not considering the low-ranking police officers).
98. Table 6.2 (Chapter 6) indicates that trust of police ranged between 8 and 48% with no apparent trend observed through the period. Table 6.12 indicates that fear of crime ranged from 26 to 60% with no observed trend observed through the period. One study by Mazaev, Yakovlev, and Kamaev (2003) suggests some marginal level of improvement on the public "index of protection" from crime; however, even in that study the number of negative responses (feel unprotected) exceeds the number of positive responses (feel protected).

99. For example, see the article "Eagle wings of Rushailo" by "Moscow Komsomolets" #21402 published on May 12, 2000. Retrieved on June 8, 2011 from http://www.mk.ru
100. For example, see the article "As we understand, this is a political appointment" by "Kommersant" #55(2185) published on March 29, 2011. Retrieved on June 8, 2011 from http://www.kommersant.ru
101. Decree of Council of Ministers of Russia #925 issued on December 7, 2000 "On subdivisions of criminal police." Retrieved on June 6, 2011 from www.consultant.ru
102. For example, see the article "Moscow criminal search is starting cadres cleansing" published on June 30, 2003. Retrieved on June 20, 2011 from http://www.newsru.com/russia/30jun2003/mur.html
103. According to FOM (2003), 33% of all surveyed did not believe that the true purpose of the campaign was to fight corruption. When asked about true reasons for the campaign, 11% of the sample reported this was done purely to improve the rating of "United Russia," while others listed a combination of reasons including "redistribution of political power among law enforcement agencies," "imitation of work," and "random actions." The experts who participated in focus groups also suggested that the "werewolves" campaign had a clear political nature and would have no impact on fighting corruption in the MVD system.
104. For example, see an article of the Russian News Agency at http://ria.ru/defense_safety/20120522/655125034.html

II

Current State of Post-Soviet Police: Structure, Identity, and Modern Policy Issues

Structure, Function, and the Workforce of the Modern Russian Police

5

5.1 Structure of MVD Agencies

5.1.1 Overall Structure (Diagram 5.1)

The structure of the MVD and the agencies of internal affairs that perform main policing functions in modern Russia follows the main structure of the country's government organization (Roudik, 2008). According to the Constitution,[1] Russia is a federation that consists of 83 "subjects of federations" (in the form of regions and republics)[2] that were grouped into eight federal districts by President Putin.[3]

Diagram 5.1 indicates that the entire MVD system has five main levels: central, district, inter-regional, regional/republican, and municipal (circuit) (Maslov, 2010). The MVD system is a federal law enforcement agency with direct hierarchical subordination to the federal authorities (Gutsenko and Kovalev, 2007). The system is officially headed by the president of Russia who appoints the MVD minister upon the prime minister's recommendation.[4] The president of Russia also appoints the deputy ministers and the highest police officers within the agency except for circuit department chairs.[5] The MVD system mainly includes a network of law enforcement agencies (see Diagram 5.1) known as the "territorial agencies of internal affairs" and the interior troops of the MVD. The interior troops represent the military forces used to support law and order in special cases, such as emergency situations or public disturbances (see Diagram 5.2).

During the 1990s, only three levels of the MVD existed: central, regional/republican, and municipal.[6] The MVD federal district level was added when the federal districts were created by President Putin in 2000.[7] Each of the eight federal districts includes a group of geographic areas known as the "subjects of federation" (regions and republics) created by their specific territorial location supervised by the presidential representative in each district.[8] The interregional levels were established by the recent 2011 presidential decree and include only limited agencies shared by several regions and/or republics. (The structure of MVD "territorial" agencies[9] is shown in Diagram 5.1.)

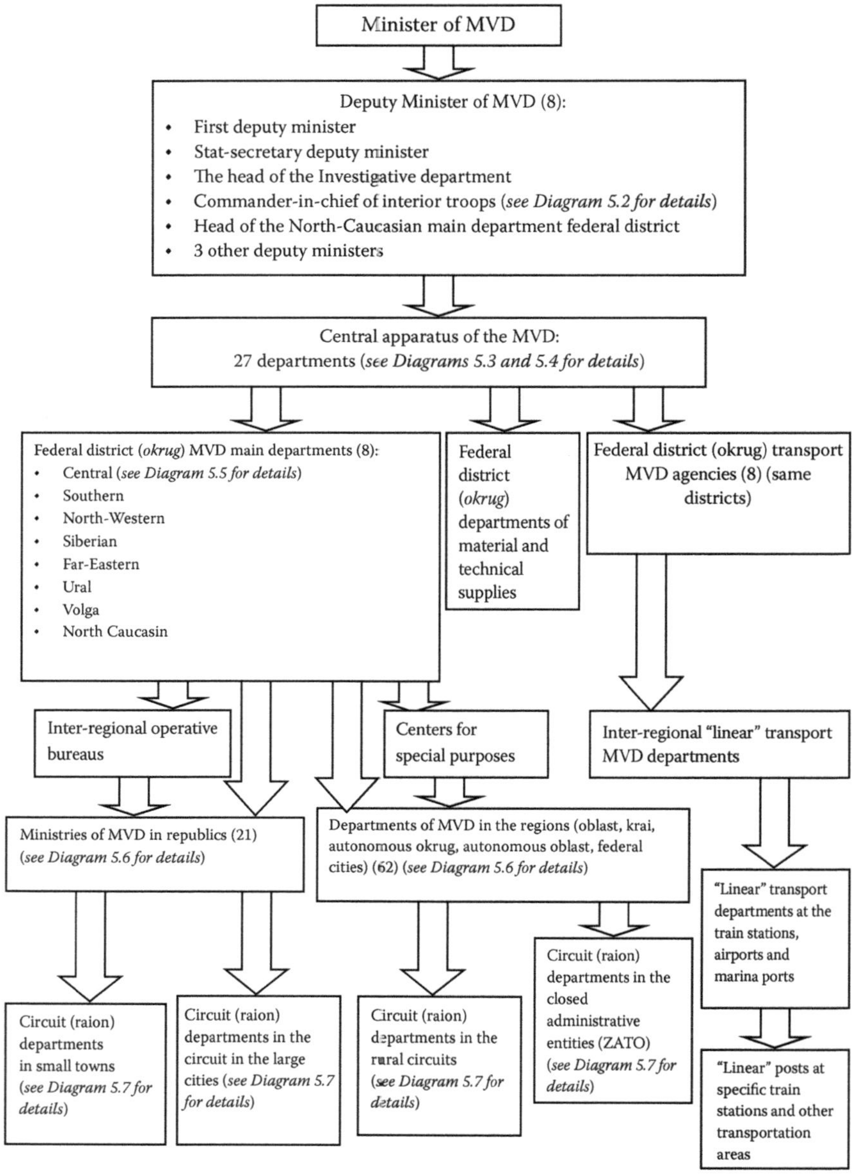

Diagram 5.1 The structure of MVD "territorial" agencies.

5.1.2 Central Apparatus of the MVD (Diagram 5.3 and Diagram 5.4)

The central MVD apparatus main functions are supervision and the overall agency leadership of internal affairs and the interior troops. It consists of 27 departments, of which 13 represent the main functions of the system (Diagram 5.3). The functions deal with crime investigation, maintenance of

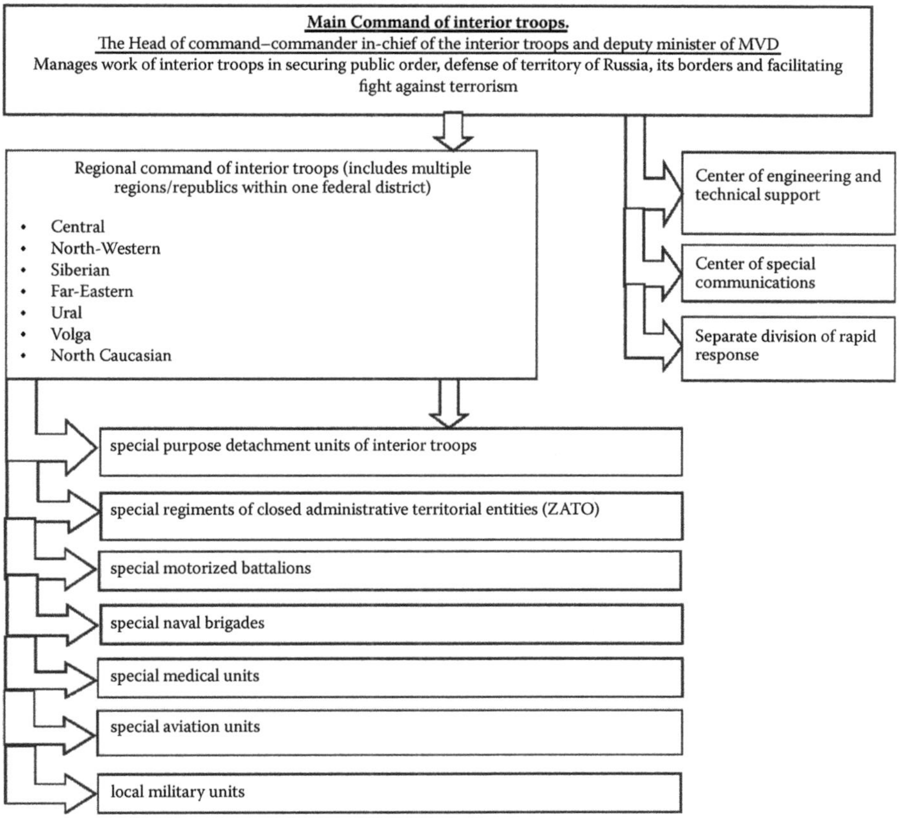

Diagram 5.2 The structure of MVD interior troops.

public order, and 14 are supplementary departments serving to facilitate and support the main functions of the system (Diagram 5.4).

Each department within the central apparatus has subdepartments and centers related to their main purposes. Since its creation in 1991, the central MVD apparatus continues to grow in both structure and staff. In 2004, the Decree of President #730 issued on November 10, 2004, listed only 17 departments of the central apparatus; the new Decree #248 issued on March 1, 2011 has 27 departments. In 1991, the MVD RSFSR had 1,500 staff employees while the Decree of President #208 issued on February 18, 2010 reported the central apparatus's size at 19,970 employees, which is 13 times more than 20 years ago. The modern reform of 2011 requires the central apparatus to be reduced to 9,264 employees.[10] The experts suggest this reduction claim is the main reason for some units (e.g., hubs of detective information) to be moved away from the central to the interregional level.

The first group of departments represents the "traditional" MVD functions, which were performed by this agency for a number of years despite

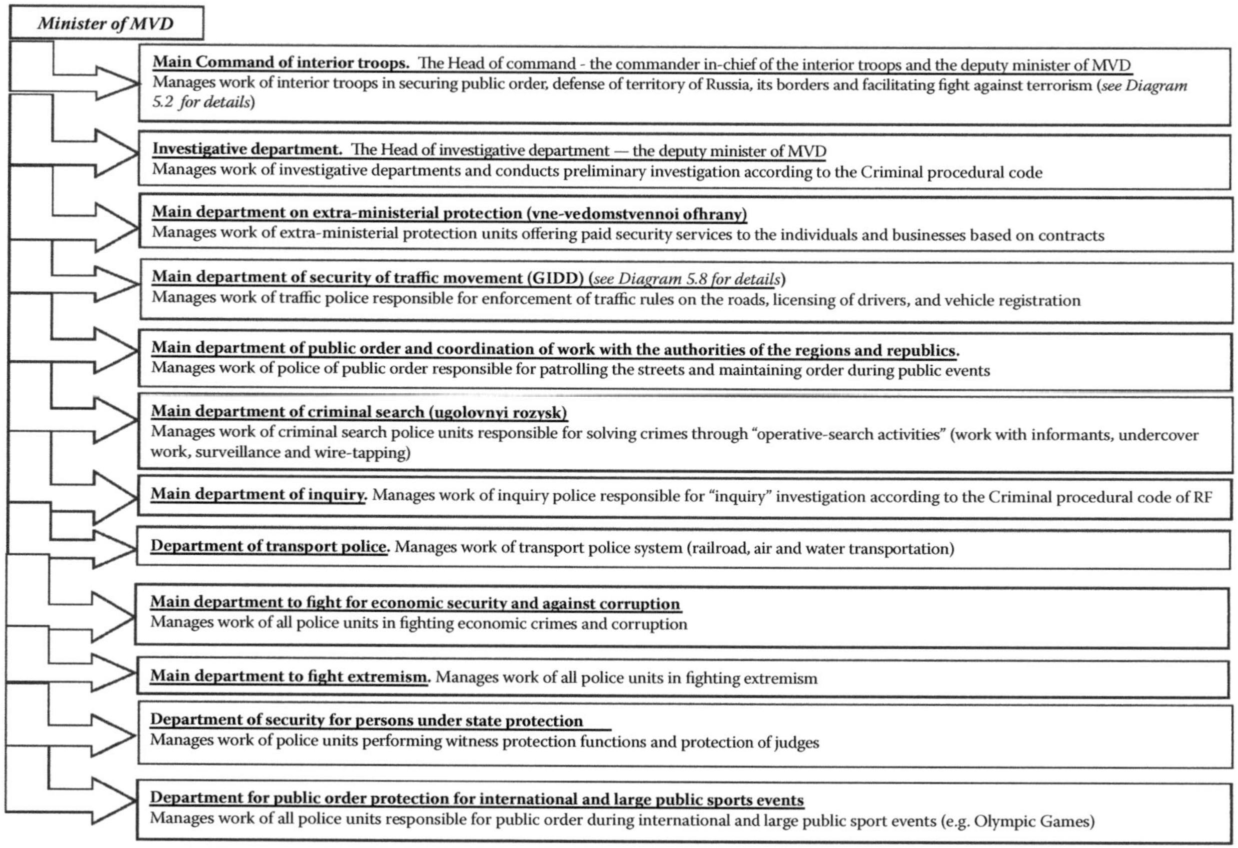

Diagram 5.3 The structure of the MVD central apparatus and the departments that perform its main functions.

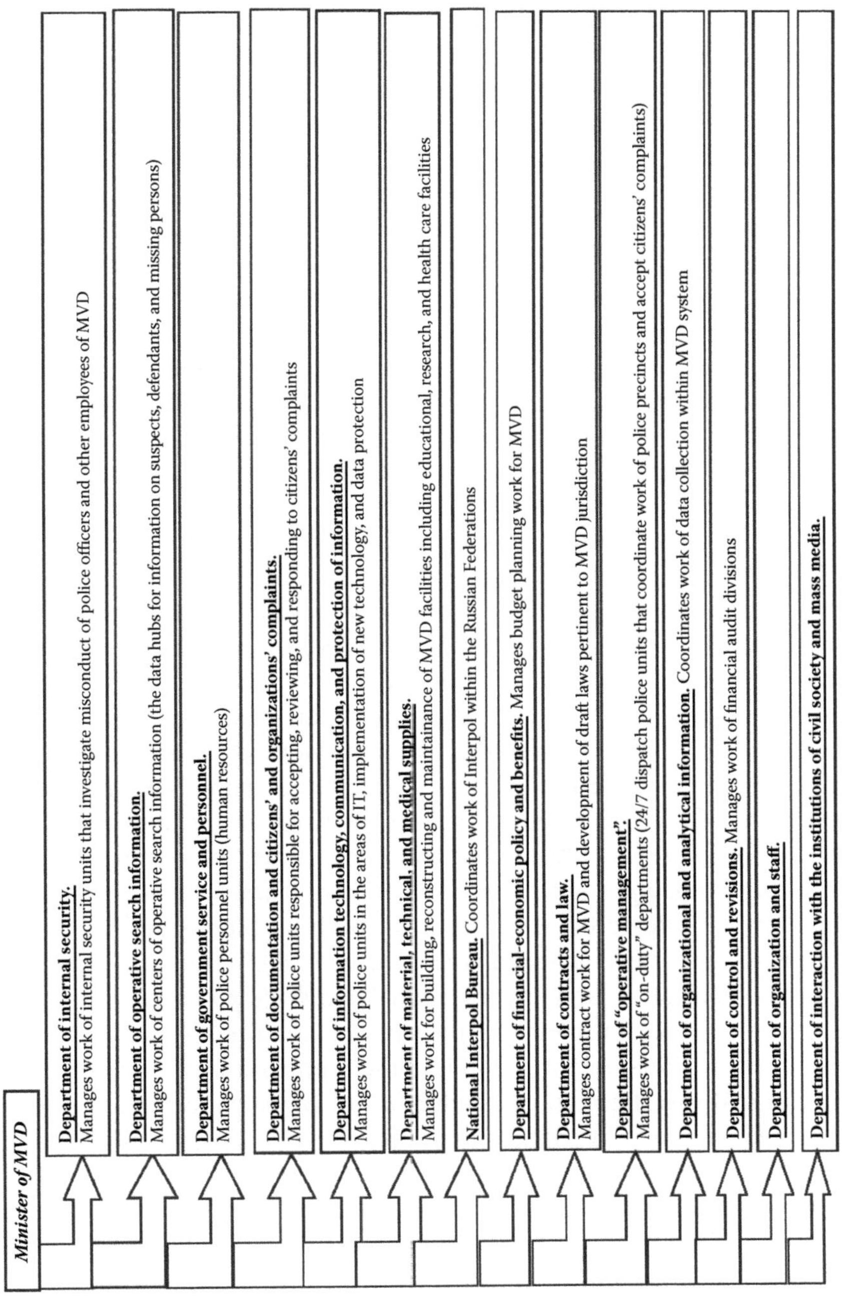

Diagram 5.4 The structure of the MVD central apparatus and the various departments performing supplementary functions.

some changes in structure or renaming of the departments. One of the major departments is the investigative department (*sledstvennyi departament*) dealing with the management of criminal investigations. This was one of the most important MVD functions acquired in 1963 after the amendments were made to the Criminal Procedural Code of the RSFSR (Bozhev, 2002a).[11] Currently more than 80% of all criminal cases are investigated by the MVD; however, only the most dangerous crimes are investigated by the employees of the investigative department of the central apparatus (Gavrilov, 2003b). Since an independent Investigative Committee was created by the president, there has been some speculation about moving the investigative functions away from the MVD to the Investigative Committee.[12] However, the recent presidential decree of March 1, 2011 does not support this theory.

The other traditional departments include the main department of public order (*glavnoe upravlenie po obespecheniyu okhrany obschestvennogo poryadka*), which is responsible for management of all public order police units including the "police of public safety" at the regional and circuit levels (Korenev, 1999).[13] The main department of "traffic" police (*glavnoe upravelnie po obespecheniyu bezopasnosti dorozhnogo dvizheniya)* leads the network of traffic police agencies responsible for enforcement of traffic rules for vehicle drivers, passengers, and pedestrians.[14] The main department of criminal search *(glavnoe upravelie ugolovnogo rozyska)*[15] manages the work of the "criminal police," the network of undercover and other detective departments dealing with felony crimes, identifying bodies, and searching for missing persons (Girko, 2006).[16] The main department of transport police *(glavnoe ypravlenie na transporte*) leads the network of separate transport police agencies enforcing public order and solving crimes committed on the territories of railroad stations, airports, marinas, trains, during flights, and boat trips (Korenev, 1999).[17] The main department of extraministerial protection *(glavnoe upravlenie vnevedomstvennoi okhrany)*[18] manages paid security services offered by MVD units for both businesses and individuals through contractual obligations (Korenev, 1999).[19] The newly created main department of inquiry organization *(upravlenie po organizatsii doznaniya)* is responsible for managing the work of "inquirers"—police officers who conduct the initial investigation into the criminal cases before transfer to the criminal investigators, or conduct a full investigation into a minor cases termed "inquiry" by the Criminal Procedural Code of Russia (Butler, 2003). The department of special purposes detachments (OMON) manages the work of special police units that were created in 1988 for rapid response to public disturbances and other emergency situations. The main command of the interior troops coordinates the work of all interior troop units and is separated from the rest of "territorial internal agencies."[20]

The other group of departments in the central apparatus was recently established ad hoc structures that reflected on MVD's growing power over the various areas of public life. One of these, the main department of economic security and corruption, was established mainly after the tax police agency was abruptly eliminated in 2003 and the duties to investigate tax crime were transferred back to the MVD.[21] The other recent additions include the department to fight extremism created in 2008 in reaction to the growing concern over religious terrorism and nationalistic extremism.[22] The department for security for persons under state protection was added in 2008 after the MVD acquired functions to protect witnesses and judges.[23] The department of public order protection for mass international events was established after the Russian Federation won the bid to conduct the 2014 Winter Olympic Games.

It is also important to discuss several units of the MVD that were not included in the structure of central apparatus by the decree of 2011. The Federal Migration Service (FMS) was established as a part of the MVD system in 2004 by transforming the existing passport–visa department of the central apparatus and also assigning the duties of managing citizens' registration and enforcement of migration regulations to the new agency (Beketov et al., 2009).[24] However, unlike the passport–visa department (Korenev, 1999), the newly created service of the FMS is not an official part of the MVD central apparatus. According to Presidential Decree #248 issued on March 1, 2011, the MVD of Russia only "coordinates and controls the activities" of the FMS. Some critics suggest that this official "removing" of the FMS from the MVD system is just another way to accomplish a reduction of MVD ranks without true cuts in personnel and they doubt that any changes will be truly achieved in a separation of passport registration control from policing. Other experts believe that the transfer of immigration functions to an independent agency is a step in releasing police from unnecessary administrative functions as proposed by President Medvedev.[25] It is unclear now whether the transfer of the FMS would be completed in reality or the separation exists only on paper. According to both the new law "On Police" of 2011 and Presidential Decree #248, the functions of the FMS are still performed within the MVD system and are controlled by the MVD minister,

Some other existing units of the MVD, such as the "expert forensic center" and "department K"[26] are not listed under the structure of the central apparatus with the new Decree #248. Because their functions are important, it is doubtful that these units will be eliminated. Instead, it is likely they will obtain some special status or will be included in one of the newly created main departments of the central apparatus as was done in the past.

One of the subunits of the MVD is the All-Russian scientific research institute of the MVD, which is the leading research institution in the area of policing. This institution is not directly included into the MVD central apparatus, but is a part of the "internal affairs agencies" (Beketov et al., 2009).[27] (The structure of the MVD central apparatus and the departments that perform main functions[28] is shown in Diagram 5.3.)

As of March 2, 2011, the central apparatus of the MVD contained 14 "supplementary" departments. Some have self-explanatory functions, such as human resources, financial audit, public relations, legal services, or internal investigations. Other departments are more unique to the functions of agencies of internal affairs. The department of "operative search information" (*operativno-razysknoi informatsii*) is responsible for management of the "operative search centers" in the regions; the data information hubs that collect, maintain, and provide information on suspicious activities; missing persons and property; escaped suspects/defendants; and other detective information collected through the work of "criminal search" departments. The department of "operative management" (*operativnogo upravelniya*) is responsible for the centers of operative management work within the district, regional, and circuit levels. The purpose of operative management units is to maintain real-time information on all important activities occurring in the district, region, or circuits, and coordinate situational efforts of law enforcement agencies (Korenev, 1999). This includes information on crimes, suspicious activities, accidents, disturbances, and other relevant information. The organizational and analytical department *(organizatsionno-analiticheskii departament)* is responsible for the coordination of the collection of massive statistical information on crimes and offenders by the MVD through its regional agencies.[29] It is interesting to note that compared to the Decree #730 of 2004, the number of supplementary departments in the MVD central apparatus in 2011 grew from 5 to 14 despite the declaration of goals to reduce the central apparatus size from 19,970 to 9,264 employees.[30] (The structure of the MVD central apparatus and the various departments performing supplementary functions[31] is shown in Diagram 5.4.)

5.1.3 Main Department of the MVD in Federal Districts (Diagram 5.5)

There are currently 8 federal districts in Russia combining 83 "subjects of federation." Each of the districts has the main MVD department that typically consists of "operative search bureaus" conducting crime-related detective work, investigative departments conducting official preliminary investigations in accordance with the Criminal Procedural Code, and an array of supplementary departments supporting work of the main department in the district. The main department on federal districts was originally established by the Decree of President #644 issued on June 4, 2001.

The structure of the typical main department was initially established by the Decree of MVD #634 issued on July 4, 2001.[32] The structure of each main department is unique and determined through the specific decrees of the MVD.[33] From the analysis of laws and literature, it is apparent that the main departments of this level only deal with solving and investigating dangerous

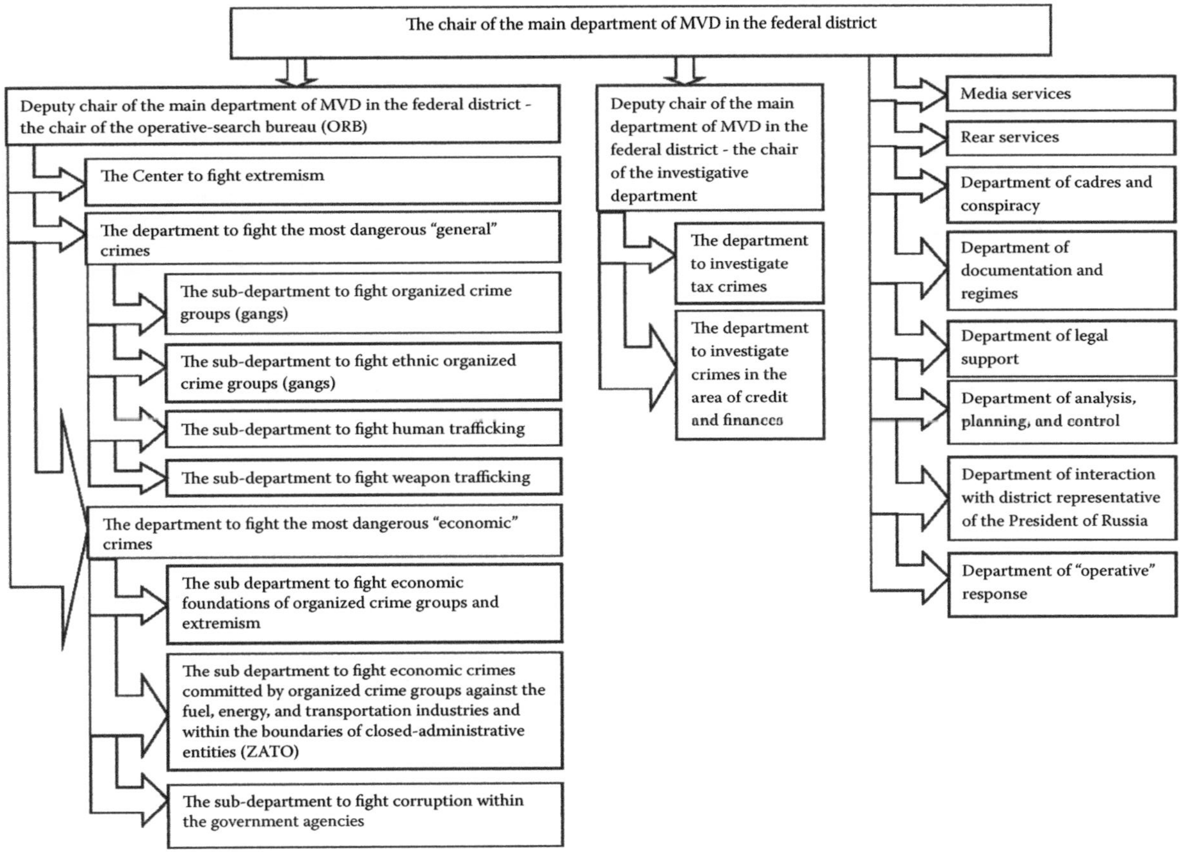

Diagram 5.5 The typical structure of an MVD main department in the federal districts (okrug).

organized crimes, crimes that require coordination of law enforcement efforts among various regions (e.g., trafficking, extremism), and crimes requiring additional investigative training (complex financial, tax, and other economic crimes).[34] The main departments also are charged with the overall coordination and management of law enforcement activities within the district. The chair of the main department and his/her deputies are appointed by the president of Russia after a recommendation by the MVD minister.[35]

Some researchers doubt whether the establishment of the main MVD departments in the federal districts was necessary (Studenikin, 2004). It has been suggested that the main goal for creating the federal districts and the main departments of MVD is to weaken the regional authorities' control of law enforcement rather than to improve MVD efficiency (Petrov and Slider, 2007). (The typical structure of the MVD main department in the federal districts (*okrug*)[36] is shown in Diagram 5.5.)

5.1.4 Ministry of MVD within the Republic or the MVD Regional Department (Diagram 5.6)

Similar to the central apparatus and the main departments in the federal districts, the departments on the republican/regional level are structured along the main functions of the Russian law enforcement system: detective (undercover) work, official preliminary investigation, and public order; a detailed description of each follows. Because the law "On Police" was issued in 1991, the agencies of internal affairs traditionally were divided between the "criminal police," which referred to the units performing detective and investigative work, and "police of public safety," which referred to police patrol and other units concerned with public order issues.

Even though the new law "On Police" of 2011 does not use these terms anymore, many regional departments continue to employ this division for their structure. Within the criminal police on the regional level, one can find departments of criminal search (dealing with solving regular felony crimes), the departments of organized crimes,[37] regional Interpol agencies, and departments of service dogs. Also considered detective departments are those that focus on economic and tax crimes.[38] In addition, there are centers to fight extremism and witness/judge protection services that are established on the basis of departmental fighting of organized crime (Beketov et al., 2009).[39]

Under the umbrella of the "police of public safety," the regional departments traditionally have a variety of units dealing with issuing private detective licenses (licensing department), providing protection and security services on a contractual basis (extraministerial department),[40] enforcing the administrative regulations in the area of consumer rights (center for protection of consumer rights) (Korenev, 1999),[41] and issuing driver's licenses,

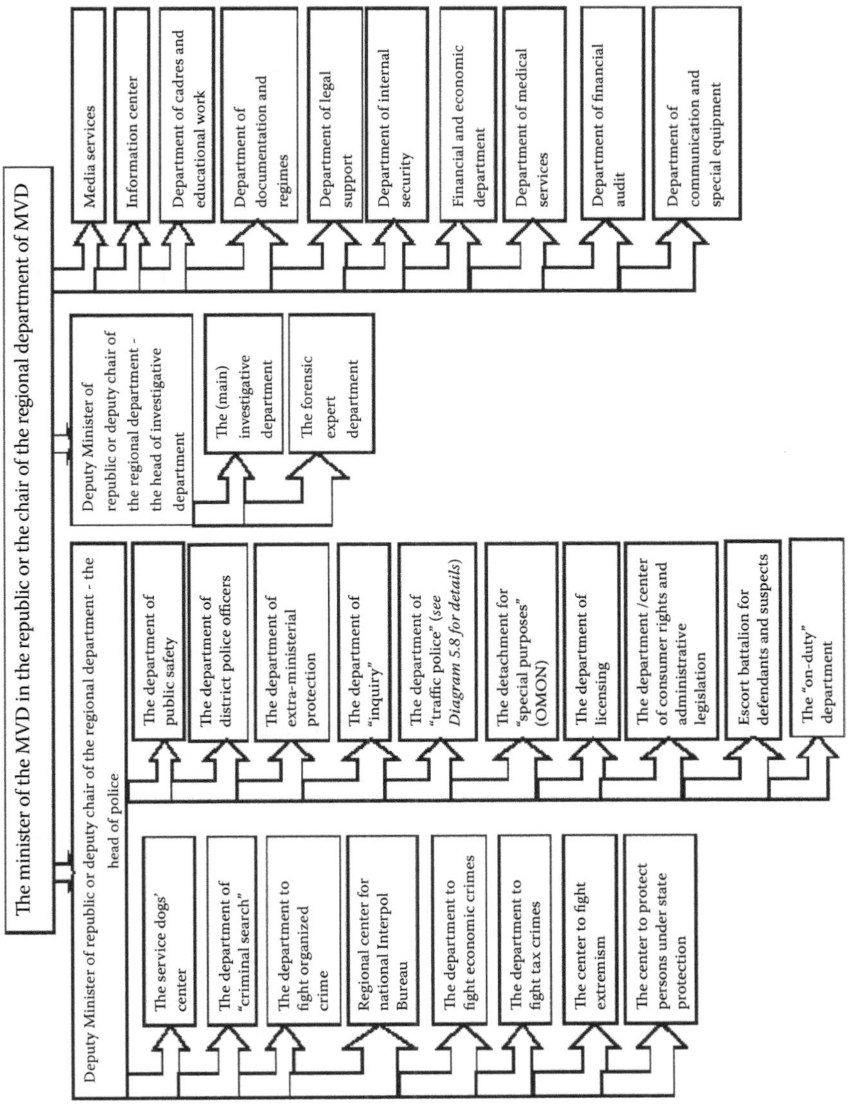

Diagram 5.6 The typical MVD structure in the republics or regions.

and conducting vehicle inspection and registrations (department of traffic police).[42] The public safety police also includes departments of district police officers (*uchastkovye upolnomochennye*) that deals with managing the work of low-ranking police officers responsible for the supervision of certain urban or rural districts.[43] At the core of the public safety police are departments managing the work of street patrols, centers to prevent delinquency, and departments of inquiry (Korenev, 1999).[44] The public safety police of the regional/republican MVD departments also typically have a detachment used for special purposes, such as the rapid response to civil disturbances and the maintenance of safety during large events (Girko, 2006).[45] The main department also has an on-duty unit (*dezhurnaya chast*) responsible for real-time information and the coordination of law enforcement efforts in the republics and regions (Panteleev, 2002).[46]

There is also a convoy battalion for escorting and transporting suspects and defendants (to court, crime scenes, interrogations, and other places that are included in the structure of the public safety police) (Korenev, 1999).[47] Unlike the criminal police, the public safety police once had a double subordination and were partially financed through the regional budgets (Bozhev, 2002a).[48] This is no longer the case since all MVD units are now funded from the federal budget and directly subordinated to the superior MVD agencies beginning in 2012.[49]

The investigative departments of the regional and republican MVD usually investigate the most important felony crimes, or crimes that occurred in multiple districts within one region or republic (Belenkov, 2003).[50] Some republican and regional departments also place expert forensic centers, charged with duties to conduct all forensic examinations during a criminal investigation, under the umbrella of investigative departments. Others list these units as independent centers.

All republican and regional departments have a variety of supplementary units supporting their functions. The MVD regional department chairs in the republics are appointed by the president from recommendations of the MVD minister.[51] The chair (or minister) has three deputies. One is the head of public police, one is the head of the investigative department, and one head is undetermined. The specific structure of the MVD in each republic/region is confirmed by the MVD minister through a special decree that explains some variations of the structure in the particular departments or ministries.[52] (The typical MVD structure in the republics or regions[53] is shown in Diagram 5.6.)

5.1.5 The Circuit Departments of the MVD (Diagram 5.7)

The circuit departments of the MVD (*rayonnye otdely vnutrennikh del*) are the lowest organizational level that performs most of its routine policing duties:

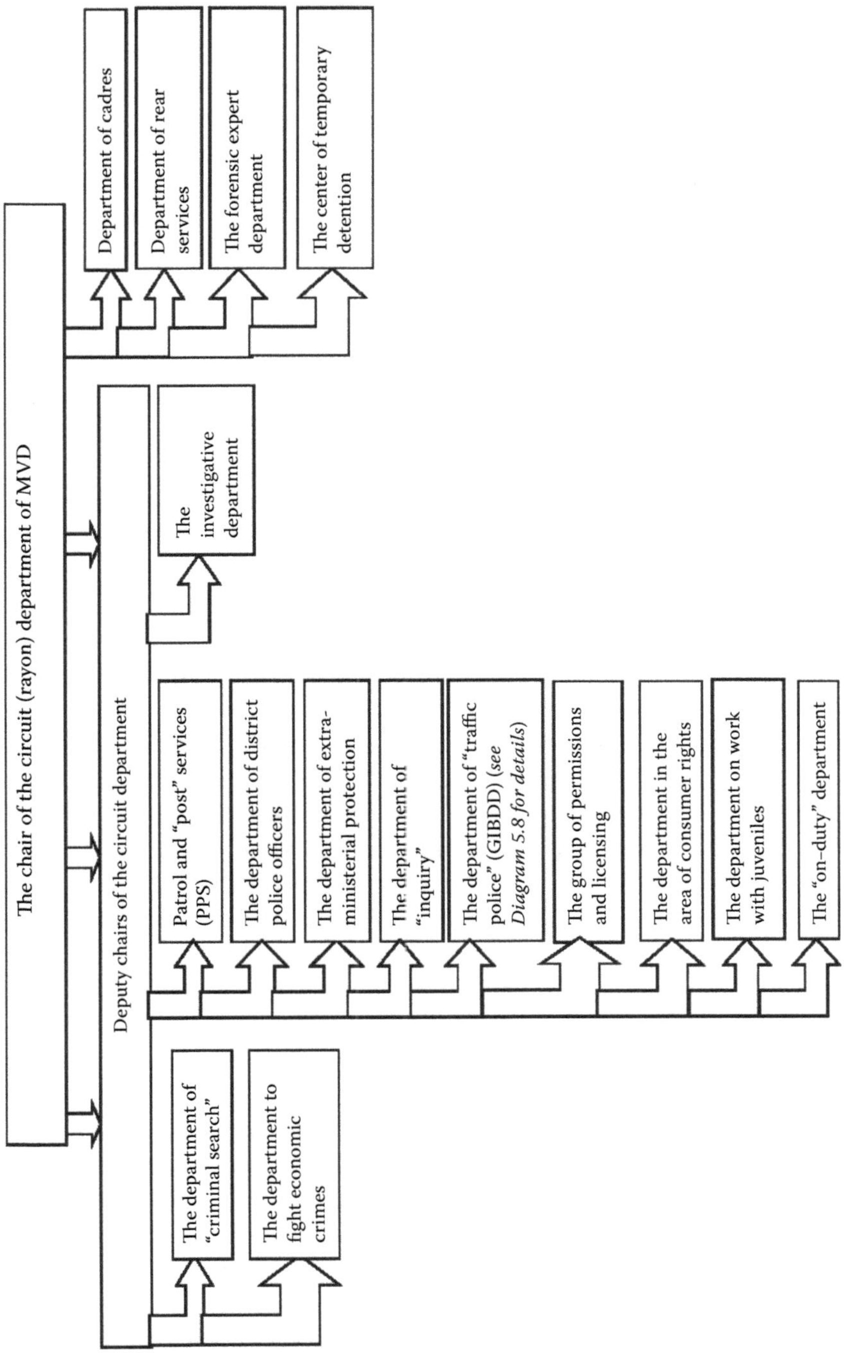

Diagram 5.7 The typical structure of the MVD circuit departments.

maintenance of public safety and investigation of crimes. The organization of the circuit police departments is based on the municipal structure of the government in the regions commonly referred as "self-government administration" (Butler, 2003).[54] Typically, the capital cities of the republics or regions are divided into multiple city circuits with each having a separate circuit police department.[55] The same is true for large noncapital cities in the regions or republics. Medium or small-sized cities may have only one circuit police department assigned to them. In the rural areas, there are typically the townships termed "circuit centers" (*rayonnye tsentry*) that are the capitals for the large rural circuits. The circuit police department located in such townships is usually responsible for both the township and the rural area. The villages located within the rural areas (*rayony*) usually do not have separate police departments, but they may have district police officers (*uchastkovyi*) who reside in the village and represent the agencies of internal affairs (Korenev, 1999).[56]

In addition, separate circuit police departments exist in the "closed administrative territorial entities" (abbreviated ZATO). ZATO refers to settlements with special regimes due to the location of some strategic entity within their territory (e.g., nuclear station or military factory).[57] Each district police department is responsible for their own territory and, in cases of interjurisdictional crimes that involve multiple city or rural circuits, an investigation is usually transferred to the regional/republican level.

The organization of each district police department is structured along similar lines as other MVD departments. There is a separation between the detective units, investigative units that conduct preliminary investigations, and a variety of units maintaining the public safety (Beketov et al., 2009). Because the circuit police departments are the lowest level of policing, their criminal search and investigative departments deal with all misdemeanors and felonies required by Article 151 of the Code of Criminal Procedure except for those that have been investigated by republican/regional or federal district-level departments.

The so-called "patrol and post services" (abbreviated PPS) are units of both on-foot and motorized patrols, and permanent locations of patrol officers in important areas (referred as "posts" of PPS) (Girko, 2006). These units are organized following military structure with battalions, companies, and platoons responsible for patrolling certain streets or areas (Korenev, 1999). The district police officers (*uchastkovyi*) are low-ranking police officers who are responsible for the supervision of certain small areas (*administrativnyi uchastok*) within the circuit of the city or villages (Panteleev, 2002).[58] Their duties are vast and include surveillance of the area, the first response to minor disturbances (often family violence), providing investigative search departments with names of suspicious persons or activities, and other daily policing functions (Pronyakin and Pronyakin, 2003).[59] The "district" police officers often interact with the departments of juvenile work to prevent juvenile truancy, other delinquency, and issues of unsupervised minors (Panteleev, 2002).[60]

The inquiry department investigates minor offenses and also conducts initial investigation into more serious offenses before transferring those into the investigative departments (Verin and Mozyakov, 2004). The employees of the inquiry department are often the first responders to the crime scene (Bozhev, 2002b). The expert forensic departments conduct basic forensic examinations to support both inquirers and investigators during their preliminary investigation. Complex forensic examinations are usually conducted by the forensic centers at the regional/republican levels (Girko, 2006).

The extraministerial departments offer security services (including alarm services) to the organizations and persons on a contractual basis within the circuit (Panteleev, 2002). The traffic departments on the circuit level typically deal with traffic fines and other minor traffic infractions. The permission and licensing department issues licenses for firearms for individuals and licenses to conduct private detective activities (Panteleev, 2002). The departments of consumer rights protection conduct surveillance and activities to prevent, or investigate, violations in the area of consumer rights. The on-duty departments (*dezhurnaya chast*) serve as real-time information and dispatch centers coordinating the work of all services and accepting citizens' complaints about potential crimes (Girko, 2006).

The services responsible for the maintenance of public order are the most numerous police agencies at the circuit level and consist of 60% of all personnel in the circuit department (Bozhev, 2002a). The chair of the circuit police department, and his/her deputies, are appointed by the chair of the MVD regional/republican department. Prior to the reform of 2011, one of the circuit department deputy chairs (responsible for the public order police) was appointed through recommendation from the local authorities in the republic or region (Pechnikov, 2005).[61] (The typical structure of the MVD circuit departments[62] is shown in Diagram 5.7.)

5.1.6 State Inspection Security of the Traffic Movement Police (GIBDD) (Diagram 5.8)

The traffic police (*gosudarstvennaya inspectsiya bezopasnosti dorozhnogo dvizheniya*, abbreviated GIBDD) are not an independent network of police agencies, but rather a police subunit in the regional, republican, and central levels charged with the enforcement of traffic rules for vehicle drivers and pedestrians. However, unlike other MVD subunits, the traffic police have a distinct identity in the Russian society. It is one of the few MVD agencies that are well-known due to its interaction with vehicle operators and pedestrians. In public polls, the traffic police are often separated from other units of the MVD system primarily due to their very low public satisfaction ratings and extremely high levels of perceived corruption. Thus, it is important to explain the structure of this subunit.

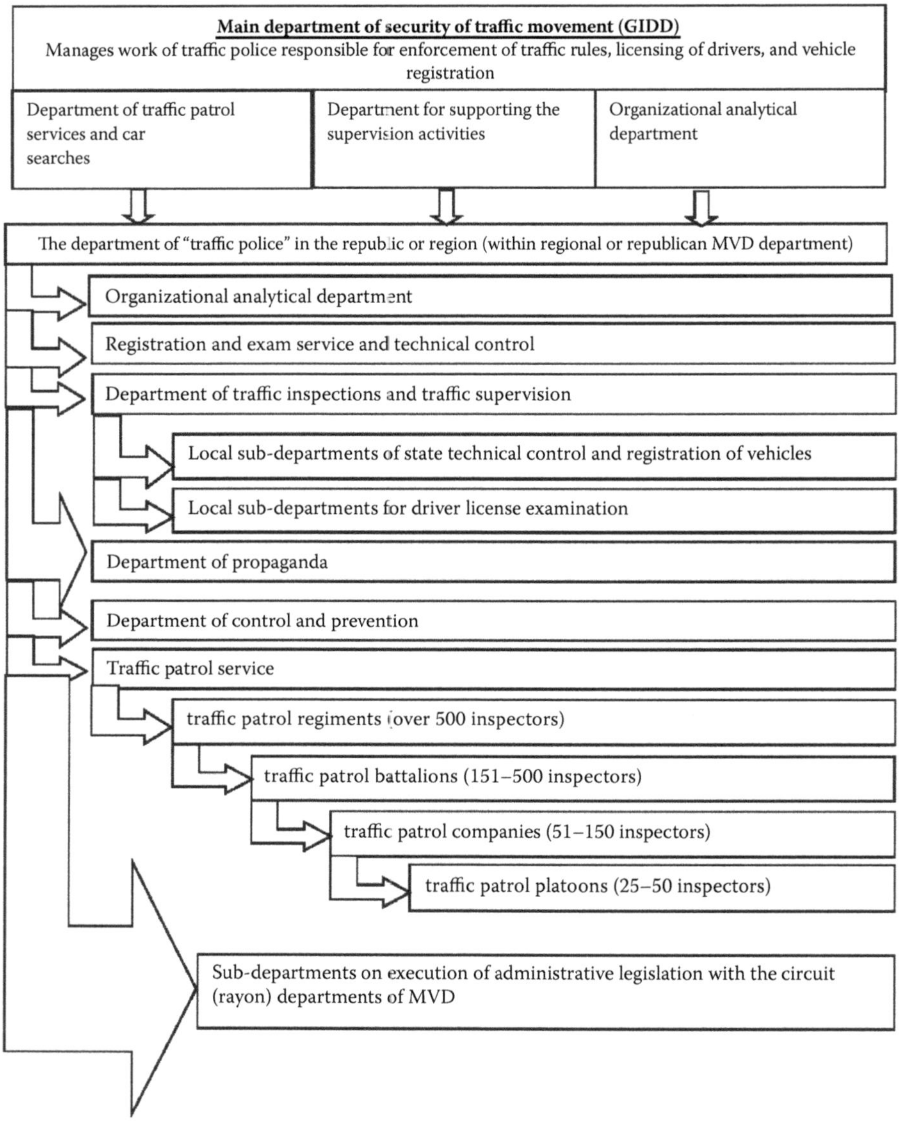

Diagram 5.8 The structure of State Inspection for Traffic Movement ("traffic police").

On the central level, the traffic police are represented by the main Department of Security of the Traffic Movement that manages and coordinates the work of all traffic police units. The major level of traffic police is either regional or republican departments that conduct most of the traffic rule enforcements. The major functions of traffic police at the republican and regional levels include issuance of drivers licenses and vehicle registration (Korenev, 1999).[63]

Until 2012, the traffic police also were responsible for conducting the vehicle safety inspections, but now this function will be performed by the licensed car dealerships and other private organizations.[64] The largest unit of the traffic police—the traffic patrol service—resembles the structure of the military organization and consists of traffic inspectors in the field enforcing the traffic rules (Panteleev, 2002). These police officers can stop drivers for speeding and other traffic violations, and issue fines (or other punishment). At the circuit level, the traffic police can have subdepartments for examination, vehicle control, and registration. At this level, there are also departments for the execution of administrative legislation that accept fines and review decisions of the traffic inspectors (Beketov et al., 2009). (The structure of State Inspection for Traffic Movement (traffic police)[65] is shown in Diagram 5.8.)

5.1.7 Interior Troops of the MVD (Diagram 5.2)

Interior troops of the MVD are not officially law enforcement agencies, but rather are auxiliary military units created to assist MVD internal agencies in performing law enforcement functions (Bozhev, 2002a). Their main duties are to assist agencies of internal affairs to maintain the public order and especially in emergency situations, protection of important public strategic objects, border protection by providing assistance to the border control agencies, and participation in counterterrorist operations.[66] The low-ranking officers of interior troops are drafted to its units under the same conditions as officers of the regular military forces in Russia.[67]

The major structural units of interior troops are regional commands that follow the organization of federal districts in the country (Beketov et al., 2009).[68] Under each of the seven regional commands, there is a variety of military units with some specialized by their type (like naval, aviation, and motorized brigades).[69] Other separate units of the interior troops exist, for each closed administrative territorial entity, that represent a settlement serving the needs of a strategic security object.[70] Also, there are special purpose units serving under the regional command. These are typically military units with advanced training used for special operations for fighting terrorism.[71] The main command in the central apparatus also has a separate division for rapid response that consists of a variety of special purpose detachments and participates in the counterterrorism operations, but does not report to any regional command. The most common are the general purposes units (*voennye chasti*) that constitute the network of the federal district territorial military detachments.[72] (The structure of MVD interior troops[73] is shown in Diagram 5.2.)

5.2 MVD Agency Authorities

5.2.1 Operative-Search Authorities of Agencies of Internal Affairs (Abbreviated ORD)

The operative search functions (*operativno-rozysknaya deyatelnost*) of MVD agencies include a variety of detective powers regulated by the Federal Law "On operative search activities" #144-FZ issued on August 12, 1995. The goals of these activities include solving crimes, preventing future crimes, finding escaped suspects and defendants, locating missing persons, finding property hidden from court-ordered confiscation, and establishing information about dangerous events and persons.[74] Operative search departments perform auxiliary functions for the investigative units of MVD, such as providing investigators with the necessary grounds to open an official investigation, searching for escaped suspects and defendants, and assisting investigators in solving crime (Goriyanov et al., 2004).

MVD agencies of every level conduct ORD functions, which depend on the type of crimes that are investigated. At the federal district level (see Diagram 5.5), the operative search activities are performed by all subunits of the operative search bureau and focus on solving very dangerous crimes, such as human and weapon trafficking, organized crime, ethnic crime, and other serious crimes. On the republican level (see Diagram 5.6), the department of criminal search addresses tax crimes, economic crimes, centers against extremism, and departments charged with the protection of witnesses and judges.

On the lowest circuit level (see Diagram 5.7), the department of criminal search and the economic crimes department perform operative search functions for their investigative departments. On the central level (see Diagram 5.3), the operative search activities of all MVD agencies are coordinated and managed through the work of the main department of criminal search, the department for economic security and corruption prevention, the department to fight extremism, and the department of security for persons under state protection.

The list of allowed operative search actions (*operativno-rozysknye meropriyatiya*) is provided by the law and includes 14 main actions:

1. Unofficial interview
2. Investigation into a person's background through database inquiries
3. Collecting samples for forensic examination
4. Control purchase
5. Examination of objects and documents
6. Surveillance
7. Identification procedures
8. Search of residences and other facilities

9. Perlustration (review) of communication
10. Phone wiretapping
11. Downloading information
12. Undercover work
13. Control supplying
14. Operative experiments[75]

These actions can be performed before the official investigation is opened, during the investigation, or at the time when the investigation is suspended (Efremov, 2002).

The unofficial interview is a consensual interview of the person, which can be recorded for the purposes of investigation, but cannot be used in court. The interviewed person cannot be detained, or in custody of the police, at the time of the interview (Vagin, Isichenko, and Chechetin, 2009). The investigation into a person's background by running search inquiries through the official databases usually returns information on criminal records, administrative violations, arrests, places of residence, family members, and other official data (Goriyanov et al., 2004). The search of forensic samples for comparative study (e.g., fingerprints, blood, hair, writing, etc.) can be consensual or done with abandoned samples within the operative search activities. The control purchase is conducted when a police officer pretends to buy a product to establish the fact of a crime or other violation through a transaction. Similar to this, control supplying refers to large-scale purchases of controlled substances or objects that are used to prove criminal activities (Efremov, 2002). The examination of documents typically occurs when a forensic expert gives an opinion on the matter without providing an official written expert conclusion (Goriyanov et al., 2004). The surveillance of persons can be done through personal observation and through the use of equipment (Vagin, Isichenko, and Chechetin, 2009). The latter requires a court order as it infringes on the constitutional rights of the persons.[76] The identification procedures are done unofficially when the identified person is placed in the natural environment and can be observed by the identifying person, such as witness or victim. The search and seizure of residences and other facilities (physical intrusion) can be done with or without the consent (and knowledge) of the person on the basis of court order (Efremov, 2002). The perlustration of communication (e.g. mail, telegraph) without a person's knowledge can be done only on the basis of a court order. A court order is also required for such actions as phone wiretapping and downloading personal data (including digital communication and fax information) (Goriyanov et al., 2004). Undercover work and operative experiment are used to allow police officers to conduct illegal activities in order to solve serious crimes.

Most of the operative search actions (even those that do not require a court order) can be performed by the operative police officer (*operativnik*) only after the official request is filed with the superior officer to justify the need for action.[77] Other agencies (such as prosecutor, investigator, and court) can request an operative search action to be taken.[78] The process of an operative search action should be recorded through video, audio, or written protocol documents when possible.[79] In cases of a control purchase and a control supplying, the actions have to be approved by a written order (*postanovlenie*) from the superior operative officer.[80] In cases when a court order is required, the superior operative officer issues an order to file the motion in court.[81] The court order is given for a duration of up to six months and can be extended by new application.[82] In cases of emergency, the operative search actions can be started without the court order, but the superior operative officer is required to file a motion within 24 hours from the beginning of the action.[83]

The results of search operative activities described above can be used as evidence during the preliminary investigation only under limited conditions (Gutsenko, 2005).[84] In most cases, the investigator in the case has to create an official document and attach the operative search action record to the criminal dossier (Article 89 of the Criminal Procedural Code of Russia). The Constitutional Court of Russia ruled that if the results of operative search actions cannot be disclosed and attached to the criminal case, they cannot be used as admissible evidence against the defendant.[85] In some situations, the results of operative search actions are not considered evidence and are used to initiate the criminal investigation, to support other investigative actions, prevent the crime, or to provide security to the witnesses or victims of the crime. In any case, the results of the ORD remain secret unless there is a decision made by the superior operative officer to disclose the materials (Vagin, Isichenko, and Chechetin, 2009).

5.2.2 Investigative Authority of the Internal Affairs Agencies

Unlike the operative search activities, the preliminary investigation (*predvaritelnoe sledstvie*) of criminal cases is done to obtain legally admissible evidence against criminal defendants (Gromov, 1998). The process of the preliminary investigation is not secret and results in compiling a criminal dossier (*ugolovnoe delo*), which is transferred to court for trial. The entire process is highly formalized and separated into the stages and regulated by the Criminal Procedural Code of Russia (CPC of Russia) (Newcombe, 2007). The term of the preliminary investigation is limited to two months, but can be extended by the procurator (Gutsenko, 2005).[86] Not all cases are subject to a preliminary investigation, only the ones listed in Article 150 of the Russian CPC. The cases that are not subjected to preliminary investigation are investigated through the process of inquiry. Typically, a preliminary investigation is mandatory for serious crimes (Butler, 1999). The prosecutor has discretion to order the preliminary investigation for cases not listed in the CPC.[87] Article 151 of the CPC determines which of the serious crimes are investigated by the agencies of internal affairs and which are investigated by other agencies (e.g., the investigative committee or the drug control agencies) (Verin and Mozyakov, 2004). Currently, over 80% of all criminal cases are investigated by MVD agencies.[88] The internal MVD regulations determine whether the case should be investigated by central, regional, district, or circuit investigative departments (Bozhev, 2002b).

As a general rule, the superior investigative departments have discretion to remand any of the cases from inferior levels for their investigation. On the federal district level (Diagram 5.5), the preliminary investigation is performed by the investigative departments for tax crimes and those related to credits and finances. They also can investigate other serious crimes that are solved by their operative search bureau. On the republic or regional level (Diagram 5.6), the main investigative department investigates any cases initiated by their operative search departments including organized crime, and economic and tax crimes. Main republican or regional departments often order high-profile criminal cases to be moved from the district level for preliminary investigation to the regional/republican level. However, the majority of the cases are investigated at the district level (Diagram 5.7) where the investigative departments deal with all crimes listed under Article 151 of the CPC, unless they are investigated by superior agencies. The overall investigative activities by the MVD agencies of all levels are coordinated and managed through the main investigative department of the MVD (Diagram 5.3).

The powers of the preliminary investigators are broad and include a variety of actions that can be taken toward the suspect, defendant, and victim. The decision to initiate the preliminary investigation is very important and determines whether someone's behavior would be considered a crime and if there will be charges.[89] Another very powerful right of the preliminary investigator is the decision to detain the suspect prior to trial.[90] Even though the investigator needs a court approval to order the detention, the initial decision on whether to release the suspect on his/her own recognizance, or to detain him/her, is made by the investigator.[91] The detention can last anywhere from 2 to 18 months for a defendant (10 days for those without charges) and can significantly impact the defendant's ability to prepare for trial.[92]

During the preliminary investigation, the investigator alone decides what evidence is entered into the criminal dossier. The decision determines what evidence would be assumed admissible in court (Gutsenko, 2005).[93] While collecting the evidence, the investigator can subpoena the witnesses;[94] order the forensic examination;[95] file a court motion to search facilities and persons, and seize property;[96] conduct identification procedures;[97] and request any of the operative search actions to be taken. The investigator also decides whether any of the defense counsel's requests about collecting evidence should be allowed and if evidence obtained by the defense counsel should be included in the dossier.[98] The investigator also determines who should be considered the official victim of the crime and whether a civil suit related to the criminal behavior would be filed during the preliminary investigation.[99] The official criminal charges are also filed initially by the investigator through the arraignment (*predyavlenie obvineniya*),[100] then later through an indictment (*obvinitelnoe zakluchenie*),[101] and finally supported by the prosecutor (Radchenko, 2006). The investigator also can determine if the investigation should be terminated in cases where no crime is established,[102] and in specially allowed circumstances when the defendant and the victim reconcile,[103] or when the behavior no longer represents a danger to society.[104]

5.2.3 Inquiry Authority of Internal Affairs Agencies

"Inquiry" (*doznanie*) is another way by which the criminal cases can be investigated.[105] Part 3 of Article 150 of the CPC specifies which crimes can be investigated using this form of inquiry. Most of these crimes are minor offenses and, therefore, the inquiry is understood as a simplified version of the preliminary investigation for less dangerous and more obvious crimes (Bradley, 2007). There are no subunits for criminal inquiry on the federal district levels because these departments usually deal only with the most serious crimes (Diagram 5.5). The departments of inquiry at regional levels are mainly concerned with the coordination of inquiry police work and rarely conduct inquires themselves (Diagram 5.6) (Girko, 2006). The departments that are fully involved in performing inquiries into crimes are district departments (Diagram 5.7), which process all minor offenses. The inquiries are conducted by the department of inquirers, but also can be performed by the operative police officers in criminal search departments when instructed by the chair (Radchenko, 2006). The department of inquiry in the central apparatus of the MVD (Diagram 5.3) was created recently in recognition of the growing role of inquiry during the criminal process. It coordinates the work of all inquiry subunits within the MVD system.

The police officer that conducts the inquiry is termed "inquirer" (*doznavatel'*) and has similar rights as the investigator. The inquirers[106] can subpoena witnesses, order forensic examinations, and file for search and seizure or pretrial detention of the defendant. The major differences between the inquiry and the preliminary investigation include a shorter term for concluding the inquiry (30 days versus 2 months)[107] and no requirements for the inquirer to arraign the defendant. Instead, the inquirer simply provides the defendant with the indictment (Verin and Mozyakov, 2004).

The other duties of the inquiry agencies are the performance of urgent investigative actions for cases subject to preliminary investigation (more serious crimes).[108] In such a situation, the agency of inquiry initiates the official investigation and conducts crime scene examinations, interviews, and other actions necessary at the time (Girko, 2006). Within 10 days after the case is initiated, the agency of inquiry transfers the case to a procurator for further preliminary investigation (Radchenko, 2006).[109] Unlike the preliminary investigation, which is always required to be conducted by the members of investigative units, the inquiry sometimes is done by the members of criminal search departments and even the commanders of interior troop units (Diagram 5.2).

5.2.4 Authorities of the Internal Affairs Agencies Related to Administrative Violations

Internal affairs are responsible for the enforcement of a variety of administrative rules under the umbrella of policing. According to the Russian Code of Administrative Violations (abbreviated KoAP),[110] the agencies of internal affairs are responsible for the prevention, investigation, and sometimes adjudication[111] of more than 40 administrative offenses, such as violations of retail trade rules,[112] public order regulations,[113] licensing violations,[114] traffic violations,[115] and violations of passport regimes and registration (Korenev, 1999).[116] Depending on the severity of the cases, the internal affairs agencies can prevent, investigate, or adjudicate for administrative violations. The volume of administrative violations handled by the MVD system is large and averages 80 million cases a year, according to official statistics (Beketov et al., 2009).

In many cases, the agencies of internal affairs can immediately issue a warning decree about an administrative violation (*postanovelnie po delu ob administrativnom narushenii*)[117] and require the violator to pay a fine. In more serious cases, police officers can issue a protocol of administrative violation (*protocol ob administrativnom narushenii*) and transfer the case for further adjudication (Beketov et al., 2009).

A person suspected of administrative violation can be summoned to the police precinct (*dostavlenie*) against his/her will if it is necessary to issue the protocol of administrative violation.[118] In some circumstances, in order to properly adjudicate the case, the person can be detained from 3 to 48 hours (*administrativenoe zaderzhanie*).[119] The detainees can be subject to a personal search[120] or search of their vehicle.[121] Contraband, fruits of the violation, and other illegal items found during the search can be seized.[122] In practice, this is routinely done when the person does not have identification or is publicly intoxicated.

If a protocol of administrative violation was issued, the case is transferred within three days to either the chief of police, peace justice, or another agency that is authorized to adjudicate.[123] Most administrative violations are immediately adjudicated by either the chief, or deputy chief, of the circuit departments (Diagram 5.7), or by the chief of the traffic departments at the regional/republican level or a designee (Diagram 5.8).[124] The information for each protocol on administrative violation is registered by the assigned police officer at the circuit level (Beketov et al., 2009). When there is not enough information to adjudicate the case within the regular three-day process, the potential violation is investigated through an administrative investigation (*administrativenoe rassledovanie*), which can take up to one month.[125] Cases for which decrees on administrative violation are issued immediately are considered adjudicated and do not require referral to the chief of police or other agency. The adjudicated decision from the chief of police can be appealed to the superior police officer or sometimes in court.[126]

5.2.5 Internal Affairs Agency Authority to Protect Public Order

The major police units responsible for providing street-level public order are patrol and post services (*patrulno-postovaya slyzhba,* PPS) of the MVD circuit departments (Diagram 5.7). They are structured as typical military units with battalions, companies, and platoons. Their main duties include patrolling the streets and providing police presence for the protection of life and property, taking original victim complaints, [127] protecting crime scenes, preventing and interrupting crimes and administrative violations, "hot pursuit" and detention of suspects, assistance of citizens in cases of emergency, and any other measures needed for public order protection (Popov, 2005).[128]

One of the major administrative violations encountered by the officers of the PPS is "petit hooliganism," a broad term used by the Code of Administrative Violations to describe actions disturbing the public peace and order (Girko, 2006).[129] In cases when the police officer witnessed the petit hooliganism or received reports about it, he could bring the perpetrator to the police precinct to issue the protocol on administrative violations following the procedure described above.

In cities like Moscow and St. Petersburg, which have special rules for the registration of residents and visitors,[130] the PPS officers are responsible for checking for the proper registration of individuals that are encountered in public. Even though these municipal rules are often in direct violation of the right to freedom of movement as provided by Russian law,[131] police officers of the PPS continue to enforce the local policies (Schaible, 2001).

Another typical administrative offense suppressed by PPS officers is public drunkenness.[132] In cases where PPS officers encounter a severely intoxicated individual, they can place him into a "sobering up" station (*vytrezvitel*). The intoxicated person can be detained in such a station for several hours until he/she sobers up (Korenev, 1999). The existence of sobering up stations within the MVD system is a grey area of Russian legislation. Officially, these MVD units were regulated through the Decree of MVD of USSR #105 issued on May 30, 1985.[133] This document is no longer in effect and no other document can be found explaining the existence of sobering up stations within the MVD police system. The new law "On Police" prescribes that all sobering up stations should be moved from the MVD to the Ministry of Health by the beginning of 2012.[134]

It is unclear now whether this change would have any effect on the level of services offered by the sobering up station, because public intoxication continues to be an administrative offense enforced by internal affairs agencies.

Unlike patrol and post services, "district police officers" (*uchastkovye upolnomochenyye*) are responsible for the protection of public order in their city district or village at the circuit department level (Diagram 5.7). District police officers conduct continuous surveillance by monitoring the most dangerous areas, visiting troubled families, and accepting citizens' complaints about disturbances of the peace, fights, and other minor issues. The district police officers are typically required to reside in the territory of their district and also should have a separate office where they hold regular hours to accept citizens' complaints (Girko, 2006).[135] The district officers are concerned with preventing use of drugs, binge drinking, prostitution, and unattended minors.[136] In cases of minor crimes, district police officers can conduct the operative search actions in order to solve the crime because they are the ones who know the territory best (Korenev, 1999).

5.2.6 Internal Affairs Agency Authorities in the Area of Juvenile Delinquency

Most police work related to juvenile delinquency is done at the circuit level by the "units on work of juvenile affairs" (*podrazdeleniya po delam nesovershennoletnikh*, abbreviated as PDN (Diagram 5.7). These police officers of juvenile units (termed PDN inspectors) are primarily concerned with juveniles who are drug addicts or truants, and those who have committed various administrative violations or crimes, before they reached the age of criminal liability. Additionally, the PDN addresses juveniles who are currently criminal suspects, juvenile defendants released on their own recognizance or bail, and juveniles who were convicted of the crimes and released on parole.[137] The major goal of the PDN is to prevent further juvenile delinquency; therefore, these units are charged with duties to conduct routine preventive interviews and to search for adult persons who encourage juvenile delinquency (Girko, 2006).

At the circuit level of MVD departments, there also are "centers of detention for juvenile delinquents" (*tsentry vremennogo soderzhaniya dlya nesovershennoletnikh pravonarushitelei*) that provide short-term detention of juveniles for PDN units.[138] The PDN units have the right to bring a juvenile suspected of committing a crime, or an administrative violation, to the police precinct and hold that person for up to three hours.[139] Juveniles detained in the police precinct can be subjected to personal searches. Juveniles who are suspected of the commission of especially heinous crimes, or those escaped from special boarding schools for juvenile offenders, can be detained in the centers for up to 48 hours.[140] Further detention in the center for up to 30 days is allowed by a court order.[141] The PDN units work closely with district police officers who typically have information on families with potential problems. PDN agencies also partner with other non-MVD structures (commissions for juvenile affairs, agencies of guardianship, and local health care institutions) (Korenev, 1999).

5.2.7 Internal Affairs Agencies with Traffic Control Authority

"Traffic" police (*gosudarstvennaya inspectsiya bezopasnosti dorozhnogo dvizheniya*, (abbreviated GIBDD) is a subunit of the MVD system in charge of traffic control for automobiles (Diagram 5.8). Its main functions include the issuance of driver's licenses, registration of automobiles, and enforcement of traffic rules for both drivers and pedestrians (Bozhev, 2002a). It is the police unit most frequently encountered by the public as car ownership rates continue to grow in Russia (Agafonov, 2008).

The traffic police are responsible for conducting both the theoretical and practical driving examination in order to issue a driver's license. The theoretical examination includes knowledge of the Rules of Traffic Movement (*pravila dorozhnogo dvizheniya*, abbreviated PDD)[142] and the practical exam includes driving skills on the road and special training area.[143] The subdepartments of driver's license examinations are located in multiple places in large cities or in the circuit centers of rural areas (Diagram 5.8).

The traffic police are also responsible for registration of all vehicles for persons in their jurisdiction.[144] Driving without registration or with an expired registration is an administrative offense.[145] Until 2012, the traffic police also conducted a technical examination (*tech osmotr*) of vehicles prior to registering them.[146] Starting in 2012, this function was transferred to privately owned dealerships or companies that are licensed and controlled by the traffic police.[147]

Numerous units of traffic patrol services (*dorozhno-patrulnaya slyzhba*, (abbreviated DPS) are responsible for enforcing driving rules of traffic movement (PDD).[148] Most violations of PDD are administrative offenses punishable by a warning, fine, or suspension of the driver's license.[149] When enforcing the rules of traffic movement, motorized units of the DPS or stationary units on the roads (*posty DPS*) can stop vehicles in order to check their registration, driver's license, or in cases when the traffic inspector witnessed a violation of the PDD. In cases when the traffic inspector has reason to believe that evidence of administrative (or criminal) violation can be found in the detained vehicle, the inspector can search the vehicle without a court order.[150] In situations where there is evidence to suspect that the driver is intoxicated, the traffic inspector can order the driver to discontinue driving (*otstranenie ot upravleniya*), order the driver to take a sobriety test (*osvidetelstvovanie na sostoyanie opyanenia*),[151] and send the driver to a healthcare institution to take a comprehensive sobriety test (*meditsinskoe osvidetelstvovanie na sostoyanie opyaneniya*).[152]

When the inspector can observe that the vehicle is apparently malfunctioning or when the use of the vehicle can be dangerous to other drivers, the inspector can order the vehicle seized and impounded to the special traffic police parking lot. [153] Vehicles also can be impounded for violation of parking rules and other municipal regulations.[154] In cases of traffic accidents, units of the DPS are called to the accident in order to provide assistance and document violations of the PDD.[155] With few exceptions, the DPS traffic inspectors follow the general rules issued for processing the administrative violations described above (Korenev, 1999).[156] Special battalions of the DPS also provide convoy services to high-ranking government officials and other designated persons. The full list of duties performed by the traffic police can be found in the administrative regulations for the GIBDD.[157]

5.2.8 Internal Affairs Agency Authorities in the Area of Licensing

The licensing duties of agencies of internal affairs mainly refer to two major areas: (1) control of guns and (2) regulation of private detective and security activities. There is no constitutional right to bear arms in Russia; however, individuals and companies can own some types of guns for hunting, sport events, conducting private detective activities (private security), and even for self-defense.[158] The individuals and companies have to obtain a license to purchase guns and also register them with the agencies of interior affairs after purchase.[159] Most licenses for purchase are issued by the license units of the circuit departments (Diagram 5.7). The republican, or regional level, departments only issue licenses to sell, exhibit, or collect guns (Diagram 5.6), and the licensing unit of the central apparatus within the main department of public order deals mainly with licenses to manufacture guns (Diagram 5.3) (Korenev, 1999).[160]

In order to obtain a license to purchase a gun, the individuals and companies have to file an application that should be reviewed within one month. The agencies of internal affairs run a background check on all applicants and can deny a license in cases when the person has a history of mental health issues or a criminal record (Agafonov, 2008).[161] The registration of purchased, or otherwise acquired guns, should be done immediately after the transaction. Failure to obtain a license or register a gun is an administrative violation punishable by a fine or administrative arrest for up to 15 days.[162]

Internal affairs agencies also are responsible for licensing of private detective and private security activities. The license to conduct private detective activities (*chastnaya-detekitivnaya deyatelnost*) is issued for individuals, whereas the license to conduct private security activities (*chastnaya okhrannaya deyatelnost*) is given to companies.[163] In both cases, the individuals and companies apply to the agencies of internal affairs and are subject to background checks. The applicants are required to have some legal education or law enforcement experience or to take special training to apply.[164] Both circuit and regional/republican departments have a right to issue the detective licenses (Korenev, 1999). Individual applicants are subject to mandatory fingerprinting as well.[165] Failure to obtain a license is an administrative violation punishable by a fine.[166]

5.2.9 Activities of the Internal Affairs' Agencies (Agencies of Federal Migration Service) in the Areas of Passport Control and Registration of Citizen Movement

Even though the federal migration service (*federalnaya migratsionnaya sluzhba,* (abbreviated FMS) is now an independent unit and not a part of the public safety police, it is still controlled by the minister of the MVD and, by this virtue, is a part of the agencies of internal affairs.[167] This service is important because, like traffic police, this is one of the most frequently publicly encountered services of the MVD system. The main duties of the FMS include issuing internal and foreign travel passports for Russian citizens, registration of citizens' and visitors' movements, issues of citizenship, and immigration control of foreigners.[168]

Following the Soviet tradition, Russia continues to issue two types of passports for their citizens: an internal passport to use within Russia and a foreign passport (*zagranpassport*) to enter and leave the Russian Federation. This division was done by the Soviet authorities to ensure control over the movement of citizens trying to leave the Soviet Union (Matthews, 1993). The internal passport is issued for every Russian citizen at the age of 14 by the FMS and should be exchanged at the ages of 20 and 45.[169] The internal passport contains not only the identification information, but also an information about marriages, divorces, children, military registrations (for males), and registration of the main place of residence.

Again, following the Soviet tradition, Russian authorities continue to control movement of their citizens within the country through the institution of registration at the main place of residence. The registration also is required for visiting other places for a period of 90 or more days.[170] Citizens of Russia are required to register within three days when they change their main place of residence.[171] Cities like Moscow and St. Petersburg adopted stricter rules, which require even short-term visitors to obtain registration. The registration stamp in the internal passport is important for the normal life of the Russian citizen (Korenev, 1999). Many government services are offered only when the person has a registration. Criminal suspects are more likely to be detained prior to trial simply because they do not have a permanent registration.[172] Residing without a registration at the permanent place of residence is an administrative violation punishable by a fine. The foreign passport to travel outside of Russia can be issued by the FMS only for citizens with unexpired internal passports and valid registration.[173] The external passports are valid for 10 years and need to be exchanged in the local agency of FSM.[174] FMS also issues invitations to apply for a Russian visa, register foreign visitors, and provide work permits for foreign visitors.[175]

5.3 Workforce of MVD Agencies

5.3.1 Training and Educational Institutions of the MVD System

There are currently 23 institutions of higher education within the MVD system. These are usually termed "universities," "academies," or "institutions" depending on the size of the student body and the number of majors. Most MVD institutions of higher education offer bachelor's degrees in law, but some also have programs in economics, finance, and social work. Some large institutions also have graduate programs (Kurushin, 2004). Until 2008, there were also 11 institutions of secondary education termed "police colleges," or schools of police. These institutions were accepting students without high school diplomas and requiring two to three years for the full course of studies (Kikot', 2004). The initial training for police is performed in the educational centers, which are organized at every regional or republican department of the MVD (Gilinskiy, 2007; Morn and Sergevnin, 1994).

In order to apply for study at an MVD educational institution, the individual needs to obtain a recommendation (*napravlenie*) from the MVD department in his/her permanent residence location. The recommendation is given when the local police department has a need of certain employees. After graduation, the applicant to the university is expected to work for the MVD department that provides the recommendation. In addition to the recommendation, the applicant has to pass a physical, a psychological examination, and a background check. All students of MVD universities also are required to participate in an internship with the MVD agencies that recommended them prior to graduating.[176]

Positions that typically require higher legal education are supervisory positions and positions of investigators conducting preliminary investigations. In exceptional cases, persons with a secondary legal education can be appointed as investigators if they have significant law enforcement experience. A secondary education is often sufficient for the jobs of inquirers. The centers for prevention of juvenile delinquency can employ persons with a pedagogical education. The patrol and post services, traffic patrol services, and district police officers often have only initial training in the educational centers.[177]

A degree in law from an MVD university is considered equivalent to the degree from a regular university. However, the curriculum of such universities often differs because MVD universities also need to train their students in military skills required for policing. This is often done by reducing the regular course hours of law and other disciplines (Botov, 2001). That is why critics of the MVD educational system suggest the system requires reforms to improve the quality of legal knowledge and provide better practical skills needed for police work (Kozchevnikov, 1999; Morozov and Sergevnin, 1996).[178]

One of the major criticisms of an MVD education is the lack of hands-on training on use of force, human rights, and ethnic conflicts (Lobachev, 2006; Potlachuk, 2008). While many MVD universities provide good theoretical knowledge on the subject, the practical application of this information is mostly nonexistent.[179] Many students feel unprepared to work in police precincts after graduating from MVD educational institutions (Morn and Sergevnin, 1994; Novikova, 2005). Another serious drawback is the quality of students that apply for MVD higher education. Research on MVD students show that many of them have serious psychological issues including tendencies toward unmotivated aggression and questionable morals (Abdrashitov, 2009).[180]

Despite a large educational system,[181] there is a continuous lack of qualified personnel within the MVD system (Galkin, 2001).[182] There are also high turnover rates among newly hired employees. As a result, 25% of all MVD employees have less than three years of experience (Kozchevnikov, 1999). Less than 50% of all higher ranking personal have higher education and 37% of MVD employees have only a secondary legal education. Only 46% of all investigators have higher legal education (Artem'ev, 2003). These problems are directly related to the issues of recruitment and retention of qualified personnel.

5.3.2 MVD Personnel Recruitment

The 2011 "On Police Service" law provided the main criteria for recruiting police officers, which include age, health, education, and other criteria. The individuals should be between 18 and 40 years old, have a clean bill of health, and no criminal record. Even though an MVD-related education is preferred, education from regular universities is accepted as well.

First, a preliminary review of the candidate is conducted including a "psycho-physical" examination and the initial interview. After the background check, full medical examination, and additional interviews with parents or family members, the head of the police department makes the final decision.[183] Starting in 2010, the medical examination included drug and alcoholism testing.[184] Newly hired police officers are commonly put on a probation period from three months to one year, and also should have a mentor (guarantor) who is a current police officer in the MVD. Starting in 2008, the police officers are subject as well to restrictions promulgated by the anticorruption laws.[185] This includes a requirement for higher ranking police officers to publish their income, the obligation to report any conflict of interest, or when someone offers a bribe to police officers.[186] Newly hired employees of agencies of internal affairs also are subject to mandatory fingerprinting.[187]

A poor public image of the Russian police, low wages, and increasing job requirements are important obstacles in recruiting qualified personnel for the MVD system (Novikova, 2005). Many applicants have questionable psychological evaluations and yet are accepted to work as police officers.[188] Another issue is the agency's inability to make graduates of the MVD universities take the jobs for which they were educated. Alumni of the MVD institutions routinely violate their duties to serve in the MVD after graduation, or do not take the jobs with the departments that recommended them for the education.[189] According to Botov (2001), only 57% of graduating MVD students said they would take MVD jobs after graduation as required by law, and 24% admitted they were never interested in the police service. Until 2012, there were no financial consequences for failing to take an MVD job or transfer to more prestigious units than the ones that provided the person with the recommendation. Therefore, students commonly enroll in MVD universities to obtain a free legal education and to avoid the mandatory military draft (for males) with little intention of becoming police officers. According to Botov (2001), 46% of all students admitted that they apply to MVD universities to get an education and 10% did so to avoid the military draft. Only 27% said they applied because they were interested in a police job. The new 2011 law "On Police Service" requires students to work in MVD agencies for at least five years after graduation or to reimburse the cost of their education.[190] The law does not provide any consequences for transferring to other units. It is unclear now what would be the impact of this law on the future graduates of the MVD education system.

5.3.3 Job Assessment and Motivation

The MVD workforce is highly militarized. The employees are assigned ranks from private to colonel general depending on the position, level of education, and experience.[191] The promotions are done based on position, experience, and work history. The criterion for the work assessment of each MVD unit is mainly quantitative and consists of a variety of statistical data. The data include unit levels of solving crimes, preventing potentially criminal situations, finding missing persons, accepting citizen complaints, and other relevant information. The statistical indicators are measured in comparison to the previous report period and are assessed as positive or negative dynamics.

Citizen police satisfaction surveys also are included in the assessment criteria, but do not play the most important role.[192] Usually, the MVD employees spend significant time collecting the data for the performance reports. The individual's performance is also based on a periodical certification (*attestatsiya*) that is typically done every five years.[193] In order to conduct the certification, the supervisor prepares paperwork for each employee that reflects their professional performance, intellectual abilities, physical preparedness, and emotional stability.[194] A review of the documents is performed by the certification commission (*attestatsionnaya komissiya*), which recommends continued employment, a promotion, demotion, a transfer, or termination. The commission's work is typically closed to the public and only includes members of the MVD community.[195] The individuals also can be motivated through one-time bonuses that can be monetary, early promotion, or simply a certificate of gratitude (Adyan, 2006).[196]

The MVD personnel are hierarchically subordinated. The legitimate order of a superior must be followed by the MVD employees.[197] MVD employee public criticism of agencies of interior affairs, or any government agencies, is prohibited and can be considered a serious violation of rules related to professional conduct.[198] The employees can be reprimanded for violation of these rules through warnings, demotion in rank or position, or dismissal (Adyan, 2006).[199]

In order to compensate for unlimited working hours and the difficult conditions of the service, employees of the MVD are awarded significant government benefits. In 2011, President Medvedev signed a new benefits law for MVD employees that includes increased payments for higher ranks, improved raises for extended experience, life insurance, retirement payments, healthcare allowances, higher compensation for overtime, allowances for housing, utility payments, and payments to family members of deceased police officers and other MVD employees.[200]

5.3.4 Gender Issues within the MVD Workforce

Even though Article 8 of the "decree on service in the agencies of internal affairs" provides for equal employment conditions for both males and females, the workforce of the MVD is dominated by male employees. The male dominance can be seen in the MVD universities where only 20% of all students are females (T.A. Ivanova, 2000). The unwritten rules often preclude female police officers from entering services, such as special detachment units (OMON), operative search activities, patrol and post activities, and traffic patrol services. These are physically demanding and sometimes dangerous workplaces, which often require overtime or around-the-clock service. Female employees are often deemed unfit for these conditions. The most common places of female employment within the MVD system include investigators, inquirers, the centers to prevent juvenile delinquency, passport and registration services, and a variety of auxiliary units (Romanova, 2007).

Female leadership within the MVD agencies also is rare.[201] Most often, female employees can be promoted to the deputy chair of the circuit department (as the head of the investigative department) or the leader of some other unit within the circuit or regional department (T.A. Ivanova, 2000). Our analysis failed to find any female head of the police departments at the circuit, regional, or republican level. Currently, in the central apparatus of the MVD, all eight deputy ministers are males. There are few high ranking female employees within the central apparatus who are typically employed as deputy chairs of the main departments or similar positions.[202]

In addition to unwritten rules related to female employment, there are official benefits as well that make hiring females in the MVD rather challenging. According to the Labor Code of Russia, female employees are entitled to up to three years of maternity leave with a guarantee of reemployment in their former position.[203] Female employees with small children also can receive additional time off to care for sick children that may include lengthy hospital stays and trips to the rehabilitative centers (sanatoriums).[204] There are restrictions as well on use of female employees with children for overtime and physically demanding jobs. These legally mandated interruptions and restrictions often limit promotion for female police officers and make them less desirable employees.

Gender differences also can be seen among male and female students of police academies and serving police officers. The majority of female students put family values over the career and professional development, and are willing to take jobs that would interfere less with their family life (Geizhan and Brazhenskaya, 2011). The family values became more evident among the female students during the fourth and fifth years of education. The majority of female students in police academies agree that police education is not only a way to get a job, but also a way to find a suitable husband. Up to 21% of female students in police academies are planning to be housewives and are not interested in professional employment as police officers (Brazhenskaya, 2011). Current female police officers also have strong family values. Many female police officers accept the fact that at some point they will have to leave police service to take care of their children and spouses. Female police officers are more likely to value a friendly environment, a good relationship with co-workers, climate, and stability of work over the potential of professional growth (Bobrova, 2005).

5.4 Concluding Remarks

Many issues experienced by the MVD system and policing in Russia can be attributed to its structure, functions, and issues of the workforce. The MVD system is a hierarchical and centralized system where one person—the president of Russia—is in control of all levels of policing. The president directly appoints chairs of all MVD levels except for the lowest level: the circuit department. There are no checks and balances for any of these vast presidential powers. Neither legislative nor court authorities have any impact on presidential control over the entire MVD system.

The structure of the MVD system is extremely formalized. Every unit of the MVD follows the structure prescribed by the minister and any deviation from it has to be approved by a ministerial decree. The centralized structure does not provide flexibility for any local or regional conditions unless approved by the central authorities. Beginning in 2011, the entire MVD system was funded from the federal budget, which disallows the local authorities to have any voice in the decisions of policing in their regions.

The MVD system appears to have an excessive number of management personnel. There are three levels of management (central, federal district, and regional/republican), but there is only one main level performing daily police work (circuit). Existing research shows that many of these management functions are redundant and require low-level police officers to spend most of their time completing reports in order to inform a variety of superiors about their activities.

The functions performed by the MVD are broad and include duties that in many other countries are not considered part of policing. Some of these functions are reminiscent of the Soviet past: addressing alcoholics through sobering up stations, juvenile delinquency prevention through centers on juvenile affairs, and control of hooliganism, are among those issues. Some functions, such as residency registration and the distinction between the internal and foreign passports, are clear violations of human rights. However, these policies continue to be enforced despite the declaration of freedom of movement in Russia. Many requirements for policing appear to be unrealistic. For example, the duty of the district police is to prevent all crimes from occurring in urban district areas along with the supervision of all juvenile delinquents for the circuit centers on juvenile affairs. Such demands motivate police officers to create either formalistic or "cooked" reports in order to satisfy these requirements.

Despite the variety of instructions, many important authorities of police officers continue to be poorly regulated and are highly discretionary. This is true for traffic stops and vehicle searches and the seizure of goods for the purposes of administrative investigation. The fact that police also can arrest a person for 48 hours prior to judicial review, even for an administrative violation, also appears to be discretionary and potentially excessive.

The police workforce is excessively militarized and includes the assignments of ranks, positions, and requirement of following the superior's orders. While these requirements may be justifiable for certain police units, such as traffic patrols, patrol and post services, or special purpose detachments (OMON), it does not appear to be necessary for positions such as detectives or investigators.

Whereas the Criminal Procedural Code of Russia requires the investigators and inquirers[205] to be independent in their legal decisions, the law "On Police Service" suggests that all legitimate orders of superiors have to be strictly followed by all MVD employees. Extreme militarization and hierarchical structure creates a fruitful environment for nepotism, corruption, and abuse of power.[206]

The educational system of the MVD is outdated and does not provide adequate training for future police officers. The requirement that a student needs a recommendation from an MVD agency to obtain an education at a MVD institution seems to be counterproductive. Without clear controls on who gets a recommendation and why, such a requirement simply promotes nepotism and further corruption. The same is true for the requirement of a mentorship for newly hired police officers. The current recruitment process is nontransparent, and many suggest that open competition should be conducted to recruit the best cadres to the Russian police service (Zentsova, 2011).

The main assessment tool of the MVD system also appears to be problematic. The quantitative indices of annual changes in solved crimes, registered incident reports, and other statistics do not always motivate police officers to perform their functions efficiently. Instead, it creates concern about poor statistics or can instigate the police to create new crimes when needed, or refuse to register potentially unsolvable crimes. It also does not account for changes that occur in the area regardless of the police work (new crimes introduced by legislation, changes in socioeconomic conditions of the regions, etc.). Public opinion obtained from a simple citizens' survey plays a limited role in these quantitative indices and can hardly be considered an effective mechanism of public police accountability.

Retention of qualified cadres remains a serious problem. According to the survey conducted by the Union of Police Workers, only 39.5% of police officers are satisfied with their work.[207] Many police officers suffer from stress and have psychological issues (Semenova, 2009). The major reasons for dissatisfaction are low wages and unpaid overtime work (Novikova, 2005). Other factors include poor conditions of police facilities, unrealistic demands from superior officers, and safety concerns (Gladarev, 2008, 2011b).

One of the major issues of policing in Russia, which is grounded in its centralized structure, broad and discretionary authorities, and hierarchical subordination of personnel, is the lack of effective accountability mechanisms. The internal security services of the MVD are not independent in their decisions and subordinated to the chairs of the corresponding departments, the minister, and the president. The certification of individual police officers is an internal process unavailable to the public, media, or other independent entities and makes the MVD prone to arbitrariness and abuse of power (Zhukov, 2004).[208] The main appointments within the system, budgeting of the MVD, and any other major decisions are nontransparent to the public as well. Little justification is given to the public about any of these decisions. Moreover, the MVD system has the right to decide which information about their work is released to the public. The newly created investigative committee, which is also highly centralized and hierarchical in structure, is responsible for conducting criminal investigations into the cases of police abuse and corruption. It continues to be questionable whether this agency, which is also directly subordinate to the president, can effectively curb police misconduct in Russia.

Endnotes

1. Article 65 of the Constitution lists the current subjects of the Russian Federation. Retrieved on July 7, 2011 from www.consultant.ru
2. Most "subjects of federation" are either republics (when there is a distinct ethnic group residing on the territory) or the regions (when there is no distinct ethnic group). Other forms of subjects include "autonomous republic," "autonomous regions," and cities of federal significance
3. Decree of the President #849 issued on May 13, 2000. Retrieved on June 15, 2011 from www.consultant.ru
4. Articles 5 and 18 of the Regulations on MVD promulgated by the Decree of President #248 issued on March 1, 2011. Retrieved on July 7, 2011 from www.consultant.ru
5. Articles 19 and 20 18 of the Regulations on MVD promulgated by the Decree of President #248 issued on March 1, 2011. Retrieved on June 15, 2011 from www.consultant.ru
6. According to the Decree of the President #1039 issued on July 18, 1996 (Article 2). Retrieved on June 15, 2011 from www.consultant.ru
7. The federal district departments of the MVD were established by the Decree of the President #644 issued on June 4, 2001. Retrieved on June 15, 2011 from www.consultant.ru
8. Decree of the President #849 issued on May 13, 2000. Retrieved on June 15, 2011 from www.consultant.ru
9. According to the Decree of the President #248 of March 1, 2011. Retrieved on June 15, 2011 from www.consultant.ru
10. Provision G of the Decree of the President #208 issued on February 18, 2010 lists 10,000 employees as the maximum number. However, the most recent document, the Decree of the President #248 issued on March 1, 2011 provides in Article 3 the number of 9,264 employees. Retrieved on July 7, 2011 from www.consultant.ru
11. Decree of MVD #500 issued on June 24, 2005. Retrieved on June 15, 2011 from www.consultant.ru
12. Originally, the independent Investigative Committee was established by the Decree of the President #1422 issued on November 23, 1998. However, it only became a working agency after the Federal Law #403-FZ was issued on December 12, 2010.
13. The description of the department's goals is taken from the official MVD site. Retrieved on July 1, 2011 from www.mvd.ru
14. Decree of MVD #982 issued on November 8, 2001. Retrieved on June 15, 2011 from www.consultant.ru

15. Decree of MVD #767 issued on November 25, 2004. Retrieved on June 15, 2011 from www.consultant.ru; Decree of MVD #396 issued on April 28, 2007 (unpublished).
16. Description of department's goals is taken from the official MVD site. Retrieved on July 1, 2011 from www.mvd.ru
17. Decree of MVD #1030 issued on November 23, 2001. Retrieved on June 15, 2011 from www.consultant.ru; Decree of MVD #828 issued on September 12, 2004 (unpublished).
18. Decree of MVD #308 issued on April 23, 2005. Retrieved on June 15, 2011 from www.consultant.ru
19. Description of department's goals is taken from the official MVD site. Retrieved on July 1, 2011 from www.mvd.ru. According to the official site, currently there are 1.45 million private apartments, 475,400 other facilities, and 5,725 cars that are protected through the extraministerial services of the MVD.
20. Decree of the President #281 issued on March 3, 1999. Retrieved on June 15, 2011 from www.consultant.ru
21. Decree of President of Russia #306 issued on March 11, 2003 "On some questions to improve government administration." Retrieved on June 15, 2011 from www.consultant.ru
22. Established on the basis of the Decree of the President #1316 issued on September 6, 2008. Retrieved on June 15, 2011 from www.consultant.ru
23. Decree of MVD #500 issued on June 24, 2005. Federal Law #119-FZ issued on August 20, 2004, and Federal Law #45-FZ issued on April 20, 1995. Retrieved on June 15, 2011 from www.consultant.ru
24. According to the Decree of the President #928 issued on July 19, 2004. Retrieved on July 7, 2011 from www.consultant.ru
25. For example, President Medvedev suggested in his public speech that separation of the FMS from the MVD is going to happen soon. See article published by *Moscow Komsomolets* on February 2, 2011. Retrieved on July 1, 2011 from http://www.km.ru/news/medvedev-zayavil-o-skorom-otdelenii-fms-ot-mvd
26. Department K currently manages detective work on computer-related crimes.
27. Article 15 of the Decree of the President #248 issued on March 1, 2011. Retrieved on June 15, 2011 from www.consultant.ru
28. According to the Decree of the President #248 of March 1, 2011. Retrieved on June 15, 2011 from www.consultant.ru
29. Decree of MVD #925 issued on December 8, 2009. Retrieved on June 15, 2011 from www.consultant.ru
30. Decree of the President #849 issued on May 13, 2000. Retrieved on June 15, 2011 from www.consultant.ru
31. According to the Decree of the President #248 of March 1, 2011. Retrieved on June 15, 2011 from www.consultant.ru
32. This decree is no longer in effect, but we failed to locate any document that would outline the structure of the general main department of the MVD in the district that replaced it. Thus, we had to rely on specific decrees and Web sites of the agencies to re-create the structure.

33. For example, see the Decree of MVD #642 issued on August 15, 2006 on establishing the Far East main department of the MVD, or the Decree of MVD #641 issued on August 15, 2006 on establishing the Siberian main department of the MVD. Retrieved on July 7, 2011 from www.consultant.ru
34. See Decree of MVD #946 issued on October 31, 2008; the main departments in federal districts are charged with fighting the most serious crimes, such as extremism, corruption, and human and weapon trafficking. For example, for details, see official Web sites for the Main Department of MVD in Volga federal district: http://www.mvdpfo.ru/ru/top/48/: Ural federal district: http://www.mvd-urfo.ru/; Siberian federal district: http://www.sibfo.ru/mvd/about.php; Far East federal district: http://www.mvddfo.ru/MVD
35. Article 5 of the Decree #634 issued on July 4, 2001. Retrieved on June 15, 2011 from www.consultant.ru
36. According to the Decree of MVD #634 issued on July 4, 2001 and the information collected from the Web sites of main departments of the MVD in the federal districts.
37. Established on the basis of Decree of MVD #634 issued on August 13, 2003. Retrieved on June 15, 2011 from www.consultant.ru
38. The services that were included in the term "criminal police" are listed in the Decree of the Government of Russia #925 issued on December 7, 2000. Retrieved on June 15, 2011 from www.consultant.ru
39. Decree of the President #1316 issued on August 6, 2008 (Article 1). Retrieved on June 15, 2011 from www.consultant.ru
40. The structure and functions of these units are determined through the Decree of MVD #715 issued on October 4, 2005. Retrieved on June 15, 2011 from www.consultant.ru
41. Decree of MVD #1065 issued on December 5, 2008. Retrieved on June 15, 2011 from www.consultant.ru
42. Decree of MVD #618 issued on September 28, 1998. Retrieved on June 15, 2011 from www.consultant.ru
43. About the duties of "district police officers" (*uchastkovye*), please see the Decree of MVD #900 issued on September 16, 2002. Retrieved on June 15, 2011 from www.consultant.ru
44. The description of department's goals is taken from the official regional MVD site. Retrieved on July 1, 2011 from http://www.krasguvd.ru/structure/; http://mvd.tatarstan.ru/rus/structure.htm ; http://www.mvdrb.ru/
45. On description of work of Moscow special purpose detachment unit, see an article by Meyr (2001).
46. Decree of MVD #174 issued on February 26, 2000 (unpublished).
47. The services that were included in the term "police of public safety" are listed in the Decree of the Government of Russia #926 issued on December 7, 2000. Retrieved on June 15, 2011 from www.consultant.ru
48. Decree of the Government of Russia #926 issued on December 7, 2000. Retrieved on June 15, 2011 from www.consultant.ru
49. Decree of the President #1468 issued on December 24, 2009 (Article 1) and Article 47 of the Federal law "On Police" #3-FZ issued on February 7, 2011. Retrieved on June 15, 2011 from www.consultant.ru

50. The description of the department's goals is taken from the official regional MVD site. Retrieved on July 1, 2011 from http://www.guvd-kuban.ru/kuban/units/
51. Article 15 of the Decree of President #249 issued on March 1, 2011. Retrieved on June 15, 2011 from www.consultant.ru
52. These decrees are not openly published, thus we had to analyze the specific structure of regional/republican departments through their official Web sites.
53. According to the Decree by the President of Russia #249 issued on March 1, 2011 and the information collected from the Web sites of departments of MVD in the republics/regions.
54. Federal Law #131-FZ promulgated on October 6, 2003 "On general principles of organization of local self-governance in the Russian Federation." Retrieved on June 15, 2011 from www.consultant.ru
55. For example, the city of Volgograd, which is the capital of the Volgograd region, has eight administrative districts and, thus, eight district police departments. There are at least 80,000 residents in each of these districts.
56. According to Beketov et al. (2009), the district police departments are established in settlements with population of at least 12,000 to 15,000 residents.
57. Law #3297-1 issued on July 14, 1992 "On closed administrative territorial entity." Retrieved on June 15, 2011 from www.consultant.ru
58. According to Panteleev (2002), there are typically 3,000 individuals residing at each administrative district supervised by one district police officer.
59. Decree of MVD #900 issued on September 16, 2002. Retrieved on June 15, 2011 from www.consultant.ru
60. Decree of the MVD #569 issued on May 26, 2000. Retrieved on June 15, 2011 from www.consultant.ru
61. Article 13 of the Decree of MVD #222 issued on April 22, 2011. Retrieved on June 15, 2011 from www.consultant.ru
62. According to the Decree by President #222 issued on April 22, 2011 and the information collected from the Web sites of circuit departments of MVD.
63. The Decree of MVD #982 issued on September 28, 1998. Retrieved on June 15, 2011 from www.consultant.ru
64. The law "On technical reviews" #170-FZ issued on July 1, 2011 was enacted on January 1, 2012. Retrieved on July 10, 2011 from www.consultant.ru
65. According to the Decree of Minister of MVD #618 issued on September 28, 1998 and the Decree of Minister of MVD #982 issued on November 8, 2001. Retrieved on June 15, 2011 from www.consultant.ru
66. Article 2 of the Law "On Interior Troops" #27FZ issued on February 6, 1997. Retrieved on June 15, 2011 from www.consultant.ru
67. Article 15 of the Law "On Interior Troops" #27FZ issued on February 6, 1997. Retrieved on June 15, 2011 from www.consultant.ru
68. The structure and functions of regional command are determined by Decree of MVD #942 issued on October 26, 2007. Retrieved on October 7, 2011 from www.consultant.ru
69. For basic organization of interior troops, please see their official Web site at http://www.vvmvd.ru/. Retrieved on October 7, 2011.
70. Law #3297-1 issued on July 14, 1992 "On closed administrative territorial entity." Retrieved on June 15, 2011 from www.consultant.ru

71. These units are likely to have their own names in addition to the numbers. For example, the Siberian regional district has two special purposes units named *Ermak* and *Kuzbass*.
72. See the following documents for more details: the Decree of the President #281 issued on March 3, 1999, the Decree of President #627 issued on June 1, 2005, and the Decree of MVD #884 issued on November 15, 2003. Retrieved on June 15, 2011 from www.consultant.ru
73. According to the Law "On Interior Troops" #27FZ issued on February 6, 1997, the Decree of the President #281 issued on March 3, 1999, the Decree of the President #627 issued on June 1, 2005, and the Decree of MVD #884 issued on November 15, 2003. Retrieved on June 15, 2011 from www.consultant.ru
74. Article 2 of the Federal Law "On Operative-Search Activities" #144-FZ issued on August 12, 1995. Retrieved on June 15, 2011 from www.consultant.ru
75. Article 6 of the Federal Law "On Operative-Search Activities" #144-FZ issued on August 12, 1995. Retrieved on June 15, 2011 from www.consultant.ru
76. Article 8 of the Federal Law "On Operative-Search Activities" #144-FZ issued on August 12, 1995. Retrieved on June 6, 2011 from www.consultant.ru
77. Details of "operative-search activities of agencies of internal affairs" can be found in the Decree of MVD #249 issued on March 30, 2010. Retrieved on July 7, 2011 from www.consultant.ru
78. Article 7 of the Federal Law "On Operative-Search Activities" #144-FZ issued on August 12,1995. Retrieved on June 15, 2011 from www.consultant.ru
79. Decree of MVD #249 issued on March 30, 2010 (Appendices 1 and 2).
80. Article 8 of the Federal Law "On Operative-Search Activities" #144-FZ issued on August 12, 1995. Retrieved on June 15, 2011 from www.consultant.ru
81. Ibid.
82. Article 9 of the Federal Law "On Operative-Search Activities" #144-FZ issued on August 12, 1995. Retrieved on June 15, 2011 from www.consultant.ru
83. Ibid.
84. Article 11 of the Federal Law "On Operative-Search Activities" #144-FZ issued on August 12, 1995. Retrieved on June 15, 2011 from www.consultant.ru
85. The Constitutional Court Ruling in the case of M. B. Nikolskyi and M. I. Sapronov issued on February 4, 1999. Retrieved on June 15, 2011 from www.consultant.ru
86. Article 162 of the CPC of Russia of 2001. Retrieved on July 1, 2011 from www.consultant.ru
87. Article 150 of the CPC of Russia of 2001. Retrieved on July 1, 2011 from www.consultant.ru
88. According to the official crime statistics for 2010 provided by MVD. Retrieved from www.mvd.ru on July 11, 2011. In comparison, the investigative committee only investigated 9% of all cases and FBS investigated 0.2% of all cases and drug control agencies investigated 4% of all cases.
89. Articles 140–149 of the CPC of Russia of 2001. Retrieved on July 1, 2011 from www.consultant.ru
90. Articles 91, 97–101, 108 of the CPC of Russia of 2001. Retrieved on July 1, 2011 from www.consultant.ru
91. Articles 91, 97–101, 108 of the CPC of Russia of 2001. Retrieved on July 1, 2011 from www.consultant.ru

92. Article 109 of the CPC of Russia of 2001. Retrieved on July 1, 2011 from www.consultant.ru
93. Articles 73–90 of the CPC of Russia of 2001. Retrieved on July 1, 2011 from www.consultant.ru
94. Articles 187–192 of the CPC of Russia of 2001. Retrieved on July 1, 2011 from www.consultant.ru
95. Articles 195–207 of the CPC of Russia of 2001. Retrieved on July 1, 2011 from www.consultant.ru
96. Articles 182–186 of the CPC of Russia of 2001. Retrieved on July 1, 2011 from www.consultant.ru
97. Articles 179–180 of the CPC of Russia of 2001. Retrieved on July 1, 2011 from www.consultant.ru
98. Articles 86, 119–122 of the CPC of Russia of 2001. Retrieved on July 1, 2011 from www.consultant.ru
99. Articles 42–44 of the CPC of Russia of 2001. Retrieved on July 1, 2011 from www.consultant.ru
100. Articles 171–175 of the CPC of Russia of 2001. Retrieved on July 1, 2011 from www.consultant.ru
101. Articles 215 and 220 of the CPC of Russia of 2001. Retrieved on July 1, 2011 from www.consultant.ru
102. Articles 24 and 212 of the CPC of Russia of 2001. Retrieved on July 1, 2011 from www.consultant.ru
103. Articles 25 and 212 of the CPC of Russia of 2001. Retrieved on July 1, 2011 from www.consultant.ru
104. Articles 26 and 212 of the CPC of Russia of 2001. Retrieved on July 1, 2011 from www.consultant.ru
105. According to Radchenko (2006), 98% of all inquiries are conducted by the agencies of the MVD.
106. For some of these actions, the inquirer needs the permission of the head of the inquiry department, which is different from the rights of the investigator, who is relatively more independent.
107. Article 223 of the CPC of Russia of 2001. Retrieved on July 1, 2011 from www.consultant.ru. It is interesting to note that Article 223 was revised twice extending the term from 15 days in 2001 to 20 days in 2003 and to 30 days in 2007.
108. Articles 40 and 157 of the CPC of Russia of 2001. Retrieved on July 1, 2011 from www.consultant.ru
109. Articles 40 and 157 of the CPC of Russia of 2001. Retrieved on July 1, 2011 from www.consultant.ru.
110. Promulgated by the Federal Law #195-FZ issued on December 30, 2011. Retrieved on July 1, 2011 from www.consultant.ru.
111. Article 23.3 of the Code of Administrative Violations lists all administrative violations under the jurisdiction of MVD. Retrieved on July 1, 2011 from www.consultant.ru.
112. Articles 14.16, 14.26, and 19.2 of the Code of Administrative Violations. Retrieved on July 1, 2011 from www.consultant.ru
113. Articles 13.24, 20.1, 20.17, 20.20, and 20.21 of the Code of Administrative Violations. Retrieved on July 1, 2011 from www.consultant.ru

114. Articles 20.8, 20.10–20.12, 20.14, 20.16, 20.23, and 20.24 of the Code of Administrative Violations. Retrieved on July 1, 2011 from www.consultant.ru
115. Articles 12.1–12.37, and 19.22 of the Code of Administrative Violations. Retrieved on July 1, 2011 from www.consultant.ru
116. Article 19.15 of the Code of Administrative Violations. Retrieved on July 1, 2011 from www.consultant.ru
117. Article 28. 6 of the Code of Administrative Violations. Retrieved on July 1, 2011 from www.consultant.ru
118. Article 27.2 of the Code of Administrative Violations. Retrieved on July 1, 2011 from www.consultant.ru
119. Article 27.3 of the Code of Administrative Violations. Retrieved on July 1, 2011 from www.consultant.ru
120. Article 27.7 of the Code of Administrative Violations. Retrieved on July 1, 2011 from www.consultant.ru
121. Article 27.9 of the Code of Administrative Violations. Retrieved on July 1, 2011 from www.consultant.ru
122. Article 27.10 of the Code of Administrative Violations. Retrieved on July 1, 2011 from www.consultant.ru
123. Article 28.8 of the Code of Administrative Violations. Retrieved on July 1, 2011 from www.consultant.ru
124. Detailed regulation of this process can be found in Decree of MVD #444 issued on June 2, 2005. Retrieved on July 1, 2011 from www.consultant.ru
125. Article 28.7 of the Code of Administrative Violations. Retrieved on July 1, 2011 from www.consultant.ru
126. On the rate of success on appealing administrative cases in court, see Burnham, Maggs, and Danilenko (2003).
127. See Decree #750 issued on September 22, 2006 on how to accept citizens' complaints and document them. Retrieved on July 1, 2011 from www.consultant.ru
128. Article 7 of the Decree of MVD #80 issued on January 29, 2008. Retrieved on July 1, 2011 from www.consultant.ru
129. Article 20.1 of the Code of Administrative Violations. Retrieved on July 1, 2011 from www.consultant.ru
130. For example, for the city of Moscow, please see Decree of the Government of Moscow #859-PP issued on October 31, 2006. Retrieved on July 1, 2011 from www.consultant.ru
131. Law #5242-1 issued on June 26, 1993 "About the right on freedom of movement, and freedom to choose the place of residence." Retrieved on July 1, 2011 from www.consultant.ru
132. Article 20.21 of the Code of Administrative Violations. Retrieved on July 1, 2011 from www.consultant.ru
133. Retrieved on July 1, 2011 from www.consultant.ru
134. Article 54 of the law "On Police" #3-FZ issued on February 7, 2011. Retrieved on July 1, 2011 from www.consultant.ru
135. See Decree #750 issued on September 22, 2006 on how to accept citizens' complaints and document them. Retrieved on July 1, 2011 from www.consultant.ru
136. For detailed duties of "district police officers," see Decree of MVD #900 issued on September 16, 2002. Retrieved on July 1, 2011 from www.consultant.ru

137. Decree of MVD #569 issued on May 26, 2000. Retrieved on July 1, 2011 from www.consultant.ru
138. Decree of MVD #215 issued on April 4, 2004. Retrieved on July 1, 2011 from www.consultant.ru
139. Article 21 of the Federal Law #120-FZ issued on June 24, 1999. Retrieved on July 1, 2011 from www.consultant.ru
140. Article 22 of the Federal Law #120-FZ issued on June 24, 1999. Retrieved on July 1, 2011 from www.consultant.ru
141. Article 2.5.2 of the Decree of MVD #569 issued on May 26, 2000. Retrieved on July 1, 2011 from www.consultant.ru
142. Promulgated by the Decree of the Government of the Russian Federation #1090 issued on October 23, 1993. Retrieved on July 1, 2011 from www.consultant.ru
143. The examinations are regulated by the Decree of MVD #1395 issued on December 15, 1999. Retrieved on July 1, 2011 from www.consultant.ru
144. Decree of the Government of Russian Federation #938 issued on August 12,1994. Retrieved on July 1, 2011 from www.consultant.ru
145. Articles 12.1 and 12.2 of the Code of Administrative Violations. Retrieved on July 1, 2011 from www.consultant.ru
146. According to the Decree of the Government of the Russian Federation #880 issued on July 31, 1998, the traffic police prior to 2011 could conduct the technical inspections itself, or contract it out to the private company.
147. Federal Law #170-FZ issued on July 1, 2011. Retrieved on July 20, 2011 from www.consultant.ru. According to this law, the traffic police will continue to conduct technical inspection of the vehicle until 2014, and the drivers would be able to choose between a privately owned company and the traffic police. Starting in 2014, all technical inspections will be done by private companies only.
148. Federal Law #196-FZ issued on December 10, 1995. Retrieved on July 1, 2011 from www.consultant.ru
149. Articles 12.1–12.37 of the Code of Administrative Violations. Retrieved on July 1, 2011 from www.consultant.ru
150. Article 27.9 of the Code of Administrative Violations. Retrieved on July 1, 2011 from www.consultant.ru
151. Decree of the Government of the Russian Federation #475 issued on June 26, 2008. Retrieved on July 1, 2011 from www.consultant.ru
152. Article 27.12 of the Code of Administrative Violations. Retrieved on July 1, 2011 from www.consultant.ru
153. Article 27.13 of the Code of Administrative Violations. Retrieved on July 1, 2011 from www.consultant.ru
154. Decree of the Government of the Russian Federation #759 issued on December 18, 2003. Retrieved on July 1, 2011 from www.consultant.ru
155. Decree of the Government of the Russian Federation #647 issued on June 29, 1995. Retrieved on July 1, 2011 from www.consultant.ru
156. Decree of MVD #444 issued on June 2, 2005 determined which traffic police officers are entitled to issue a protocol on the administrative violation for certain groups of administrative charges. Retrieved on July 1, 2011 from www.consultant.ru
157. Promulgated by the Decree of MVD #185 issued on March 2, 2009. Retrieved on July 1, 2011 from www.consultant.ru

158. Federal Law #150-FZ issued on December 13, 1996. Retrieved on July 1, 2011 from www.consultant.ru
159. Article 9 of the Federal Law #150-FZ issued on December 13, 1996. Retrieved on July 1, 2011 from www.consultant.ru
160. Decree of MVD #288 issued on April 12, 1999. Federal Law #150-FZ issued on December 13, 1996. Retrieved on July 1, 2011 from www.consultant.ru
161. Decree of MVD #288 issued on April 12, 1999. Federal Law #150-FZ issued on December 13, 1996. Retrieved on July 1, 2011 from www.consultant.ru
162. Article 20.8 of the Code of Administrative Violations. Retrieved on July 1, 2011 from www.consultant.ru
163. Law #2487-1 issued on March 11, 1992. of the Code of Administrative Violations. Retrieved on July 1, 2011 from www.consultant.ru
164. Decree of MVD #447 issued on June 19, 2006. Retrieved on July 1, 2011 from www.consultant.ru
165. Article 9 of the Federal Law #128-FZ issued on July 25, 1998. Retrieved on July 1, 2011 from www.consultant.ru
166. Article 20.16 the Code of Administrative Violations. Retrieved on July 1, 2011 from www.consultant.ru
167. Decree of the President of Russia #248 issued on March 10, 2011. Retrieved on July 1, 2011 from www.consultant.ru
168. Decree of the President of Russia #928 issued on July 19, 2004. Retrieved on July 1, 2011 from www.consultant.ru
169. Article 7 of the Decree of the Government of Russia #828 issued on July 8, 1997. Retrieved on July 1, 2011 from www.consultant.ru
170. Article 9 of the Decree of the Government of Russia #713 issued on July 17, 1995. Retrieved on July 1, 2011 from www.consultant.ru
171. Article 31 of the Decree of the Government of Russia #713 issued on July 17, 1995. Retrieved on July 1, 2011 from www.consultant.ru
172. Article 91 Part 2 of the Criminal Procedural Code of Russia. Retrieved on July 1, 2011 from www.consultant.ru
173. Federal Law #114-FZ issued on August 15, 1996. Retrieved on July 1, 2011 from www.consultant.ru
174. Ibid.
175. Decree of the President of Russia #928 issued on July 19, 2004. Retrieved on July 1, 2011 from www.consultant.ru
176. Decree of MVD #158 issued on April 7, 1993. Retrieved on July 1, 2011 from www.consultant.ru
177. General requirements for education corresponding to the appropriate police rank are established in Article 9 of the 2011 law "On service in the agencies of internal affairs" FZ #342 issued on November 30, 2011. Retrieved on December 1, 2011 from www.consultant.ru
178. On issues of police training, please see report by Public Verdict at: http://publicverdict.ru/articles_images/10169_56719_suslov.pdf
179. For details on proposed changes to police education, see, for example, "The Concept of MVD Reforming" developed by the group of nongovernmental organizations (NGOs) in 2010. Retrieved on July 25, 2012 from http://publicverdict.ru/topics/reform/8104.html

180. According to the official MVD statistics, 21% of MVD students have serious psychological issues and are not recommended for police service. Data retrieved from report by the Human Resources Department of MVD "Psychological climate in OVD." Retrieved on July 25, 2012 from http://sartraccc.ru/Pub/suharenko.pdf
181. According to Kurushin (2004), in 2004 there were 101,592 students in all educational institutions of MVD.
182. According to Galkin (2001), the lack of personnel in MVD in general ranges from 5 to 15%.
183. Articles 10–39 of the Decree of MVD #386 issued on May 19, 2009. Retrieved on July 1, 2011 from www.consultant.ru
184. Article 8 of the Decree of Supreme Council of Russian Federation #4202-1 issued on December 23, 1992. Retrieved on July 1, 2011 from www.consultant.ru
185. Articles 9.1 ad 12 of the Decree of Supreme Council of Russian Federation #4202-1 issued on December 23, 1992. Retrieved on July 1, 2011 from www.consultant.ru
186. Articles 8–11 of Federal Law #273-FZ issued on December 25, 2008. Retrieved on July 1, 2011 from www.consultant.ru; see also Decree of MVD #1038 issued on December 14, 1999. Retrieved on July 1, 2011 from www.consultant.ru
187. Federal Law #128-FZ issued on July 25, 1998. Retrieved on July 1, 2011 from www.consultant.ru
188. According to the official MVD statistics, 339 applicants who failed psychological evaluations were hired in 2009. Nine percent of the entire police workforce has documented psychological issues. On the management level, 526 were found to have "inadequate" capabilities due to psychological problems. Data retrieved from report by the Human Resources Department of MVD "Psychological climate in OVD." Retrieved on July 25, 2012 from http://sartraccc.ru/Pub/suharenko.pdf
189. On common psychological profiles of MVD students and applicants to the MVD institutions, see, for example, Borodavko (2005), Gavrilin (2001), Panina (2006), and Shelepova (2004).
190. Article 76, Par 12 of the law "On Police Service" #342-FZ issued on November 30, 2011. Retrieved on January 12, 2011 from www.consultant.ru
191. Article 6 of the Decree of Supreme Council of Russia #4202-1 issued on December 23, 1992. Retrieved on July 1, 2011 from www.consultant.ru
192. For details, see Decree of MVD #25 issued on January 19, 2010. Retrieved on July 1, 2011 from www.consultant.ru
193. Article 17 of the Decree of Supreme Council of Russia #4202-1 issued on December 23, 1992. Retrieved on July 1, 2011 from www.consultant.ru
194. Article 9.7 of the Decree of MVD #1039 issued on December 14, 1999. Retrieved on July 1, 2011 from www.consultant.ru
195. Articles 9.16–9.27 of the Decree of MVD #1039 issued on December 14, 1999. Retrieved on July 1, 2011 from www.consultant.ru
196. Article 36 of the of the Decree of Supreme Council of Russia #4202-1 issued on December 23, 1992. Retrieved on July 1, 2011 from www.consultant.ru
197. According to Article 286.1 of the Criminal Code of Russia, the intentional noncompliance of an order by a superior police officer can be deemed a criminal offense and punished by two years of imprisonment.

198. Article 34 of the Decree of Supreme Council of Russia #4202-1 issued on December 23, 1992. Retrieved on July 1, 2011 from www.consultant.ru
199. Article 37 of the of the Decree of Supreme Council of Russia #4202-1 issued on December 23, 1992. Retrieved on July 1, 2011 from www.consultant.ru
200. Federal Law #247-FZ issued on July 19,2011. Retrieved on July 25, 2011 from www.consultant.ru
201. According to Akhamadiev (2007), there are only 27 colonels and 97 lieutenant colonels in the entire law enforcement and military systems of Russia.
202. For example, see the biography of Tatyana Moskalkova who worked as the deputy chair of the legal department within the central apparatus before getting elected to the State *Duma*. Retrieved on July 22, 2011 from http://ria.ru/spravka/20100929/280535740.html
203. Articles 254–256 of the Labor Code promulgated by Federal Law #197-FZ issued on December 30, 2001. Retrieved on July 25, 2011 from www.consultant.ru
204. Articles 262–263 of the Labor Code promulgated by Federal Law #197-FZ issued on December 30, 2001. Retrieved on July 25, 2011 from www.consultant.ru
205. Articles 38 and 41 of the Code of Criminal Procedure of Russia of 2001. Retrieved on July 1, 2011 from www.consultant.ru
206. The psychological studies of police culture suggest that police organizational culture is extremely hierarchical, formalized, and bureaucratic. The police superiors often value industrious and loyal officers who execute their orders without questions. As a result, police officers admit to valuing orders of superiors over the rule of law (Berezin, 2011).
207. The survey conducted by unions of police officers in Moscow in 2001. The report retrieved on July 11, 2012 from http://www.prof-police.ru. It is interesting to note that in the study conducted by Pelfrey (2005), the high-ranking police officials and managers demonstrated high levels of job satisfaction.
208. According to Zhukov (2004), 33% of surveyed police officer did not believe that certification contributes to professional development of police officers, 50% believed that their chair was professionally unprepared to conduct certification, and 21% believed that the certification decision was biased and arbitrary.

Public–Police Relations in Modern Russia[1] 6

6.1 General Public Views of the Russian Police

Prior to 1989, public views on the Russian police were considered a state secret and were not openly available (Inkeles, 1950). Without releasing specific data, the Soviet literature traditionally insisted that the public prestige of police officers was high and an absolute majority of Soviet citizens were satisfied with the work of police (Efremova et al., 1984). However, the studies published after *perestroika* suggested otherwise (Krivel'skaya, 1990). The summary of major studies on public police satisfaction conducted between 1990 and 2011 is presented in Table 6.1. Whereas the studies differ in methodology and sampling, the findings clearly indicate that, in the past 20 years, Russian society was predominately dissatisfied with police work (Shepeleva, 2005b). At any given time during the past 20 years, less than 50% of respondents were satisfied with the police, and public dissatisfaction ranged anywhere between 27% and 86.7%. A similar situation can be found when looking at the public trust of the Russian police. Table 6.2 presents a summary of major Russian studies on police trust published between 1989 and 2010. According to this research, public trust of the police ranges between 11% and 45% and public distrust in some years was as high as 75%.

In addition to low levels of public police satisfaction and trust, many Russian respondents do not see any improvements in police work. Table 6.3 indicates that at any time, except for the 1997 study, there were more respondents indicating the Russian police were getting worse than those that indicated the police were improving. Studies shown in Table 6.4 (conducted in the Volgograd region between 1998 and 2011) are consistent with the extant literature. Public police satisfaction remained under 50% during the 10 years of this research and trust ranged anywhere between 40.2% and 58.4%.

Public satisfaction with the Russian police varies and depends on the specific police unit and its functions. Table 6.5 consists of data from the Volgograd region and suggests that passport services were among the top-rated police units, followed by the district police officers (*uchastkovyi*), and on-duty police departments (responsible for dispatching police patrols for immediate assistance and coordination of services). The least satisfying were

Table 6.1 Summary of empirical findings measuring public satisfaction with police from 1990 to 2011

Author(s)	Year	Police Satisfaction		
		Yes	No	Don't Know
Krivel'skaya	1990	2.9%	61.5%	35.6%
ICVS	1992	13.3%	86.7%	—
Zvekic	1996	10.2%	47.7%	19.8%
FOM	1996	10%	47%	43%
ICVS	1996	9.8%	46.9%	43.3%
Egoryshev	1997	24%	32.4%	43.6%
Mazaev[2]	1997	10%	30%	60%
ICVS	2000	24.7%	50.1%	25.2%
WCIOM[3]	2001	32%	68%	—
WCIOM	2001	25%	74%	—
WCIOM[4]	2002	30%	69%	—
WCIOM	2002	28%	72%	—
FOM[5]	2003	11%	33%	24%
FOM [6]	2004	10%	34%	25%
WCIOM	2004	38%	56%	
FOM	2005	43%	38%	19%
Cherkasov	2006	36%	43%	21%
Nevirko et al.	2006	42.7%	29%	28.3%
WCIOM[7]	2006	35.9%	73.1%	8%
Levada	2007	27%	22%	14%
FOM	2007	21%	55%	24%
FOM	2008	24%	52%	23%
Levada	2008	27%	58%	
WCIOM[8]	2009	14%	27%	10%
FOM	2009	21%	58%	—
WCIOM[9]	2010	27%	29%	12%
FOM	2010	20%	30%	19%
WCIOM	2011	32%	48%	—
FOM	2011	45%	27%	28%

the traffic police, then the street patrol services (PPS), and finally the district police officers. The fact that district police officers were mentioned in both categories of satisfied and unsatisfied respondents probably suggests their position of high public visibility. These findings are somewhat consistent with other studies about public satisfaction of different police units.

Nevirko, Shenkevich, and Gorbach (2006) reported that police units with the highest levels of public dissatisfaction included district police officers (24.7%) and patrol police services (32%). Research by Nevirko, Shenkevich, and Gorbach also suggests that public dissatisfaction for both units increased

Table 6.2 Summary of empirical findings measuring police trust from 1989 to 2011

		Trust of Police		
Author(s)	Year	Yes	No	Don't Know
WCIOM	1989	18.6%	26.9%	18.4%
WCIOM	1990	18.2%	27%	11.2%
WCIOM	1991	16.7%	27.5%	20.2%
IS RAN[10]	1992	25.4%	68%	6.7%
WCIOM[11]	1993	12.6%	63.4%	22.9%
WCIOM	1994	14.7%	63.7%	21.6%
WCIOM[12]	1995	45.7%	39.5%	14.7%
IS RAN[13]	1995	20.7%	73.6%	5.7%
IKSI	1996	42.9%	49.4%	7.7%
FOM	1997	19%	55%	7%
WCIOM	1998	18.3%	68%	13.7%
FOM	1998	18%	52%	7%
FOM	1999	23%	50%	9%
IKSI	1999	19.5%	57.1%	24.2%
Bezaev	1999	—	57%	—
ROMIR[14]	2000	47.3%	47.5%	5.2%
WCIOM	2000	18%	50%	—
FOM	2001	—	55%	—
IKSI	2002	15.7%	67.1%	17.1%
FOM	2002	—	48%	—
WCIOM	2002	26%	74%	—
FOM[15]	2002	8%	31%	—
Levada	2004	23.7%	71.8%	4.5%
Gudkov et al.	2004	48%	40%	12%
ROMIR	2005	5%	—	—
Andreev	2005	11.5%	67.6%	—
Dzuev et al.[16]	2005	26%	46.2%	27.8%
Robertson	2005	45%	39%	16%
Gryaznova	2006	25%	70%	4%
Gudkov, Dubin	2006	24%	65%	11%
Nevirko	2006	41.7%	—	—
WCIOM	2006	33%	61%	6%
Verdict	2008	25%	75%	—
FOM	2008	39%	46%	15%
WCIOM	2009	38%	53%	10%
WCIOM	2010	40%	47%	12%
FOM	2011	11%	40%	—
Levada	2011	35%	56%	—

Table 6.3 Summary of empirical findings measuring the dynamics of police work assessment: "Did the work of the police become better or worse from 1990 to 2010?"

		Did the Work of Police Become Better from 1990 to 2010?		
Author(s)	Year	Better	Worse	The Same
Levada	1990	9%	38%	29%
Levada	1994	8%	43%	39%
FOM[17]	1997	15%	15%	19%
WCIOM	2002	14%	24%	—
FOM[18]	2003	9%	22%	12%
WCIOM	2003	19%	21%	7%
WCIOM	2004	19%	21%	9.8%
WCIOM	2005	16.8%	22.8%	36%
LEVADA	2007	17%	39%	—
FOM	2009	5%	15%	72%
FOM[19]	2010	13%	18%	24%
WCIOM[20]	2010	15%	16%	69%
Levada	2010	15%	16%	57%

in 2004 when compared to similar data in 1998. WCIOM in 2006 reported that passport services and on-duty police services are the highest public ranked units, whereas traffic police and district police officers (*uchastkovyi*) are the lowest-ranked units (WCIOM, 2006). The study by INDEM (2007) reported that in both large cities and small towns, the top-ranked police units are passport services and extraministerial units that provide paid security services to citizens. The lowest-ranked units were traffic police, patrol services, and district police officers. The traffic police led all police units in a negative public perception of corruption and bribery while the patrol services were top-ranked in public perceptions of physical abuse and violence against citizens (INDEM, 2007). Makarova (2011) also reported that passport services were the top-ranking units, whereas the district police officers and the investigative departments were the lowest-ranking units.

When examining public views of the Russian police, some studies take a qualitative approach by asking respondents about the typical characteristics of an average police officer. The overall image of policemen appears to be rather negative. A study conducted in 1990 listed "rudeness," "indifferent," "lacking culture," and "dishonest" as qualities of the typical police officer (Gudkov, 2000). The study by Mazaev (2004), conducted during the 1998 to 2001 period, listed "rudeness," "bribery," and "dishonesty" as the top features of Russian police officers. Similar research conducted in 2005 suggested "cruel," "impolite," and "indifferent" as the major characteristics of police officers (Andreev, 2005b). In a study by Cherkasov (2006), the qualities of Russian police included "rudeness" (54%), "corruption" (47%), and

Table 6.4 Public views of police from surveys conducted in the Volgograd region[21]

Variable	1998	1999	2000	2001	2002	2003	2004	2005	2006	2007	2008	2009	2010	2011
Satisfaction with police	42.8	42.5	47.0	47.6	42.4	47.4	48.0	48.0	42.0	46.1	—	—	—	—
Trust of police	50.8	45.1	46.6	43.2	40.2	46.6	50.8	51.6	43.2	47.3	28.1	46.6	58.4	42.7
Trust of courts	45.0	38.9	47.8	48.4	39.4	41.4	45.0	40.4	48.4	45.5	40.3	—	—	49.2
Trust of prosecutor's office	44.2	32.7	24.8	45.3	29.0	41.6	44.2	43.0	45.3	42.7	40.1	26.4	—	50.3
Trust of FSB	46.6	25.9	42.6	47.3	32.4	40.4	46.6	48.2	47.3	47.3	47.3	20.3	—	—
Fear of police	—	—	—	—	—	—	—	—	—	—	21.3	25.9	27.1	24.5
Avoidance of police	—	—	—	—	—	—	—	—	—	—	60.1	60.2	41.3	51.5
Contact with police	58.9	62.7	50.0	54.4	53.5	51.7	58.9	75.9	54.4	58.3	37.1	40.3	13.6	—

Table 6.5 Public satisfaction of police units: 1998–2007 in the Volgograd region[22]

Type of Police Unit	Satisfied	Unsatisfied
Passport services	44.0%	19.8%
District police officers	38.7%	23.7%
On-duty police departments	35.9%	14.5%
Street patrolling services	33.2%	28.1%
Criminal detective departments	32.6%	17.2%
Traffic police	32.0%	34.1%
Criminal investigative departments	29.7%	17.2%
Juvenile inspectors	23.1%	17.8%

"alcoholism" (38%). In a qualitative study, Bondarenko (2006b) found that most negative stereotypes about police are pertinent to the services provided by police officers to the citizens.

It is also interesting that Russian police officers are often compared unfavorably to Soviet police, which typically are viewed as more honest, trustworthy, and brave (Andreev, 2005a).

Findings depicted in Table 6.6 show the demographic characteristics of respondents pertinent to their views on police satisfaction and trust in the Volgograd region. From these findings, it appears that older respondents have more trust and are more satisfied with police. Female respondents reported less police distrust and dissatisfaction than males. More educated respondents showed less police trust and satisfaction than less educated groups. Almost an equal number of lower-income and high-income groups appear to distrust police, but more higher-income respondents indicated trust of the police. These findings are somewhat consistent with the existing literature.[24]

The study by Public Verdict (2010) also suggests that older Russians are more likely to trust the police. The same study indicates that lower-income Russians and those who live in the large urban areas are more dissatisfied with police than higher-income individuals and those who live in the rural areas. The study by Gudkov, Dubin, and Leonova (2004) also indicated that retired respondents are more likely to trust police, whereas students and unemployed individuals are less likely. The research by Mazaev (2004) concluded that older, retired individuals, and residents of rural areas are more satisfied with the police. Dzutsev, Khugaeva, and Tsogoev (2005) found no relationship between age or gender and trust of police, but it was reported that less-educated individuals were more likely to trust the police. Bondarenko (2002) also found that rural residents are more satisfied with police work. Gryaznova (2006) and Dzutsev (2010) similarly reported that respondents with higher levels of education are less likely to trust the police or be satisfied with their work.[25]

Table 6.6 Trust and satisfaction of police: Demographic characteristics: 1998–2007 in the Volgograd region[23]

Demographics	Trust	Distrust	Don't Know	Total	Mostly Satisfied	Mostly Unsatisfied	Don't Know	Total
Age								
Under 18	38.4%	33.1%	28.4%	100%	37.2%	28.9%	33.9%	100%
18–24	39.4%	32.3%	28.3%	100%	42.6%	30.8%	26.6%	100%
25–29	42.7%	31.5%	25.8%	100%	48.0%	29.6%	22.4%	100%
30–39	42.9%	27.7%	29.4%	100%	44.9%	32.1%	23.0%	100%
40–49	40.0%	30.8%	29.2%	100%	41.1%	32.3%	26.6%	100%
50 +	48.2%	27.3%	24.5%	100%	49.1%	27.2%	23.6%	100%
Gender								
Male	41.8%	31.5%	26.7%	100%	46.7%	30.4%	22.9%	100%
Female	42.0%	27.4%	30.7%	100%	44.2%	29.6%	26.2%	100%
Income								
<4K	9.4%	36.5%	54.1%	100%				
4–7 K	13.3%	31.0%	55.7%	100%				
7–11 K	11.7%	29.9%	58.4%	100%				
11–18 K	7.1%	30.0%	63.0%	100%				
18–25 K	21.1%	34.2%	44.7%	100%				
Education								
Elementary	44.3%	26.4%	29.3%	100%	44.7%	26.5%	28.8%	100%
Secondary	40.1%	30.7%	29.1%	100%	48.4%	27.3%	24.4%	100%
Technical	42.9%	28.8%	28.2%	100%	45.3%	29.8%	24.9%	100%
College+	41.4%	29.4%	29.2%	100%	43.2%	33.4%	23.3%	100%
Victimization								
Yes	33.9%	37.4%	28.7%	100%	37.3%	42.1%	20.6%	100%
No	42.3%	26.8%	30.8%	100%	48.3%	25.6%	26.1%	100%

Whereas overall research consistently suggests that retired, rural, and lower-educated individuals are more likely to trust the Russian police, some researchers conclude that such a trust is simply a reflection of higher levels of vulnerability for these groups. These individuals simply have no other means to protect themselves and, therefore, have to trust the police (Public Verdict Fund, 2010). It is clear from all the data that no demographic group of Russian society, including the most vulnerable ones, expresses high levels of support for or satisfaction with the police. On the contrary, all demographic groups indicate serious concerns with the legitimacy of the Russian police.

The police is not the only government institution that suffered from lack of public satisfaction and trust. Table 6.4 indicates that other criminal justice institutions including the courts, prosecutor's office (*Procuracy*), and the Federal Security Service (FSB) have low levels of public trust through the entire period from 1998 to 2011. This data is corroborated by findings from other studies that report low levels of trust for all law enforcement and justice agencies in Russia (Mishler and Rose, 2005; Nevirko, Shenkevich, and Gorbach, 2006; ZIRCON, 2005). Some research suggests the police are viewed as the least trustworthy institution among all agencies and institutions (Gudkov, Dubin, and Leonova, 2004).[26] For example, according to the Index of Criminal Justice Institutions' Trust, measured quarterly by the Levada Center between 1994 and 2006, the trust rating of the police remained the lowest in 12 years followed by the courts, the *Procuracy*, and then the FSB (Gryaznova, 2006). In the study by WCIOM, distrust of both the courts and *Procuracy* ranged from 38% to 43% between 1991 and 2000 and trust ranged from 8% to 14% (Gudkov, 2000).

The low levels of public satisfaction and trust of all criminal justice institutions are not unique to Russia. Comparative research suggests that most post-Soviet countries in Eastern Europe and the former Soviet Union experienced similar problems due to their authoritarian past and lack of a clear plan for reform (Kaariainen, 2007; Los, 2002; Mishler and Rose, 1998; Uidriks and Reenen, 2005). The International Crime Victimization Survey (ICVS), a cross-country study that was repeatedly conducted in Eastern Europe from 1992 onward, ranked all post-Soviet countries at the bottom when measuring public satisfaction with police (ICVS, 1992, 1996, 2000). However, even within the post-Soviet countries, Russian levels of public dissatisfaction and distrust of police are considered high. Findings in Table 6.7 from the ICVS suggest that public satisfaction with the police in North American and Western European countries ranges anywhere from 66% to 84% compared to a range of 10% to 30% rates for the post-Soviet countries. The results of the 2004 Barometer study ranked Russia the second-lowest county among 13 post-Soviet countries on public trust of police (Mishler and Rose, 2005).[27]

Table 6.7 Findings from the ICVS on police satisfaction: 1992–2002

Country	Satisfied	Ranking
Canada	84.6%	1
United States	83.9%	2
United Kingdom	70.1%	3
Germany	66.7%	4
Lithuania	31.0%	5
Estonia	30.5%	6
Georgia	29.1%	7
Belarus	26.9%	8
Russia	**24.7%**	**9**
Ukraine	23.8%	10
Latvia	21.8%	11
Kyrgyzstan	10.7%	12

6.2 Crime Rates, Victimization, Fear of Crime, and Contact with Police

The criminological literature traditionally inversely relates low levels of public satisfaction with the police in post-Soviet countries with high crime rates as a result of the process of rapid transition (Gudkov, 2000; Shelley, 1996; Uidriks and Reenen, 2005). Table 6.8 presents official statistics of registered crimes in Russia for the past 20 years. An analysis of the main crime categories in Table 6.8 suggests that, with the exception of drug-related crimes, crimes committed by foreigners, and crimes committed by repeat offenders, all other major categories of registered crimes began a decline starting in the period from 2000 to 2001.

The overall number of registered crimes per 100,000 residents was recorded at 1,839 in 2010 compared to 2,039 in 1999 when it had reached its highest level. Other crime rates also showed significant declines when compared to their highest values from 1997 to 1999. The number of serious offenses was registered at 684,347 in 2010, which is almost three times less than what it was in 1997. The number of juvenile crimes in 2010 also was almost three times less than in 1999. Registered crimes committed by organized groups dropped more than three times in 2010 compared to 1999. One of the most impressive declines in crime rates was in firearms-related offenses, which dropped almost five times when compared with the years 1997 through 2010. However, the improvement in registered crimes does not appear to be a result of an improvement in the public image of Russian police officers.

The analysis of Table 6.1 through Table 6.4 does not indicate any clear upward trend in either public trust or satisfaction with the police. Levels of

Table 6.8 Registered crime rates reported by the Ministry of Internal Affairs: 1990–2010[29]

Years/Crime Rates	1990	1991	1992	1993	1994	1995	1996	1997	1998	1999	2000
Total number of registered crimes per 100,000 residents	1,243	1,461	1,859	1,886	1,774	1,857	1,772	1,621	1,748	2,039	2,028
Total number of serious and very serious crimes	415,755	513,910	984,078	1,633,367	1,466,388	1,422,931	1,560,764	1,847,835	1,735,198	415,755	513,910
Total number of drug-related crimes	—	53,169	74,798	79,948	96,762	184,832	190,127	216,364	243,572	53,169	74,798
Total number of crimes committed by juveniles	162,718	173,375	199,291	223,651	221,649	209,777	202,935	182,798	189,293	208,313	195,426
Total number of crimes committed by repeat offenders	257,853	274,339	320,330	346,672	343,940	459,602	493,983	565,373	604,557	692,134	651,522
Total number of crimes committed by organized group	188,511	213,951	278,158	355,498	349,343	349,464	345,464	359,887	374,262	450,930	418,973
Total number of crimes committed by alcohol intoxicated offenders	334,740	356,189	438,543	518,876	600,120	650,261	637,012	508,928	485,160	488,067	442,656
Total number of crimes committed by drug intoxicated offenders	—	—	—	6,842	8,388	9,402	11,253	15,514	16,482	18,518	18,894
Total number of crimes committed by foreigners and individuals without citizenship	—	—	—	17,302	27,107	32,258	37,065	27,953	31,000	32,286	35,120
Total number of crimes committed by use of firearms	—	—	—	22,116	16,780	12,160	9,549	19,650	18,584	15,591	13,025

(continued)

Table 6.8 Registered crime rates reported by the Ministry of Internal Affairs: 1990–2010[29] (continued)

Years/Crime Rates	2001	2002	2003	2004	2005	2006	2007	2008	2009	2010
Total number of registered crimes per 100,000 residents	2,033	1,739	1,907	2,012	2,484	2,706	2,521	2,261	2,110	1,839
Total number of serious and very serious crimes	1,769,565	1,347,237	1,080,151	936,804	1,076,988	1,07,4501	961,133	851,392	796,224	684,347
Total number of drug-related crimes	241,598	189,576	181,688	150,096	175,241	212,019	231,218	232,613	238,523	222,564
Total number of crimes committed by juveniles	185,379	139,681	145,368	154,414	154,734	150,264	139,099	116,090	94,720	70,955
Total number of crimes committed by repeat offenders	622,040	418,826	420,666	434,669	517,383	534,283	534,072	521,552	531,798	530,742
Total number of crimes committed by organized group	376,939	254,997	245,989	250,763	246,669	239,102	225,155	198,138	170,598	145,448
Total number of crimes committed by alcohol intoxicated offenders	408,072	325,580	315,098	301,407	311,799	302,255	262,278	231,785	214,371	237,283
Total number of crimes committed by drug intoxicated offenders	15,798	8,537	8,387	7,528	8,526	10,759	11,713	12,837	14,090	14,828
Total number of crimes committed by foreigners and individuals without citizenship	37,166	35,712	40,570	48,927	51,225	53,014	50,139	53,876	57,955	48,992
Total number of crimes committed by use of firearms	12,580	12,285	11,746	9,641	9,171	7,648	5,509	4,365	4,388	4,040

public distrust and dissatisfaction have remained low and steady during the past 20 years. Several plausible explanations can be offered for the lack of correlation. One suggestion would be to look at the rates of police effectiveness to see if poor police performance could be responsible for consistently low rates of public trust and satisfaction with the Russian police despite the declining crime rates. Table 6.9 summarizes data available for the number of criminal cases under investigation, and clearance rates. The clearance rates are used in Russia as the official measure of law enforcement performance.

Table 6.9 Official statistics on criminal investigation: 2003–2010[30]

Year	Type	Total Percent of Criminal Cases	Percent of Very Serious Crimes	Percent of Crimes That Are Subject to Preliminary Investigation	Percent of Crimes Subject to "Inquiry"	Percent of Crimes Investigated per Each Year by MVD
2003	Total	2,756,398 (100%)	39.18%	44.77%	55. 23%	
	Solved	55.10%	21.77%	25. 89%	29. 20%	
	Unsolved	42.04%	17.08%	18. 35%	23. 69%	
2004	Total	2,893,810 (100%)	32.37%	34.56%	59.72%	
	Solved	54.23%	16.70%	22.12%	32.11%	
	Unsolved	43.71%	15.19%	17.12%	26.60%	
2005	Total	3,554,738 (100%)	30.30%	38.76%	61.24%	
	Solved	47.79%	14.32%	19.97%	27.82%	
	Unsolved	46.67%	14.46%	16.64%	30.02%	
2006	Total	3,855,373 (100%)	27.87%	36.94%	63.06%	3,576,542 (92.77%)
	Solved	46.55%	13.20%	19.40%	27.14%	
	Unsolved	52.72%	14.53%	17.13%	35.57%	
2007	Total	3,582,541 (100%)	26.83%	49.86%	50.14%	3,348,859 (93.47%)
	Solved	49.55%	13.82%	22.74%	26.81%	
	Unsolved	52.02%	13.08%	23.48%	28.55%	
2008	Total	3,209,862 (100%)	26.52%	58.22%	41.78%	2,997,642 (93.39%)
	Solved	53.38%	14.14%	27.50%	25.88%	
	Unsolved	46.09%	11.74%	30.01%	16.08%	
2009	Total	2,994,820 (100%)	26.59%	57.79%	42.21%	2,788,067 (93.09%)
	Solved	55.12%	14.35%	27.98%	27.14%	
	Unsolved	43.71%	11.36%	28.73%	14.99%	
2010	Total	2,628,799 (100%)	26.03%	57.48%	42.52%	2,437,114 (92.71%)
	Solved	54.43%	13.79%	27.27%	27.17%	
	Unsolved	45.39%	11.68%	29.71%	5.68%	

The analysis of Table 6.9 suggests that, irrespective of declining crime rates shown in Table 6.8, the number of open criminal cases continued to grow in 2005 and 2006. The growth of criminal cases can possibly be explained by the fact that, at any given year, police clearance rates did not exceed 55%. This suggests that 45% of the cases continued to be investigated for some period of time. It is also evident from Table 6.9 that despite changes in the absolute number of investigations, law enforcement agencies continued to clear cases at very similar rates. This is true for all crime categories including very serious crimes, crimes subjected to preliminary investigation (serious and very serious crimes), and cases subject to inquiry (minor offenses).

Based on the previous analysis, it appears that poor performance of Russian law enforcement (regardless of a decline in crime rates and the number of cases under investigation) can be responsible for continuously low levels of public trust and satisfaction with the police. However, caution needs to be applied to this conclusion because the official Russian crime statistics are known to be biased (Skomorokhov and Shikhanov, 2006). The literature indicates that official crime rates can be used only as an approximation of true national crime (Inshakov, 2007). Since crime rates and clearance of cases are used as the main measure of police performance, the official statistics are

Table 6.10 Victimization percentages and reported crimes in Russia (ICVS)

Variable	1992	1996	2000
Theft			
Victimized	72.2	79.7[31]	80.7[32]
Reported	31.7	30.5[33]	29.7[34]
Assault			
Victimized	12.8	13.5	11.0
Reported	19.7	27.0	26.7
Robbery			
Victimized	7.7	9.8	8.9
Reported	17.6	25.0	34.6
Rape			
Victimized	9.0	7.3	6.7
Reported	6.3	14.6	16.9
Embezzlement/Fraud[35]			
Victimized	54.6	48.4	46.5
Reported	1.6	4.1	1.3
Corruption[36]			
Victimized	—	18.0	16.7
Reported	—	2.2	2.4
Other			
Victimized	9.0	14.5	15.1
Reported	21.6	17.6	10.6

known to be manipulated for better outcome (Gilinskiy, 2000).[28] Thus, the real numbers of crimes are believed to be much higher and the numbers of truly solved crimes appear to be much lower than reported.

The study by INDEM (2001b) reports that police officially refuse to initiate criminal investigations in at least 50% of all cases and that the number is correlated with reported clearance rates. According to Gavrilov (2001), up to 90% of these refusals are illegal and are made in an attempt to hide crimes that are difficult to solve. Inshakov (2007) estimates that actual crime rates are at least five times higher than registered crimes. Using the official clearance rates of 55% of registered crimes, one can estimate that police are solving only 7% to 8% of all crimes in Russia. Kolennikova (2006) concludes that only 15% to 20% of all crimes are registered by the police and only 10% of offenders are apprehended. The study suggests that for the crimes of fraud and embezzlement the actual numbers are even lower with only 1% to 5% of these being investigated (Kolennikova, 2006). Makarova (2011) indicated that only 18% of reported criminal complaints were sent to courts for adjudication, 20% of complaints were refused further investigations, and the rest remained uninvestigated for various reasons. Considering that only 44% of crimes are reported, this study estimates that only 8% of all crimes are solved and sent for adjudication. Thus, it can be suggested that the inability to investigate the majority of crimes plays an important role in low levels of public police satisfaction and trust.

The issues related to the official statistics require a closer examination of the rates of victimization and fear of crime in Russia. Unfortunately, there is no periodic victimization survey conducted in Russia, so the data on victimization is often fragmented and difficult to compare due to methodological differences. Findings from the International Crime Victim Survey (ICVS) conducted in 1992, 1996, and 2000 are presented in Table 6.10. Even though the ICVS does not provide victimization totals, it gives a detailed breakdown on types of victimization. According to Table 6.10, the top three crimes that were reported were theft, fraud/embezzlement, and corruption. The victimization rates for each crime appeared to be stable during the survey years of 1992, 1996, and 2000.

Volgograd citizen surveys conducted annually from 1998 to 2010 on victimization are reported in Table 6.11. Unlike the ICVS, these surveys measured victimization during one year prior to the data collection, which may explain discrepancies with other studies. Similar to the ICVS, the Volgograd study concludes that theft is the leading crime reported by victims. Unlike the ICVS, in the Volgograd study in Table 6.11, hooliganism (public disturbance of the peace) and personal assault were among the greatest number of crimes committed. Volgograd studies of 1998–2010 also measured total victimization, which appeared to range from 20% to 30% of the sample. Similar to the ICVS, findings in Table 6.11 failed to find any significant change within

Table 6.11 Victimizations and reported crimes in the Volgograd region[37]

Variable	1998	1999	2000	2001	2002	2003	2004	2005	2006	2007	2008	2009	2010
Victimization													
Assault	3.4	3.0	3.6	3.3	1.4	2.4	3.4	3.6	3.3	4.4	—	—	—
Rape	.4	.6	1.8	.7	1.6	.8	.4	—	.7	.2	—	—	—
Theft	10.4	16.0	15.8	8.3	13.2	9.2	10.4	10.4	8.3	11.4	—	—	—
Embezzlement	3.0	2.2	1.6	3.5	2.0	2.6	3.0	1.8	3.5	2.0	—	—	—
Robbery	1.2	2.4	2.4	1.5	2.8	2.4	1.2	2.0	1.5	3.6	—	—	—
Blackmailing	2.2	1.8	2.6	1.7	3.2	3.4	2.2	.2	1.7	3.2	—	—	—
Hooliganism	5.8	6.0	7.2	3.5	7.6	4.4	5.8	4.2	3.5	5.4	—	—	—
Other	.6	1.2	.2	.7	.2	.6	.6	—	.7	1.0	—	—	—
Total Victimization	26.4	30.7	29.2	20.8	28.6	23.2	26.4	22.2	20.8	28.3	21.7	24.0	26.1
Total Reporting	59.8	62.7	50.0	54.9	53.5	51.7	58.9	75.9	54.4	58.3	—	—	—

the observed period of time during 1998–2010. When looking at public trust of police and satisfaction pertinent to victimization, as shown in Table 6.6, victimization has a clear negative impact on citizen perceptions of the police.

Findings on victimization from Volgograd surveys administered from 1998–2010 are supported by other research. Goriyanov (1994) reported that 23.7% of those surveyed were victimized in the past five years and 9.4% were victimized during the last year. In his study, personal theft, assault, and burglary of a dwelling comprised the greatest numbers of crimes. In a study by Bezaev (1999), one-third of the respondents were victimized in the past 12 months and 44.7% were theft victims. Similar to Volgograd surveys administered from 1998 to 2010, hooliganism and assault were among other leading crimes identified in his work. Beck and Robertson (2003) also reported that one-third (29%) of respondents were victimized in the previous 12 months. Theft was the leading crime and males between the ages of 30 and 39 were three times more likely to become victims of a crime than older males (A. Beck and Robertson, 2003). Similarly, Kopkareva (2007) suggests that victimizations rates for Russian university students (e.g., younger respondents) were much higher (45%) than the average victimization rate (30%). Makarova (2011) also reported that only 21% of Russians were victimized in their lifetime; the leading crime of victimization also was theft. Younger and less educated respondents were more likely to report victimization. Thus, it can be suggested that steady, low public–police satisfaction and trust is a result of continuously high levels of victimization. Beck and Chistyakova (2004), in a Ukrainian study, also found that both public–police trust and satisfaction were negatively impacted by victimizations.

Another important variable in the context of public–police trust and satisfaction is public fear of crime, and safety concerns. Traditionally, the individuals that have greater levels of fear of crime and safety concerns have lower levels of trust of and satisfaction with law enforcement (A. Beck and Chistyakova, 2004). The summary of studies conducted in Russia on fear of crime is shown in Table 6.12.

An analysis of Table 6.12 suggests that fear of crime levels remains high in Russia. The fear of crime ranges from 30.6% to 74.1% and appears to have remained steady during the past 20 years (Reynolds, Semukhina, and Demidov, 2008). Considering that official crime rates (Table 6.8) have dramatically declined since the 2000–2001 period, it would follow that fear of crime also would decline. However, we found no support for this proposition, which questions the validity of official crime statistics. Other researchers have raised serious concerns over discrepancies between the official crime rates and reported levels of victimization in Russia (Gilinskiy, 2000). The Russian public concerns with personal safety are higher than similar values in other countries that include the former Soviet countries of Eastern Europe. The information contained in Table 6.13, derived from the ICVS, ranks Russia at the bottom of the former Soviet countries for perceived levels of public safety.

Table 6.12 Summary of empirical findings on fear of crime: 1989–2011

		Fear of Crime	
Author(s)	Year	Yes	No
WCIOM	1989	42.4%	52.2%
Krivel'skaya	1990	74.1%	25.9%
ICVS	1992	70.4%	29.5%
Gudkov	1993	70%	—
FOM	1996	70%	30%
ICVS	1996	69.9	30.1%
Shubkin	1997	66%	—
Bezaev	1999	30.6%	—
ICVS	2000	64.8%	31.6%
Glinskiy	2000	64%	—
Beck, Robertson	2003	61%	39%
Ivanova, Shubkin	2005	34%	—
Lelekov, Tyamin	2005	60%	—
Reynolds, et al.	2008	48%	52%
Dzuev	2010	63.7%	30.1%
FOM	2011	46%	43%

Table 6.13 Findings from the ICVS on fear of crime of selected countries: 1992–2002

Country	Feel Safe	Ranking
Canada	78.4%	1
United States	77.6%	2
United Kingdom	71.0%	3
Germany	67.1%	4
Estonia	59.5%	5
Georgia	45.0%	6
Latvia	39.6%	7
Kyrgyzstan	36.3%	8
Lithuania	35.8%	9
Belarus	35.6%	10
Ukraine	31.6%	11
Russia	**31.6%**	**12**

Several Russian researchers studied public concerns by ranking their level of importance to the public. One of the most comprehensive studies conducted annually by WCIOM is presented in Table 6.14. The study by WCIOM measured public concerns that ranked in the top 10 over the past 20 years. *Rising* crime rates were at the top of the list every year; however, there was a decline from 52.9% in 2001 to 19.1% in 2009. This declining trend follows the official

Table 6.14 Ranking of public concerns in Russia: 1991–2009

Study	Concerned with Rise of Crime Rates	Concerned with Corruption	Concerned with Police Abuse
WCIOM, 1991	28.8%	—	—
WCIOM, 1992	37.5%	—	—
WCIOM, 1993	65.4%	19.3%	—
WCIOM, 1993	51.8%	—	—
WCIOM, 1994	67.8%	22.4%	—
WCIOM, 1995	57.7%	23.0%	—
WCIOM, 1995	48.7%	—	—
WCIOM, 1996	41.9%	19.2%	—
WCIOM, 1997	40.1%	—	—
WCIOM, 1998	49.6%	31.9%	—
WCIOM, 1999	44.7%	29.1%	—
WCIOM, 2000	43.8%	30.9%	
WCIOM, 2001	52.9%	34.8%	—
WCIOM, 2002	43.3%	23.1%	—
WCIOM, 2003	25.4%	36.7%	7.5%
WCIOM, 2004	27.1%	38.0%	9.8%
WCIOM, 2005	27.0%	31.7%	7.8%
WCIOM, 2006	29.4%	25.2%	7.7%
WCIOM, 2007	26.2%	24.6%	8.9%
WCIOM, 2008	26.7%	27.0%	8.7%
WCIOM, 2009	19.1%	23.2%	6.5%

statistics of registered crimes presented in Table 6.8. However, when examining data on public concerns with crime in general, or concerns of personal safety, the same declining trend was not discernible. Except for issues of poverty, unemployment, and health, concerns with crime and public safety were always the top-ranked public fears in Russia at any given year between 1991 and 2010. In retrospect, most respondents reported feeling "much safer"[38] (Gudkov, 2000) and less concerned about crime prior to 1991 (Gilinskiy, 2000; Shubkin, 1997).

Shubkin (1997) measured the fears of Russians in 1996 and concluded that crime and safety concerns were the three top-ranked fears (66%) and preceded only by fear of poverty (67.2%) and "lawlessness" (66.7%). He also compared public fears with those of recent Russian immigrants in the United States. The immigrants that had left Russia less than one year ago reported their fear of crime declined by 15% (Shubkin, 1997). Bezaev (1999) indicated that in 1998, 30.6% of respondents were afraid of becoming a crime victim, which was preceded only by fear of poverty (ranked first), fear of disease (ranked second), and fear of unemployment (ranked third). In 2000, a study conducted by INDEM (2001b) found fear of becoming a crime victim was ranked as the number one public concern (55%), followed by fear of unemployment (35.3%). V. A. Ivanova and Shubkin (2005) used 2003 data to conclude that safety concerns are the leading group of public fears, with 36% concerned with crime, 34% with terrorism, and 27% concerned with the war in Chechnya.

Lelekov and Tyamin (2005) measured public concerns in 2004 and concluded that 64% of respondents were concerned, or very much concerned, with their safety in Russia. He found that small businesspersons and retired individuals are more concerned with their safety than younger groups of the population, or those that are employed by the government agencies. INDEM (2007) ranked concerns with street crime among the top seven fears, preceded only by issues of high prices, poverty, and other economic concerns. When asked directly about the safety of their cities and townships, many Russians concluded that their places of residence were unsafe. INDEM (2007) reported only 3.5% of residents from the large cities and 3.3% of those in small towns reported their places of residence to be safe. A number of studies on Russian police and police of other post-Soviet countries reported that public concerns with crime and personal safety negatively influenced public trust and satisfaction with police (A. Beck and Chistyakova, 2004; A. Beck and Robertson, 2003). The literature indicates that public concerns with crime strongly relates to victimization in Russia (A. Beck and Robertson, 2003).

Actual police contact is another important factor to consider when examining issues of public trust and satisfaction with police (Davis et al., 2004). The persons who contact the Russian police traditionally included victims of crimes (voluntary contacts) and those stopped, or arrested, by police (involuntary contacts). Also, due to the large volume of police administrative functions, significant numbers of citizens contact the police for routine purposes, such as the issuance of the driver's licenses, registrations, or passports. Table 6.15 summarizes various studies on Russian police contacts.

Table 6.15 Summary of empirical findings on contact with the Russian police: 2000–2010

		Personal Contact		
Author(s)	Year	Yes	No	Don't Know
Davis	2000	34%[39]	18%	3%
FOM[40]	2003	36%[41]	52%	3%
FOM	2004	24%[42]	74%	2%
Andreev	2005	—	49.2%	
FOM	2008	34%[43]	60%	2%
WCIOM	2009	25%	72%	3%
WCIOM[44]	2009	28%	71%	1%
WCIOM	2010	25%	72%	3%

Table 6.15 indicates that on any given year between 24% and 51% of all Russians had contact with police. Davis et al. (2004), in a comparative study of New York City, and St. Petersburg, Russia, reported that 34% of those in St. Petersburg versus 23% in New York City were stopped by police. The same study indicated that New York City residents voluntarily contacted police almost twice as often (41%) than St. Petersburg residents (27%). Younger males of non-Russian ethnicity were more likely to be stopped by police in St. Petersburg (Davis et al., 2004). Rural residents were more likely to have voluntary contact with police than urban residents (Bondarenko, 2002). Similar to victimization and fear of crime, contact with the Russian police negatively influences public trust and police satisfaction. Several studies confirm this correlation over a variety of samples and contact types (A. Beck and Chistyakova, 2004; Dzutsev, Khugaeva, and Tsogoev, 2005; Public Verdict Fund, 2010).

An analysis of the literature indicates that factors of victimization, fear of crime, public concern for safety, and contact with police play an important role in explaining low levels of public trust and police satisfaction in Russia. In the past 20 years, levels of victimization, fear of crime, and public concern for safety remained high, which is consistent with the steady low levels of trust and satisfaction with police. However, when respondents are asked directly about their dissatisfaction and distrust of police, the predominant reasons are not safety concerns, but instead: corruption, abuse of power, violence, lack of accountability, and public oversight of the police. This theme is echoed in a variety of studies including some conducted by police-affiliated research centers (Andreev, 2005b; Blagoveschenskyi et al., 2006; Dzutsev, Khugaeva, and Tsogoev, 2005; Egoryshev, 1997; Goncharov and Kozchevnikov, 1996; Gryaznova, 2006; INDEM, 2001b; Public Verdict Fund, 2010). Findings from Table 6.14 also support this proposition. Studies by WCIOM shown in Table 6.14 indicate, beginning in 2003, police abuse appeared in the top 10 public concerns. Furthermore, public concern with general government corruption was greater than concern with rising crime rates. Since the issue of police abuse of power and corruption has emerged as one of the central themes in Russia, it will be discussed in more detail in Chapter 7.

6.3 Issues of Public–Police Cooperation in Russia

Low levels of public trust and police satisfaction clearly have negative impacts on public–police cooperation. One of the major manifestations of this issue is a refusal of victims to officially report crimes. Findings of the International Crime Victimization Survey (ICVS), shown in Table 6.10, indicate that a large percentage of crime is not officially reported to police. The failure to report was especially high for crimes of fraud. With fraud, less than 5% filed official reports and less than 3% for corruption.

Theft-related crime, the most prevalent type of crime, is also dramatically underreported. The ICVS found theft reports were just above 30%. These findings were corroborated in a study by FOM (Public Opinion Foundation), which indicates that 27% of thefts and 25% of robberies were reported in comparison to 4% of frauds and 3% of bribery solicitations (FOM, 1996). Longitudinal findings from the Volgograd region in Table 6.11 show that between 50% and 76% of all victims made official reports during the period from 1998 to 2007. These numbers may be different because the Volgograd 1998–2007 study did not separately measure reports for each category of crime.

The literature supports the notion that many crime victims do not make official reports. Goryanov (1994), based on 1993 data, concluded that 60% of all crimes were reported by victims. Egoryshev (1997), using data from 1995 to 1996, indicated that between 29.3% and 40.3% of victims did not make a report. INDEM (2001b), based on year 2000 data, concluded that 55% of victims reported crimes, which leaves 17 to 18 million crimes unreported. Lelekov and Tyamin (2005) relied on data collected between 1998 and 2000 and found 56% of victims made official reports. In a study by INDEM (2007), it was found that 23.4% of crimes were officially reported by residents of large cities, whereas 28.6% were reported in small towns. According to study by the Public Verdict Fund (2010), when respondents were asked a hypothetical question of whether they would report the theft of a purse or an office bag, 30% responded no. Makarova (2011) indicated that 44% of victims reported crimes to police in 2010.

The problems of not reporting crimes are shared by other post-Soviet countries that are experiencing similar issues of rapid transition (Zvekic, 1996). According to ICVS, in developed countries anywhere from 75% to 85% of crimes are reported to the police, whereas in Russia it is somewhere between 30% to 50% (ICVS, 1992, 1996, 2000).

It is even more disturbing that crime victims in Russia typically identify the inability of the police to solve crimes and police corruption as the leading reasons for not making reports. According to Goryanov (1994), 39% of victims blamed their nonreporting on ineffective or corrupted police. Goncharov and Kozchevnikov (1996) found 55% of victims in 1994 did not make reports because they did not believe the crimes would be solved. Egoryshev (1997) stated that "disbelieve that police can help" was listed as the leading reason not to report crimes by 23.6% to 32.9% of respondents during the period from 1995 to 1996. A study by INDEM (2001b) concluded that 47.9% of those did not report a crime because of police distrust and their inability to solve the crime.

In an INDEM (2007) study, victims in large cities (48.3%) and in small towns (33.6%) failed to report crimes because they did not believe in the "police ability to help." Also, 37.8% and 28.9%, respectively, had no confidence that the police would seek justice on their behalf. Then, urban (25.4%)

and nonurban (23.4%) victims did not believe the police could find the perpetrators. The Public Verdict Fund (2010) study relied on 2009 survey results and found that 54% of victims that failed to file reports were unconvinced that the police could solve the crime. It's worth mentioning that, in all the aforementioned studies, decisions to not report a crime because of fear of the perpetrator, shame associated with publicity, or lack of time were only mentioned by 5% to 10% of the victims.

A potentially serious consequence of poor public–police cooperation concerns the measures that citizens are willing to take in dangerous situations. Unlike other countries where the police are trusted, Russians are more likely to rely on themselves, family members, or even criminals for their own protection. Only the most vulnerable population groups that have limited resources consider the police as their best option for personal safety.

In a study by FOM (1998), 40% of Russians reported they would contact police in life-threatening situations or when their property is in danger. Both female and older respondents were more likely to contact the police for help, while those younger and more educated preferred to seek help from private security or organized criminals. Bezaev (1999) suggested that 75.2% of respondents would contact police in life-threatening situations, whereas 19.1% would protect themselves. Mitroshenkov (2004) found that in 2002 only 34.3% would contact the police for protection of their rights and, in 2003, this number dropped to 23%. At the same time, 15.2% (in 2002) and 18.7% (in 2003) of respondents reported that there is no person, or institution, that they could contact in such a threatening situation for assistance. Gefter, Petrova, and Reznichenko (2006) found that in 2003 16.1% of respondents reported they would contact police in case their rights were violated. Gudkov, Dubin, and Leonova (2004) reported that only 67% of citizens were willing to contact the police even in cases of life-threatening situations. Ermolaev and Verem′eva (2007) found that 69% of police officers themselves reported they would not contact police in hypothetical life-threatening situations.

According to Gudkov, Dubin, and Leonova (2004), retired individuals (80%), housewives (71%), and government employees (68%) were much more likely to contact the police. Those less willing to contact police were private businessmen (53%) and blue-collar employees (54%). Gudkov, Dubin, and Leonova (2004) also reported a strong relationship between trust of police and the willingness to contact police in case of danger. Only 8% of respondents who trusted police would prefer to resolve their life-threatening situations themselves, compared to 48% that did not trust the police.

In an INDEM (2004) study, 29% of crime victims indicated that they would rather protect themselves than contact the police, 1% would rely on private security services, and 4% would prefer the assistance of organized crime groups instead of the police. Andreev (2005b) reported that only 14% of those surveyed were counting on police to protect them in cases of danger or emergencies. Urban dwellers from areas like Moscow and St. Petersburg were less likely than others (7%) to rely on or have confidence in the police (Andreev, 2005b). Sakhno (2005) reported a strong correlation between contact with the police and a willingness to seek police assistance in dangerous situations. Those individuals who had previous contact with police were more likely to rely on themselves or organized crime groups for protection (Sakhno, 2005). Makarova (2011) also reported that 24.8% of crime victims would prefer to protect themselves and 11.5% would seek protection from private security organizations rather than report the crime to police. Younger males were more likely to rely on themselves, whereas older females were more likely to seek assistance from police.

Public perceptions of police fear and avoidance have created serious issues with public cooperation with the police. Table 6.4 indicates that between 2008 and 2011, from 41.3% to 60.1% of citizens in the Volgograd region reported the best way to deal with the police is avoidance. During the same period, anywhere from 21.3% to 27.1% of respondents feared an approaching police officer. Findings in Table 6.4 from the Volgograd 1998–2007 study are confirmed by other researchers. Fear of the police and abuse appear to be one of the leading public concerns. FOM (1997) found that 24% of respondents admitted that they are afraid of police abuse. WCIOM (1998) indicated that 20.8% of citizens are afraid of the police. Table 6.12 also depicts that longitudinal survey data by WCIOM beginning in 2003 found police abuse had become one of the top public national concerns. Gryaznova (2006) reported that 47% of Russians are either afraid of, or seriously concerned about, police abuse. In a study of the Ossetian police, Dzutsev, Khugaeva, and Tsogoev (2005) reported that 13.8% of citizens felt anxiety and 4.7% fear an approaching police officer. Older and less educated respondents were more likely to fear the police. Lelekov and Tyamin (2005) reported that Russians are seriously afraid of government abuse (2.8 out of 5 on a fear scale) and police abuse (2.7 out of 5). Also, the respondents were afraid of crime (2.1 out of 5) and ecological disasters (1.6 out of 5). In 2008, FOM reported that 22% experienced anxiety and 3% experienced fear from an approaching police officer (FOM, 2008). The Public Verdict Fund (2010) found that 28% of respondents are afraid of police and found little variation among different demographic groups.

The crisis of Russian police legitimacy is also evident when examining public views about the justification of police resistance. WCIOM (2005) found 60.2% of respondents suggested that it is justifiable to resist the police. Andreev (2005b) reported that only 34% of respondents suggested that police resistance cannot be justified. In 2007, WCIOM reported that 46% of respondents justified police resistance. Males, along with the younger and more educated, were more likely to justify police resistance than females and older individuals (WCIOM, 2007).

Cooperation with the Russian police is dramatically reduced by the major issues of crime underreporting, a failure to seek police assistance in dangerous situations, police avoidance, police fear, and resistance. When asked directly about a willingness to assist the police, a significant number refused to cooperate under any conditions and a majority only in some cases. Goncharov and Kozchevnikov (1996) indicated that only 5% were unconditionally willing to assist the police, whereas 20% completely refused. Bezaev (1999) reported that, in 1998, 24.5% of Russians were willing to unconditionally assist the police. WCIOM (2004) found only 19.8% of the survey sample agreed to unconditionally assist the police, whereas 18.9% unconditionally refused to the assist police. Older respondents were more likely to unconditionally assist police compared to younger respondents. A Public Verdict Fund (2008) study found 32% reported they were likely, or definitely likely, not to assist the police. In a 2011 study by WCIOM (2011b), 22% were willing to assist police occasionally and 4% reported not to assist police in any case. Residents of large urban cities are less likely to assist police than rural inhabitants. Similar results were reported in the Ukraine where 26% refused to help the police and 30% agreed to help without any conditions (A. Beck and Chistyakova, 2004).

6.4 Perceptions of Police Officers in Public–Police Relations

For the purposes of our analysis of public–police relations, it's important to understand the views of police officers themselves about their job and performance. The dynamics related to personal motivation to become a police officer are interesting. In a 1991 study by Vorob'ev (1992), 75% of all police officers reported the need to punish offenders and reduce crime rates as their main reason for becoming an officer. Five percent of police officers suggested that benefits were the main motivating factor to join the police force. Kuztnetsov (2009) found in a 2008 study that 52.4% of police officers said that a "stable job" was the main motivating factor to serve, while 39.2% were attracted by advanced benefit levels and 26% stated the guaranteed salary was the main reason to join. Almost 10% stated they became police officers to improve their "material conditions" and use their position "for personal reasons." Other quantitative studies confirm that in an environment of high levels of public distrust of the police, the motivation to serve as a police officer rarely has anything to do with the ideals of serving the people and fighting crime. Instead, personal gain through advances, benefits, abuse of power, and broad discretion are reasons identified as motivators to join the police force (Sakhno, 2005).

However, many officers clearly understand the levels of performance-related deficiencies. INDEM (2004) found 39% of police officers agreed that citizens are not protected from crime by police (compared to 43% of the general population), 15% of the officers admitted that actions against organized crime are completely ineffective (compared to 19% of the general population), and 38% admitted that citizen rights are not guaranteed (compared to 39% of the general population). Gudkov and Dubin (2006) reported that only 59% of officers agreed that it is necessary to protect all citizens, while 26% reported that the government and powerful individuals obtain priority protection, and 25% suggested that those with money receive priority services.

The police and public have much different attitudes about why police provide poor performances that result in public dissatisfaction. Citizens identify corruption, lack of personal responsibility, lack of transparency, and lack of superior officer accountability as the top reasons for poor police performance (INDEM, 2004).[45] In the opinion of police officers, the main reasons for their poor performance are insufficient funding, low wages, lack of equipment, and outdated facilities (Novikova, 2005; Savchenko, 2011). According to Nevirko, Shenkevitch and Gorbach (2006), 77.3% of police officers in 1998 and 69.7% in 2004 reported that insufficient "material technical" support is the main reason for poor performance. Comparatively, only 5% of police officers in 1998 and 20.3% in 2004 suggested that a lack of accountability should be blamed for their deficient performance.

INDEM (2004) found that only 14% of police officers agreed that rude behavior by officers is responsible for public dissatisfaction (compared to 28% of the general public). Similarly, only 13% of police officers agreed that the inability of police to solve crime is the main reason for low satisfaction with the police (compared to 36% of the general population). Police officers think the poor quality of Russian laws, a lack of proper training, and a biased media interfere with their ability to work efficiently (Gudkov and Dubin, 2006; INDEM, 2004; Yanbukhtin, 2005). Many police officers suggest they are forced to violate laws by their immediate superiors for the purposes of personal gain and to falsely report for better performance indicators (Kuztnetsov, 2009; Yanbukhtin, 2005).[46] Some researchers suggested that police officers blame the public for their own deficiencies by claiming that citizens don't know the laws, and do not comply with laws or cooperate with the police to achieve efficient enforcement (Andreev, 2005a; Gudkov and Dubin, 2006). Police officers often claim to feel unappreciated by both the citizens and government (Savchenko, 2011).

6.5 Media and Public–Police Relations

Media is an important source of public information about the Russian police. Findings from the Volgograd 1998–2007 study presented in Table 6.16 depicts that, for any given year, at least 35% of respondents considered media

Table 6.16 Finding on source of information about police from surveys conducted in the Volgograd region[47]

Sources of Information	1998	1999	2000	2001	2002	2003	2004	2005	2006	2007	2008	2009	2010
Personal experience	41.0	42.3	38.6	46.0	43.8	44.6	47.8	35.6	—	43.5	—	—	—
Print media publications	26.8	24.0	13.1	23.8	13.6	8.6	8.0	18.0	—	8.4	57.8	38.0	38.5
TV and radio	38.0	37.9	37.0	31.4	25.6	26.0	22.8	24.4	—	22.9	—	59.8	71.1
Talking to friends/family	0.2	—	29.6	—	32.0	26.6	24.6	28.0	—	28.3	—	—	32.1
Police	—	—	—	—	—	—	—	—	—	—	—	—	9.5
Internet	—	—	—	—	—	—	—	—	—	—	—	18.5	21.8

to be their main source of police information (Reynolds, Semukhina, and Demidov, 2008). For most Russians, the TV and radio appear to be the leading information sources. These findings are consistent with other studies. Komlev, Demidov, and Tolchinskiy (1997) reported that two-thirds of all Russians obtain their information about the police from the mass media. According to Bondarenko (2006a), urban and rural residents, (43% and 22%, respectively) listed the media as their main source of police information. Egoryshev (1997) also suggested that TV is the leading source of police information (33.6%), followed by newspapers (33%). Savel'ev (2010) found that 25% of residents receive their information from TV and radio.

Federal TV channels appear to be, in general, the most important source of information for most Russians. According to ZIRCON (2009), 81% of Russians watch federal TV channels at least one hour a day. The importance of federal TV channels as police-related information sources is higher for retired and unemployed individuals, whereas younger working professionals are more likely to rely on online sources (Cherkasov, 2006). The information about police obtained by seniors from the federal TV channels is based primarily on drama series, films, and much less on news and documentary programs (Mazaev, 2004). Bondarenko (2006a) found a positive correlation between the frequency of watching crime dramas and a positive attitude about police.

Crime and law enforcement became a significant part of Russian media content in the past 20 years (MacFadyen, 2008; Prokhorova, 2003; Rogatchevski, 2004). The content analysis of newspapers, TV news, shows, and series indicates that, overall, the Russian media portrays the Russian police in a negative manner.[48] Borovikova (2002) analyzed printed media in 2001 and found only 15% of all articles about the police had positive connotations compared to 57% that contained negative perceptions. Bondarenko (2006a) also reported that, in crime dramas and police TV series, 80% of the police imagery was negative.

Whereas the media's portrayal of the Russian police is overall negative, most Russians believe that media's representations are fair. Cherkasov (2006) found 21% of those surveyed believed the media portrayal of the police is biased. Mazaev (2004) similarly reported that only 20% believed the media smears the reputation of Russian police, while 40% stated the media flatters Russian police. Mazaev discovered that respondents who are not satisfied with the work of the police are more likely to complain about media's positive image of the police. At the same time, police officers frequently complain about the media's negative bias and blame the media for poor public attitudes (Gudkov and Dubin, 2006).

During the Soviet period, the media was fully controlled by the Party through a network of government censorship (Tomin, 1976). Thus, media coverage of the police was carefully regulated and typically included only positive police stories. Critical information was released carefully and scarcely and most crime statistics were considered a state secret. The dissolution of the Soviet Union created a variety of independent media that was no longer controlled by the Party or government. These new media outlets launched critical coverage of the police, which continued through the entire decade of the 1990s. In early 2000, government took control over the federal channels and took action to reduce the number of independent media outlets through additional regulations and licensing (Koltsova, 2006). The Media Sustainability Index (MSI) is an instrument developed by the International Research Exchange Board (IREX) to measure the country's development of the media's independence and professional journalistic growth. The Russian MSI indicates that between 2001 and 2011 the media sector suffered a significant loss of its independence, plurality, and journalist professionalism (IREX, 2011). Nevertheless, the Russian media continues to exhibit critical attitudes toward the police.

In order to understand the Russian police media strategy, four high-profile cases were analyzed that occurred between 2009 and 2011. The circumstances of these cases are outlined in Table 6.17. One hundred articles were reviewed in six different media outlets[49] and we concluded that the police failed to develop an effective strategy when dealing with the independent Russian media. Four major interrelated problems can be outlined from the analysis.

First, the most common police reaction when a high-profile story emerges in the news is to delay providing any public information. For example, in the case of the Primorye partisans, the head of the regional office refused to provide any comments on the June 8th police shooting.[50] At that time, the "partisans" already committed four different assaults on police, and the media were circulating rumors on possible connections and their motivations. The same tactic was used in the Sagra case concerning self-defense where the head of the investigative department refused to provide any comments on the shooting.[51] Later, the journalists interviewed the residents of the village and got some controversial information about the case.

Second, the common strategy used by police in high-profile cases is restricting the sources of information for the public and media. For example, in the case of the Yevsyukov shooting, access to the Web page of the entire police office was restricted by the day following the incident.[52] In the case of the Kushchevskaya massacre, access to the village was restricted for all journalists two weeks from the incident when local police claimed that journalists were interfering with the investigation.[53]

Third, when providing information about the case, police officials often downplay the case's importance. For example, in the Yevsyukov shooting, in an early interview, his immediate superior suggested that Yevsyukov was a good police officer who had "family issues" that caused him to open fire in the supermarket.[54] However, the next day after this statement, the journalists found that Yevskyukov had known issues with alcoholism and other incidents of public shootings.

Table 6.17 Case studies of media–police relations

Story Name	Story Summary	Sequence of events and Media's Coverage of the Story
Yevsyukov case	The head of a district police office, Denis Yevsyukov, opened fire in a local supermarket in Moscow on April 24, 2009. As a result, two people died and seven were injured. Yevsyukov was arrested at the scene. He was later tried and received a life sentence.	The story immediately drew national attention of the media. In early comments, Yevsyukov's immediate superior claimed that he was a good police officer. However, the media soon discovered the suspect had problems in the past including alcoholism and incidents of public shooting. Despite this, he was promoted to head of the district police office at the age of 32. Several days after the shooting, President Medvedev fired the head of the Moscow police office and the minister of the MVD fired three deputy heads of the city district police office.
Primorye partisans	An organized group of six young men in the Far East committed four attacks on police officers on May 25, 27, 29, and June 8, 2010. The group was originally surrounded by police in their village, but was able to escape through the forest to a local city. Four of the men were surrounded on June 11 in a city apartment; two committed suicide and two were arrested. Two other members of the group were arrested separately.	Whereas the incidents were reported in the local and central media, it was after June 8th when the four attacks were clearly linked by journalists. Even at that point, the local police refused to comment on the situation and denied the group's existence. It was only after June 11th, when the regional police provided information on the incident, that there was an immediate variety of rumors and speculations. At the same time, prior to June 11, 2010, members of the group published video Internet messages explaining their actions were caused by local police abuse. Parents of the young men also gave interviews accusing the police of abuse, which motivated the men to commit violent crimes. Police officials reported to the media the abuse allegations were unsubstantiated after the official investigation was conducted. The head of the district police office where the alleged abuse took place was suspended during the internal investigation.

(continued)

Table 6.17 Case studies of media–police relations (continued)

Story Name	Story Summary	Sequence of events and Media's Coverage of the Story
Kushchevskaya massacre	On November 4, 2010, 12 people, including four children, were killed in the village of Kushchevskaya located in Southern Russia. Sergei Tsapok, a leader of an organized group and local businessman, is currently charged with ordering the murders. There are five other defendants in the case including a local deputy and member of United Russia. The motive of the murders appeared to be the refusal of a victim, a private farmer, to pay racketeering fees to Tsapok's group.	The story immediately received national headlines because of the large number of victims including small children. Within two to three days, the police provided little information to the media "in the interests of the investigation." This produced a variety of speculations over the reasons for the crime including the fact that the murders were ordered by an organized group that took over the village with the help of corrupt police. Between November 10 and November 24, the media reported that several suspects were arrested including Sergei Tsapok. On November 18, the head of the district police department retired and, on November 24, the head of the local center to fight extremism (MVD) was arrested on suspicion of assisting Tsapok's group.
Sagra self-defense case	On July 1, 2011, residents of Sagra, a small village in the Ural mountains, had to defend themselves against an armed group of people who came to the village for revenge. As a result one assailant was killed. The police arrived two hours later and were unable to arrest anyone except for residents of the village.	The original story in the news was brief and reported the death of one man in a small village from a shooting. However, a few days later the new details emerged that the deceased was part of large group of people who came to the village with guns and threatened the residents. The media alleged the assailants were part of the organized crime group that came to the village to protect one of their members. This member resided in the village and distributed drugs. Two residents of Sagra were immediately arrested. The local police did not arrest any of the assailants and did not find the cars that they used in the crimes. Only two weeks later, when the Investigative Committee took over the case, 15 assailants were arrested and charged with shooting and hooliganism. The majority of the assailants were residents of the North Caucasus area. The head of the district police office was fired and charged with the crime of neglecting his professional duties that caused a death.

In the case of the Kushchevskaya massacre, the head of the district police office insisted there were no organized gangs in his village. This proclamation came even after the investigative committee already had admitted the fact that murders were committed by the organized group under Tsapok's leadership.[55] In the Sagra case, the police maintained in the beginning that the altercation was "a simple fight between village residents and urban visitors over personal issues" and that it had nothing to do with organized crime, ethnic conflicts, or drug dealing.[56] However, the interviews of the villagers suggested otherwise.

Finally, the fourth interrelated problem is that the police ignore the "alternative stories" of crime that often flourish online and in the media when other more reliable information is not available. For example, in the Yevskyukov shooting case, from interviews with the suspect's colleagues, the journalist deduced that Yevskyukov had known alcohol abuse issues and a past history of public shootings. Regardless, he was promoted to a prestigious position as the head of the MVD district office. This information, in combination with comments from Yevskyukov's immediate superior about his putative good character, created a variety of rumors. These were primarily about Yevskyukov being a corrupt police officer who was promoted despite his substandard performance. The rumors were intensely discussed by bloggers and the online media, but the MVD remained silent for some period of time.[57]

The only official reaction was that the head of the Moscow police was fired by President Medvedev along with three deputy heads of city district offices by the MVD minister without any explanation.[58] This government reaction only strengthened public suspicions that Yevskyukov was an example of a corrupt police officer who became publicly dangerous.

An even more apparent example of ignoring the "alternative story" is the case of the Primorye partisans. In this case, some of the young men involved provided online video and text messages for several weeks describing their assaults on the police as vengeance against police brutality and abuse they were subjected to in the past.[59] The police made no comments about these allegations until the suspects were caught and two committed suicide during the attack. As a result, the online messages created an image of the men fighting against police corruption and subsequently convinced a large group of online users that killing the police officers was justified.[60] Massive online discussions in the blogosphere, and even national representative surveys about the actions of the Primorye partisans, indicated that many were sympathetic to those who had killed the police officers.[61] Some media sources suggested that village residents helped young men to escape from the police because they were also sympathetic with their cause.[62]

The analysis of the police–media interaction suggests the police have not learned how to build a constructive dialog in the modern period with either the traditional or modern media outlets. Instead, they continue to use methods employed during the Soviet period that includes delay and the restriction of information. These antiquated methods may not be very harmful in societies where high levels of public–police trust exist. However, in post-Soviet modern Russia, where more than half of the citizens do not trust the police any time, these methods are proving to be devastating.

When clear, timely, and precise official police information is not available, Russians tend to imagine the worst-case scenario and almost always interpret the silence unfavorably for the police. This process has even become more intense since the development and availability of social media throughout the country. Whenever there is a new crime story emerging, the Russian blogosphere is flooded with rumors, discussions, videos, and even communication from the alleged offenders. This information often becomes so popular that even traditional media, such as newspapers, feel the need to report it.[63] In such conditions, silence from police officials, or dry statements made only after long periods of time, are viewed with public suspicion.[64]

6.6 Concluding Remarks

The research studies reviewed data from the Volgograd 1998–2007 surveys, which clearly indicate that public–police relations in Russia are seriously strained. The public trust of and satisfaction with police has remained low during the past 20 years. The majority of Russians believe the police situation is continuing to deteriorate despite policy reforms or other government actions. All Russian demographics groups demonstrate distrust and dissatisfaction of the police; however, the retired, rural residents, and those with little education are more likely to support the police. Many studies speculate these groups are simply left with no other means to protect themselves, and therefore have to rely on the police in the absence of some other more reliable options.

When compared to that of other countries, Russia's police situation appears to be one of the worst. Russia consistently ranks at the bottom of public–police satisfaction, trust of the police, and safety concerns even among other post-Soviet countries. Traditional factors, such as fear of crime, victimization, and concerns with safety play an important role in explaining the low levels of public trust and satisfaction with the police. Nevertheless, the official crime rates have been found to be inconsistent with public opinions about the police.

Many researchers suggest that the official crimes rates are manipulated and do not reflect the true level of crime. The consequences of low police public trust and satisfaction are devastating for Russian society. The most serious concerns include high levels of unreported crime, lack of police cooperation, avoidance, overt fear of the police among law-abiding citizens, and tolerating the resistance of police.

The police officers themselves are often aware of the low public satisfaction, but tend to blame the lack of funding and the quality of legal regulations for their poor performance. Police officers also blame Russian citizens for legal noncompliance and ignorance of the law. The mutual blame clearly indicates the extreme level of alienation between the citizens and the police.

Public survey research repeatedly suggests that Russians often view police as an alien and dangerous organization that only serves the interests of powerful bureaucrats and wealthy individuals. Unsurprisingly, very few Russians are interested in assisting the police. The police media strategy is ineffective and frequently involves limitations on media access to information and deleterious delays. This often leads to a spread of rumors and speculations by the media, which typically are unfavorable to the police. The process has intensified in the past several years with the availability and development of social networking and online media sources that are often beyond the control of the traditional media or police.

Endnotes

1. In this chapter, we used the results of more than 200 surveys conducted by well-known pollsters and research organizations in Russia, such as WCIOM (All-Russian Center for Research of Public Opinion), FOM (Fund of Public Opinion), Levada Center (named after famous sociologist Yuri Levada), ROMIR (Russian Public Opinion and Research of Market), and ZIRCON (company comprised of several research institutes of the Russian Academy of Sciences). Many of these studies were only published on the companies' official Web sites or included in their databases maintained online. Most of these companies used representative samples of the Russian Federation in their studies, which allowed us to generalize their findings to the entire country. However, these companies used different methodology and instruments for their surveys, which made direct comparison of their data somewhat difficult We also used studies conducted annually by authors and partners from the Volgograd Academy of MVD in the Volgograd region during 1998–2011. The stratified multistage sample technique allowed us to obtain a representative sample of the Volgograd region. Because comparison of major demographic characteristics of the Volgograd region yielded only a few differences with the known parameters of the Russian Federation population, we concluded that our findings from the Volgograd region can be, to a certain degree, generalized to the entire country.
2. Satisfaction with police was measured as a positive/negative change in what occurred in the last three years.
3. Refers to satisfaction with the work of the police in the neighborhood.
4. Refers to satisfaction with the work of the police in the neighborhood.
5. Refers to the Moscow police only.
6. Refers to the traffic police only.
7. Refers to the Ministry of Internal Affairs in general.
8. Refers to the local police only.

9. Ibid.
10. Measures trust of all law enforcement agencies.
11. Ibid.
12. Ibid.
13. Ibid..
14. Measures trust of the Ministry of Internal Affairs only.
15. Refers to law enforcement agencies.
16. Only refers to the public trust of police in the Ossetia region of Russia.
17. Refers to the traffic police only.
18. Refers to police of the Moscow city only.
19. Refers to the work of the police in the neighborhood only.
20. Refers to the traffic police only.
21. These data were collected by the authors of this book in the Volgograd region. The sample is representative of the Volgograd region's population, which is similar to the population of the Russian Federation. Thus, data presented in this table can be generalized to the entire Russian Federation.
22. These data were collected by the authors of this book in the Volgograd region. See previous endnotes on details of sampling and representativeness.
23. Ibid.
24. This can be partially due to the fact that the Volgograd study contains a large number of "don't know" answers.
25. These findings are in line with other research on public trust of police around the world. The 2012 study of 50 nations reported that elderly, female, married, and retired persons tend to have higher confidence in police in the overall sample (Cao, Lai, and Zhao, 2012).
26. For example, in the study by Gudkov (2000), police officers ranked second lowest on public trust followed only by politicians.
27. The mean for Russia was 3.1 compared to 3.8 for Poland, 3.9 for Romania, and 4.0 for Hungary (Mishler and Rose, 2005).
28. The fact of data manipulation was confirmed officially by the Attorney General of Russia whose agency conducted a review of statistical reporting within the MVD system in 2010. For example, see an article by the Public Council of Media Outlets affiliated with the Moscow district department of MVD at http://www.os-guvd.ru/news/20110429/250097056.html (retrieved on September 20, 2011).
29. The data collected from the official Web site for the State Department of Statistics of Russia (*Komitet gosudarstvennoi statistiki*), which obtained it directly from the MVD. Retrieved on June 6, 2011 from www.gks.ru
30. This data was only available for 2003–2010 and was collected and estimated from semiannual reports on crime statistics and investigation published by the Ministry of Internal Affairs. Retrieved on June 6, 2011 from www.mvd.ru
31. Data missing for "theft from garages" for these years.
32. Ibid.
33. Ibid.
34. Ibid.
35. Data for these variables are only available within the last year. All other variables are within the past five years.
36. Ibid.

37. These data were collected by the authors of this book in the Volgograd region. The sample is representative of the Volgograd region's population, which is similar to the population of the Russian Federation. Thus, data presented in this table can be generalized to the entire Russian Federation.
38. According to Gudkov (2000), in 1993, fear of crime reached 70%; when respondents were asked in retrospect, only 19% reported fear of crime five years prior to the survey.
39. Refers to involuntary contacts only.
40. Refers to the district officers only (*uchastkovyi*).
41. Measured the period of time from one week to three years.
42. Measured a bad experience as well as good experience.
43. Measured the period of time from 1 or 2 years to 20 years.
44. Refers to the citizens of Moscow and St. Petersburg only.
45. For example, see the list of the most serious police problems identified by Oks (2010). The top issue is corruption, followed by the lack of control, illegal and antisocial behavior of police officers, and nontransparent decision making.
46. On the contradictions between the illegal orders of superior officers and laws and its reflection in the media, see an article by Kolyushkina (2005).
47. These data were collected by the authors of this book in the Volgograd region. The sample is representative of the Volgograd region's population, which is similar to the population of the Russian Federation. Thus, data presented in this table can be generalized to the entire Russian Federation. Note: Percentages were calculated based on the number of people who responded to each question. Participants could indicate more than one source of information.
48. On the underlying meaning of Russian media imagery on police, see the work by MacFayden (2008).
49. This includes newspapers *Komsomolskaya Pravda*, *Arguments and Facts*, *Utro*, *Rosbalt*, *Trud*, and *Ekho Moskvy*. These outlets represent a variety of political affiliations available in Russia.
50. See, for example, an article "In Primorie the patrol car of traffic police was shut at...": http://lenta.ru/news/ 2010/06/08/obstrel/ (retrieved December 1, 2011).
51. See, for example, an article "Massive fight in Sagra village": http://www.kp.ru/onlin e/news/926535/ (retrieved on December 1, 2011).
52. See, for example, an article "Internet site of UVD for Southern district of Moscow where information on Yevsyukov was deleted": http://kp.ru/online/news/479109/ (retrieved on December 1, 2011).
53. See, for example, an article "Kushchevskaya is becoming a closed area": http://www.kp.ru/online/news/779982/ (retrieved on December 1, 2011).
54. See, for example, an article "Drunk police major opens fire in the supermarket in South of Moscow": http://www.kp.ru /online/news/4 77803 (retrieved on December 1, 2011).
55. See, for example, an article "The head of the Kushchevskaya ROVD: We don't have any band here!": http://kp.ru/daily/2 4593.4/761482/ (retrieved on December 1, 2011).
56. See, for example, an article "The criminal charges are filed against assailants on Sagra village": http://kp.ru/d aily/25716.4/914542/ (retrieved on December 1, 2011).

57. See, for example, an article "How the police generals were promoting the police major-murderer": http://www.kp.ru/daily/2428 5/481055/ (retrieved on December 1, 2011).
58. See, for example, an article "The major police—murderer has a deadly dose of alcohol in his blood": http://www.kp.ru /daily/24286/481 664/ (retrieved on December 1, 2011).
59. For example, this video was allegedly shot by "Primorye partisans" while hiding in the forest from police. See: http://www.youtube.com/watch?v=pQqnhZiBzL8 (retrieved on December 6, 2011).
60. For example, even now the Internet is flooded with video messages glorifying the "Primorye partisans." See: http://www.yout ube.com/watch? v=7mp AmkODjxM (retrieved on December 6, 2011).
61. The representative survey of Russia conducted by the Levada Center in June of 2010 indicated that only 37% of all respondents believed "Primorye partisans" were criminals, 34% stated that they were simply young men frustrated with the abuse of police, and 13% suggested they were "vigilantes" who were fighting against corruption. Moreover, 55% agreed that the case of "Primorye partisans" was reflective of public attitudes about police in Russia and only 35% suggested this was a separate incident of violence. See the report by the Levada Center, "Public Opinion–2010": http://www.levada.ru/sites/default/files/levada_2010_rus.pdf (retrieved on December 6, 2011. The nonrepresentative polls, taken through the Internet, suggested that an even higher number of young online users were supporting the group.
62. For example, see the interview with the faculty of local university at: http://www.svobodanews.ru/content/article/2067836.html (retrieved on December 6, 2011).
63. For example, see an article about the first review of Russian blogs published by traditional media in 2009 at: http://kp.ru/daily/2 4327/520156/ (retrieved on December 12, 2011).
64. For information on Russian blogosphere, see, for example, the report by Harvard University "Public Discourse in the Russian Blogosphere" (Etling et al., 2010).

Police Corruption and Abuse of Power in Russia

7

7.1 General Problem of Police Corruption in Russia

The term *police corruption* has multiple meanings in the literature. In this chapter, the definition that was developed by Ivkovic (2005, p. 16) will be used:

> An action or omission, a promise of action of omission, or an attempted action or omission committed by a police officer or a group of police officers, characterized by the police officer's misuse of the official position, motivated in significant part by the achievement of personal gain.

This definition is broad enough to encompass not only police bribery, but also the abuse of power in the form of arbitrary detention, misuse of physical force, and crime statistic manipulations, which will be discussed in this chapter.

In the past 10 years, Russia made significant improvement in its socioeconomic development. The Human Development Index (HDI) of the United Nations provides a composite measure of the three most important aspects of a country's human development: health, education, and income. For the Russian Federation, the HDI value increased from 0.66 in 2000 to 0.75 in 2011. Currently Russia ranks 66th among 187 comparable countries.[1] Yet Russia's record of corruption remains poor. The measures of corruption developed by Transparency International indicate that Russia continues to be a highly corrupt country with no improvement during the past 10 years.

Russia's Corruption Perception Index (CPI) in 2000 was 2.1 out of 10 possible points. During the years 2000–2011, the CPI scores for Russia ranged anywhere between 2.1 and 2.8. In 2011, the CPI was 2.4. In comparison to former Soviet countries, Russia remains at the bottom of CPI ranking. Other countries in the region improved their corruption scores with values above 3 and 4.[2]

Another data point that indicates a troublesome situation with corruption in Russia is a set of World Governance Indicators (WDI) that was developed by the World Bank Group. Among other factors, WDI measures the government's ability to control corruption by ranking the countries in percentiles. Based on the WDI during the past seven years, the Russian government's ability to control corruption decreased from 29.1% in 2003 to 12.9%

in 2010. This placed Russia at the bottom 15% of all the countries measured related to corruption abatement efforts.[3]

Many studies suggest that police corruption in Russia contributes significantly to the overall problem of government corruption along with the government's inability to decrease corruption (INDEM, 2001b; Ryvkina, 2000).[4] The majority of studies also agree the Russian police have been highly corrupted over the past 20 years regardless of numerous reform attempts by the government (A. Beck and Robertson, 2009b; Uidriks and Reenen, 2005; Weiler, 2004). Public surveys in Russia indicate that citizens consider the police to be one of the most corrupt government institutions (INDEM, 2007). According to Mazaev (1997), public perceptions of police corruption grew significantly between 1993 and 1996. A study by FOM (Public Opinion Foundation) demonstrates that between 1998 and 2006, public perception of police corruptness continued to grow from 46% to 57%.[5] Table 7.1 summarizes selected findings from various surveys about police corruption. The table indicates that at any point during the past 20 years anywhere between 48% and 83% of Russians considered the police corrupt, or very corrupt. When the participants were asked to rank the pervasiveness of corruption among various political and societal institutions, the police were ranked at the top of corrupted Russian institutions (INDEM, 2005a; Ministry of Economic Development, 2011).

Within the Ministry of Internal Affairs (MVD), the traffic police led the perceived level of corruption (50%), followed by criminal investigators (36%), and then street patrol services (27%) (Gudkov, Dubin, and Leonova, 2004). In the study by Medvezhevsky, Girin, and Mizeryi (1999), 23.4% of drivers and 20% of pedestrians said all traffic police are corrupt and dishonest. Only 10% of drivers and 8.2% of pedestrians believed traffic police officers were honest. In a government-sanctioned study by the Ministry of Economic Development of Russia, 77% of the respondents considered the traffic police dishonest and corrupt (Ministry of Economic Development, 2011). Also, the perceived corruption for police, in general, and traffic police specifically, remained the same between 2001 and 2010 (Ministry of Economic Development, 2011).

The surveys indicated levels of direct experience with police corruption are lower than the overall perception of police corruption and ranges from 9% to 53% in any given year (Table 7.1). However, when estimating the total number of incidents of police misconduct, there is a minimum of 16.4 million acts of police misconduct during a two- or three-year period (Gerber and Mendelson, 2008). Blue collar male respondents between the ages of 24 and 50 without a college degree were more likely to report direct experience with police abuse (Gudkov, Dubin, and Leonova, 2004). Similar findings are reported by Gerber and Mendelson (2008), who suggest that higher status

Table 7.1 Summary of empirical findings related to the variable "do you believe that police officers are in general corrupt" from 1999 to 2010

		Believe that Police Are Corrupt			Ranking of Police Corruption among Other Institutions[a]	Have First-Hand Experience with Corruption		
Author(s)	Year	Yes	No	Don't Know		Yes	No	Don't Know
FOM	1998	47.0%						
FOM	1999	48.0%	—	—	1			
INDEM	2001	67.4%	17.7%	14.9%	1			
		73.6%[17]	15.5%	11.7%	2			
INDEM	2002	73.6%[18]	14.3%	12.2%				
		71.9%	21.3%	9.7%				
FOM	2002	55.0%			1	28.0%[19]	66.0%	9.0%
INDEM	2004	52.2%[20]	17.5%	30.3%				
		74.2%[21]	12.5%	13.3%				
		83.6%[22]	8.5%	7.8%				
WCIOM	2004					18.0%	69.0%	
Andreev	2005	46.0%						
Levada	2004	80.0%	—	—		26.0%		

[a] 1 = Highest level of corruption

(continued)

Table 7.1 Summary of empirical findings related to the variable "do you believe that police officers are in general corrupt" from 1999 to 2010 (continued)

		Believe that Police Are Corrupt			Ranking of Police Corruption among Other Institutions[a]	Have First-Hand Experience with Corruption		
Author(s)	Year	Yes	No	Don't Know		Yes	No	Don't Know
INDEM	2005	81.4%	13.9%	4.7%				
WCIOM	2005					23.2%	66.2%	10.6%
FOM[23]	2006	57.0%			1	27.0%	70.0%	3.0%
WCIOM[24]	2006				3	44.0%	53.0%	3.0%
WCIOM	2007				2			
FOM	2007	61.0%[25]						
FOM	2008						87.0%	1.0%
WCIOM	2008				3			
Gerber						9.0%		
Levada	2010	60.0%	2.0%					
WCIOM[26]	2010					44.0%	48.0%	9.0%
Ministry of Economic Development	2011	71.0%	14.0%			53.0%	46.0%	

[a] 1 = Highest level of corruption

groups, and Slavic Russians, are somewhat less likely to be victimized by police than blue-collar lower status non-Slavic Russians.

As with perceived corruption, the units of the traffic police were listed among the top violators of human rights during direct citizen contacts with the police (Public Verdict Fund, 2010). A report by the Ministry of Economic Development indicated that 65% of citizens had first-hand experiences with traffic police corruption (Ministry of Economic Development, 2011). Similar findings were reported by the Public Council of Russian Federation. The report disclosed that 63% of all reported corruption was related to law enforcement agencies (Obschestvennaya Palata, 2011a). Table 7.1 presents a significant gap between perceptions and personal experiences of police abuse and corruption. Differences between the levels of perceived and direct experiences with corruption also were reported by Rose and Mishler (2010) who concluded that perceptions of corruption do not always suggest there is direct experience with corruption. Instead, they found that political awareness is the most important predictor for perception of corruption, whereas the probability of contact is an important factor in predicting experience with corruption.

Despite the relatively low proportion of those reporting personal experiences with police corruption in the past, the majority of respondents believe that future victimization by police is very probable. According to Gryaznova (2006), 71% of those surveyed in 2005 reported that it is probable that they will become victims of police abuse, and only 3% indicated it was unlikely. In 2010, the Levada Center published a new report in which 66% of respondents considered that future police victimization is possible and 3% reported it was unlikely.

The study by Gryaznova also reported that in 2006, 81% of respondents thought they were not protected against police abuse, and 59% did not believe the Russian criminal justice system would offer protection from police abuse (2006). According to Levada, in 2010, 54% believed the Russian criminal justice system would not protect them against police abuse (2010). Young males (and females of all ages) reported higher chances for potential police abuse than older groups. However, all Russian demographic groups were convinced they are equally unprotected against police abuse and corruption (Gryaznova, 2006). In the Volgograd study conducted in 2011, 40.6% reported that future victimization by police is likely, or very likely.[6] It was found that only 52.4% of respondents believed the Russian criminal justice system will protect them from police abuse. As in studies by Gryaznova and Levada, the Volgograd research in 2011 reveals that younger males were more likely to believe in future victimization by police and were less convinced the Russian criminal justice system would offer protection.

The problem of widespread police corruption and abuse was the focus of an annual report from the Russian Ombudsman spanning the years 1998 through 2010 concerning human rights violations.[7] The Ombudsman reported that the police ranked among the top violators of human rights with at least 25% of complaints directed against the police every year.[8] Similar findings were reported by the All-Russian nongovernment organization, Clean Hands, which was established to fight corruption. In 2009, Clean Hands received 2,436 viable complaints about corruption within the MVD that represented 30% of their annual complaints (Chistye Ruki (Clean Hands), 2009). Internationally recognized organizations, such as Amnesty International and Human Rights Watch, published reports that outlined specific cases and estimates of police corruption and abuse in Russia (Amnesty International, 2002; Human Rights Watch, 1999). Russian human rights organizations, such as Committee against Torture,[9] the Public Verdict,[10] the Memorial,[11] and the Moscow Helsinki Group[12] also routinely publish specific cases of police abuse and corruption and applicable legal remedies.

An analysis of European Court of Human Rights (ECHR) practices against the Russian government also provides strong evidence that police mistreat their citizens and abuse their power.[13] A significant number of cases against Russia in the ECHR jurisdiction deal with police brutality, arbitrary pretrial detention, and inhumane conditions in pretrial detention centers (Rudinsky, 2008).[14]

Lastly, the Ministry of Internal Affairs statistical reports on disciplinary actions provide some insight on the scope of police corruption even though many experts believe the data are unreliable (Skomorokhov and Shikhanov, 2006). In 2009, for example, according to the MVD, 101,000 offenses were committed by police officers including 4,202 that were criminal offenses (Tagaev, 2010).[15] In 2011, the MVD reported 50,000 violations were committed by police officers during the period of January through May of 2011 alone. Some 2,000 of these were criminal offenses.[16] However, experts in this area believe the true number of violations is exponentially higher than the MVD official statistics (INDEM, 2001a; Jurkanin and Sergeev, 2012).

7.2 Underlying Factors of Police Corruption in Russia

A variety of factors that explain Russian police corruption are discussed in the literature. These include insufficient funding and training, lack of external supervision, and a lack of decision-making transparency (A. Beck and Robertson, 2005, 2009b; Gilinskiy, 2005; Roudik, 2008). For the purposes of our analysis, we divided all the studies into four large groups.

The first group is focused on a historical analysis of the Russian government. The analysis concludes that corruption, including police corruption, is an "old Russian habit" embedded in the national culture from past experiences. Some address the phenomena of "feeding" (*kormlenie*) back to the ninth century where regional heads appointed by the tsar were expected to be "fed" by the local population through legalized donations (i.e., bribery) (Gilinskiy, 2004; Shergina, 2001). The analysis of other periods in prerevolutionary Russia also suggests that corruption, including police corruption, remained a serious problem at any given period of time (Moller and Skaaning, 2010).

Whereas the prerevolutionary period of Russian history is important for understanding the roots of corruption, some studies suggest that police corruption should be viewed primarily as the problem of "Soviet heritage." The Soviet period brought to life the system of corrupt government officials intertwined with organized crime (INDEM, 2001a; Shelley, 1996). The planned economy and Party nomenclature privileges created a system known as *blat.* It prevailed and became widely accepted during the Soviet period seen in the 1970s and 1980s (Krastev, 2002). *Blat* was an interconnected system of personal favors used for the exchange of consumer goods during a period of commodity scarcity and shortages of other resources (Ledeneva, 2002).

Blat, to some degree, was tolerated by the Soviet government as the acceptable way to increase a planned economy's efficiency for both average Soviet citizens and high echelon members of the nomenclature (Finckenauer and Voronin, 2001). Unlike bribery and modern-day corruption, *blat* typically did not involve money. It was well-structured and concealed within each societal group (Ledeneva, 2002). On a larger scale, *blat* was transformed into the "shadow economy," black markets, and illegal enterprises through the misuse of state property by government officials (Finckenauer and Voronin, 2001). The other "Soviet heritage" that shaped corruption is the lack of social (interpersonal) trust during the post-Soviet period. This resulted from both the authoritarian political regimes and the existence of black markets and networks of economic "fixers" (Paldam and Svendsen, 2001).

Some of the literature on corruption emphasizes that the early post-Soviet period is the main cause of modern Russian police corruption. The experiences of rapid political and economic transitions from a planned economy to a free market during the early 1990s were often blamed for contemporary Russian police corruption (Sajo, 1998; Salagaev, Shashkin, and Konnov, 2008). Corruption is thought to be a result of deteriorating economic and social conditions and a by-product of growing interconnections between former Party nomenclature (transformed into new business elite and government officials) and members of organized crime (Glinkina, 2002; Ryvkina, 2000; V. Volkov, 2002). Corruption is closely tied to the maturation of Russian organized crime during the societal transition and its penetration into the police and other weakening government agencies (Galeotti, 2004; Serio, 2008; Shelley, 2002; V. Volkov, 2002). This argument is supported by similar processes and connections observed in other former Soviet countries (Holmes, 2009; Ivkovic and Shelley, 2008).

The second group of studies focuses on the structural and functional attributes of the modern Russian police that led to the facilitation of police corruption. One of the most serious problems was the unnecessary centralization and hierarchical structure of the police combined with the extreme militarization of the workforce (Kuztnetsov, 2009; Shepeleva and Novikova, 2005). The recent laws only seem to intensify these issues. The new 2011 law on "Police Service" not only makes orders from superior officers mandatory for execution, but also lists noncompliance with such orders as grounds for serious reprimands including criminal liability.[27] Russian police officers often reported that they were given and obeyed what were apparently illegal orders (Gladarev, 2011a; Public Verdict Fund, 2005).

The tradition of blind compliance with orders is also known to be practiced at the police academies and MVD higher education institutions (Public Verdict Fund, 2005; Shelepova, 2004). The monthly bonuses for low-ranking police officers, which constitute a significant part of their income, often depend on their performance as determined by a superior's assessment, which makes the compliance almost absolute (Public Verdict Fund, 2005). Many police officers reported feeling helpless and unprotected from the potential retaliation of their superiors. Some of the superiors are known to have psychological problems (Borisova, 1998; Yanbukhtin, 2005).[28] Thus, the current structure of the Russian police and its workforce prevents transparency decision making and encourages hierarchal subordination, which eventually leads to higher levels of corruption and lower levels of public trust (A. Beck and Robertson, 2005).

One result of the centralization and militarization is the lack of a viable and independent agency to oversee police activities and to investigate corruption (Robertson, 2004). The internal service of the MVD is apparently inefficient due to its subordinate role. Many police officers reported that investigations conducted by the internal service are mostly formalistic and superficial (Shepeleva and Novikova, 2005).[29] The new Investigative Committee that is charged with combating corruption is also hierarchically structured and fully dependent upon the president.[30]

So far, the Investigative Committee has not been effective regarding addressing police corruption even though it initiated several high-profile cases. The survey results from 2011[31] indicated that only 38.2% of Russians believed the creation of the new Investigative Committee would make any difference in the levels of police corruption. The WCIOM findings from a 2010a study are similar and indicate that only 36% believed the new Investigative Committee can effectively fight corruption; a large number of the respondents (37%) were undecided.[32]

The Prosecutor's Office (*Procuracy*) traditionally charged with "supervision of legality" during investigations conducted by the criminal police has the same problem as the Investigative Committee and does not appear to be effective in addressing corruption (Chikov, 2005; Shepeleva and Novikova, 2005).[33]

Moreover, the *procuracy* itself was recently involved in corruption scandals that further undermined its reputation as a guardian against corruption.[34]

The ineffective government control over police is coupled with insufficient civilian oversight. Nontransparent decision making and a hierarchical structure impede the effective control of the police by Russia's institutions of civil society and media (Simonov, 2005). The new law "On Police Service" directly banned police officers from releasing any information to the media and makes any oversight by the media very difficult.[35]

The media also is known to be threatened by successful defamation suits filed by police officials in cases when the media has reported cases of potential corruption (Ombudsman, 2010). Police whistleblowers like Dymovskyi and Matveev were charged with various crimes shortly after revealing information about corruption to the public.[36]

The lack of a mature civil society in Russia also contributes to the problem even though some examples of plausible partnerships between the police and Russian society do exist (Uhlin, 2006). As a part of the 2011 police reform, the "public councils" were reestablished at the central and regional levels of the MVD. They are intended to provide police oversight by prominent members of Russian society. However, from an analysis of the law, it appears that "public councils" have little authority when it comes to the investigation of police corruption.[37] They serve primarily as hubs that receive and transfer complaints to the government agencies and can be present at the meetings when citizens file complaints to the police. However, the selection of the public councils' membership is controlled by the police and their decisions are treated only as recommendations. Not surprisingly, most public councils at the regional and local levels are criticized by the media for being ineffective and only a formality.[38]

The lack of effective control from both the government and civil society results in a lack of police accountability (A. Beck and Lee, 2002; Shergina, 2001). The analysis of court practices related to bribery and information presented by the Russian Supreme Court, the Public Council, and reported in the media show that only a small number of low-ranking police officers have been prosecuted for taking small bribes.[39] Moreover, most of the sentences for defendants convicted of bribery were suspended with few sentencing restrictions (Obschestvennaya Palata, 2011a).[40]

According to official government statistics, only 1,000 of all criminal defendants in 2010 were sentenced for bribery and were banned from their professional activities.[41] Reports by the Russian Ombudsman,[42] the media, and cases published by human rights organizations, such as the Public Verdict, the Committee against Torture, and the Memorial, provide numerous examples where police officers suspected of bribery, physical abuse, and other misconduct avoided responsibility or received minor reprimands.[43] This is often done by firing the police officers immediately after the incident occurs without further investigation,[44] or by subjecting victims to prolonged bureaucratic procedures that results in dismissing the complaint.[45]

The third group of studies addresses the economic roots of Russian police corruption. Police corruption in these studies is understood as "business" with a maximization of income and a minimization of risks by the officers. Economic studies on corruption emphasize that if the risk of prosecution and other social costs remain low, corruption will prevail as one of the most lucrative business transaction (Rimskyi, 2008). The cost of anticorruption regulation and enforcement is often too high to make it an effective public policy (Michael, 2010). It is also suggested that low wages and poor equipment are among the economic reasons for pervasive police corruption in Russia (A. Beck and Robertson, 2009b; Dzutsev, Khugaeva, and Tsogoev, 2005). For example, in 2001 and 2002, Uildriks and Reenen (2003) reported the base salary for an ordinary police officer was 2,000 rubles a month (approximately $67) with a regional police officer earning no more than $200 per month.

This point of view is especially popular with police officers themselves, which provides a moral justification of their behavior (A. Beck and Lee, 2001, 2002; Public Verdict Fund, 2010). However, most researchers agree that poor funding could be a short-term stimulus for taking bribes, but may not explain the further development and maturation of police corruption (INDEM, 2001a). Previous increases in police wages had no impact on the levels of perceived police corruption among Russian citizens (Kuztnetsov, 2009). On the contrary, despite increasing the wages of the officers, the frequency of bribe solicitation continues to grow exponentially (INDEM, 2005b; Ministry of Economic Development, 2011).[46]

Finally, the fourth group of studies examined corruption as a manifestation of a larger cultural phenomenon in Russia. The widespread disrespect of the law, which causes unprecedented public tolerance to corruption, also reinforces preexisting corruptive subcultures within the police (Artemov, 2000; Khludova, 2004). Russians, in general, indicate high awareness levels about appropriate standards of police behavior and show genuine concern about corruption (Gerber and Mendelson, 2008).[47]

Yet recent public surveys show that 69% of Russians are willing to offer a traffic police officer a bribe and 28% are willing to bribe a criminal investigator if necessary (Ministry of Economic Development, 2011). INDEM (2001a) reported that 20.3% of respondents provided a bribe "just in case" it was needed in a situation that did not clearly indicate a bribe would be required.

The data also show that many police officers, and especially in the investigative departments, have a clear understanding of the normative standards required for appropriate behavior (Uidriks and Reenen, 2003). Beck and Lee (2001, 2002) found that a variety of dubious practices were "morally unacceptable" for the majority of officers and police academy students that were interviewed. Regardless of the normative standards, many police officers continue to be involved in corrupt practices. This clear disconnect between normative expectations and behavior is often explained by the "unique" Russian legal culture that typically includes a lack of respect for the law (Borisova, 1998; Gudkov, 2000; Korneeva, 2008; Shepeleva, 2005a). This widespread disrespect of the law is often related to the historic experiences of Russia during the prerevolutionary and Soviet periods (Nethercott, 2007). According to this group of studies, the general public culture of poor legal consciousness reinforces a subculture of police corruption and creates a perfect reinforcement cycle of corruption (Shepeleva, 2005a).

It is emphasized in the literature that the roots of Russian police corruption should be viewed as part of the larger phenomena of a corrupt government (Webster et al., 2000). The police are representatives of the government and the most visible and coercive institution. The police are seen or encountered more often than other agencies and, therefore, its corruptive nature is more evident to the public. But other branches of the government are also as corrupt and this implies that police corruption cannot be solved without improving the larger corruption problems within the government, generally (Obschestvennaya Palata, 2011a). Experience of other post-Soviet countries indicates the political will of the government is among the most important factors in successfully combating corruption (Holmes, 2009).

7.3 Common Forms of Police Corruption in Russia

7.3.1 Physical Abuse and Torture

Physical abuse and torture are among the most grievous forms of police corruption in Russia (Weiler, 2004). The true scope of these violations is unknown and most evidence is presented in the form of cases published by human rights activists, the media, and self-report victimization surveys. Human Rights Watch, in one of its earliest reports on Russian police torture, estimated that at least 50% of all criminal suspects may be subjected to torture and ill-treatment by police (1999). The Committee against Torture reported that 4.12% of those surveyed were victims of police torture within the past year and 21.3% were physically abused by police during their lifetimes (Committee against Torture, 2006). The findings of Gudkov, Dubin, and Leonova (2004) support previous research. He concluded that 24% of urban residents experienced police physical abuse in their lifetimes. Gerber and Mendelson (2008) indicated that through 2002 and 2004, between 4.8% and 5.5% of those surveyed experienced police physical abuse each year. Gilinskiy (2011) reported that 25.5% of respondents in St. Petersburg were unlawfully ill-treated by police at least once in their lifetimes and 5.9% in 2005 alone.

Reports by Amnesty International (2002), Human Rights Watch (1999), and the Committee against Torture (2006) found that common forms of police torture and ill-treatment include prolonged beating, asphyxiation, suspension by the arms and legs, denial of food and drink, and electroshock. Many of these practices are done during the preliminary criminal investigation, short-time administrative detention, and at the sobering-up stations (Amnesty International, 2002; Ombudsman, 2010). The most common police units involved in physical abuse are police detectives (*operativniki*), patrol and post services (PPS), and the sobering-up station's staff (Amnesty International, 2002; Committee against Torture, 2006; Ombudsman, 2010).

Human Rights Watch (1999) found younger, less-educated males are more likely to be detained and maltreated. Gerber and Mendelson (2008) indicates that males under 40 experienced more police violence (11.2%) than other age groups, or females (9% average). Gudkov, Dubin, and Leonova (2004) reported that Russian citizens view the most vulnerable population subgroups that experience police abuse as drunk individuals (67%), youth and teenagers (48%), the homeless (23%), and individuals of non-European ethnic origin (17%). Gerber and Mendelson (2008) also found the odds of police victimization is 43% higher for non-European Russian citizens. Gilinskiy et al. (2002) concluded that 90% of ex-convicts, 70% of the homeless, and 20% of students residing in dorms reported police physical abuse during their detention.

The majority of experts and victims agree that the leading motive for torture and abuse are forced criminal confessions followed by a motivation to steal, or misappropriate, valuables of detained persons, racial discrimination and hatred, and the pathological cruelty of police officers (Amnesty International, 2002; Committee against Torture, 2006; Human Rights Watch, 1999). Misappropriation of valuables most often occurs in the sobering-up stations, and is perpetrated by the staff or members of the postpatrolling services who deliver publicly intoxicated individuals (Amnesty International, 2002).[48] Police detectives (sometimes together with criminal investigators) are reported to be involved in the psychical abuse of suspects to elicit confessions and solve crimes (Human Rights Watch, 1999).

Russian police officer surveys show that physical abuse is somewhat a morally accepted practice. Gudkov and Dubin (2006) reported that only 31% of the officers found that subjecting suspects to physical violence was unacceptable under any circumstances. Sixty-six percent indicated that it is acceptable to violently abuse an individual who verbally assaulted a police officer. Goncharenko (1999) found that 65% of criminal investigators thought the use of *illegal* violence toward suspects was justifiable. Both Gudkov and Goncharenko indicated that more educated and highly ranked officers are less likely to accept and justify physical abuse against suspects and defendants.

The public surveys demonstrate that Russian citizens are aware of the physical abuse conducted by police. Mazaev (1997) reported that 44% of respondents in 1993 and 58% in 1996 believed that police were using torture during investigations. A survey by the Committee against Torture (2006) found 28.3% of respondents in five Russian regions considered torture a systematic police practice, while only 13.2% said that police rarely torture suspects or defendants.

However, surveys also show citizens are quite tolerant of the physical abuse by the police. These views are often based on a dubious believe that only guilty criminals are tortured and these deserve the treatment. Mazaev (1997) reported that 57% of citizens find physical abuse of suspects justifiable. The Committee against Torture (2006) reported that 22.1% of those surveyed in five regions did not feel that any protection against police torture is needed because only the guilty are subject to torture. Gilinskiy (2011) reported that 25.5% of respondents in St. Petersburg agreed that "innocent people are not being tortured."

The public acceptance of police physical abuse could result from an inadequate understanding of the presumption of innocence and the general disregard for the rule of law by citizens (Andreev, 2005a; Gudkov, 2000). In the Volgograd study conducted in 2008,[49] it was found that 12.8% of the respondents did not think that physical force and abuse is ever used by police during interrogations. A relatively small number (2.6%) reported that police use physical abuse all the time, with 9.4% reporting that it does happen often. Crime victims were more likely to agree that police use physical abuse for interrogations. According to a Volgograd 2008 study,[50] younger males with university degrees were more likely to agree that police abuse occurs during interrogations.

The Russian law provides a variety of legal remedies to report and investigate torture and ill-treatment by police (Uidriks and Reenen, 2003). The ban of torture and other inhumane treatment is one of the key principles outlined in the Russian Constitution, the Code of Criminal Procedure, and the new law "On Police."[51] The victims of police abuse can file a criminal complaint with the police officer's superior (typically the head of the district police office),[52] with the Office of the Investigative Committee,[53] and with the Procurator's Office.[54] Additionally, if there is an open criminal investigation, a complaint can be filed by the suspect, or defendant, directly to the court.[55] The decisions of district police heads, heads of the Investigative Committee, and the district procurators can be appealed to regional superiors and eventually to the court. In proven cases of physical abuse, criminal charges can be filed for "torture without significant bodily injury,"[56] "forceful confession with the use of torture,"[57] or "assault and bodily injury."[58] A combined civil lawsuit can be brought by the prosecutor during the criminal trial on behalf of alleged police abuse victims (Roudik, 2008). A separate civil lawsuit also can be filed independently by the victims of crime for damage compensation and moral sufferings in the court system.[59]

Despite an abundance of legal remedies, the investigation of torture and ill-treatment is largely ineffective. Annual reports by Russian Ombudsman[60] and various human right organizations[61] are filled with examples of superficial, delayed, and ineffective investigations of alleged cases of physical abuse. The European Court of Human Rights (ECHR) has reported that violations of Article 3 of the European Convention of Human Rights is a frequent practice of the Russian police (Rudinsky, 2008).[62] During 2011, the ECHR issued over 50 decisions against the Russian government for torture and inhumane and degrading treatment by law enforcement agencies that included the police.[63] In six weeks during 2012, there were 10 additional decisions by the ECHR against Russia on the same issue.[64] In 13 of these decisions, the ECHR also found the Russian government in violation of Convention Article 13, which demands effective legal remedy in the form of a prompt and efficient government investigation into allegations of torture.[65]

On multiple occasions, the ECHR emphasized that legal remedies provided by the Russian government for police torture victims are inadequate, inaccessible, tainted with "repeat suspensions, plagued by critical delays, and omissions, and has been pending for many years with no tangible results."[66] In 2010, 115,700 complaints were filed with Russian courts against criminal investigators of which only 13.1% were resolved.[67] Civil lawsuits combined with the criminal process filed by prosecutors on behalf of victims have been almost nonexistent. According to Roudik (2008), only two lawsuits of this kind were reported in the last 15 years. The separate civil lawsuit approach to seek a remedy has been found to be ineffective by the recent decisions of the ECHR.[68] The ECHR criticized both the formalistic approach and low levels of compensation awarded by Russian courts to the claimants.[69] According to 2010 Russian government statistics, only 22% of all civil lawsuits filed by detainees for compensation were granted and 35% were dismissed as inadmissible without a trial.[70]

In addition to superficial and often delayed investigations, victims of police torture often face problems accessing medical treatment and finding forensic experts (Human Rights Watch, 1999). While in detention, many victims of police torture are denied timely access to professional medical care (Amnesty International, 2002). Due to the inability to access medical treatment, victims of alleged physical abuse often lose any forensic evidence of injuries, which leads to the dismissal of cases (Uidriks and Reenen, 2003). Even when victims of police abuse are able to get medical treatment from the state hospitals, emergency medical vehicles (*"skoraya pomosch"*), and stationary offices for traumatic injuries (*travmpunkty*), there are barriers. The medical professionals are instructed by the government to report physical abuse to the same police office, or simply the medical staff does not know where to report the incidents (Gudkov, Dubin, and Leonova, 2004).

Also, health professionals that work primarily in government institutions are reluctant to get involved in cases of police torture for fear of being pressured from the police not to document the injury or provide the testimony. Gudkov, Dubin, and Leonova indicated that only 67% of surveyed healthcare professionals reported having no cases where police made a request not to document a suspect or defendant's injuries and 13% admitted being requested to suppress documentation. Additionally, the law of criminal evidence often requires that medical documentation of injuries has to be provided by the authorized office of the forensic medical experts (*sudmedexpert*).[71] The documents from hospitals and private doctors are often found unacceptable as they lack indicia (indications) of reliability required by Russian law (Amnesty International, 2002). Most victims of police torture have no direct access to forensic medical experts and have to obtain requests from the court, or the investigator, to access these resources. Often such requests are denied, or delayed, which results in a loss of evidence by the victims (Uidriks and Reenen, 2003).[72]

Another factor that encourages police torture and physical abuse is the judiciary's reluctance to exclude evidence obtained by torture (Rudinsky, 2008). According to Human Rights Watch (1999), evidence obtained by torture was not excluded from any of the cases analyzed and included in its report.

An issue closely related to police torture and physical abuse is the problem of arbitrary and excessive police detention (Rudinsky, 2008). The majority of police torture cases occur while victims are in detention prior to trial or stopped by the police for a short-term administrative detention.[73] The conditions in Russian pretrial centers (SIZO) are so grave that the ECHR repeatedly found prolonged detention in these facilities alone equivalent of torture and inhumane treatment. Inmates in SIZO are deprived of food, access to medical professionals, and suffer from extreme overcrowding (Weiler, 2004). In the recent case of *Ananyev v. Russia* (2012), the ECHR noted that only 0.9% of Russian pretrial facilities are compliant with international standards and 40% are not even complaint with the Russian penitentiary standards.[74] Whereas the administration of the SIZO has been officially transferred to the Ministry of Justice, police investigators are responsible for ordering and extending the pretrial detention.

Prior to 2002, investigators were authorized to order pretrial detention with approval of the appropriate procurator (Conquest, 1968b).[75] The procurator also was allowed to extend the pretrial detention. [76] The procurators, who were to supervise the legality of the preliminary investigation, including the pretrial detention, were required to support the prosecution in court as well (Osakwe, 1983). With no checks and balances for implementation of impartiality in the criminal process, police investigators and procurators had natural tendencies for accusatory biases (Ananyev, 2006). In such conditions, the decision to detain the accused prior to trial provided the investigator with exclusive access to the accused and an opportunity to extract confession by use of threats, coercion, or deception. The ECHR repeatedly condemned this procedure emphasizing that the procurator cannot be considered an independent tribunal within the meaning of Article 5 of Convention. The Court stressed that judicial review is paramount to establishing "lawfulness" of detention and to avoid arbitrary detentions and abuse of power by the police.[77]

After the new Criminal Procedural Code (CPC) was adopted in 2001, the authority to approve detention was transferred to the judges. According to the new CPC, a criminal investigator needs to obtain judicial approval to detain an individual with support of the procurator within 48 hours of the arrest (Solomon, 2005a). The detainee has the right to legal counsel within 24 hours of the actual arrest, and the family should be informed of the detention.[78]

The pretrial detention is limited to 18 months and extensions require judicial approval.[79] Only persons accused of crimes punishable by at least two years of imprisonment can be detained prior to trial (Radchenko, 2006). New CPC rules clearly improved the problems with pretrial detention and Russia's compliance with international law (Ananyev, 2006; Fillipov, 2003).[80] However, the CPC was ineffective in completely eliminating the arbitrary detention and physical abuse by police.

First, the police continue to have substantial discretion authority to execute detentions (Roudik, 2008). The Ombudsman 2010 report points out the police continue to only apply the term "detention" to handcuffed persons who are locked inside the cage (*camera*) at the police office. Individuals also are held by force in investigator's offices and interrogated against their will. They are treated as a "witness" or a "person of interest" and the new rules of CPC are not applied to these individuals (Ombudsman, 2010, p. 30). The new CPC also provides police discretion regarding which family members should be informed of the arrest and in what form the notice should be communicated (Roudik, 2008).

Another issue is that Russian courts do not always critically access the necessity of pretrial detention. This is especially true when extending detention that is already authorized (Ombudsman, 2011). According to official 2011 Russia Supreme Court statistics, the courts approved 90% of motions to detain and 97% of motions to extend the detention. Similar data were reported for the period from 2007 through 2010.[81] In 2010, 23.5% of criminal defendants were detained prior to trial, which was 134,400 cases nationwide.[82] Cases described by the Committee against Torture, Public Verdict, and those analyzed by the ECHR after the adoption of the CPC reforms show that police officers continue to misuse pretrial detention (A. Beck and Robertson, 2009b). The abuse of detention also is supported by a pervasive accusatory culture among Russian police officers. In a study by Rudinsky (2008), 67% of investigators considered pretrial detention as a form of punishment, and 93% reported that pretrial detention occurring before charges are filed is acceptable, which essentially rejects the very essence of a presumption of innocence.

7.3.2 Bribery and Other Illegal "Income Activities" by Police Officers

The Russian police are known to be notorious for participating in bribery and other forms of illegal activities that result in "additional income" (A. Beck and Robertson, 2009b). The law "On Police" prohibits any additional employment by police officers other than teaching and research.[83] Yet research literature demonstrates that police officers routinely engage in additional activities including illegal services and bribery. A survey of police officers conducted by Kolennikova et al. (2002) demonstrated that 50% of the officers are involved in illegal activities to earn additional income. Kolennikova et al. also reported that police officers spend 24% to 29% of their work time and 45% to 55% of their free time engaging in illegal activities.

Public awareness about police bribery in Russia is high. According to Gudkov, Dubin, and Leonova (2004), only 2% of Russians believed that bribery is a nonexistent practice among police officers, while 35% consider that bribery is endemic, and 48% think it is a pretty widespread practice. Gilinskiy (2004) indicated that public concern with police bribery is growing in Russia. In 1998, 36.5% of citizens considered it to be a significant issue compared to 46.5% in 2001. A comprehensive study of bribery by INDEM (2001a) demonstrated that the traffic police are the leaders in perceived levels of bribery followed by the "regular police." Medvezhevskyi, Girin, and Mizeryi (1999) indicated that 10.6% of citizens thought a bribe given to a traffic officer would never resolve a problem and 17.1% were convinced that a bribe always can be a solution.

In the 2008 Volgograd study,[84] 50.3% of respondents agreed that citizens pay bribes in order to terminate criminal investigations. Seventy percent agreed that traffic police typically solicit bribes when stopping vehicles. Victims of a crime, and younger individuals with university degrees (regardless of gender) were more likely to agree that the traffic police solicit bribes. Individuals with university degrees of both genders were more likely to believe that criminal investigators accept bribes to terminate an investigation. Similarly, in the 2011 Volgograd survey,[85] 58.8% believed that citizens have to pay bribes to have a criminal investigation terminated while 74% agreed that the traffic police solicit bribes when a vehicle is stopped. Younger male respondents, students, and private businessmen were more likely to believe in police bribery. Females, both older and retired respondents, along with government employees, were less likely to believe that police bribery occurs.

This awareness and concern of bribery is grounded in both personal experiences and information from secondary sources, such as personal communication and the media. There is a multitude of reported personal incidents involving police bribery among studies. Dzutsev, Khugaeva, and Tsogoev (2005) described that 34.6% of respondents either admitted bribing an officer or were a witness to a bribe involving another person. In a 2001 study by INDEM, the "risk of corruption" (calculated by a the probability of being involved in a bribery situation) was reported to be 27.4% for "regular" police, 59.3% for the traffic police, and 19.7% for passport services (2001a). The same "risks of corruption" calculated for 2005 demonstrated a significant increase for regular police and passport services, but remained the same for traffic police: 40.2% (regular police), 32.7% (passport services), and 59.6% (traffic police) (INDEM, 2005b). A Ministry of Economic Development study reported similar findings. A citizen's risk of being involved in a bribery situation in 2010 was highest for the traffic police (52%), followed by the regular police (26%), and passport services (23%) (Ministry of Economic Development, 2011).

Estimates have been made related to the scope of corruption controlled by the police. These estimates indicate the illegal activities produce significant financial resources. Kolennikova et al. (2002) surveyed police officers in 2000 and reported that 42% of their monthly income is from "additional activities" that include illegal behavior. Considering the average 2000 salary was 2,349 rubles ($78.3[86]) per month, there was an additional monthly income of 1,701 ($56.7) rubles per month. Kolennikova et al. also indicated that at least 40% of the officer's "additional income" came from clearly illegal behavior including bribery (Wilson et al., 2008). Taking into consideration the number of police officers who reported they participate in these additional activities, it was estimated the officer's annual "additional" income nationally in 2000 was between $1.5 billion and $3.3 billion (all following amounts are in U.S. dollars). The specific sources were $600 million from illegal "trade," $170 million from the traffic police, $300 million from the control of illegal drug markets, $60 million derived from controlling prostitution, and $50 million from the illegal immigration markets (Stremoukhova, 2008). INDEM conducted a study in 2000 that was based on a survey of citizens and produced similar estimates. The total annual amount of bribes taken by the "regular police" was estimated to be $30 million and $368.4 million by the traffic police (INDEM, 2001a). The average bribe amount for a traffic police officer in 2001 was $29 and $57 for a "regular police" officer (INDEM, 2005a).

It was estimated in 2005 that the total amount of bribes taken by the regular police was the same amount, $30 million, as in 2000. The traffic police total amount in 2005 decreased to $183.3 million (INDEM, 2005a, 2005b). The average bribe given to a traffic officer increased by $1 to $30 compared to 2000 and that given to the regular police decreased from $57 to $30 (INDEM, 2005a). Another government-based study estimated bribery amounts for the regular police to be $42 million in 2005. However, the same study reported that, in 2010, bribery estimates increased 13 times for the regular police, thus reaching an amazing $540.3 million. The 2010 bribery estimates for the traffic police doubled from 2005 and reached $814.5 million. The average size of a bribe in 2010 for the traffic police was $81.50 compared to $419 for the regular police (Ministry of Economic Development, 2011).

In the 2008 Volgograd study,[87] 29.1% believed that a bribe between $1,500 and $3,000 was necessary to terminate a criminal investigation, with 34.4% of the respondents stating more than $3,000 was required. Twenty-three percent reported that up to $6 is sufficient to bribe traffic officers, while 27.9% believed the amount should be up to $10, and 28.5% estimated it would be more than $10. It is interesting to note that only 24.4% reported the amount was unknown for an investigator and 10.8% replied the necessary amount for a traffic officer was unknown.

Bribery committed by the traffic police is the most common and involves violations, such as speeding, running red lights, and DUI (driving under the influence). The average bribe amount is relatively small, but very frequent.[88] The media have reported the greatest bribe amounts are for DUI violations, followed by speeding, then illegally passing cars, and, finally, failing to stop at railroad crossings.[89] The issuance of driver's licenses and car registrations also are common forms of bribery. Bribes are given for passing both the "theoretical" and "practical" tests of drivers license exams. Bribe incentives are provided as well to expedite the drivers license issuance process along with car registrations. The same technique applies to the technical examination of cars for safety certification. Larger bribes are offered to illegally obtain "privileged" car license plate numbers and blue roof-top emergency lights installed on cars that provide extra driving privileges (INDEM, 2002; Medvezhevskyi, Girin, and Mizeryi, 1999).[90]

The term *regular police* includes criminal investigators that have been shown to accept bribes to initiate or terminate criminal investigations, release a detainee, or place the person in pretrial detention. The patrol and post services (PPS) are known to accept bribes from small businessmen and entrepreneurs that sell goods on the street as well as those selling goods in farmer's markets or kiosks. The PPS also elicit bribes from citizens on the street for the lack of proper registration or a passport. The district police officers (*uchastkovyi*) often secure bribes from illegal immigrants and for resolving small conflicts in lieu of making an official report to the distinct police office. The district police officers *(uchastkovyi)* also are known to sell personal information about citizens residing in their city districts (*uchastki*) to both business and organized crime groups (INDEM, 2001a, 2005a; Shepeleva, 2005a).

In the passport services, bribes are accepted to expedite the process of registration, the issuance of both internal and external passports, and immigration registration.[91] Other police licensing agencies are known to take bribes for expediting or "simplifying" the procedure to license firearms, license detectives, and register detective bureaus. Kolennikova et al. (2002) listed over 50 varieties of "additional income activities" for police officers of which almost half were related to bribery.

Whereas public opinion about police corruption is generally negative (Gilinskiy, 2004), citizens are not reluctant to offer bribes (Obschestvennaya Palata, 2011a). Using a comprehensive analysis of corruption, INDEM calculated the "corruption demand index" to estimate the probability (readiness) of citizens to offer bribes in certain situations. In 2000, the "corruption demand index" for the regular police was calculated to be 77.3%, and 86% for the traffic police, which suggested that a majority of Russians are willing to offer a bribe when it is felt to be necessary (INDEM, 2001a). Similar data was collected in 2004 by INDEM that estimated the corruption demand index at 48.9% for the regular police and 68.9% for the traffic police (INDEM, 2005a).

A 2010 Ministry of Economic Development study found 28% of Russians were willing to bribe a regular police officer (compared to 55% in 2005). Forty-six percent would attempt to bribe services responsible for passports, the registration or licensing of a firearm, and 69% would bribe a traffic officer. The study reported the willingness to bribe a traffic officer remains the highest among all possible situations including education, health services, the military draft, and child care. It appears the general public's willingness to participate in bribery diminished in the past 10 years, but the absolute numbers remain high with at least one third of all Russians willing to bribe a police officer (Ministry of Economic Development, 2011).

When examining the motivation for initiating a bribe, it appears that the majority of these corrupt transactions occur with the implied understanding that, given the situation, a bribe is necessary (54.3%). Only in 25.1% of the cases was the bribe directly solicited and, in 18.3%, it was offered without an implied understanding, but instead, "just in case" (INDEM, 2005b).

The public's willingness to avoid bribery doesn't necessary mean that it is a morally unacceptable practice in Russia. INDEM reported that only 20.2% of Russians reported they did not engage in bribery because it violates their moral principles, whereas 16.3% said that they would not feel good doing it. Almost half of those who would not offer a bribe said that it was due to a lack of funds (25.7%) or because they did not know how to do it (23.7%) (INDEM, 2001a).

7.3.3 Abuse of Power and Manipulation of Statistics

The existing Russian police crime reporting system is problematic and facilitates corruption (Democracy Fund, 2009). Current police effectiveness is measured through a set of quantitative indicators, such as crime clearance rates or the number of registered crimes. Each indicator is compared with the previous year (abbreviation known as APPG) and the system penalizes police officers, and their respective units, if the numbers are lower or higher than those of a previous year (INDEM, 2004). In this organizational environment, police officers are encouraged to falsify solved crimes (slang term *palki*). Another method is to conceal information about actual crimes to keep their statistics at an acceptable level and, therefore, receive their full salary and bonuses (INDEM, 2001b).[92] There are some media reports that officers even engage in the practice of exchanging and trading cases (*palki*) among the departments to keep their performance numbers high.[93] Many police officers find the system counterproductive, but have to follow orders given by their superiors in order to receive salaries and bonuses.[94]

One of the major issues related to the manipulation of crime statistics is the refusal by the police to accept criminal complaints that are difficult to resolve. Such cases apparently reduce the clearance, which is a major crime-reporting issue. Hiding existing crimes is accomplished by convincing the victim not to file the complaint or by officially refusing to initiate a criminal investigation after the complaint is registered (Shepeleva, 2005a).[95] In a 2005 representative study by WCIOM, 4.69% of those surveyed reported they witnessed the police illegally refusing to register a complaint.[96] When a decision is made to reject the case, victims are rarely informed in a timely manner, thus precluding the opportunity for appealing the decision. INDEM demonstrated in 2000 that 62% of car theft victims, 71% of burglary victims, and 63% of robbery victims in Moscow were not informed of the police actions after filing the official report (INDEM, 2001b). In a nine-month period during 2011, the Prosecutor's Office found over 1,200 police decisions to reject a criminal investigations were unreasonable and illegal.[97]

Another problem pertinent to reporting and assessment is the "creation" of unnecessary police actions with the purpose of fulfilling quotas in police reports (INDEM, 2001b). Some examples of unnecessary police actions designed to artificially inflate police performance are the unnecessary and unjustified passport security checks. Other actions relate to the administrative detentions of homeless alcoholics, illegal immigrants, and other vulnerable persons. These police actions are used to improve performance indicators for the district police officers, patrol services, and detectives (Weiler, 2004).[98]

Multiple cases of ungrounded searches and detentions of minority religious leaders were described in the latest reports by the Ombudsman (2010, 2011). Some media reports suggested the purpose of such harassment is to fulfill the police report quotas related to addressing extremism and has nothing to do with religious minorities itself.[99] Other examples of police-based power abuse include falsifying criminal cases using vulnerable groups of the population, planting evidence in cases of "convenient suspects" (e.g., ex-felons), or forcing defendants to confess to other unrelated crimes (Gladarev, 2009).[100] A WCIOM study reported that, in 2005, 6.85% of Russian respondents in a representative sample witnessed officers attempting to falsify cases.[101]

The falsification of crime reporting in Russia designed to benefit the police is a serious problem. The true scope of the falsification is difficult to estimate; however, a *procuracy* report suggested that massive manipulations of statistics by the MVD were found in 80 regions of Russia.[102] Manipulation of the data leads to an ineffective use of police resources and further undermines public trust of the police. Moreover, it encourages the use of force and results in the conviction of innocent citizens (Democracy Fund, 2009; Skomorokhov and Shikhanov, 2006).

7.3.4 High-Order Police Corruption and Corruption Networks in Russia

The use of force, torture, bribery, and the manipulation of crime reports are serious problems. However, the most dangerous form of Russian police corruption is so-called "high-order" activities that typically relate to invisible, but well-coordinated services, provided to organized crime groups by the police along with business racketeering.

The most common term used to describe high-order police corruption is "roofing" (*krysha*). The liberalization of the economy in the early 1990s and emergence of the free market created numerous businesses. During this time, the function of roofing was mainly performed by organized criminal groups and businesses were targeted. The roofing activities mainly included a variety of protections against attacks from other organized crime groups. During the early 1990s, many legitimate businesses were blackmailed into using a roof. It was generally understood that every serious business, both legitimate and illegitimate, needed a roof for normal functioning (Serio, 2008). During the early 2000s, the roofing changed since various police units assumed and replaced the old "blue" roofs provided by organized crime groups with new "red" roofs performed by police units themselves (Salagaev, Shashkin, and Konnov, 2008).[103]

Very few cases of successful investigation into the red roofing phenomena exist, so neither its scope nor its exact forms are well known. Most researchers are basing their information on interviews with former and current police officers or public surveys about the perceptions of roofing (Serio, 2008). The literature describes red roofing as a variety of services provided to both legal and illegal businesses. This includes securing prosecutorial immunity for members of crime organizations and, owners of the business, "leaking" information about criminal cases to the members of organized groups, and using criminal prosecution to disrupt business competitors (Galeotti, 2004). Salagaev, Shashkin, and Konnov (2008) list over 15 different police activities that involved support of organized crime groups for the purpose of roofing.

Radaev (1998) found the majority of businessmen admitted being involved with a roof and most said they preferred the red roof to the blue roof because the police provided more services for a lower price. The Public Council of Russia reported that up to 90% of businesses that were surveyed pay bribes and fees for roofing and included the expenses for bribery as the cost of doing business in Russia (Obschestvennaya Palata, 2011a). Levada reported in 2010 that 60% of Russians think that roofing by police is a normal practice within law enforcement and only 2% believe that it does not exist.[104]

In many situations, "roofing by police" is related to the creation of legal or semilegal private companies that deal with private security. They also perform middleman functions between police and their clients (businesses and other individuals) (V. Volkov, 2000). These satellite companies employ former police officers, or members of police officers' families, who use their ties with police to provide services or protection. The middleman companies are often used by citizens to expedite passport issuance (or to illegally obtain a passport), registrations, immigration permission, licenses for firearms, or detective activities. Some research shows that police officers intentionally slow down service delivery, consequently encouraging citizens to seek middleman companies (Rimskyi, 2008).

One example of a "beneficial partnership" with organized crime is police participation in an illegal hostile takeover of businesses, which is known as "black raiders." This elaborate criminal scheme is typically based on falsifying company documents, and paying judges bribes to take ownership of the company, along with physical attacks on the company's facilities assisted by police units of rapid reaction (Borzov, 2006). Another example of a "police business" conducted in conjunction with organized crime is their participation in "black real estate schemas" (*chernye rieltrory*). Here, single, elderly or vulnerable owners of apartments are targeted and killed, and then their apartments are sold through illegal, or semilegal, real estate agencies. The media have reported that some police units offered these groups "protection" by preventing prosecution of their members.[105] The media also highlighted that officers in various regions provided roofing protection to poachers,[106] prostitution businesses,[107] drug dealers,[108] and illegal dealers of antiques.[109]

In most cases, roofing and other illegal police activities pertinent to organized crime are performed by high-ranking police officers or with their implied consent (Salagaev, Shashkin, and Konnov, 2008). For the successful completion of most cases, these corruption schemes require participation from other government agencies including judges, prosecutors, and public notaries. Thus, most researchers agree that roofing is a part of the larger issue of Russian corruption networks (Borzov, 2006; INDEM, 2001a). These networks are more dangerous than standalone acts of police corruption because they allow a complete coverup of most illegal activities conducted by highly ranked participants (Rimskyi, 2007). It was also found that highly ranked officers who participate in "additional income activities" are encouraging lower-ranked officers in the same unit to participate in corruption (Kolennikova et al., 2002).

7.4 Police Corruption and Ethnic Minorities

The Russian Federation is a multifaith and multiethnic country even though the Slavic Russians are the ethnic majority. According to the latest 2010 census, at least 8 million residents did not consider themselves ethnic Russians.[110] From this group, the leading ethnic minorities include Muslim-practicing groups of Tatars (3.87% of the population) and Chechens (3.7%).[111] Also, the Federal Migration Services reported that at least 10.2 million immigrants are currently residing in Russia with the majority from the North Caucasian and Central Asian regions (Voronkov and Gladarev, 2011).

As in many other countries, the relationship among police and ethnic minorities and immigrants is strained. Gerber and Mendelson (2008) reported that Russians of non-European origin are more likely to be stopped by the police. Ethnic immigrants are at higher risk of police harassment for passport and registration violations (Gladarev and Tzinman, 2010; Weiler, 2004). Such harassment typically intensifies when politicians and government officials bring ethnic issues and immigration policies to the top of the public agendas (Voronkov and Gladarev, 2011).

Illegal immigrants also are more likely to be used by police to support the falsification of criminal or administrative cases for official reporting (Democracy Fund, 2009; Gladarev and Tzinman, 2010). The police and the Federal Migration Service (FMS) are more likely to solicit bribes from ethnic minorities for both legal and illegal immigrants (Human Rights Watch, 2009). Some evidence exists that owners of businesses would conspire with the FMS to deport illegal immigrants to avoid paying their salaries at the end of the season (Voronkov and Gladarev, 2011). Many experts have suggested that businesses that routinely use illegal immigrants' labor (e.g. construction) are under protection by police red roofs (Gladarev, 2011a).

The surveys indicate that many officers maintain racist and discriminatory biases toward ethnic minorities.[112] Some of views are not personal, but rather a reflection of the unofficial practices of ethnic discrimination prevailing within the MVD. Lack of proper training also contributes to the tension. Ethnic immigrants are often viewed by police as the most suitable group for harassment due to their vulnerable position in the society (Gladarev and Tzinman, 2010). The participation in the armed conflicts in Chechnya and other North Caucasian regions have contributed to discriminatory views by police officers (Gladarev, 2011a). The prevailing, but questionable, presumption that ethnic immigrants commit more crime than Slavic Russians also contributes to the discriminatory views held by some officers toward ethnic minorities (Obschestvennaya Palata, 2011b). Most police officers admit that they have no training and skills on how to deal with ethnic minorities (Tudupova and Ochirov, 2009; Zhukova, 2008).

Paradoxically, there are surveys that indicate many Russians believe the police favor ethnic minorities like North Caucasians and provide them with preferential treatment (Andreev, 2005b). However, this contradiction is understandable. Whereas the true scope of this phenomenon is unknown, existing evidence indicates that "ethnic diasporas" take advantage of the police corruption to prevent criminal prosecution against their members, or arrange for the red roofing of their businesses[113] (Obschestvennaya Palata, 2011b). Russian ethnic diasporas are influential, stable, and well-organized ethnic minority groups that allegedly have ties with organized crime.[114] Ethnic diasporas are known to lobby the interests of their members, but they rarely offer protection against police for individuals with similar ethnicity that are considered to be "nonsignificant" (Obschestvennaya Palata, 2011b).

Police "assistance" provided to ethnic diasporas is often seen by the public as preferential treatment of all ethnic minorities and especially those from the North Caucasian region. Such beliefs contribute to the growing problem of Russian nationalism and xenophobia that has become prevalent among younger Russians during the past five years (Obschestvennaya Palata, 2011b). The 2010 riot in Moscow's Manezhnaya Square clearly demonstrated that the perception of preferential treatment of ethnic minorities by the police is a major concern. The December 11, 2010, riot was triggered by the release of four North Caucasian suspects from police custody who were accused of killing Egor Sviridov, a Russian national. The riot attracted thousands of participants that resulted in dozens being injured and arrested.

The public reaction was even more important. In a follow-up survey, the Public Council of Russia found that 76% of younger respondents supported the riot.[115] In a representative study by WCIOM, 11% of the respondents had a desire to participate and 18% said they supported the cause.[116] The majority (53%) were convinced the suspects were released by the police because of money and corruption (Obschestvennaya Palata, 2011b). Thus, corruption and the abuse of police power contribute to the growing Russian–ethnic tensions in two major ways: (1) the selective enforcement and harassment of ethnic minorities by the police further alienates these groups from the mainstream Russian society and government, and (2) the preferential treatment of ethnic diasporas and organized crime groups alienates citizens from the police and contributes to their extreme nationalistic views.

7.5 Analysis of Modern Anticorruption Measures in Russia

Since its creation in 1991, the MVD leadership acknowledged police corruption as one of the major institutional problems and offered numerous measures to fight it. However, most of these measures were focused on increased funding and establishing new anticorruption agencies. However, in the past five years, the government developed some new anticorruption policies that differed from previous attempts.

One of the new measures is a requirement for highly ranked police officers[117] to disclose information related to their income and valuable property.[118] Accordingly, officers and immediate family members provide information about their annual salary, other income, real estate possessions,, vehicles, and other means of transportation. The information has been published annually on the MVD Web site beginning in 2009.[119] Both the traditional and social media paid significant attention to this information. Reports were published related to a variety of questionable circumstances where police officers and family members owned expensive property that exceeded their means for financial acquisition or support.[120] These reports, however, had no significant consequences.

Most police officers continue their MVD service and the media reported no criminal investigations were filed. Even when the prosecutor's office reviewed and found over 9,000 violations of income declarations in 2010, all the violators (1,700 police officers) were only subjected to disciplinary measures, such as a reprimand.[121] At best, some police officers who had questionable possession of expensive properties or those who falsified their income were fired, but no corruption charges were filed against them.[122] Unsurprisingly, most Russians did not view the new measure as an effective anticorruption reform (Obschestvennaya Palata, 2011a).

Another recent anticorruption measure is termed *administrative reform*, which focuses predominantly on limiting the discretionary authority of all government agencies, including the police. This is done primarily by implementing so-called "anticorruption" expertise of draft legislation and adopting new administrative regulations. The anticorruption expertise of draft legislation was introduced by President Medvedev in 2009. It required that all major draft laws should be subjected to examination of potential corruption risks by both government agencies and independent nongovernment organizations. The findings of anticorruption experts were published and discussed prior to implementing the new laws.[123] In 2010, the MVD issued a document containing the types of proposed MVD legislation that require anticorruption expertise.[124] An analysis of the methodology used to conduct an anticorruption expertise[125] of draft legislation and published anticorruption expert opinions[126] was undertaken. The results indicated that the major focus of anticorruption experts is to clarify any uncertainties in the laws that are enabling the possibility of corruption and limit the discretion of government officials and the police.

Another method of limiting problematic police discretion is new administrative regulations (*administrativenye reglamenty*) focused on police "services" provided to persons and organizations. These regulations provide detailed instructions related to the application of police services, the deadlines for each step of service provision, and who are the responsible officials. For example, separate administrative regulations were issued related to vehicle registration by the traffic police,[127] the procedure to obtain documents related to criminal records,[128] and the procedure to obtain internal[129] and external passports.[130]

Whether these documents are effective anticorruption measures is debatable. Whereas it is possible that these regulations curb some police discretion and create clear deadlines for service delivery, they also make police work extremely formalized and inflexible. The operational guidelines for each service contain at least 50 extremely detailed pages along with the mandatory forms and other requirements. Due to the detailed regulations, some administrative regulations require frequent amendments, thus making it more difficult for both government officials and individuals to follow.[131] Also, as with the police income declaration, the administrative rules violations are not easily enforceable. At the present time, citizens have to file a court complaint to effectively punish police violations of the administrative regulations, which is a costly and time-consuming procedure.[132] The media rarely reports any consequences suffered by policemen resulting from the administrative rule violations.[133]

As part of the anticorruption campaign, the Russian government also took measures to increase the criminal liability for corruption. One of the major steps was Amendments to the Criminal Code of Russia (CC). The 2011 Amendments made significant changes to the provisions of Articles 290 and 291 pertaining to bribery. Prior to 2011, the sentence for bribery could be imprisonment, community service, or a fine. The fine was estimated in rubles and was insignificant. For example, for a simple bribe, the fine was up to 500,000 rubles (approximately $16,666) and, for a significant bribe, it was up to 1,000,000 rubles ($33,333).[134] Many argued these amounts would not effectively deter bribery (Chistye Ruki, 2010).

The new 2011 Amendments made the fine directly related to the amount of the attempted or actual bribe. For example, the fine for accepting a bribe is determined to be as much as 50 times the amount received.[135] The Amendments also created three separate crimes for bribery including accepting a bribe, accepting a significant amount, and accepting a very significant amount.[136] In addition, the CC Amendments introduced separate criminal liabilities for facilitating or mediating bribes.[137]

Another 2010 CC Amendment focused on increasing the criminal liability of the police. In the new provisions, a crime committed by a police officer should be considered as an aggravating circumstance during sentencing.[138] The new law "On Police" requires that all officers report any solicitations related to corruption with reprimands for failure to do so through disciplinary actions and other liability.[139] These measures are intended to increase the liability for corruption and are positive anticorruption policy steps; however, without proper enforcement the efficacy is doubtful.

An analysis of current court practices related to bribery indicated that only low-ranking officers that had received small bribes are typically charged with a crime. Thus, if the current practice continues, an increase in the penalties would have little impact on the extremely dangerous corruption networks of the higher ranking officers. It is also questionable how the requirement to report a solicitation will be enforced since the officer is part of the corruption activity.

As a part of the anticorruption reform, measures were also taken to improve the police reporting system and performance assessments. After examining the current reporting system,[140] the MVD declared the previous reporting system was being replaced by a new and improved system.[141] A careful review of the police reporting MVD regulations and assessment contradicts the MVD declaration.[142] The regulations (decrees) related to police reporting and assessment requirements are not publically available from any official databases. Instead, the available information is restricted to unofficial copies of decrees published online by members of the police communities.[143]

A comparison of the 2005 Decree of MVD #650[144] to the new 2010 Decree #25[145] and 2011 Decree #1310[146] demonstrates the old quantitative indicators were not eliminated, but simply became more complex and elaborate.[147] For example, in Appendix 1 of Decree #25, the effectiveness of reported crime by the police (criterion #1.5) is assessed positively when the overall number of written complaints from citizens decreases every year. The criterion can be easily manipulated by concealing the officially written complaints.

Criterion #2.1 requires that the number of crimes committed by ex-felons, juveniles, and drunken perpetrators per capita should decrease annually to achieve positive police performance. Because many factors that are independent from police work can influence the rate of crimes per capita in any given region, it is not difficult for the police to achieve the necessary data by concealing the true rates of crime from official reports.

Decree #1310 consists of similar shortcomings. Criterion #4.2 penalizes police units for the number of cases that are terminated due to defendant's innocence or for those in which there was an acquittal. This criterion directly encourages accusative biases by the police and courts as well as the conditions for coerced confessions and abuse of power. Criterion #7.1, found in the decree of 2011, penalizes the traffic police for annual increases in traffic fatalities. Because the police cannot control all extraneous factors related to the causation of traffic fatalities that are beyond police performance alone, this requirement facilitates the false manipulation of actual traffic-related fatalities.

Another major problem related to the new police performance regulations is the very vague policy description pertaining to how public survey results will be factored into the overall police assessment. Both documents suggest that surveys should be included, but give no explanation as to how this would be done and what weight the public surveyed will have.[148] The document mentions that surveys would adhere to a methodology developed by the MVD, but the process is not transparent or public. The public MVD Web site survey information includes items about personal safety, police trust and satisfaction, and willingness of citizens cooperate with the police.[149] Because the collection and analytical methodologies are not provided to the public, it is unclear how the polling organizations are selected to conduct the surveys. The media have reported that regional police managers are to select their own survey organizations, which makes the independence of the surveys questionable.[150]

Additionally, several recent anticorruption measures were undertaken that included the creation of new government agencies and an increase in police funding. The Anti-Corruption Council was created in 2008 to coordinate national anticorruption policies.[151] Currently, there is little evidence the new agency has had much impact on reducing police corruption. Recent public surveys by Levada indicate that 40% of the respondents had no knowledge of the Council's existence and only 16% reported any familiarity with the agency's anticorruption measures (Levada, 2011b).

In 2011, a new law pertaining to the social benefits of police officers was adopted with the intention of increasing both benefits and wages.[152] MVD Minister Rashid Nurgaliev announced that, beginning in 2012, all police officers will receive at least $1,000 monthly and those with college degrees $1,500 along with a variety of social benefits. According to the minister, the increase of salary and benefits should deter officers from taking bribes.[153] However, many experts and media commentators doubt that these measures alone will effectively reduce police corruption.[154] To the contrary, some media outlets suggest the wage increase will only escalate the bribe amounts solicited by the police.[155]

A majority of survey respondents did not find the new anticorruption measures effective. The Public Council report found only 12% believed that modern anticorruption policies can effectively change police corruption (Obschestvennaya Palata, 2011a). Many surveys indicate citizens are favoring increased penalties for corruption, such as lengthy imprisonment terms and the confiscation of property obtained through corruptive activities (INDEM, 2001a, 2005a; Levada, 2011b). Both surveys and interviews of experts in the field emphasize the main problem of the recent anticorruption campaign is the lack of uniform enforcement. Only a small group of respondents (9.1%) consider the wage increase an important anticorruption measure.[156] Instead, the majority think what is needed is an increase in control from both police superiors, members of civil society, and the media to curb police corruption (Obschestvennaya Palata, 2011a).[157] These recommendations are in line with the successful anticorruption measures implemented by other former Soviet countries (Wolf, 2009).

7.6 Concluding Remarks

Russian police corruption is an old and complex issue. It has historical roots extending to both the tsarist and Soviet periods. Many believe that it is embedded in both the Russian legal culture as well as the law enforcement institutions. However, the problem of police corruption became extremely acute during the past 20 years after the Soviet Union collapsed. Police corruption became one of the major reasons for the pervasive public–police alienation that has exacerbated public distrust and dissatisfaction with the police.

Many factors have contributed to police corruption, including Russia's rapid economic and political transition to a free market and democracy during the early 1990s. The transition resulted in severe underfunding and large attrition rates among qualified police officers. Whereas the funding and quality of the police workforce improved by the early 2000s, the issue of police corruption remained critical. The extreme centralization and unnecessary militarization of police forces facilitated the growth of corrupt police practices. The lack of independent police oversight either from government or civil society shaped the continuous growth of police corruption.

Now, the most common forms of police corruption include torture and other physical abuses of suspects, bribery, falsification of criminal charges, and the manipulation of crime statistics. The most dangerous forms include beneficial "partnerships" with organized crime and corruption networks among various law enforcement and government officials.

Despite the general public disapproval of police corruption, Russians are rather tolerant of the physical abuses and are willing to participate in bribery, if required. These public attitudes perpetuate the cycle of corruption and erode any anticorruption policies. The most recent reform efforts include the requirements to publish the incomes of high ranking officers, limiting the activities of officers through detailed regulations, changes in the performance assessment and reporting system, improved criminal liability for bribery, and the increase in police wages and benefits. Most experts agree the measures can effectively deter corruption if the enforcement is applied uniformly in all violations. However, currently the enforcement is selective, thus allowing the majority of police corruption cases to remain unpunished.

It is clear that the leadership's political will, along with citizen activism, is needed to effectively combat police corruption. Some cases of effective public–police cooperation already exist in Russia, but they are rare exceptions. The police continues to be a closed institution that regularly rejects any attempts by civil society to oversee its activities.[158] Citizens are disappointed with the government's anticorruption rhetoric and are less and less likely to report acts of corruption.[159] At this point, it is unclear whether mutual alienation will continue to grow or steps will be taken toward strengthening the public–police partnership to address the issue of corruption.

Endnotes

1. For more details on HDI, see the Human Development Report at http://hdrstats.undp.org/en/countries/profiles/RUS.html.
2. For more details, see the Corruption Perception Index Report at http://cpi.transparency.org/cpi2011/results/.
3. For more details, see the World Governance Indicators database at http://info.worldbank.org/governance/wgi/mc_countries.asp.
4. The study by INDEM demonstrates that 78.7% of surveyed businessmen consider police corruption one of the main reasons for widespread corruption in the country. Questions #69–25 from a study "Diagnostics of Russian Corruption: The Survey of the Businessmen, 2001, at http://sophist.hse.ru/.
5. The study by FOM titled "Corruption and corrupted individuals," at http://bd.fom.ru/report/map/dd0600113.
6. The study was conducted by the authors of this book during 2011 in the Volgograd region with a representative sample of 500 residents.
7. The office of Ombudsman was established in 1997. For 14 years, the office published annual reports that outline dozens of cases of police corruption. The reports can be found at http://ombudsmanrf.org/.
8. For details, please see annual reports published by the Office of Ombudsman at http://ombudsmanrf.ru/.
9. See official Web site for specific publications at http://www.pytkam.net/web/.
10. See official Web site for specific publications at http://www.publicverdict.org.
11. See official Web site for specific publications at http://www.memo.ru.
12. See official Web site for specific publications at http://www.mhg.ru/.
13. See the HUDOC database of ECHR for specific cases at http://www.echr.coe.int/ECHR/EN/Header/Case-Law/Decisions+and+judgments/HUDOC+database/.
14. The list of many cases can be found in the Appendix to the decision on the case of *Ananyev v. Russia* (2011).
15. More data is available from the report by VNII MVD Russia, Vladivostok, 2010. Retrieved on July 25, 2012 from http://sartraccc.ru/Pub/suharenko.pdf.
16. See an article published in Komsomolskaya Pravda at http://kp.ru/daily/25709.5/909933/.
17. Sample of private businessmen only.
18 Sample of private businessmen only.
19. Sample of experts only.
20. Sample of government employees only.
21. Sample of general population only.
22. Sample of private businessmen only.
23. Measured involvement in all state corruption.
24. Measured only involvement in the bribery of traffic police.
25. Measured only opinion about traffic police.
26. Measured only involvement in the bribery of traffic police.

27. Article 4 part 2 paragraph 3 and Article 49 part 1 of the Federal Law "On police service" issued on November 30, 2011 #342-FZ. The full text of this document can be obtained at www.consultant.ru.
28. Even official MVD statistics found a significant number of psychologically "inadequate" police superiors within the MVD ranks. According to the article in Infox, 526 chiefs were flagged by staff psychologists as inadequate in 2009 and over 1,900 of superiors were found to have problems with "psychological adaptation." Full text can be found at http://infox.ru/authority/state/2010/05/18/V_MVD_vyyyavlyeno_52.phtml.
29. Examples of superficial internal investigations within MVD also can be found in Reports by Ombudsman. For example, in the annual report of 2009, Ombudsman describes a case of individual M. who was killed by police in Dagestan and the materials of investigation were unavailable even to Ombudsman's office (Ombudsman, 2009).
30. For details on structure, jurisdiction, and responsibilities of the new Investigative Committee, see the Federal Law "On Investigative Committee" issued on December 28, 2010 #403-FZ. The full text of this document can be obtained at www.consultant.ru.
31. The survey conducted by the authors during May of 2011 in the Volgograd region with a representative sample of 500 citizens.
32. Findings from the WCIOM Omnibus study conducted on August 28, 2010. The results can be found at http://wciom.ru/zh/print_q.php?s_id=531&q_id=38070&date=23.03.2008 *or by search at* www.wciom.ru.
33. For examples of formalistic and superficial investigations into police violations conducted by the *Procuracy,* see the annual report of Ombudsman in 2009 who describes responses by the *Procuracy* of Moscow investigating complaints into police actions against public protesters (Ombudsman, 2009).
34. One of the most significant is a case of several high-ranked procurators in the Moscow region, who are charged with protecting illegal gambling businesses. For details of this story, please see, for example, articles at http://www.kp.ru/daily/25637.5/802332/ *and* http://kp.ru/daily/25683/888739/.
35. Article 49, part 2 paragraph 15 of the Federal Law "On police service" issued on November 30, 2011 #342-FZ lists the dissemination of information about police in the media as an "aggravated disciplinary offense" for any police officer. Such a violation can lead to a variety of punishments including termination from police service (Article 50 part 1 of the same law). The full text of this document can be obtained at www.consultant.ru.
36. For example, see articles about Matveev at http://www.kp.ru/online/news/896855/ *or* http://dv.kp.ru/daily/25749/2735834/ *and* Web site dedicated to news on Dymovskyi at http://www.dimovsky.ru/.
37. The activities of "Public Councils" are regulated by the Presidential Decree "About public councils at MVD and its regional agencies" issued on May 23, 2011 #668, the Presidential Decree "About confirming the Provisions on the public council at MVD" issued on July 28, 2011 #1027, and the Decree of Minister of MVD "About confirming the order in which the members of public councils at MVD and its regional agencies can be present at the personal meetings accepting complaints" issued on August 31, 2011 #988. The full text of these documents can be obtained at www.consultant.ru.

38. For example, see the article "Vrednye Sovety" at http://www.profile.ru/article/vrednye-sovety-60858.
39. The analysis of court practice reported in the Decree of the Supreme Court of Russia "About some questions of court practice for the corruption-related cases" issued on December 8, 2010. The full text of the decree can be found at http://www.vsrf.ru. The statistical analysis of cases adjudicated by Russian courts can be found at Judicial Department of the Supreme Court at http://www.cdep.ru. The full texts of actual court decisions can be found through the court search engine at www.sudrf.ru. Also see media reports at http://www.me-journal.ru/352/46447 *and* http://www.rg.ru/2012/02/14/vziatki-anons.html.
40. According to the Public Council report of 2011, only one out of every 25 sentences on bribery involves imprisonment. Other defendants receive a suspended sentence or fine (Obschestvennaya Palata, 2011a). The decree by Supreme Court issued on December 8, 2010, reported that only 26% of all defendants convicted for bribery were sentenced to imprisonment. For the rest, the sentence was suspended. Others received suspended sentences or were fined.
41. The analysis of court practices in 2010. The full text can be found at Judicial Department of the Supreme Court at http://www.cdep.ru/index.php?id=5&item=577.
42. For an example, see a description of the case for defendant P. who died in police detention in St. Petersburg in 2008. In his report from 2010, Ombudsman openly states that police authorities allowed the responsible officers to avoid the legal liability by prolonging the investigation of the incident (Ombudsman, 2010, p. 22).
43. For example, see an article at http://kp.ru/daily/25670.5/831729/.
44. For example, see the article on firing the head of the St. Petersburg regional MVD office at http://www.corrupcia.net/articles/fact-5800.html. Only after he was fired, the internal investigation into his activities began. See, for example, an article by Public Verdict at http://www.publicverdict.org/topics/news/10042.html.
45. For example, the Committee against Torture describes a case of the defendant whose complaint of police torture was overturned nine times by the local *Procuracy* office (Committee against Torture, 2006, p. 45). Also see an annual report by the Ombudsman in 2009 that describes cases of a citizen who unsuccessfully appealed the denial to investigate his case five times within one year (Ombudsman, 2009).
46. The Report by the Ministry of Economic Development of Russia "On lower level corruption" showed that the amount of bribes paid by citizens to the police increased 13 times between 2005 and 2010 and consisted of 16.211 billion rubles (Ministry of Economic Development, 2011).
47. According to the recent studies by Levada, 77% of Russians consider police abuse and corruption to be very serious problems (Levada, 2010).
48. An example of such abuse can be found in the annual report of Ombudsman in 2009 about citizen O. from Kaluga city. He was beaten by police in a sobering-up station for asking to call his lawyer and asking for a doctor for a medical examination to document his injuries (Ombudsman, 2009).
49. The 2008 study was conducted by the authors in the Volgograd region using a representative sample of 500 citizens.
50. Ibid.

51. Article 21 of the Russian Constitution, Article 5 part 3 of the law "On Police," and Article 9 part 2 of the CPC of Russia. Full text can be found at www.consultant.ru.
52. Articles 123–123 of the CPC of Russia. Full text can be found at www.consultant.ru.
53. Article 11 of the Federal Law "On Investigative Committee" issued on December 28, 2010 #403-FZ. Full text can be found at www.consultant.ru.
54. Articles 10, 27 of the law "On Procuracy" issued on January 17, 1992 #2202-1. Full text can be found at www.consultant.ru.
55. Articles 46, 47, and 125 of the CPC of Russia. Full text can be found at www.consultant.ru.
56. Article 117 of the Russian Criminal Code. Full text can be found at www.consultant.ru.
57. Article 302 of the Russian Criminal Code. Full text can be found at www.consultant.ru.
58. Articles 110–118 of the Russian Criminal Code. Full text can be found at www.consultant.ru.
59. Articles 12, 150–151, 1069–1070, 1100 of the Russian Civil Code and Articles 254–258 of the Russian Criminal Procedural Code. Full text can be found at www.consultant.ru.
60. For example, in the Annual Report of 2010, the Ombudsman describes the story of defendant P. who died in police custody in Voronezh in 2009. The police investigation conducted revealed that P. died from self-inflicted wounds that he sustained when he "fell multiple times from the chair and jumped multiple times from the window without any visible reasons" (Ombudsman, 2010, pp. 22–23). Another example can be found in the 2009 Ombudsman report regarding citizen O. from Kaluga who was beaten in a sobering-up station and denied investigation multiple times despite medical documentation of his injuries (Ombudsman, 2009).
61. For example, see the case of Evgenyi Shishov who was severely beaten by police in 2007. For three years, Shishov was filing multiple complaints to the Investigative Committee, the *Procuracy,* and courts. His complaints were denied on local and regional levels by all agencies. Only after the complaint reached the Attorney General was a case initiated against police officer—three years after the incident. The case is featured by Public Verdict at http://www.publicverdict.org/topics/cases/8896/1144.html. Another example is the case of Alexander Kamesnky who was illegally detained and beaten by police in 2005. Despite a court decision that the detention was illegal, the Investigative Committee and the police refused to initiate a criminal investigation against the police officers. For six years, the *Procuracy* issued 28 decisions rejecting an initiation of an investigation into the police actions. The case is featured by the Committee against Torture at http://www.pytkam.net/web/index.php?go=Facts&in=view&id=159.
62. The Committee against Torture alone filed 67 complaints of torture as of February 23, 2012 to the ECHR. See list of cases on their site http://www.pytkam.net/web/index.php?go=Content&id=251.
63. The decisions include *Ergashev v. Russia* (2011), *Ivantoc and others v. Moldova and Russia* (2011), *Filatov v. Russia* (2011), *Sambiyeva v. Russia* (2011), *Yakubov v. Russia* (2011), *Aleksandra Dmitriyeva v. Russia* (2011),

Vanfuli v. Russia (2011), *Naboyshchikov v. Russia* (2011), *Ushakov v. Russia* (2011), *Buldashev v. Russia* (2011), *Cherkasov v. Russia* (2011), *G. O. v. Russia* (2011), *Shuvalov v. Russia* (2011), *Khatayev v. Russia* (2011), *Beksultanova v. Russia* (2011), *Kondratishko and others v. Russia* (2011), *Shishkin v. Russia* (2011), *Gadamauri and Kadyrbekov v. Russia* (2011), *Velkhiyev and others v. Russia* (2011), *Chudun v. Russia* (2011), *Giriyeva and others v. Russia* (2011), *Makharbiyeva and others v. Russia* (2011), *Isayev and others v. Russia* (2011), *Orlov v. Russia* (2011), *Gerasiyev and others v. Russia* (2011), *Kosumova and others v. Russia* (2011), *Vitayeva and others v. Russia* (2011), *Khodorkovskiy v. Russia* (2011), *Maayevy v. Russia* (2011), *Malika Alikhadzhiyeva v. Russia* (2011), *Popandopulo v. Russia* (2011), *Vadim Kovalev v. Russia* (2011), *Ilyadi v. Russia* (2011), *Shokkarov and others v. Russia* (2011), *Matayeva and Dadayeva v. Russia* (2011), *Nikolay Fedorov v. Russia* (2011), *Vasyukov v. Russia* (2011), *Esmukhambetov and others v. Russia* (2011), *Murtazovy v. Russia* (2011), *Vladimir Sokolov v. Russia* (2011), *Khambulatova v. Russia* (2011), *Kuptsov and Kuptsova v. Russia* (2011), *Tsarenko v. Russia* (2011), *Khakiyeva, Temirgeriyeva and others v. Russia* (2011), *Dolgov v. Russia* (2011), *Kapanadze v. Russia* (2011), *Dorogyaykin v. Russia* (2011), *Dudarovy v. Russia* (2011), *Premininy v. Russia* (2011), *Yevgeniy Alekseyenko v. Russia* (2011), *Gisayev v. Russia* (2011), *Popandopulo v. Russia* (2001), and *Petrenko v. Russia* (2011). The full text can be found at http://cmiskp.echr.coe.int/tkp197/search.asp?skin=hudoc-en.

64. The decisions include *Ananyev v Russia* (2012), *Valyayev v. Russia* (2012), *Mitrokhin v. Russia* (2012), *Nechto v. Russia* (2012), *A. A. v. Russia* (2012), *Alchagin v. Russia* (2012), *Arutyunyan v. Russia* (2012), *Sakhvadze v. Russia* (2012), *Vladimir Vasilyev v. Russia* (2012), *Sokurenko v. Russia* (2012). The full text can be found at http://cmiskp.echr.coe.int/tkp197/search.asp?skin=hudoc-en.
65. The cases include *Gisayev v.* Russia (2011), *Popandopulo v. Russia* (2001), *Orlov v. Russia* (2011), *Esmukhambetov and Others v. Russia* (2011), *Ananyev and Others v. Russia* (2011), *Beksultanova v. Russia* (2011), *Ivanţoc and Others v. Moldova and Russia* (2011), *Isayev and Others v. Russia* (2011), *Aleksandra Dmitriyeva v. Russia* (2011), *Buldashev v. Russia* (2011), *Yakubov v. Russia* (2011), *Sambiyeva v. Russia* (20110, and *Fetisov and Others v. Russia* (2012). The full text can be found at http://cmiskp.echr.coe.int/tkp197/search.asp?skin=hudoc-en.
66. *Gisayev v. Russia* (2011). The full text can be found at http://cmiskp.echr.coe.int/tkp197/search.asp?skin=hudoc-en.
67. Analysis of court practices in 2010. The full text can be found at Judicial Department of the Supreme Court at http://www.cdep.ru/index.php?id=5&item=577.
68. See Paragraph 115–118 of case *Ananyev v. Russia* (2012). The full text can be found at http://cmiskp.echr.coe.int/tkp197/search.asp?skin=hudoc-en.
69. See *Ananyev v. Russia* (2012) and case of *Aleksandr Makarov v. Russia* (2009). The full text can be found at http://cmiskp.echr.coe.int/tkp197/search.asp?skin=hudoc-en. An example of low compensation received for illegal detention is the case of Igor Velichkov who spent three years in prison on the basis of a forced confession he gave after a prolonged beating. The Russian court awarded 300,000 rubles ($10,000) as compensation for unlawful detention. The case is featured by Public Verdict at http://www.publicverdict.org/topics/cases/9585/1169.html.

70. Statistics analyzed in the case of *Ananyev v. Russia* (2012) (paragraph 68). The full text can be found at http://cmiskp.echr.coe.int/tkp197/search.asp?skin=hudoc-en.
71. Article 157 of the Russian CPC. The full text of these documents can be obtained at www.consultant.ru.
72. The case of Kirill Schiborsch featured by the Public Verdict is one of the examples of how obstacles in accessing forensic medical professionals can cause a loss of evidence of police abuse. The case is featured at http://www.publicverdict.org/topics/cases/8823/1134.html.
73. Examples of police abuse and denial of the facts of short-term detention can be found in the annual report of Ombudsman in 2009. The report describes cases of citizen N. in Tula and multiple citizens in Moscow who were forcibly delivered to police precincts without any records of their detention. The lack of documentation was treated by both internal investigations by the MVD and *Procuracy* as sufficient evidence that the detentions never occurred (Ombudsman, 2009).
74. See Annex 1 in case of *Ananyev v. Russia* (2012). The full text can be found at http://cmiskp.echr.coe.int/tkp197/search.asp?skin=hudoc-en.
75. Articles 89, 92, and 96 of the Criminal Procedural Code of RSFSR. Full text can be found at www.consultant.ru.
76. Article 97 of the Criminal Procedural Code of RSFSR. Full text can be found at www.consultant.ru.
77. ECHR reiterates in paragraph 460 of the case of *Ilascu v. Moldova and Russia* (2004) that "the word 'tribunal' used in the French text of Article 5 (court) and other Articles of the Convention, in particular Article 6 (tribunal), refers in the first place to a body 'established by law' satisfying a number of conditions, which include independence, particularly vis-à-vis the executive, impartiality, the duration of its members' terms of office and guarantees of a judicial procedure." In *Salov v. Ukraine* (2005) paragraph 58, the court instructs that "The prosecution authorities not only belong to the executive branch of the State, but they also concurrently perform investigative and prosecution functions in criminal proceedings and are party to those proceedings. The Court, therefore, reiterates its position as to the status of the prosecutor, who cannot be regarded as 'an officer authorized by law to exercise judicial power'." See also *Klyakhin v. Russia* (2005). The full text can be found at http://cmiskp.echr.coe.int/tkp197/search.asp?skin=hudoc-en.
78. Article 108 of the CPC of Russia. The full text of these documents can be obtained at www.consultant.ru.
79. Article 109 of the CPC of Russia. The full text of these documents can be obtained at www.consultant.ru.
80. According to the judge (Ananyev, 2006), the requests of pretrial detention were reduced by 40% once the judicial approval of the pretrial detention became a requirement.
81. See paragraph 57 in the case of *Ananyev v. Russia* (2012). The full text can be found at http://cmiskp.echr.coe.int/tkp197/search.asp?skin=hudoc-en.
82. Analysis of court practices in 2010. The full text can be found at Judicial Department of the Supreme Court at http://www.cdep.ru/index.php?id=5&item=577.

83. Article 34 Paragraph 4 of Federal law "On Police Service," issued on November 30, 2011 #342-FZ. The full text of these documents can be obtained at www.consultant.ru.
84. The 2008 study was conducted by the authors in the Volgograd region with a representative sample of 500 citizens.
85. Ibid.
86. All estimates are based on 30 rubles per $1 ratio, which indicates an average conversion rate during 2000–2012.
87. The 2008 study was conducted by the authors of this book in the Volgograd region with a representative sample of 500 citizens.
88. On some estimates of traffic police bribery, see, for example, an article at http://kp.ru/daily/25662/824358/.
89. For example, see self-reported statistics on the bribe size and the violation type at http://www.vashamashina.ru/bill.php.
90. For information on the community of Russian online activists who are documenting potential violations by legal and illegal users of "special signals" and "special car registrations," please see http://ru-vederko.livejournal.com/.
91. For example, see an article about a police officer of the Federal Migration Service who illegally issued passports to 341 citizens of Kazakhstan, Moldova, and Tajikistan in Kursk at http://www.rg.ru/2011/04/07/reg-roscentr/pasport.html. Another example is a story of Tryapitsina who was administratively fined for illegally issuing Russian passports to immigrants and who committed similar crimes again in Chelyabinsk. The details can be found at http://www.kasparov.ru/material.php?id=4E85BD69B9084.
92. On issues of police refusal to investigate crime, see an article at http://kp.ru/daily/25756/2742388/.
93. For example, see an article "Mentalnyi ishod" (mental outcome is the literal translation, but this also means police officers' departure) published at http://www.kommersant.ru/doc/1310438.
94. For example, see an article from *Moscow Komsomolets* about resistance of some police officers to comply with the assessment system. The full text of the article can be found at http://www.mk.ru/editions/daily/article/2001/11/26/101150-palochnyiy-bunt.html.
95. An example of prolonged police failure to take criminal complaints from victims of racketeering can be found in the Report by the Clean Hands organization published in 2009 (Chistye Ruki (Clean Hands), 2009, p. 17).
96. For details, see WCIOM Omnibus study from December 28, 2005 at www.wciom.ru.
97. For example, see an article at http://kp.ru/daily/25756/2742388/.
98. For example, see an article on Moscow police detectives who falsified burglary and robbery cases by using homeless and alcoholics they found on the streets. Full details, see http://www.newsland.ru/news/detail/id/506519/.
99. For example, see an article at http://www.mospravda.ru/issue/2011/12/09/article29965/.
100. For an example of police falsifying economic crime against small businessmen, please see the Report by Clean Hands organization published in 2009 (Chistye Ruki (Clean Hands), 2009, p. 20). Also see an example from the

Tatarstan Republic where an ex-felon homeless person was used to falsify the case of robbery by the police. See more details at http://s-pravdoy.ru/regions/13718-2011-12-13-104156.html.

101. For details, see the WCIOM Omnibus study from December 28, 2005 at www.wciom.ru.
102. For example, see an article at *Komsomolskaya Pravda* at http://kp.ru/daily/25674/834484/.
103. For some details on development of "red roofs," see article at http://www.aferizm.ru/criminal/ops/ops_bez_grima.htm.
104. See an article titled "Opinion of Russians about police" published on November 10, 2010 by Levada Center at http://www.levada.ru/press/2010111001.html.
105. For example, see an article about the Moscow regional police at http://www.corrupcia.net/articles/fact-5252.html *or* an article about the Magnitogorsk police at http://reporter.by/incident/V-Magnitogorske-uvoleny-sotrudniki-OBEhP-zameshannye-v-kvartirnyh-aferah-Vlasti-obewajut-predostavit/.
106. For example, see article about MVD Minister of Kalmyk republic at http://www.compromat.ru/page_13083.htm.
107. For example, see an article about a police officer in Ulan-Ude at http://police-russia.info/index.php/2011/10/13/policejskij-krysheval-prostitutok-v-ulan-ude/.
108. For example, see an article about police from Komi Republic at http://gulagu.net/index.php?option=com_content&view=article&id=645:v-komi-vysokopostavlennye-oficzery-kryshevali-narkobiznes-odnoj-iz-syktyvkarskix-ops&catid=81:11-respublika-komi&Itemid=94.
109. For example, see an article about Moscow police at http://vz.ru/news/2011/10/26/533691.html.
110. This number is calculated based on 19.1% of all Russian citizens calling themselves "individuals with non-Russian origins." Statistical data is retrieved from http://www.perepis-2010.ru.
111. Statistical data is retrieved from http://www.perepis-2010.ru.
112. For example, according to Gudkov and Dubin, 67% of police officers report negative feelings toward immigrants from North Caucasus (Gudkov and Dubin, 2006).
113. For example, see an article about an Azerbaijani drug dealing ring protected by the police in the Irkutsk region at http://salam.vesti.az/news.php?id=91953.
114. For example, see an article on ties between the Chechen diaspora and organized crime in the Republic of Mary El at http://www.compromat.ru/page_9662.htm. Also see an article on Azerbaijani "mafia" in Moscow at http://www.compromat.ru/page_13207.htm.
115. For example, see an article at http://www.rosbalt.ru/main/2011/04/21/842011.html.
116. For example, see an article at http://www.newsru.com/russia/24dec2010/besporyadki.html.
117. The exact list of positions to which the income requirement is applicable can be determined from Presidential Decree #557 issued on May 18, 2009. Full text can be retrieved from www.consultant.ru.
118. Decree of MVD #205 issued on April 19, 2010. Full text can be retrieved from www.consultant.ru.
119. Full information can be found at http://www.mvd.ru/mvd/info/.

120. For example, see an article on a recently fired head of the St. Petersburg regional police office at http://www.compromat.ru/page_29258.htm *or* an article about the wife of a police officer who made five times more than the president of Russia, at http://www.aif.ru/money/article/43052.
121. For example, see an article at http://www.baltinfo.ru/2011/05/03/Bolshe-vsego-narushenii-pri-zapolnenii-deklaratcii-o-dokhodakh-vyyavleno-v-sisteme-MVD---Buksman-202648. [The largest number of violations has been recorded by State Attorney's office among police officers declaring their income].
122. For example, see an article about general Khorev at http://realty.newsru.com/article/20jan2012/horev.
123. The Federal Law #172-FZ titled "About anticorruption expertise of normative legal acts" issued on July 17, 2009. Full text can be retrieved from www.consultant.ru.
124. Decree of MVD #15 issued on January 15, 2010. Full text can be retrieved from www.consultant.ru.
125. Decree by the Government of Russian Federation #96 titled "On anticorruption expertise of normative legal acts" issued on February 26, 2010. Full text can be retrieved from www.consultant.ru.
126. For example, see the anticorruption expert opinion of Transparency International about Federal Law "On Police" at http://crimpravo.ru/blog/reforma_mvd/1116.html *or* reports by the Presidential Council for Human Rights and Interaction with Civil Society at http://www.president-sovet.ru/structure/group_corruption/materials/index.php.
127. Decree of MVD #1001 issued on November 24, 2008. Full text can be retrieved from www.consultant.ru.
128. Decree of MVD #1121 issued on November 7, 2011. Full text can be retrieved from www.consultant.ru.
129. Decree of FMS #339 issued on December 7, 2009. Full text can be retrieved from www.consultant.ru.
130. Decree of FMS #26 issued on February 3, 2010. Full text can be retrieved from www.consultant.ru.
131. For example, see an article about multiple drafts of administrative regulations for traffic police at http://www.rg.ru/2012/02/28/ekzamen.html.
132. See an article on this at http://www.rbcdaily.ru/focus/opinion/562949979455246.shtml.
133. On future measures taken by government to enforce the administrative rules, see, for example, an article by the Ministry of Economic Development at http://www.ar.gov.ru/about/publications/index.php?id_13=1957&from4=79&from_13=3.
134. Article 290 of the CC of Russia as amended by the Federal Law #162-FZ issued on December 8, 2003. Full text can be retrieved from www.consultant.ru.
135. Article 290 of the CC of Russia as amended by the Federal Law #97-FZ issued on May 4, 2011. Full text can be retrieved from www.consultant.ru.
136. Ibid.
137. Article 291-1 of the CC of Russia as amended by the Federal Law #97-FZ issued on May 4, 2011. Full text can be retrieved from www.consultant.ru.
138. Article 63 of the CC of Russia as amended by the Federal Law #18-FZ issued on July 22, 2010. Full text can be retrieved from www.consultant.ru.

139. Article 27 par 14 and Article 30.1 of the Federal Law "On Police" #3-FZ issued on February 7, 2011. Full text can be retrieved from www.consultant.ru.
140. According to the official MVD Web site, the study into an assessment system for police was conducted in 2009 by the Highest School of Economics. The report on the study can be found at http://www.mvd.ru/reform/research/.
141. For example, see an interview with the MVD Minister, Rashid Nurgaliev published at http://www.rg.ru/2010/01/22/karera.html.
142. For example, see some analysis of old and new performance systems at http://www.rabkor.ru/news/4829.html. Also see the analysis at http://www.kommersant.ru/doc/1307852.
143. We were able to find the full text of Decree of MVD #650 issued on August 5, 2005, Decree of MVD #25 issued on January 19, 2010, and Decree of MVD #1310 issued on December 26, 2011 at the forum of police officers at www.police-russia.com. We were unable to authenticate these documents because they contain no official signatures, but after comparison with several other sources, we believe that these documents are valid unofficial copies.
144. Decree of MVD of Russia #650 issued on May 6, 2005 titled "The questions of performance assessment of the agencies of interior affairs, units of criminal police and police of public safety, the agencies of preliminary investigation and investigation of crimes pertinent to transportation."
145. Decree of MVD #25 issued on January 19, 2010 titled "Questions of performance assessment of agencies of internal affairs, police units of criminal police and police of public safety, and agencies of preliminary investigation."
146. Decree of MVD #1310 issued on December 26, 2011 titled "Questions of performance assessment for the territorial agencies of interior affairs."
147. For example, see an article from 2011 about the traffic police superior officer demanding his employees "find" more traffic violators on the roads to fill the quota; at http://radiovesti.ru/articles/2011-10-11/fm/14206.
148. Provision 2.5 of Decree #25 of 2010 and provision 4.2 of Decree #1310 of 2012.
149. The report titled "Brief summary of sociological results on public safety and opinions about agencies of internal affairs" published at www.mvd.ru/userfiles/file/2012/ban/yanvar/analiz_oad.doc.
150. For example, see an article at http://crimpravo.ru/blog/reforma_mvd/1227.html.
151. Decree of President of Russia #815 issued on May 19, 2008. Full text can be retrieved from www.consultant.ru.
152. Federal law #247-FZ issued on July 19, 2011. Full text can be retrieved from www.consultant.ru.
153. For full text of the interview, see an article at www.pda.mvd.ru/presscenter/interview/minister/show_94818/.
154. For example, see an article at http://www.trud.ru/article/07-03-2012/273391_rossijskoj_politsii_ispolnilsja_god_chto_izmenilos.html The Russian police is one year old, did anything change? *and* an article at http://www.rb.ru/topstory/economics/2010/04/29/161654.html.
155. For example, see an article at http://kp.ru/daily/25688/892760/ *and* an article at http://region15.ru/news/main/2011/12/18/01-24/.
156. Study titled "Kourier" by Levada conducted in November of 2007, question # 14A. Retrieved from http://sophist.hse.ru/.

157. Study titled "Kourier" by Levada conducted in April of 2007, question #11-1. Retrieved from http://sophist.hse.ru/.
158. For example, see an article about a young woman who fights online pedophiles and police reaction to this at http://kp.ru/daily/25716.3/914323/.
159. According to the report by Public Council, the number of citizens who are willing to report police corruption decreased from 31% to 22% in just a one-year period (Obschestvennaya Palata, 2011a).

Conclusion: The Path to Reforms 8

Since the Soviet Union's collapse, the Russian Federation has implemented polices with the objectives of creating a democracy. As a part of the transformation, efforts have been made to establish democratic police institutions. While forms of democratic policing vary between nations, the institutions generally share similar traits. The common understanding of democratic policing includes public accountability, transparent decision making, responsiveness to the citizens, representativeness of the general population, respect for human rights, commitment to the rule of law, and a minimum use of force (Can, 2005; Das, 2000). A democratic police agency is assumed to be acting on behalf of the people, guided by the moral consensus and shared values of security (Caparini and Marenin, 2004).

The ideals of democratic policing are difficult to achieve even in countries with mature democracies. The inherently coercive nature of police activities to accomplish social control often conflict with notions of democracy (Haberfeld and Cerrah, 2008). Building democratic policing is an extremely challenging task in the former Soviet countries. In addition to "immature" democratic forms of government, post-Communist countries are often plagued with issues of corruption, a minimal civil society structure, the lack of commitments from political elites, the lack of state institutional autonomy, an undeveloped middle class, and lack of social capital (Mawby, 2001; Pino and Wiatrowski, 2006). While some former Soviet countries of Eastern Europe have made progress in the past 10 years related to established democratic policing (Can, 2005; Caparini and Marenin, 2004; Das, 2000; Haberfeld and Cerrah, 2008; Mawby, 1999), Russia continues to struggle. Constant reforms in the past 20 years have produced limited outcomes in the area of democratic policing (Robertson, 2004).[1]

One of the latest attempts to reform the Russian police was undertaken by President Medvedev in 2011. The reform consisted of four major measures that included personnel cuts, increased wages and benefits, review of personnel files ("re-attestation"), and the centralization of funding. The reform was promulgated by the new 2011 "On Police" statute that streamlined the existing regulations of police service (Gall, 2011).[2] The reform called for a 20% reduction in personnel among the MVD staff. Russia has one of the highest number of police officers per capita among European countries (Kalabekov, 2010). The maximum number of MVD personnel also was restricted to 1.1

million officers.[3] Another element of the reform was an officer salary increase. According to Interior Minister Nourgaliev, an officer's salary was increased by at least four times and the monthly salary should constitute an average of $1,000.[4] The reform also required a full review of all personnel files in order to "cleanse" the police ranks of bad apples and fight corruption. This process, known as *pereattestatsiya*, was completed by August 1, 2011, with 90% (875,000) of existing officers and 94% of management personnel passing the review.[5] Finally, the reform called for the centralization of all police funding into the federal budget, thus eliminating regional funding for the "police of public security." Because many regions struggle to maintain balanced budgets, the regional police funding was often delayed and varied significantly between regions. The centralization of funding was posited as a measure to provide stable and uniform support to the entire Russian police system.[6]

The critics of the 2011 reforms maintain these measures are ineffective and can hardly facilitate a drastic transformation toward democratic policing (Kosals, 2011; D.E. Petrov, 2011; Poduzov, 2010). The media have often reported the majority of personnel cuts were done among low-ranking officers while the large managerial staff was untouched. Instead, police precincts were closed in small rural areas making police services inaccessible to a large number of residents.[7] The process of existing personnel review (re-attestation) was nontransparent to the public, NGOs (nongovernmental organizations), or the media.[8] As a result, many Russians believe that corrupt officers were retained and the mechanism of re-attestation was used to terminate honest policemen.[9] The officers themselves found the review process arbitrary and prone to abuse from superior officers. There were media reports that a $300 bribe was sufficient to pass the re-attestation during the 2011 reforms.[10]

Many researchers are skeptical as well about the impact of increased wages and benefits on police culture (Novikova, 2005; Chistye Ruki, 2012). First, between 2000 and 2010, funding was increased ninefold for law enforcement, yet this made no difference in the levels of effectiveness or the corruption rates (Kalabekov, 2010). Second, even after the reform, a large part of an officer's salary continues to depend on the supervisor's assessment. Without changes in the reporting system and the elimination of the existing crime statistics requirements, honest police officers will continue to struggle and may not receive full salary.[11] Finally, the idea of the new centralized funding system also has been criticized. Exclusive federal funding strengthened presidential authority over the police and diminished decentralized regional authority over the local police offices.[12] This measure is simply a redistribution of power and appears to have little effect on democratizing the Russian police (D.E. Petrov, 2011).[13]

Generally, the 2011 police reforms have suffered from the same problems as prior reform attempts. The reform was designed as a top-down process where the MVD was ordered by the president to reform itself. The MVD leadership alone was responsible for developing the reform agenda, the implementation, and oversight of the process.[14] Whereas civil society organizations were actively involved in the discussion of the 2011 law, only a few of their suggestions were accepted.[15] Human rights advocates and NGO representatives were essentially ignored by the MVD officials when discussing the draft reform, "On Police," and other reform initiatives. Some provision of the 2011 police reforms clearly contradicted the suggestions developed by NGOs including calls for MVD decentralization and demilitarization.[16] The MVD's rank-and-file members also were excluded from the discussion (Poduzov, 2010). Despite the many suggestions to conduct a thorough analysis of the situation and develop a better plan for reforms, the 2011 reforms were rushed by the president and MVD leadership in an extremely short period of time.[17]

It has been suggested that the true meaning of the 2011 reforms had little to do with enhancing democratic policing at all (Kosals, 2010).[18] Instead, it was precipitated from drastic public dissatisfaction with the police and the need of political elites to reassert their control over the MVD security apparatus.[19] A public opinion survey demonstrated that citizens in general are skeptical about the 2011 reform outcomes. Table 8.1 indicates that only 16% to 19% of citizens expected positive reforms outcomes, whereas the majority did not anticipate any changes, or actually expected things to get worse. These findings arguably reflect the overall public dissatisfaction and disapproval of the ongoing continuous reform efforts over the past 20 years.[20] The police officers themselves are also skeptical about the reform outcomes.[21]

Based on the discussion of institutional development, structure, authorities, workforce, and continuous issues presented in Chapters 1 through 7, it is clear that several important changes have to be made in order to improve the performance and integrity of the Russian police:

1. *Reducing political subservience.* Even though legal regulations forbid the Russian police from any political involvement, the agency remains far from apolitical (A. Beck and Robertson, 2009b). Following Soviet traditions, the police continued to be involved in the processes of power redistribution and accession (Gilinskiy, 2000). To a large extent this is explained by the hierarchical structure of the MVD, whereby the president alone controls the key appointments. Political allegiances and personal loyalty appear to play a critical role in the selection of MVD leadership. These allegiances are transferred down to the lower ranks. Officers admit that loyalty to the government officials and allegiances to local authorities, and their interests, is an important part of successful police service (Gladarev, 2008). Political manipulation of the

Table 8.1 Summary of empirical findings related to the variable public attitudes toward adoption of a new federal law on "Police" from 2010 to 2011

		Level of Public Awareness about Adoption of a New Federal Law on "Police"			Impact on the daily Work of the Police (Militia)			
Author(s)	Year	Yes	No	Don't Know	Positive	Negative	Nothing Changes	Don't Know
WCIOM	2010				16%	7%	49%	28%
FOM	2010	51%	47%	3%				
LEVADA	2010	73%	24%	3%	19%	52%	—	29%
FOM	2011	97%	2%	1%	19%	4%	61%	16%
ROMIR	2011	84%	16%					

police further undermines public legitimacy. According to surveys, many Russians believe the police are primarily serving the interests of government officials and wealthy individuals (Gilinskiy, 2003).[22] Some officers admit these are who they serve. Decreasing the MVD's political subservience may not be easily achieved as this requires significant changes in political will and organizational structure. The most plausible solutions can include checks and balances from the legislative branch (*Duma*) related to leadership appointments, and transparency in the area of major decision-making processes achieved through public hearings of policy changes.

2. *Decentralization of the MVD structure.* Whereas a decentralization of the police structure does not necessarily mean democratic policing (Bayley, 1985), centralization appears more prone to the abuse of power and corruption (Can, 2005). The centralization of the police forces in Russia is extreme. The entire structure, authorities, and performance are centrally controlled by the MVD apparatus in Moscow. The MVD centralized management process has proved to be cumbersome, bureaucratic, and inefficient. The highly formalized centralization is not flexible enough to consider the local conditions in the regions that are idiosyncratic vis-à-vis' the levels of crime rates, socioeconomic factors, and ethnicity.[23] Extreme centralization also exacerbates political subservience and facilitates an environment for the abuse of power and corruption (Committee of Civil Initiatives, 2012). The 2011 reforms appear only to strengthen the centralized control as now the entire MVD system is funded exclusively from the federal budget. The centralization has a long history as a part of the continental police system, so it is unlikely that a fully decentralized police structure would ever be developed. What is more likely is a slight decentralization of police functions through the redistribution of federal power. This can be done by emulating the Soviet system of double subordination that continued through the 1990s. In this system, the public security police are funded and controlled through the governor's office in the region, while the criminal investigators and detectives are funded by the federal budget.[24] There is also a proposal in which the lowest police levels (circuit police departments) are funded and controlled by the municipal authorities.[25] This would only be possible if regional and municipal authorities were to develop and control sustainable budgets and reduce their federal government dependency.
3. *Demilitarization of the police workforce.* By its very nature, the police are inherently a coercive and paramilitary agency of social control (Haberfeld and Cerrah, 2008). However, countries with democratic policing forms attempt to curb militarization to ensure

accountability and compliance with the rule of law (Das, 2000). Modern Russia inherited a militaristic policing system from the Soviet Union (Mawby, 1990) and continued this tradition during the past 20 years (Kosals, 2011).[26] In 2010, the refusal to follow an order of a superior became a criminal offense. Police militarization creates an absolute dependency of the officers on their superiors (Kuztnetsov, 2009).[27] In the current conditions of pervasive corruption, this dependency contributes to an abuse of power and its subsequent replication among all members of the various police units (Yanbukhtin, 2005). Police officers report feeling humiliated, insecure, and forced to follow apparently illegal orders of superiors (Gladarev, 2011b; Novikova, 2005). In the current system, a superior's command appears to be more important than the rule of law and public interest (Kosals, 2010). The Russian militarized organizational structure has a lengthy historical tradition making the full demilitarization highly unlikely.[28] The alternatives include the demilitarization of criminal investigators and detective units along with licensing divisions that include the traffic police.[29] Currently, members of the Federal Migration Service have been demilitarized via the 2011 police reforms. This is a positive step toward democratizing the Russian police.

4. *Improving the performance assessment and reporting system.* The Russian police reporting system is based on preset quantitative indices that measure unit outcomes or offense types based on present year to past year. Officers' salary and promotions depend on achieving a set of quantitative criteria that include registered crime rates, crime clearance rates, and the number of convicted offenders. The MVD assessment regulations are typically unavailable to the public. The current system encourages the manipulation of data, falsifications of charges against innocent individuals, and abuse of power to conceal existing crimes (Gladarev, 2008; Novikova and Shepeleva, 2005). On multiple occasions, the MVD announced a reform of the performance reporting criteria; however, the changes were mainly superficial.[30] Public surveys of police performance and satisfaction were finally included in evaluations, but their overall assessment weight is unclear. It is also unclear whether sociological centers conducting the surveys are independent from police influence.[31] Alternative reporting systems have already been developed and tested by various NGOs and research centers (Democracy Fund, 2009; INDEM, 2001b, 2004).[32] Some recommendations of these organizations are to eliminate the use of statistical indices to determine officers' salaries. Instead, these organizations recommend the use of official statistics only for future planning of crime control and

prevention strategies; they also propose to use the public surveys as a major criteria to assess police performance. Currently, it appears that the surveys are only supplementary to the crime statistics indices. It also has been suggested that citizen surveys should be conducted by independent sociological organizations that are recruited by municipalities or other sources that are independent from police agencies. Performance and measurement units, other than registered crime, have been suggested as well for a new statistical reporting process (INDEM, 2001b, 2004). Overall, the process of police assessment needs public transparency and should include the participation of stakeholders, such as human rights advocates and NGOs.[33]

5. *Increasing the transparency of decision making and public accountability of police.* One of the main goals of the 2011 police reforms was to increase public accountability and the transparency of daily police activities. The new law "On Police" declared the need for the public to control the police through the Federal Public Council (*Obschestvennaya palata*) and regional public councils.[34] Yet the presidential decrees and MVD regulations provide public councils with little authority to investigate the potential of police abuse and other violations.[35] There is little independence as the MVD itself controls the membership of public councils (Panchenko, 2010). This lack of independence can interfere with inquiries into allegations of police abuse.[36] The transparency of police activities is also declared as one of the main principles of police work by the new 2011 law "On Police." In compliance with the new law, the regional heads of the MVD now provide annual reports to the regional legislative agencies. Yet the "On Police"[37] reform of 2011 allows the MVD to determine how, when, and what is reported to the legislative agencies, media, and public.[38] Despite the declaration of transparency, many police buildings are inaccessible to the public due to security checkpoints and other requirements.[39] The prevailing police culture is one of the major obstacles for attaining an increase in transparency and public accountability (Savchenko, 2011). Many police officers perceive citizens only as potential victims, or witnesses, and reject the idea of civilian oversight.[40] On the other hand, many Russians are convinced that police reform will fail unless a true mechanism of public–police accountability is implemented (S.V. Egoryshev and Egorysheva, 2010; Levada, 2010).[41] Changes in police culture can be achieved gradually through the process of establishing a civil society. Of course, this interaction is possible only if civil society members are provided with real authority to investigate police violations and are given better access to police information.

6. *Integrating civil society into future police reforms.* Whereas the overall situation with civil society in Russia remains difficult, there are indications it is slowly maturing (Levada, 2011a; Uhlin, 2006).[42] During the period from 2009 through 2011, citizens demonstrated a significant interest in police reform issues. Table 8.1 shows that anywhere between 51% and 97% of Russians were aware of the police reforms and provisions of the proposed law. Over 20,000 responses were published during the Internet public discussion period related to the draft law "On Police" in 2010.[43] Several prominent international and Russian NGOs, leading academic institutions, and government-authorized organizations conducted examinations of the draft law and published their expert opinions.[44] Despite this level of activity and participation, only a few recommended amendments to the draft law that were suggested by NGOs and the public were accepted.[45] Many citizens felt disappointment with the results (Taubina, 2011). They perceived the online discussions of the draft were conducted to ease the public's dissatisfaction with the police and not to actually improve their performance (Kosals, 2011).[46] On the other hand, there is a growing consensus among various societal members that the MVD is incapable of self-reform and more civil society involvement is needed to legitimize future police reforms.[47] Nevertheless, top-down reforms are consistent with the national government's tradition of centralization and militarization. At this point, it is unclear if the political elites will be willing to engage in an additional dialog with members of the growing civil society over future police reforms.[48] However, it is certain the future legitimacy of police reforms depends on a constructive dialog between the citizenry and government.
7. *Developing realistic expectations about the role and functions of the police.* It appears that both the MVD leadership and the citizens are still uncertain about the exact role and functions of the contemporary police. Soviet criminology was based in part on the idealistic premise that crime can be completely eradicated by the actions of the police, preventing all crimes through the active involvement in the lives of citizens (Solomon, 1996). Soviet-style proactive policing included police authority to forcefully institutionalize the mentally ill, drug addicts, alcoholics, homeless, and preventive police involvement into family disputes. It appears from interviews with current police officers, that these expectations are still embedded in the system of police management.[49] Of course, the ability to fulfill these expectations failed then and now since the police authority to interfere with the private lives of Russian citizens has diminished in the past 20 years.[50] This contradiction often leads to the manipulation of statistical reporting and hypocritical attitudes of police officers

about their duties (Gladarev, 2011b). Citizens also send mixed signals about the mission of the police, who are often blamed for not successfully controlling the situation with drug addicts, the mentally ill, the homeless, alcoholics, and family violence.[51] On the other hand, citizens expect a minimum level of invasion into their privacy and protection of their human rights. This situation is a clear contradiction between the values of the proactive policing style inherited from the Soviet period contrasted with the more recent adoption of democratic values.[52] If the dialog about police reform between civil society elements and government continues, it is possible that a consensus will be reached eventually. However, the Soviet legacy of the Russian legal and police culture, which contains some elements of the historic proactive policing, will more than likely survive into the future. If this is the case, the citizens must cede the police more authority and resources to achieve the goals of a Soviet style of proactive policing.

These suggested changes are just a few among many other measures that can achieve a more democratic Russian police force. Other traditional recommendations include advanced training regarding the use of force, human rights, strengthening the police officers' unions, and restructuring the internal security service into a more independent agency (Can, 2005). [53]

Future police reforms depend primarily on two interrelated factors: the development of civil society and the transformation of a larger political system into a multiparty democracy to provide government checks and balances. The experiences of former Soviet countries suggest that political will and the level of democracy are key factors to facilitate democratic policing (Pino and Wiatrowski, 2006). Another important factor is if the citizenry can consolidate and strengthen the political pressure that is necessary to transform the police institution. The national government did take some steps to recognize the need for a dialog with citizens and NGOs when reforming the police, but it failed to effectively include recommendations from the citizenry in the recent police reforms.

Endnotes

1. On public opinion about reforms in general including transformation of law enforcement, see the report by the Institute of Sociology of Russian Academy of Sciences (IS RAN, 2011).
2. Federal Law "On Police" issued on February 7, 2011 #3-FZ. Retrieved July 7, 2012 from www.consultant.ru.
3. Decree of President issued on March 1, 2011 # 252. Retrieved July 7, 2012 from www.consultant.ru.

4. The interview with the MVD minister Nourgaliev published in *Komsomolskaya Pravda* on November 17, 2011. Retrieved on July 7, 2012 from http://kp.ru/daily/25789.4/2771871/.
5. Statistics provided according to the article in *Komsomolskaya Pravda* published on July 25, 2011. Retrieved on July 7, 2012 from http://kp.ru/daily/25723.5/2715985/ and the interview with the MVD minister Kolokoltsev published in the newspaper *Grani* on June 25, 2012. Retrieved on July 7, 2012 from http://grani.ru/tags/police/m.198621.html.
6. For example, see articles at http://www.vz.ru/society/2010/4/28/397239.html *and* http://www.memoid.ru/node/Perspektivy_reformy_MVD_v_sovremennoj_Rossii#cite_note-oreanda-30.
7. The interview with the MVD minister Kolokoltsev published in the newspaper *Grani* on June 25, 2012. Retrieved on July 7, 2012 from http://grani.ru/tags/police/m.198621.html.
8. For example, see the interview with the Public Council member, advocate Kucherna, who was given the access to the meetings of the "attestation commission" only after the public outcry. The article retrieved on January 5, 2011 at http://www.gzt.ru/topnews/accidents/-kucherena-zanyalsya-sborom-kompromata-na-/358913.html.
9. For example, according to a WCIOM survey, 46% of Russians believe that "re-attestation" of police was biased and only 24% reported it was an honest process. Retrieved on July 7, 2012 at http://wciom.ru/index.php?id=459&uid=111883. Also, see an interview with the director of Public Verdict, Natalia Taubina, at http://publicverdict.ru/topics/lib_experts/10214.html.
10. For example, see an interview with the head of the Union of Moscow police, Pashkin at http://radiovesti.ru/articles/2012-03-15/fm/38001. According to the survey conducted by the Union of the Moscow police officers, 90% of officers agreed that "re-attestation" was arbitrary. For details, see an article published on March 17, 2011 at http://www.gudok.ru/sujet/militsiya-reforma/?pub_id=391302.
11. Public opinion on increased police wages is divided. According to WCIOM (2011c), 55% of Russians approve of the increased wages; however, only 13% reported that increased wages can improve the situation with police corruption.
12. See, for example, the report by the Oxford Analytica. Russia: Police reform fails to address key challenges. Retrieved on July 7, 2011 from http://www.oxan.com/display.aspx?ItemID=DB156958.
13. The police officers themselves also consider that new police reform is mostly protecting the interests of federal authorities (Savchenko, 2011). Also, see an article by Alexander Podrabinek "The reform of MVD is impossible and not needed." Retrieved on July 7, 2012 at http://www.ej.ru/?a=note&id=9892.
14. For example, see an article by Vladimir Voronov, "Police syndrome." Retrieved on July 7, 2012 at http://www.sovsekretno.ru/magazines/article/2815.
15. For example, the expert opinion of the presidentially authorized Public Council on the draft law "On Police" and the Moscow Committee against Corruption concluded that the draft law was "unripe" and required further development before it could be implemented. Despite these opinions, the draft law was adopted without any major changes proposed by these organizations. Expert opinions can be retrieved from http://mosmakk.ru/ and at http://www.oprf.ru/1449/1537/views/1545/. Also, see an article on discussion of the draft law

by members of NGOs and human rights advocates at http://www.gazeta.ru/social/2010/09/08/3417305.shtml. Also, see an article by Public Verdict that describes successful public initiative to change the draft law "On Police" at http://publicverdict.ru/topics/articles/10175.html. Another set of proposals for reform was developed by the Interregional Union of police officers and published in 2010 at http://www.policemagazine.ru/bez1.html.

16. See the "Concept of MVD reform" developed by the group of leading NGOs in 2010 at http://publicverdict.ru/topics/reform/8104.html, and a report by the Solidarity movement at http://www.rusolidarnost.ru/perestroika-mvd-ot-militseiskogo-proizvola-k-professionalnoi-politsii.
17. For example, see an article by Tikhonova calling for postponing of the new law and police reforms and needs to improve the new law "On Police" (2010).
18. For other criticism of reforms, see, for example, the report by the oppositional democratic movement Solidarity titled "Perestroika of MVD: From militia abuse to professional police" published at http://www.rusolidarnost.ru/perestroika-mvd-ot-militseiskogo-proizvola-k-professionalnoi-politsii.
19. See, for example, a report by the Oxford Analytica. Russia: Police reform fails to address key challenges. Retrieved on July 7, 2012 from http://www.oxan.com/display.aspx?ItemID=DB156958.
20. According to the survey by FOM conducted in March 2012, the failure of police reform is viewed by Russians as among the top 10 failures of Medvedev's government. Retrieved on July 15, 2012 at http://fom.ru/politika/10369.
21. According to Savchenko (2011), 48% of police officers consider the new 2011 reform a "political intrigue" and 16% reported that it is just a "PR action." Only 28% of officers suggested that the new law was intended as a true transformation of police.
22. For example, a representative survey conducted by WCIOM on August 15, 2002 reported that only 2% believed that police are always protecting their interests, and 38% believed that it never happens. Retrieved on July 7, 2012 from http://wciom.ru/zh/print_q.php?s_id=302&q_id=23839&date=15.08.2002. In a 2008 study conducted by the authors of this book in the Volgograd region, 57% reported that police protects primarily powerful and wealthy individuals.
23. For examples of an extremely centralized management system, see interviews with police officers conducted by Public Verdict in 2010, at http://publicverdict.ru/articles_images/9936_56250_police.pdf.
24. For possible decentralization models, see, for example, "Concept of MVD reform," a report developed by a group of leading NGOs in 2010. Published at http://publicverdict.ru/topics/reform/8104.html. For more discussions on potential decentralization of police, see, for example, an article by Alexander Tretyakov at http://www.business-gazeta.ru/text/61691/. Also, see an article on potential of municipal police at http://top.rbc.ru/society/24/11/2011/626717.shtml.
25. See the report by the oppositional democratic movement Solidarity at http://www.rusolidarnost.ru/perestroika-mvd-ot-militseiskogo-proizvola-k-professionalnoi-politsii.
26. See the report by the Oxford Analytica. Russia: Police reform fails to address key challenges. Retrieved on July 7, 2011 from http://www.oxan.com/display.aspx?ItemID=DB156958.

27. For example, see an interview with the former police officer. Retrieved on July 28, 2012 at http://www.kazan.aif.ru/society/article/24896.
28. On resistance of police demilitarization, see, for example, police interviews conducted by Public Verdict in 2010 at http://publicverdict.ru/articles_images/9936_56250_police.pdf.
29. For discussion on potential "demilitarization," please see an article at http://www.newsland.ru/news/detail/id/452496/. Also, see "The concept of MVD reform" developed by a group of leading NGOs in 2010 at http://publicverdict.ru/topics/reform/8104.html.
30. For example, see the analysis by Oleg Kashin in the newspaper *Kommersant* at http://www.kommersant.ru/doc/1310438.
31. For discussion of reporting and assessment shortcoming, see an article at http://m.forbes.ru/article.php?id=65506.
32. Also, see the recommendation by Asmik Novikova from Public Verdict at http://publicverdict.ru/articles_images/10166_56713_novikova.pdf.
33. For report by the Council on Human Rights of Russia, see http://publicverdict.ru/topics/lib_experts/10166.html.
34. Article 50 of the Federal Law "On Police" issued on February 7, 2011 #3FZ. Retrieved from www.consultant.ru.
35. The activities of "Public Councils" are regulated by the Presidential Decree "About public councils at MVD and its regional agencies" issued on May 23, 2011 #668, the Presidential Decree "About confirming the Provisions on the public council at MVD" issued on July 28, 2011 #1027, and the Decree of Minister of MVD "About confirming the order in which the members of public councils at MVD and its regional agencies can be present at the personal meetings accepting complaints" issued on August 31, 2011 #988. The full text of these documents can be obtained at www.consultant.ru.
36. For examples of biased and nontransparent selection of regional Public Councils, see an article by Alexander Nazarov at http://publicverdict.ru/articles_images/10168_56716_nazarov.pdf.
37. Article 8 of the Federal Law "On Police" issued on February 7, 2011 #3FZ. Retrieved from www.consultant.ru.
38. In the current situation, the regional legislative agencies (*Dumas*) are highly dependent on the federal authorities and unlikely to provide an independent control. The current police reports to the public contain mainly the official statistics collected by the MVD. For example, see the report by the head of Moscow city police in 2011 at http://petrovka38.ru/gumvd/Stats/272/.
39. For example, see the report by Public Verdict at http://publicverdict.ru/articles_images/10170_56722_taubina.pdf *and* the interview with Natalia Taubina, the director of Public Verdict at http://publicverdict.ru/topics/lib_experts/10214.html.
40. According to Gudkov, the majority (48%) of police officers do not think that police need to be more transparent, compared to 43% who support more transparency. Gudkov and Dubin (2006) also found that only 26% of officers reported that more public accountability is needed to improve the work of police.
41. According to Levada (2010), 42% of those who are skeptical about 2011 police reforms reported that a real public control is needed for police transformation.

42. On examples of police cooperation with representatives of civil society, see the work by Revin (2004) and Taylor (2006).
43. For details on public discussion, please see an archive at http://zakonoproekt2012.ru/#law/police. The May 2011 survey conducted by this book's authors in the Volgograd region demonstrates that 68% knew about the online discussion of the draft law "On Police."
44. Among those organizations are Transparency International (the full report can be found at http://www.transparency.org.ru/reforma-politcii/zakliuchenie-po-zakonu-o-politcii), Independent Expert Council (full report can be found at http://www.neps.ru/node/1665), Presidential Council of Human Rights (www.president-sovet.ru/structure/group_corruption/materials/zakon.doc), The Institute of State and Law by Russian Academy of Sciences (http://www.igpran.ru/public/articles/Zaklyuchenie_IGPRAN_na_roekt_fz_o_policii.pdf), Regional Coalition of NGOs "Agora" (http://old.novayagazeta.ru/file/pdf/zaklMVD.pdf), Ural State Law Academy (www.gfurfo.tmweb.ru/wp-content/uploads/2010/.../nauchno-pravovoe.doc), and Working Group of NGOs (http://www.polit.ru/article/2010/08/27/npomvd, http://hro.org/node/8908).
45. The accepted amendments included five provisions suggested by Transparency International and supported by an online petition of Internet users. See full details at http://www.police2010.ru/. Also, see an article at http://www.newsland.ru/news/detail/id/578410/.
46. For example, Levada (2010) reported that 53% of Russians believed that police reform was done to "release the steam" of public disappointment with police.
47. In a study by Levada (2010), 42% were reported to believe the MVD is incapable of reforming itself without effective public control and involvement of civil society. In a study by WCIOM (2010a), 25% reported that the existing police culture is the leading obstacle to successful police reforms.
48. Some discussion of this can be found at http://www.levada.ru/14-11-2011/den-cheloveka-s-dubinkoi-grazhdane-ne-ulavlivayut-raznitsy-mezhdu-politsiei-i-militsiei.
49. For example, see interviews with police officers conducted by Public Verdict at http://publicverdict.ru/articles_images/9936_56250_police.pdf. Also, refer to the book by Popov (2005) on description of variety of police functions.
50. For example, see an article by Kharlamov (2011) on the obstacles of family violence prevention and need of new police authorities.
51. For example, see an article on reinstitution of "sobering-up" stations at http://www.echomsk.spb.ru/projects/goryachaya-tema/glavnyy-narkolog-rossii-prizyvaet-vernut-vytrezviteli.html.
52. On contradictions between human rights and determinate crime prevention by police, see Bayley (1994).
53. See the report from Public Verdict on the situation with police education at http://publicverdict.ru/articles_images/10169_56719_suslov.pdf.

References

Abbott, R. J. (1973). Police reform in the Russian Province of Iaroslavl, 1856-1876. *Slavic Review, 32*(2), 292–302.

Abbott, R. J. (1977). Crime, police, and society in St. Petersburg, Russia, 1866–1878. *Historian, 40*(1), 70.

Abdrashitov, E. E. (2009). Pravosoznanie sovremennogo sotrudnika militsii [Legal consciousness of modern police officer]. *Social Research, 5*, 146–152.

Abdulmalikov, A. M. (2007). Normativno-pravovoe regulirovanie bor'by politsii s pravonarusheniyami v sfere ekonomiki dorevolutsionnoi Rossii [Normative-legal regulation of police work against the economic crimes in pre-revolutionary Russia]. *Bulletin of the Russian Pedagogical University, 12*(33), 11–14.

Abdurakhmanova, I. V. (2006). Obraz politsii v massovom pravosoznanii nakanune i vo vremya Fevral'skoi burzhuazno-demokraticheskoi revolutsii 1917 [The image of police before and during the February democratic revolution of 1917]. *Bulletin of Rostov State Economic University, 1*, 27–31.

Adyan, A. O. (2006). *Sovershenstvovanie sistemy stimulirovaniya truda sotrudnikov organov vnutrennikh del [Improving the system of job stimulation for the employees of the agencies of Interior Affairs]*. Institute of State and Law, Russian Academy of Sciences, Moscow.

Agafonov, S. I. (2008). *Administrativnye protzedury i ikh realizatsiya v deyatel'nosti organov vnutrennikh del Rossiskoi Federatsii* [Administrative proceedings and their realization in the work of agencies of interior affairs of Russian federation*]*. Moscow Humanitarian University, Moscow.

Akhmadiev, I. A. (2007). Feminizatsiya gosudarstvennykh silovukh struktur [Feminization of the state law enforcement]. *Successes of the Modern Sciences, 1*, 88.

Amnesty International. (2002). The Russian Federation. Denial of Justice Available from www.amnesty.org.

Ananyev, V. N. (2006). Monitoring UPK vzglyad sudiy [Monitoring of CPC: judicial opinion]. In E. B. Mizulina and V. N. Pligin (Eds.), *Uroki reformy ugolovnogo pravosudiya v Rossii [The lessons of criminal justice reforms in Russia]* (pp. 110–133). Moscow: Yurist.

Andreev, A. L. (2005a). Pravovoi mentalitet i otnoshenie k militsii v Rossiskom obschestve: sotsiokulturnye aspekty [Legal mentality and public attitudes of police in Russian society: socio-cultural aspects]. *Monitoring of Public Opinion, 4*(72), 26–37.

Andreev, A. L. (2005b). Vzaimootnoshenia grazgdan i militsii [Relations between the citizenry and police]. *Bulletin of Academy of Science, 75*(4), 291–297.

Anuchin, E. N. (1872). *Istoricheskii obzor razvitiya administrativno-politseiskih ucherezhdenii v Rossii c Ucherezhdeniya o gubernoyakh do nashih dnei [Historic review of development of the administrative-police institutions in Russia from Establishment of provinces, 1775 to present time]*. St. Petersburg: Tipographia MVD.

Artem'ev, A. M. (2003). *Realizatsiya kadrovoi politiki MVD Rossii v sfere podgotovki kadrov [Implementation of personnel policy in MVD of Russia in the area of training the staff]*. Moscow: Zakon i Pravo.

Artemov, V. M. (2000). Sotsial'no-kul'turnaya orientatsiya pravookhranitel'nykh organov [Social-cultural orientation of law enforcement agencies]. *Social Research, 1*, 51–55.

Association for Criminology. (1996). *Kriminal'naya situatsiya v Rossii o ee izmeneniya [Criminal situation in Russia and its changes]*. Moscow: Association for Criminology.

Association for Criminology. (1997). *Prestupnost i reformy v Rossii [Crime and reforms in Russia]*. Moscow: Association for Criminology.

Avrutin, Y. E. (2006). Sotsial'no-politicheskie i organizatsionno-pravovye predposylki stanovleniya rossikoi militsii [Social, political, organizational, and legal conditions of Russian militia development]. *Bulletin of Moscow University MVD, 3*, 132–136.

Babanov, A. A. (2004). *Silovye struktury v sisteme politicheskoi vlasti pravovog gosudarstva [Law enforcement agencies in the political system of legal state]*. Volgograd: Volgograd State University Press.

Bakhanskaia, N. (1975). New legislation on the volunteer auxiliary police. *Soviet Law and Government, 2*, 3–11.

Balmuth, D. (1979). *Censorship in Russia, 1865–1905*. Washington, D.C.: University Press of America, Inc.

Barber, M. L. (2000). Reforming criminal justice in Russia: Progress report for twenty-first century. *Journal of Transnational Law, 13*, 319–362.

Barnes, J. (1939). The great Bolshevik cleansing. *Foreign Affairs, 17*(3), 556–568.

Baron, S. W. (1976). *The Russian Jew under Tsars and Soviets*. London: Macmillan Publishing, Inc.

Bayley, D. H. (1985). *Patterns of policing*. New Brunswick, NJ: Rutgers University Press.

Bayley, D. H. (1994). *Police for the future*. New York, Oxford: Oxford University Press.

Beck, A., and Lee, R. (2001). Valeurs et pratiques professionnelles dans la police russe. *Les Cahiers de la sécurité intérieure, 44*(2), 115–142.

Beck, A., and Lee, R. (2002). Attitudes to corruption among Russian police officers and trainees. *Crime, Law and Social Change, 38*, 357–372.

Beck, A., and Robertson, A. (2003). Crime in Russia: Exploring the link between victimization and concern about crime. *International Journal of Crime Prevention and Community Safety, 5*(1), 27–46.

Beck, A., and Chistyakova, Y. (2004). Closing the gap between the police and public in post-Soviet Ukraine: A bridge too far? *Police Practice Research, 5*(1), 43–65.

Beck, A., and Robertson, A. (2005). Policing in post-Soviet Russia. In W. A. Pridemore (Ed.), *Ruling Russia. Law, crime and justice in a changing society* (pp. 247–260). New York: Rowman and Littlefield Publishers, Inc.

Beck, A., and Robertson, A. (2009a). The challenges to developing democratic policing in post-Soviet societies: The Russian experience. *Police Practice and Research, 10*(4), 285–293.

Beck, A., and Robertson, A. (2009b). Policing in the "new" Russia. In M. S. Hinton and T. Newburn (Eds.), *Policing developing democracies* (pp. 50–73). London and New York: Routledge.

Beck, F., and Godin, W. (2006). Russian Purge and the Extraction of Confession. In P. Hollander (Ed.), *From the gulag to the killing fields* (pp. 21–38). Wilmington, DE: ISI Books.

Beketov, O. I., Bocharov, S. N., Kaplunov, A. I., Kokorev, A. N., Maslov, A.E., Oparin, V. N., et al. (2009). *Administrativnaya deyatel'nost' organov vnutrennikh del [Administrative activity of the agencies of interior affairs]*. Moscow: TsOKR MVD.

Belenkov, R. A. (2003). *Pravookhranitel'nye organy [Law enforcement agencies]*. Moscow: Prior-Izdat.

Benvenuti, F. (1997). The "reform" of the NKVD, 1934. *Europe-Asia Studies, 49*(6), 1037.

Berezin, G. N. (2011). Organizatsionnaya kultura v rossiskoi politisii: problemy i perspektivy [Organizational culture in the Russian police: problems and prospects]. *Bulletin of Adygei State University, 4*, 180–186.

Berezina, L. V. (2003). *Dokazyvanie v stadii vozbuzhdeniya ugolovnogo dela po UPK Rossiskoi Federatsii [Proof during the stage of case initation under the CPC of RF]*. Saratov Law Institute, Saratov.

Berg, G. P. V. D. (1985). *The Soviet system of justice: Figures and policy*. Dordrecht, Boston, and Lancaster: Martinus Nijhoff Publishers.

Berman, H. J. (1950). *Justice in Russia*. Cambridge: Harvard University Press.

Berman, H. J. (1963). *Justice in the USSR. An Interpretation of Soviet Law*. Cambridge and London: Harvard University Press.

Berman, H. J. (1966). *Soviet criminal law and procedure. The RSFSR codes*. Cambridge, Massachusetts: Harvard University Press.

Bescherevnykh, T. G. (1973). Direction of interior affairs organs by local Soviets. *Soviet Law and Government, 3*, 75–87.

Bezaev, M. N. (1999). Obschestvennoe mnenie o kriminogennoi obstanovke i deyatel'nosti vnutrennih del [Public opinion about the criminal conditions and the work of police]. *Social Research, 12*, 100–105.

Bezlepkin, B. T. (2001). *Sudebnaya sistema, pravookhranitel'nye organy i advokatura Rossii [Court system, law enforcement and public defender office in Russia]*. Moscow: Yurist.

Blagoveschenskyi, Y. N., Golovschinkyi, K. I., Krasnov, M. A., Parkhomenko, S. A., Rimskyi, V. L., and Satarov, G. A. (2006). *Opredelenie faktorov vliyayuschikh na effektivnost' predostavleniya uslug po bezopasnosti ot prestupnykh posyagatelstv [Determining factors that infleunce the effectivness of providing services on safety and protection from crime]*. Moscow: Fund INDEM.

Bobrova, I. A. (2005). *Psikhologicheskie osobennosti lichnosti zhenschin-sotrudnikov organov vnutrennikh del MVD Rossii [Psychological features of female police officers employed by MVD]*. St. Petersburg: St. Petersbury MVD University.

Boffa, G. (1990). *Storia dell'Unione Sovietica*. Rome: Unità.

Bolotin, B., and Godunov, N. (1977). Responsibility for offenses against the life, health and dignity of policemen and the unarmed volunteer police auxiliaries. *Soviet Law and Government, 4*, 55–60.

Bondarenko, T. A. (2002). *Avtoritet sotrudika militsii [Reputation of a police officer]*. Academy of Management of MVD, Moscow.

Bondarenko, T. A. (2006a). Imidg organov vnutrennih del MVD v "militseiskih" teleserialah [The image of Agencies of Interior Affairs in the "police" soap operas]. *Social Research, 9*, 114–119.

Bondarenko, T. A. (2006b). Stereotip vospiytiya pravoohranitelnyh organiv na Dal'nem Vostoke [The stereotype about the law enforcement activities in Far East Region]. *Social Research, 1*, 99–102.

Bondarenko, T. A., and Dorokhov, V. Z. (2006). Formirovanie prestizha organov vnutrennikh del SSSR v 50-60e gody XX veka [Shaping the prestige of the bodies of interior affairs of USSR in 1950–1960s of 20th century]. *History of State and Law, 4*, 42–44.

Borisenko, G. F. (1925). *Ugolovnyi protsess. Predvaritel'noe proizvodstvo [Criminal procedure. Preliminary proceeding]*. Kazan': Tipo-litography "Vostok."

Borisova, S. V. (1998). *Professional'naya defomatsiya sotrudnikov militsii i ee lichnostnye determinanty [Professional deformation of police officers and their personality]*. Academy of Management of MVD, Moscow.

Borodavko, L. T. (2005). *Professional'noe vospitanie sotrudnikov pravookhranitel'nykh organov v vuzakh MVD [Professional education of law enforcement personnel in the universities of MVD system]*. St. Petersburg: St. Petersbury MVD University.

Borovikova, V. V. (2002). *Problemy osvesheniya prestupnosti v sredstvah massovoi infomatsii o profilakticheskaya deyatel'nost' organiv vnutrennikh del [The problems of media coverage of crime and prophylactic work of police]*. Moscow Academy of MVD, Moscow.

Borzov, A. A. (2006). Korruptsia i dolzhnostnye prestuplenia v pravookhranitel'nykh organakh [Corruption in the law enforcement agencies]. *Bulletin of St. Petersburg Academy of MVD, 3*(31), 239–243.

Botov, A. I. (2001). *Organizatsiya i pravovoe regulirovanie professional'noi podgotovki kadrov v sisteme MVD [Organization and legal regulation of professional training within the MVD system]*. Law Institute of MVD Russia, Moscow.

Bozhev, V. P. (2002a). *Pravookhranitel'nye organy Rossiskoi Federatsii [Law enforcement agencies of Russian Federation]*. Moscow: Spark.

Bozhev, V. P. (2002b). *Ugolovnyi protsess [Criminal procedure]*. Moscow: Spark.

Bradley, C. M. (2007). *Criminal procedure. A worldwide study*. Durham, NC: Carolina Academic Press.

Brazhenskaya, N. E. (2011). Sootnoshenie orientatsi na semyu i kareru u kursantov-devushek v vuze MVD Rossiii [The relationship between family and career values among female students of police academies of MVD of Russia]. *Bulletin of St. Petersburg MVD University, 2*(50), 179–183.

Brjuhanov, I. V. (2009). Pravookhranitel'naya deyatel'nost' protiv ugolovnogo banditisma na territorii Irkutskoi gubernii i Irkutskogo okruga v 1920e gody 20 veka [Law enforcement of criminal banditism on the territory of Irkutsk province and the Irkutsk district in 1920s of 20th century]. *Siberian Law Bulletin, 3*(46), 11–14.

Brunovskii, V. (1928). Delo bylo v S.S.S.R [The case was in the USSR]. *Archive of Russian Revolution, 19*, 5–156.

Burdin, K. I. (1999). Voprosy stanovleniya militseiskih profsoyuzov [Issues of developing police civil unions]. *Social Research, 9*, 51–55.

Burds, J. (1996). A culture of denunciation: Peasant labor migration and religious anathematization in rural Russia, 1860–1905. *Journal of Modern History, 68*(4), 786.

Burnham, W., Maggs, P. B., and Danilenko, G. M. (2003). *Law and legal system of the Russian Federation*. Huntington, NY: Juris Publishing.

Butler, W. E. (1999). *Russian law*. Oxford, U.K.: Oxford University Press.

Butler, W. E. (2003). *Russian law*. Oxford, U.K.: Oxford University Press.

Can, S. H. (2005). A comparative model of democracy, respect for human rights, and the rise of democratic policing reforms. In C. B. Fields and R. H. Moore (Eds.), *Comparative and international criminal justice. Tradition and nontraditional systems of law and control* (pp. 150–173). Long Grove, IL: Waveland Press, Inc.

Cao, L., Lai, Y.-L., and Zhao, R. (2012). Shades of blue: Confidence in the police in the world. *Journal of Criminal Justice, 40*(1), 40–49.

Caparini, M., and Marenin, O. (2004). Police transformation in Central and Eastern Europe: The challenge of change. In M. Caparini and O. Marenin (Eds.), *Transforming police in Central and Eastern Europe: Process and progress* (pp. 3–22). Munster, Germany: Lit Verlag.

Carothers, T. (2006). *Promoting the rule of law abroad*. Washington, D.C.: Carnegie Endowment for International Peace.

Carter, A. (1922). The Bolshevist substitute for a judicial system. *Illinois Law Review, 16*(5), 340–360.

Carton, S. F. (1992). American popular culture's view on the Soviet militia: The end of the police state? *Nova Law Review, 16*, 1023–1078.

Chalidze, V. (1977). *Criminal Russia. Essays on crime in the Soviet Union*. New York: Random House.

Chel'tsov, M. A. (1948). *Ugolovnyi protsess [Criminal procedure]*. Moscow: Legal publishers of Ministry of Justice of USSR.

Cherkasov, R. V. (2006). SMI o obschesvennoe menie o militsii [Mass media and public opinion about police]. *Social Research, 4*, 85–88.

Chikov, P. (2005). *Narushenie prava na effektivnoe sredstvo pravovoi zaschity v ugolovnom protsesse [Violations of right for effective legal remedies in criminal process]*. Paper presented in Moscow at the Naruscheniya prav cheloveka Rossiksimi pravookranitel'nymi organami [Violations of human rights by Russian law enforcement]. Retrieved from http://www.publicverdict.org/topics/library/DOKLAD_05_06.html.

Chistye Ruki (Clean Hands). (2009). *Doklad Vserossiskoi Antikorruptsionnoi Obschestvennoi Priemnoi [The report of All-Russian Anti-Corruption Civil Office]*. Retrieved on January 3, 2013 from http://www.rusadvocat.com/node.

Chistye Ruki (Clean Hands). (2012). *Doklad politistia v zakone* (Report. Police in law]. Retrieved on January 3, 2013 from http://www.rusadvocat.com/node.

Chudakova, M. S. (2011). Pravookhranitel'nye organy Rossii (fevral-oktyabr 1917) [Law enforcement agencies of Russia (February–October 1917)]. *History, philosophy, law, culture, and art. Issues of theory and practice, 6*(1), 221–224.

Clarke, W. A. (1993). *Crime and punishment in Soviet officialdom*. New York, London: M.E. Sharpe.

Collins, D. N. (1972). A note on the numerical strength of the Russian Red Guard in October 1917. *Soviet Studies, 24*(2), 270–280.

Collins, D. N. (1976). The Russian Red Guard of 1917 and Lenin's utopia. *Journal of Russian Studies, 32*, 3–12.

Committee against Torture. (2006). Sotsiologiya nasiliya. Proizvol pravookranitelnykh organov glazami grazhdan [Sociology of violence. Police abuse in the eyes of citizens] Available from www.pytkam.net.

Committee of Civil Initiatives. (2012). Pravookhranitelnaya deyatelnost v Rossli: struktura, funstsionironvanie, puti reformirovaniya [Law enforcement in Russia: Structure, functions and paths of reform]. Available from http://komitetgi.ru/projects/70/

Confino, M. (1985). Russian customary law and the study of peasant mentalities. *Russian Review, 44*(1), 35–43.

Connor, W. D. (1972a). *Deviance in Soviet society. Crime, delinquency, and alcoholism.* New York and London: Columbia University Press.

Connor, W. D. (1972b). The manufacture of deviance: The case of the Soviet Purge, 1936–1938. *American Sociological Review, 37*(4), 403–413.

Conquest, R. (1968a). *Justice and the legal system in the U.S.S.R.* New York and Washington, D.C.: Frederick A. Praeger Publishers.

Conquest, R. (1968b). *The Soviet police system.* New York and Washington, D.C.: Frederick A. Praeger Publishers.

Curfman, R. S. (1997). *Russian police transition to democracy: Revising the Russian police attitute toward the rule of law.* Monterey, CA: Naval Postgraduate School.

Curtis, G. E. (1998). *Russia: A country study.* Washington, D.C.: Federal Research Division, Library of Congress.

Czap, P., Jr. (1967). Peasant-class courts and peasant customary justice in Russia, 1861–1912. *Journal of Social History, 1*(2), 149–178.

Dallin, D. J., and Nicolaevsky, B. I. (1947). *Forced labor in Soviet Russia.* New Haven: Yale University Press.

Daly, J. W. (1998). *Autocracy under siege, security police and opposition in Russia 1866–1905.* DeKalb, IL: Northern Illinois University Press.

Daly, J. W. (2004). *The watchful state: Security police and opposition in Russia 1906–1917.* Dekalb, IL: Northern Illinois University Press.

Das, D. K. (2000). Challenges of policing democracies: A world perspective. In D. K. Das and O. Marenin (Eds.), *Challenges of policing democracies. A world perspective* (pp. 173–194). Amsterdam, Netherlands: Gordon and Breach Publishers.

Davis, R. C., Ortiz, C. W., Glinskiy, Y., Ylesseva, I., and Briller, V. (2004). A cross-national comparison of citizens' perception of the police in New York City and St. Petersburg, Russia. *Policing. An International Journal of Police Strategies and Management 27*(1), 22–36.

Democracy Fund. (2009). Postroeni effekstivnoi sistemy otsenki podrazdelenii MVD Rossii po borbe s korruptsiei [Building an effective system to evaluate the anti-corruption work of MVD of Russia units] Available from www.democracyfund.ru.

Dergileva, S. Y. (2011). Suschnost politseiskogo gosudarstva kak predmet osmysleniya politseistov vtoroi poloviny XIX - nachala XX veka [Nature of police state as the topic of police studies research in the second half of 19th and beginning of 20th century]. *Bulletin of St. Petersburg MVD University, 3*(51), 15–20.

Deriuzhinskii, V. F. (1911). *Politseiskoe pravo. Posobie dlya studentov [Police law. Study book for students].* St. Petersburg: Senatskaya tipographia.

Dormin, A. N. (2006). *The limits of Russian democratization. Emergency powers and states of emergency.* London and New York: Routledge.

Dunaeva, A. Y. (2009). Politsia Moskovskoi gubernii v nachale 20 veka: uslovia sluzhby i material'noepolozhenie [Moscow police at the beginning of 20th century: conditions of service and salary]. *New Historic Bulletin, 1*(19), 80–86.

Dzhakishev, A. U. (2007). Deyatel'nost' organov militsii Kirgistana po presecheniyu mezhetnicheskogo konflikta v oshskoi oblasti letom 1990 goda [The police activity to prevent an ethnic conflict in Oshkaya oblast of Kyrgyzstan in summer of 1990]. *Bulletin of Tumen State Unversity, 1*, 228–233.

Dziak, J. J. (1988). *Chekisty. A History of the KGB*. Lanham, MD, Toronto: Lexington Books.

Dzutsev, H. V. (2010). Sotsiologiya kriminogennosti v respublike Severnaya Osetiya-Alaniya [Sociology of crime in the republic of Ossetia]. *Social Research, 12*, 80–84.

Dzutsev, H. V., Khugaeva, A. A., and Tsogoev, T. N. (2005). *Monitoring obschestvennogo mneniya o deyatel'nosti MVD RSO-Alaniya [Monitoring of public opinion about work of MVD RSO-Alania]*. Vladikavkaz: Russian Academy of Science. Northern Ossetian Center of Social Research. Institute of Social-Political Studies. MVD.

Easter, G. M. (2002). The Russian tax police. *Post-Soviet Affairs, 18*(4), 332.

Efremov, A. M. (2002). *Osnovy-operativno-rozysknoi deyatelnosti [Basis of the operative-search activities]*. Irkutsk: Baikal State University of Economics and Law.

Efremova, G. K., Lezchava, G. S., Ratinov, A. R., and Shavgulidze, V. G. (1984). *Obschestvennoe mnenie i prestuplenie [Public opinion and crime]*. Tbilisi: Mezniereba.

Egoryshev, S. V. (1997). *Organy vnutrennih del kak sotsial'naya organisatsiya: problemy ih reformirovaniya i povysheniya effectivnosti deyatel'nosti* [The agencies of Interior Affairs as a social organization: The problems of their reforming and improving the effectiveness of their activity]. Ufa, Russia: Bashkir State University.

Egoryshev, S. V., and Linkevitch, A. E. (2008). *Iz istorii vzaimodesitbiya praookhranitel'nykh organov's institutami grazhdanskogo obschestva i naseleniem Rossiskoi Federatsii* [From the history of interaction of police and the institution of civil society and people of Russian Federation]. *Bulletin of East Economic State University, 5*(37), 11–18.

Egoryshev, S. V., and Egorysheva, N. V. (2010). Sotsialnty audit organov vnutrennikh del: ponyatie i vozmozhnosti [Social audit of the agencies of interior affairs: the understanding and the opportunities]. *Euroasian Legal Journal, 7*(26). Retrieved from http://www.eurasialaw.ru/.

Elizarov, I. E., and Petryuk, M. Y. (2006). Ot konseptsii "pravo sily" k kontsepsii "sila prava" v deyatel'nosti Rossiskoi militsii [From the concept of authority of power to the concept "authority of the law" in work of Russian police]. *Bulletin of Moscow University MVD, 3*, 38–39.

Emelin, S. M. (2008). Sozdanie, osobennosti i osnovnye napravleniya deyatel'nosti militsii v Bashkiriiv 1917–nachale 1919 [Creation and main directions of police work in Bashkortostan during 1917, beginning of 1919)]. *Bulletin of Bashkir University, 13*(3), 619–623.

Engelstein, L. (1988). Gender and the juridical subject: Prostitution and rape in nineteenth-century Russian criminal codes. *The Journal of Modern History, 60*(3), 458–495.

Erin, D. A. (2009). Promyshlennaya militsiya v sisteme spetsialnykh vidov sovetskoi militsii SSSR 1919-1921 [Industrial police in the system of special police of USSR, 1919-1921]. *Bulletin of the Volgograd Law Institute 1*(10), 198–202.

Erin, D. A., and Bubnova, Y. G. (2008). Kadrovoe obespechenie promyshlennoi militsii Vladimirskoi gubernii (1920–1921) [Staff of industrial police in Vladimir province 1920–1921]. *Bulletin of the Vladimir Law Institute, 3*(8), 240–243.

Ermolaev, V. V., and Verem'eva, E. A. (2007). K probleme izucheniya organizatsionnoi kultury i imidga militsii [The problem of organizational culture and image of police]. *Bulletin of the Voronezh Institute of MVD, 2*, 85–87.

Etling, B., Alexanyan, K., Kelly, J., Faris, R., Palfrey, J., and Berkman, U. G. (2010). Public discourse in the Russian blogosphere: Mapping RuNet politics and mobilization. Retrieved on May 5, 2011, from http://cyber.la w.harvard.ed u/sites/cyber.la w.harvard.edu/files/ Public_Discourse_in _the_Russian_Blo gosphere_2010.pdf.

Fadin, M. A. (2006). Zakon RF o "Militsii" - put dlinoi v pyatnadtsat let [The law "On Police"—the path of fifteen years]. *Bulletin of Moscow University MVD, 3*, 137–138.

Fastov, A. G. (2005). *Organy vnutrennih del Rossii: istoriya stanovleniya i razvitiya [The Agencies of Interior Affairs of Russia: History of establishment and development]* Volgograd: Volgograd Law Academy.

Favarel-Garrigues, G. (2002). La bureacratie policiere et la chute du regime sovietique. *Societe contemporaines, 1*(57), 63–81.

Favarel-Garrigues, G. (2011). *Policing economic crime in Russia.* New York: Columbia University Press.

Fedorenko, S. A. (2009). Stavropol'skaya militsiya v 20-e gody XX veka [Police forces of Stavropol region in the 1920s of the 20th century]. *Scientific Problems of Humanities, 11*, 124–133.

Field, M. G. (1991). Soviet health problems and the convergence hypothesis. In A. Jones, W. D. Conno and D. E. Powell (Eds.), *Soviet social problems* (pp. 78–93). Boulder, San Francisco, Oxford: Westview Press.

Fillipov, V. V. (2003). New Russian code of criminal procedure: The next step on the path of Russia's democratization. *Demokratizatsiya, 11*(3).

Finckenauer, J. O., and Voronin, Y. I. (2001). *The threat of Russian organized crime.* Washington, D.C.: U.S. Department of Justice. Office of Justice Programs.

Foinitskyi, I. Y. (1912). *Kurs ugolovnago sudoproizvodstva [The course of criminal procedure]* (Vol. 1). St. Petersburg: Tipographiya obschestvennaya pol'za.

FOM. (1996). Moskvitchi nedovolny rabotoi mestnoi militsii [Residents of Moscow are unhappy about their local police]. Retrieved on September 10, 2006, from http://bd.fom.ru/report/cat/power/pow_l/of19963004.

FOM. (1997). Chetvertaya chast Rossiyan botisya tekh kto ikh dolzhen zaschishat [A quarter of Russians are afraid of those who should be protecting them]. Retrieved on June 23, 2011, from http://bd.fom.ru/report/cat/power/pow_l/of19974205.

FOM. (1998). Esli vy pochustvuete ugrozu dlya svoego imuschestva ili lichnoi bezopasnosti, k komu vy obratites za pomoschyu v pervuyu ochered [If you feel threat to your property or life, where would you seek assitance in the first place]. Retrieved on October 11, 2011, from http://bd.fom.ru/report/cat/power/pow_l/t8033109.

FOM. (2003). Operatsiya "Obortni v pogonakh" [Campaign "werewolves in uniform"]. Retrieved July 1, 2011, from http://bd.fom.ru /report/map/projects/dominant/dominant2003/839_177/dd032727.

FOM. (2008). Uroven' doveriya militsii [The level of trust of police]. Retrieved on November 24, 2010, from http://bd.fom.ru/report/cat/power/pow_l/d082723.

Frank, S. P. (1987a). *Cultural conflict and criminality in rural Russia, 1861–1900.* Providence, RI: Brown University.

Frank, S. P. (1987b). Popular justice, community and culture among the Russian peasantry, 1870–1900. *Russian Review, 46*(3), 239–265.

Frank, S. P. (1999). *Crime, cultural conflict and justice in rural Russia 1865–1914.* Berkley, Los Angeles, London: University of California Press.

Freedom House, Radio Free Europe/Radio Liberty, and Radio Free Asia. (2009). Undermining democracy. 21st Century Authoritarians. Retrieved April 1, 2011 from http://www.underminin gdemocracy.org/.

Frolov, V. V., and Tyshkovets, N. K. (2009). Obespechenie pravoporyadka v Rossiskoi imperiiv nachale 20 veka, svyaz' istorii i soverennosti [Law enforcement in Russian Empire at the beginning of the 20th century, connection of history and modernity]. *Bulletin of the St. Petersburg University of MVD, 3*(43), 21–26.

Galeotti, M. (1993). Perestroika, perestrelka, pereborka: Policing in Russia in a time of change. *Europe Asia Studies, 45*(5), 769–786.

Galeotti, M. (2004). The criminalization of Russian state security. *Global Crime, 7*(3–4), 471–486.

Galkin, A. S. (2001). *Pedagogicheskie osnovy kadrovoi raboty v organakh MVD [Pedagogical basis for human resources in MVD system].* Moscow: Scientific Research Institute of MVD of Russia.

Gall, C. (2011). Das neue russische Polizeigesetz. *Russland-Analysen, 219*, 2–4.

Gamerman, E. V. (2005). Politsiya dal'nego vostoka vo vtoroi polovine XIX - nachale XX veka [Police of Far East in the second half of 19th–early 20th century]. *Bulletin DVO RAN, 5*, 164–168.

Gavrilenko, D. A. (1975–1976). Disciplinary answerability in organs of the Ministry of Interior Affairs. *Soviet Law and Government, 3*, 53–66.

Gavrilin, S. A. (2001). *Formirovanie pravosoznaniya slushatelei vuzov MVD kak faktor sovershenstvovaniya ikh professional'noi podgotovki [Legal consciousness of MVD students as factor for improving their professional training].* Moscow: Academy of Management of MVD.

Gavrilov, B. (2001). Sposobna li Rossiskaya statistika o prestupnosti stat' realnoi? [Can the crime statistics in Russia become real?] *State and Law, 1*, 47–62.

Gavrilov, B. (2003a). Novelly ugolovnogo protsessa na fone kriminal'noi statistiki [Novelties of the criminal procedure and the criminal statistics]. *Russian Justice, 10*, 5–9.

Gavrilov, B. (2003b). Sledstvennyi apparat organov vnutrennikh del [Investigative bodies of agencies of internal affairs]. *Otechestvennye zapiski [Native notes], 2*(10). Retrieved from http://www.strana-oz.ru/?ozid = 11andoznumber = 2.

Gavrilov, B. (2006). Monitoring UPK RF v sisteme Ministerstva vnutrennikh del [Monitoring of CPC of RF within the system of Ministry of Internal Affairs]. In E. B. Mizoulina and V. N. Pligin (Eds.), *Uroki reformy ugolovnogo pravosudiia v Rossii [Lessons of reforming criminal justice in Russia]* (pp. 155–198). Moscow: Yurist.

Gefter, V. M., Petrova, E. P., and Reznichenko, L. A. (2006). Prava cheloveka glazami sotsiologa [Human rights in the eyes of sociologist]. *Monitoring of Public Opinion, 2*(78), 32–42.

Geizhan, N. F., and Brazhenskaya, N. E. (2011). Gendernoe vospitanie devushek v vedomstvennykh vuzakh [Gender education of girls in departmental institutions of higher education]. *Pedagogical Education in Russia, 5*, 193–199.

Gerber, T. P., and Mendelson, S. E. (2008). Public Experiences of Police Violence and Corruption in Contemporary Russia: A Case of Predatory Policing? *Law and Society Review, 42*(1), 1–44.

Gerson, L. D. (1976). *The secret police in Lenin's Russia.* Philadelphia: Temple University Press.

Gessen, I. V. (1905). *Sudebnaya reforma [Court reform].* St. Petersburg: Tipo-Lyatographia F. Vaisberga i P. Gershunina.

Gessen, V. M. (1905). *Politseiskaya reforma v trudakh komissii stat sekretarya Kakhanova [Police reform in the work of Kakhanov commission].* St. Petersburg: Tipo-litographiya Schredera.

Gessen, V. M. (1908). *Lektsii po politseiskomu pravu [Lectures on police law].* St. Petersburg: Tipographia "Sever."

Getty, J. A. (2002). Excesses are not permitted: Mass terror and Stalinist governance in the late 1930s. *Russian Review, 61*(1), 113.

Getty, J. A., Rittersporn, G. T., and Zemskov, V. (1993). Victims of the Soviet penal system in the pre-war years: A first approach on the basis of archival evidence. *American Historical Review, 98*(4), 1017.

Gilinskiy, Y. (2000). Challenges of policing democracies: The Russian experience. In D. K. Kas and O. Marenin (Eds.), *Challengers of policing democracies. A world perspective* (pp. 173–194). Amsterdan, Netherlands: Gordon and Breach Publishers.

Gilinskiy, Y. (2003). Politsiya i naselenie: kto dlya kogo [Police and public: who for whom?]. *Otechestvennye zapiski [Native notes], 2*(10). Retrieved from http://www.strana-oz.ru/?ozid = 11&oznumber = 2.

Gilinskiy, Y. (2004). Korruptsiya: teoriya o rossiskaya real'nost' [Corruption: theory and Russian reality]. In L. E. Kessel'man (Ed.), *Aktual'nye problemy transformatsii cotsial'nogo prostranstva [Actual problems of social space transformation]* (pp. 151–172). St. Petersburg: GP MTsSEI "Lento'evskyi center."

Gilinskiy, Y. (2005). Corruption: Theory and Russian reality. In R. Sarre, D. K. Das and H. J. Albrecht (Eds.), *Policing corruption. International perspectives* (pp. 157–168). New York: Lexington Books.

Gilinskiy, Y. (2007). Police training and education. In D. K. Kas and P. C. Kratcoski (Eds.), *Police education and training in a global society* (pp. 161–166). New York: Lexington Books.

Gilinskiy, Y. (2011). Torture by the Russian police: An empirical study. *Police Practice and Research, 12*(2), 163–171.

Gilinskiy, Y., and Zazulin, G. (2001). Drugs in Russia: Situation, policy and the police. *Police Practice and Research, 2*(4), 345–364.

Gilinskiy, Y., Kostyukovskyi, Y., Eliseeva, I., Gordienko, N., and Bozhkov, O. (2002). *Naselenie i militsiya v bolshom gorode [Population and police in the large city].* Unpublished manuscript, St. Petersburg.

Girko, S. I. (2006). *Deyatelnost militsii v ugolovnom protsesse [Activities of police in criminal procedure]*. Moscow: Examen.

Gissi, S. A., and Sokolovskyi, D. A. (1879). *Doznanie, ego tseli i sposoby proizvodstva. Rukovodstvo ldya chinov politsii. [Preliminary investigation, its purposes and methods. Manual for the police officers]*. Kazan': Tipographiya Gladysheva.

Gladarev, B. (2008). Opasnost' militsii obschestvennoi bezopasnosti [The danger of police of public security] *Sotsiologiya vchera, segodnya, zavtra [The sociology yesterday, today, and tomorrow]* (pp. 151–174). St. Petersburg. Retrieved on January 3, 2013 from http://www.cisr.ru/Gladarev.html.

Gladarev, B. (2009). Militsionery i etnicheskie migranty na ultisakh sankt-peterburga [Police and ethnic immigrants on the streets of St. Petersburg] *Puti Rossii [Ways of Russia]* (Vol. 16, pp. 486–495). St. Petersburg: University Books.

Gladarev, B. (2011a). Korni rasizma v Rossiskoi militsii [Roots of racism in Russian police]. In B. Gladarev, V. Voronkov, and L. Sagitova (Eds.), *Militsiya i etnicheskie migranty: praktiki vzaimodeistviya [Police and ethnic immigrants: practices of interaction]* (pp. 424–507). St. Petersburg: Aleteya.

Gladarev, B. (2011b). Professiya "rossioskiyi militsioner": usloviya sluzhby i vnutri-institutsionnaya logika [Profession of Russian police officer: conditions of service and inter-institutional logic]. In P. V. Romanov and E. R. Yuarskoi-Smirnov (Eds.), *Antropologiya professii [Anthropology of professions]* (pp. 113–134). St. Petersburg: Variant.

Gladarev, B., and Tzinman, Z. M. (2010). Militsionery i gasterebaitery: praktiki perespredeleniya resursov [Police officers and gasterarbeiters: practice of resource redistribution] *Sociology Journal, 1*, 37–63.

Glinkina, S. P. (1994). Privatisatsiya and Kriminalizatsiya [Privatization and Criminalization]. *Demokratizatsiya, 2*(3), 385–391.

Glinkina, S. P. (2002). Privatizatsiya and Kriminalizatsiya: How organized crime is hijacking privatization. In M. Galeotti (Ed.), *Russian and post-Soviet organized crime* (pp. 249–256). Dartmouth: Ashgate.

Goldman, W. Z. (2003). The internal Soviet passport: Workers and free movement. In M. Siefert (Ed.), *Extending the borders of Russian history* (pp. 315–332). Budapest, New York: CEU Press.

Golovizina, M. V. (2005). Politika sotsial'nogo kontrolya prestupnosti nesovershenno-letnikh v SSSR (1917-konetz 1980s) [Social control policy of juvenile delinquency in USSR (1917-end of 1980s)]. *Journal of Social Policy Studies, 3*(2), 223–240.

Golunskyi, S. A., Kalashnikova, N. Y., Karev, D. S., Savgirova, N. M., Tarasov-Rodionov, P. I., and Yakub, M. L. (1953). *Sovetskyi ugolovnyi protsess [Soviet criminal procedure]*. Moscow: Gosyurizdat.

Goncharenko, V. D. (1999). *Pravo cheloveka na svobodu ot pytok, i drugikh zhestokikh, peschelovechnykh i unizhayuschikh dostonistvo vidov obrascheniya ili nakazaniya: teoretiko-pravovye aspekty [Individual's right against torture and other cruel and abusive treatment or punishment: theoretical and legal aspects]*. Volgograd Law Institute of MVD, Volgograd.

Goncharov, V. B., and Kozchevnikov, V. V. (1996). Obschestvennoe mnenie omichei o militsii [Public opinion of Omsk residents about police]. *Social Research, 7*, 106-108.

Gonyukhov, S. O., and Gorobtsov, V. I. (2002). *MVD Rossii [MVD of Russia]*. Moscow: Reitar.

Gorbatenko, G. V. (2011). Professional'noe obrazovanie sotrudnikov OVD SSSR vo vtoroi polovine 30 godov- nachale 50 godov XX veka [Professional education of police in 1930s-1950s]. *Bulletin of Voronezh Institute of MVD, 4*, 183–188.

Gordon, V. M., Kisilev. A. D., Palienko, N. P., Popov, B. V., P., Raevskiy, A. A., Temnikovskyi, E. N., et al. (1911). *Administrativnoe pravo iz kursa pravovedeniya po Narodnoi entsiklopedii. Polutom 12. Obschestvenno-yuridicheskie nauki [Administrative law according to the jurisprudence course from the People's encyclopedia. Volume 1. Social-legal sciences]*. Moscow: Tipographiya tovarischestva I.D. Sytina.

Gorer, G., and Rickman, J. (1949). *The people of Great Russia. A psychological study*. London: The Cresset Press.

Goriyanov, K. K. (1994). *Latent crime in Russia*. Moscow: UNICRI, United Nations.

Goriyanov, K. K., Ovchinskii, G. K., Sinilov, A. Y., and Shumilov, A. Y. (2004). *Operativno-rozusknaya deyatelnost [Operative-search activities]*. Moscow: Infra-M.

Govorov, I. V., and Remneva, S. V. (2007). Iz istorii razvitiya obschestvennykh formirovanii po sodeistviyu organam militsii v SSSR v 20-80e gody [The history of development of the public formations on assistance to the law enforcement bodies in the USSR in the years 1920–1980]. *Bulletin of the St. Petersburg University of MVD, 4*(36), 25–31.

Gregory, F., and Brooke, G. (2000). Policing economic transition and increasing revenue: A case study of the federal tax police service of the Russian Federation 1992–1998. *Europe-Asia Studies, 52*(3), 433.

Gromov, N. A. (1998). *Ugolovnyi protess Rossii [Criminal procedure of Russia]*. Moscow: Jurist.

Gryaznova, O. (2006). Otnoshenie zschitelei Rossii k pravoohranitel'nym organam [The attitude of Russian residents toward the law enforcement agencies]. *Bulletin of Public Opinion, 2*(82), 32–46.

Grzybowski, K. (1965). Soviet criminal law. *Problems of Communism, 14*(March-April), 53–62.

Gudkov, L. (2000). Otnoshenie k pravovym institutam v Rossii [The attitude toward the legal institutions in Russia]. *Monitoring of Public Opinion: Economic and Social Changes, 3*(47), 30–39.

Gudkov, L. (2009). Priroda "putinisma" [The nature of "putinism']. *Bulletin of Public Opinion, 3*(101), 6–21.

Gudkov, L., and Dubin, B. (2006). Privatisatsiya politsii [Privatization of police]. *Bulletin of Public Opinion, 1*(81), 58–71.

Gudkov, L., Dubin, B., and Leonova, A. (2004). Militseiskoe nasilie i problema "politseiskogo gosudarstva" [Police violence and the problem of 'police state"]. *Bulletin of Public Opinion, 4*(72), 31–47.

Gusak, V. A. (2010). Osobennosti deyatelnosti sovetskoi militsii v usloviyakh osadnogo i voennogo polozheniya (1941–1945) [The details of police work during the war time: 1941-1945]. *Bulletin of Chelyabinsk State University, 9*(190), 114–117.

Gusman, L. Y. (2002). *Stanovlenie tsenzurnogo zakonodatel'stva v Rossii (pervaya polovina 19 veka) [Development of censorship legislation in Russia in the first half of 19th century]*. St. Petersburg: St. Petersburg State University of Aerospace machinery.

Gutman, M. Y. (2007). Pravovye osnovy organizatsii i deyatel'nosti militsii Vremennogo pravitel'stva, rabochei militsii i Krasnoi gvardi Petrograda (mart-oktyabr' 1917) [Legal and organizational basis of police activities of the Provisional Government, militia of workers and Red Guards, March-October 1917]. *Bulletin of the St. Petersburg University of MVD, 4*(36), 32–43.

Gutsenko, K. F. (2005). *Ugolovnyi protsess Rossii [Criminal procedure of Russia]*. Moscow: Zertsalo.

Gutsenko, K. F., and Kovalev, M. A. (2007). *Pravookhranitel'nye organy [Law enforcement bodies]*. Moscow: Zertsalo-M.

Haberfeld, M. R. (2002). *Critical issues in police training*. Upper Saddle River, NJ: Prentice-Hall.

Haberfeld, M. R., and Cerrah, I. (2008). *Comparative policing. The struggle for democratization*. Los Angeles: Sage.

Hagenloh, P. M. (1999). *Police, crime and public order in Stalin's Russia 1930–1941*. Austin: University of Texas at Austin.

Haimson, L. (1964). The problem of social stability in urban Russia, 1905–1917 (Part One). *Slavic Review, 23*(4), 619–642.

Haimson, L. (1965). The problem of social stability in urban Russia, 1905–1917 (Part Two). *Slavic Review, 24*(1), 1–22.

Handelman, S. (1995). *Comrade criminal. Russia's new mafia*. New Haven and London: Yale University Press.

Hasegawa, T. (1973). The formation of the militia in the February Revolution: An aspect of the origins of dual power. *Slavic Review, 32*(2), 303–322.

Hasegawa, T. (1992). Crime, police, and mob justice in Petrograd during the Russian revolution of 1917. In C. E. Timberlake (Ed.), *Religious and secular forces in late Tsarist Russia* (pp. 241–271). Seattle and London: University of Washington Press.

Hingley, R. (1971). *The Russian secret police*. New York: Simon and Schuster.

Hinton, M. S., and Newburn, T. (2009). Introduction: Policing developing democracies. In M. S. Hinton and T. Newburn (Eds.), *Policing developing democracies* (pp. 1–28). London and New York: Routledge.

Holmes, L. (2009). Crime, organized crime and corruption in post-communist Europe and the CIS. *Communist and Post-Communist Studies, 42*(2), 265–287.

Holodny, M. A. (2010). Deformatsiya ekonomicheskogo myshleniya naseleniya Rossii i bor'ba militsii c prestuplenoyami protiv sobstvennosti: istoricheskyi opyt 1924–1929 [Deformation of economic thinking of the population of Russia and struggle of militia against crimes against the property: historical experience 1924–1929]. *Bulletin of Chuvash University, 1*, 101–105.

Huerou, A. L. (2002). Des pratiques locales de sécurité hybrides. *Les Cahiers de la sécurité intériere, 50*(4), 19–42.

Human Rights Watch. (1999). *Confessions at any cost. Police torture in Russia*. New York, Washington, D.C., London, Brussels: Human Rights Watch.

Human Rights Watch. (2009) *Are you happy to cheat us?* New York, Washington, D.C., London, Brussels: Human Rights Watch.

Huskey, E. (1986). The politics of the Soviet criminal process: Expanding the right to counsel in pre-trial proceedings. *The American Journal of Comparative Law, 34*(1), 93–112.

ICVS. (1992). Database. Cross-tabulations. Retrieved on August 4, 2006, from https://easy.dans.knaw.nl/dms.

ICVS. (1996). Database. Cross-tabulations. Retrieved on August 4, 2006, from https://easy.dans.knaw.nl/dms.

ICVS. (2000). Database. Cross-tabulations. Retrieved on August 4, 2006, from http://www.unicri.it.

INDEM. (2001a). *Diagnostika rossiskoi korruptsii [Diagnostics of Russian corruption]*. Moscow: INDEM.

INDEM. (2001b). *Uluchshenie vzaimootnoshenii grazhdan i militsii [Improving the public-police relations]*. Moscow: INDEM.

INDEM. (2002). *Korruptsiya na dorogakh [Corruption on the streets]*. Moscow: INDEM.

INDEM. (2004). *Uchet mneniya grazhdan v planirovanii i otsenke deyatel'nosti militsii [Considering public opinion on evaluation of police work]*. Moscow: Fund INDEM.

INDEM. (2005a). *Corruption process in Russia: level, structure, trends*. Moscow: INDEM.

INDEM. (2005b). *Vo skol'ko raz uvelichilas' korruptsiya za 4 goda. [How the corruption increased in the last 4 years]*. Moscow: INDEM.

INDEM. (2007). *Opredelenie faktorov vliyayuschikh na effektivnost' predostavleniya uslug po bezopasnosti ot prestupnykh posyagatel'stv [Determining the factors impacting the effectiveness of protection services from crimes]*. Moscow: INDEM.

Inkeles, A. (1950). *Public opinion in Soviet Russia. A study of mass persuasion*. Cambridge: Harvard University Press.

Inshakov, S. M. (2007). *Latentnya prestupnost' v Rossiskoi Federatsii: 2001-2006 [Latent crimes in Russian Federation, 2001–2006]*. Moscow: Unity. Statute and Law.

Inshakov, S. M. (2008). Research of criminal latency and paradoxes of social denial of criminality. *Criminology Journal of Baikal State University of Economics and Law, 4*(6), 5–10.

IREX. (2011). Media Sustainability Index. Russia. Retrieved on December 1, 2011, from www.irex.org.

IS RAN. (2011). Dvadtsat let reform glazami rossiyan [Twenty years of reform in the eyes of Russians]. Retrieved on July 10, 2011, from www.isras.ru.

Isaev, M. M., Karev, D. S., and Utevskyi, B. S. (1948). *Sovetskoe pravo v period velikoi otechestvennoi voiny. Ugolovnoe pravo. Ugolovnyi protsess [Soviet law during the Great Patriotic War. Criminal law. Criminal procedure]* Moscow: Legal publishers of Ministry of Justice of USSR.

Ivanov, K. D., and Sedunov, A. V. (2005). Kadrovyi sostav pravoohranitel'nykh organov na Severo-Zapade Rossii v 1920-e gody: professional'naya i ideino-politicheskaya podgotovka [Staffing of the law enforcement in North-Western Russia in the 1920s: professional and ideological-political preparedness]. *Bulletin of the St. Petersburg University of MVD, 2*(26), 92–96.

Ivanov, S. A. (2008). Obschestvennaya samorganizatsia i militsia na territorrii Irkutskoi gubernii 1917 [Social self-organization and police on the territory of Irkutsk province in 1917]. *Bulletin of the Russian State Pedagogical University, 70*, 183–186.

Ivanova, T. A. (2000). *Organisatsionno-pravovye problemy raboty s zhenschinami-sotrudnikami organov vnutrennihk del, militsii [Organizational and legal issues of working with female police officers and employees of the Ministry of Interior Affairs]*. Moscow Academy of MVD, Moscow.

Ivanova, V. A., and Shubkin, V. N. (2005). Massovaya trevozschnost' Rossiyan kak prepyatstvie k integratsii obschestva [Massive anxiety of Russians as the obstacle to the societal integration]. *Social Research, 2*, 22–28.

Ivkovic, S. K. (2005). *Fallen blue knights: Controlling police corruption*: Oxford, U.K.: Oxford University Press.

Ivkovic, S. K., and Shelley, T. O. C. (2008). The contours of police integrity across Eastern Europe. *International Criminal Justice Review, 18*(1), 59–82.

Jasny, N. (1951). Labor and output in Soviet concentration camps. *The Journal of Political Economy, 59*(5), 405–419.

Jones, T., Newburn, T., and Smith, D. (1996). Policing and the idea of democracy. *British Journal of Criminology, 36*(2), 182–198.

Jurkanin, T. J., and Sergevnin, V. (2012). An examination of police corruption in Russia. *Law Enforcement Forum, 12*(2), 63–75.

Juviler, P. (1974). Crime and its study. In H. W. Morton and R. L. Tökés (Eds.), *Soviet politics and society in the 1970s* (pp. 200–238). London: Collier Macmillan Publishers.

Juviler, P. (1976). *Revolutionary law and order.* New York and London: The Free Press.

Kaariainen, J. T. (2007). Trust in the police in 16 European countries: A multilevel analysis. *European Journal of Criminology, 4*(4), 409–435.

Kaiser, D. H., and Marker, G. (1994). *Reinterpreting Russian history. Readings 860-1860s.* New York and Oxford: Oxford University Press.

Kalabekov, I. G. (2010). *Rossiksie reformy v tsifrakh i factakh [Russian reforms in numbers and facts].* Moscow: Rusaki.

Kalinichenko, V. I. (1998). Delo o 140 milliardakh ili 7060 dnei iz zhizni sledovatelya [The case about 140 billion or 7060 days from the life of the investigator]. Retrieved on April 22, 2011, from http://www.abogado.su/.

Kalinin, A. Y. (2007). Problemy, slyzhba i byt sotrudnikov Altaiskoi militsii v gody velikoi otechestvennoi voiny [Problems, service, and conditions of the Altay police during the WWII]. *Fundamental Research, 9*, 18–19.

Kalmykov, V. V. (2008). Korruptsia v pravookhranitel'nykh organakh Yuzhnogo Urala v poslevoennyi period,1945-1953) [Corruption in the law enforcement of the Southern Ural region during the after-war period, 1945-1953]. *Bulletin of the Chelyabinsk State University, 34*, 55–59.

Kamalova, D. T. (2008). Teoreticheskie osnovy stanovleniya sovetskoi modeli pravookhranitel'noi sistemy (1921-1929) [Theoretical basis of developing the Sovit police model, 1921–1929]. *Bulletin of Altay State University, 4*, 71–78.

Kantsev, A. B. (2008). Pravovye osnovy sozdaniya i funktsionioraniya organov politsii v chernomorskoi gubernii v kontse 19 nachale 20 veka [Legal basis for establishment and functioning of police in Chernomor province in the end of 19th and beginning of 20th centuries]. *Bulletin of the Russian State Pedagogical University, 60*, 119–122.

Karklins, R. (1987). Nationality policy and ethnic relations. In J. R. Millar (Ed.), *Politics, life, and work in the USSR* (pp. 301–331). Cambridge: Cambridge University Press.

Karnitskyi, D. A., and Strogovitch, M. S. (1925). *Ugolovno-protessualnyi kodeks RSFSF. Tekst i postateinyi kommentarii [Criminal procedural Code of RSFSR. Text and article-by-article commentary].* Moscow: Legal publishers of NKViU of RSFSR.

Kennan, G. (1889). The Russian police. *Century Illustrated Magazine XXXVII*(6), 890–892.

Kharlamov, V. S. (2011). Aspekty deyatelnosti organov vnutrennikh del po prfilaktike pravonarushenii v semeino-bytovoi sfere v svete federal'nogo zakona "O politsii" [The aspect of police work to prevent violations in areas of family after the adoption of federal law "On Police"]. *Bulletin of St. Petersburg MVD University, 4*(52), 89–94.

Khlevnyuk, O. (2003). The economy of the OGPU, NKVD and MVD of the USSR, 1930–1953. In P. Gregory and V. Lazarev (Eds.), *The economics of forced labor. The Soviet GULAG* (pp. 43–66). Stanford, CA: Hoover Institution Press, Stanford University.

Khludova, O. V. (2004). *Psikhologicheskie osobennosti professional'nogo rosta lichnosti [Psychological issues of professional development]*. Tambov: Tambov Technological State University Press.

Khoroshun, K. Y. (2007). Rossiiskaya politsiya i zhandarmeriya v 60-90kh gg19 veka [Russian police and the Corps of Gendarmes in the 1860-1890s of 19th century] *Bulletin of the Tomsk State University, 2*(46), 141–144.

Kikot', V. Y. (2002). *Organizatsionno-pravovoe i informatsionnoe obespechenie realizatsii kadrovoi politiki MVD Rossii v sfere podgotovko kadrov [Organizational, legal and informational support of human resource policy of MVD of Russia]*. Moscow University of MVD, Moscow.

Kikot', V. Y. (2004). Mesto i rol' organov MVD v politike Rossikogo gosudarstva po obespecheniyu mezchdunarodnoi zakonnosti i pravoporyadka [The role of MVD agencies in the politics of strengthening the international public and order]. *State and Law, 1*(55–61).

Kladov, V. Y. (2007a). K voprosu o sovershenstvovanii kadrovogo sostava provintsial'noi politsii v nachale 20 veka na primere penzenskoi gubernii [The problems of staffing of provincial police at the beginning of 20th century using the example of Penza province]. *Bulletin of the Russian Pedagogical University, 14*(37), 87–90.

Kladov, V. Y. (2007b). Organizatsiya sluzhby Penzenskoi gorodskoi politisii v nachale 20 veka [Oranzation of urban police in Penza at the beginning of 20th century]. *Bulletin of Penza State Pedagogical University, 3*(7), 108–112.

Kladov, V. Y. (2007c). Razrabotka penzenskim politseiskim nachal'stvom sistemy mer po povysheniyu kachestva kadrovogo sostava v nachale 20 veka [Development of educational measurements to improve the quality of the police work by Penza police at the beginning of 20th century]. *Bulletin of the Penza State Pedagogical University, 3*(7), 103–108.

Knight, A. (1984). Soviet politics and KGB-MVD relationship. *Soviet Union, Union Sovietique, 11*(2), 157–181.

Knight, A. (1988). *The KGB. Police and politics in the Soviet Union*. London: Unwin Hyman.

Kolemasov, V. N. (2011). Opyt vzaimodeistviya militsii s obschestvennymi formirovaniyami 1917-1941 [Expereince of police interaction with public formations]. *History, Philosophy, Law, Culture, and Art. Issues of Theory and Practice, 5*(11), 109–113.

Kolemasov, V. N., Mil'shin, Y. N., Pomogalova, Y. V., Puzyrev, S. V., Chanov, S. E., and Yur'eva, Y. S. (2007). *Kommentrai k Zakonu Rossiskoi Federatsii O Militsii [Commentary to the Statute "About Police"]*. Moscow: Os'-89.

Kolennikova, O. A. (2002). Rynochnye reformy i oslablenie bezopasnosti naseleniya [Market reforms and diminished public safety] *Rossia 10 let reform. Sotsialno-demograficheskaya situatsiya [Russia: ten years of reform. Social-demographic situation]* (pp. 272–281). Moscow: Russian Academy of Science.

Kolennikova, O. A. (2006). Transformatsiya pravoohranitel'nyh organov v Rossii: sotsial'no-politicheskie posledstviya [Transformation of law enforcement agencies in Russia: social-political consequences]. *Social Research, 2*, 69–75.

Kolennikova, O. A., Kosals, L., Ryvkina, R., and Simagin, Y. (2002). Ekonomicheskaya aktivnost' rabotnikov pravookhranitelnykh organov v postsovetskoi Rossii: vidy, masshtaby i vliyanie na obschestvo [Economic activities of law enforcement agencies in post-Soviet-Russia: types, scope, and the impact on the society] Available from www.transparency.org.ru/center/DOC/book07.doc.

Koltsova, O. (2006). *News media and power in Russia.* London and New York: Routledge.

Kolyushkina, L. Y. (2005). Rossiksie pravookhranitel'nye organy v usloviyakh transformatsii sotznetal'noi sistemy: otsenka situatsiii samopresentatsii [Russian law enforcement in the conditions of transformation: assessment of situation and self-presentation]. *Law Bulletin of the Rostov State Economic University, 3*(35), 70–75.

Komlev, Y. Y., Demidov, V. N., and Tolchinskiy, L. G. (1997). Sredstva massovoi informatsii i formirovanie obschestvennogo mneniya o pravoohranitel'noi deyatle'nosti [Mass media and formation of the public opinion about law enforcement'. *State and Law, 8*, 110–114.

Kondrashev, B. P., Solovei, Y. P., and Chernikov, V. V. (2006). Kontseptualnye idei rossikogo zakona o militsii [Conceptual ideas of Russian law "On Police"]. *Bulletin of Moscow University MVD, 3*, 16–23.

Koni, A. O. (1914). *Otsy i deti sudubnoi reformy. K 50-ti letiyu sudebnoi reformy [The fathers and the sons of the judicial reform. For the 50th anniversary of judicial reform].* Moscow: Tipographia tovarischestva I.D. Sytina.

Kopkareva, S. I. (2007). Otnoshenie studencheskoi molodezhi k zakonam i pravookhranitel'nym organam [Public attitudes of students to law and police]. *Power, 2*, 56–60.

Korenev, A. P. (1984). The rights of the Soviet police and socialist legality. *Soviet Law and Government, 4*, 80–95.

Korenev, A. P. (1999). *Administrativnaya deyatel'nost' organov vnutrennikh del [Administrative functions of agencies of interior affairs].* Moscow: Moscow Law Institute of MVD. Schit-M Press.

Korneeva, G. K. (2008). Sotrudnik pravookhranitel'nykh organov v rossiskom obschestve: suschnost' problemy pravovogo nigilisma [Staff Member of Law Enforcement Bodies on Russian Society: the Issues of Legal Nihilism]. *An individual, 4*, 146–148.

Kosals, L. (2010). Police in Russia: Reform or business restructuring? *Russian Analytical Digest, 84*, 2–6.

Kosals, L. (2011). Russlands Polizei- Reform oder neues Geschäftsmodell? *Russlandanalysen, 219*, 5–8.

Kozchevnikov, V. V. (1999). Problemy professionalisma sotrudnikov vnutrennikh del [Problems of professionalism of police officers]. *Social Research, 9*, 55–59.

Kramer, J. M. (1991). Drug abuse in the USSR. In A. Jones, W. D. Conno, and D. E. Powell (Eds.), *Soviet social problems* (pp. 94–118). Oxford: Westview Press.

Krastev, I. (2002). *The corruption paradox: Why post-Communism is/looks more corrupt than Communism*. Budapest, Hungary: Collegium Budapest.

Krivel'skaya, N. V. (1990). *Obshestvennoe mnenie i ego uchet v upravlenii organami vnutrennih del [Public Opinion and Its Role in the Management of Agencies of Internal Affairs]*. Academy of MVD USSR, Moscow.

Kucherov, S. (1970). *The organs of Soviet administration of justice: Their history and operation*. Leiden, The Netherlands: E.J. Brill.

Kuritsyna, E. V. (2008). Razvitie organizatsionnoi struktury rossiskoi militsii, 1953–1964 [Development of organization structure of the Russian police, 1953–1964]. *The Bulletin of the Penza State Pedagogical University, 6*(10), 50–53.

Kuritsyna, E. V. (2009). Deayatel'nost' militsii po bor'be s prestupnost'yunesovershen olletnikh v 1953–1964 gody [Activity of Militia in the Struggle against Juvenile Delinquency in 1953–1964 (by the example of the Penza region)]. *Bulletin of the Russian State Pedagogical University, 97*, 72–75.

Kurushin, V. I. (2004). Professional'naya podgotovka kadrov v sisteme ministerstva vnutrennikh del RF: perspektivy modernisatsii [Professional training in the system of the Ministry of Internal Affairs of Russian Federation: prospects of modernization]. *The Bulletin of Samara State University, 33*(3), 149–151.

Kuztnetsov, E. V. (2009). Prfessional'no-nravstvennaya deformatsiya [Professional ethical deformation]. *The Bulletin of the Russian State Pedagogical University 117*, 322–325.

Lapenna, I. (1961). The new Russian criminal code and code of criminal procedure. *The International and Comparative Law Quarterly, 10*(3), 421–453.

Lapenna, I. (1968). *Soviet penal policy*. Chester Springs, PA: Dufour.

Lauchlan, I. (2005). The Okhrana: Security policing in late imperial Russia. In I. D. Thatcher (Ed.), *Late imperial Russia* (pp. 44–63). Manchester and New York: Manchester University Press.

Lavrik, T. M. (2008). Politika po formirovaniyu karovogo sostava zhadarmerii na rubezhe 19-20 vekov [Staffing policy of gendarmerie between 19th–20th centuries]. *Bulletin of the Tomsk State University, 8*(64), 297–300.

Lavroff, D.-G. (1963). *Les libertés publiques en Union Sovietique*. Paris: Editions A. Pedone.

Le Donne, J. (1970). The provincial and local police under Catherine the Great, 1775–1796. *Canadian Slavic Studies, 4*(3), 513–528.

Le Donne, J. (1974). Criminal investigations before Great Reforms. *Russian History, 1*, 101–118.

Ledeneva, A. V. (2002). Practices of exchange and networking in Russia. In M. Galeotti (Ed.), *Russian and post-Soviet organized crime* (pp. 257–272). Dartmouth, U.K.: Ashgate.

Leggett, G. H. (1975). Lenin, terror and the political police. *Survey, 21*(4), 157–187.

Leggett, G. H. (1980). The Cheka and a crisis of Communist conscience. *Survey, 25*, 122–137.

Lelekov, V. A., and Tyamin, A. V. (2005). Zaschishennost' lichnosti ot prestupnyh posyagatelstv [Personal security from crime acts]. *Social Research, 6*, 107–108.

Lemke, M. (1909). *Nikolaevskie gendarmes and literature of 1826-1855*. St. Petersburg: Published by S.V. Bunin.

Levada. (2010). Ot mnenii k ponimaniyu [From opinions to understanding] Available from www.levada.ru.

Levada. (2011a). Perspektivy grazhdanskogo obschestva [The perspectives of civil society] Available from www.levada.ru.

Levada. (2011b). Problema korruptsii v Rossii [The problem of corruption in Russia] Available from http://bd.fom.ru/pdf/d04pkvr11.pdf.

Levytsky, B. (1972). *The uses of terror. The Soviet secret police 1917–1970*. New York: Coward, McCann and Geoghegan, Inc.

Lewin, M. (1985). Customary law and Russian rural society in the post-reform era. *Russian Review, 44*(1), 1–19.

Lieven, D. C. B. (1989). The security police, civil rights, and the fate of the Russian Empire, 1855–1917. In O. Crisp and L. Edmondson (Eds.), *Civil rights in Imperial Russia* (pp. 235–262). Oxford: Clarendon Press.

Lincoln, B. W. (1994). The genesis of an enlightened bureaucracy, 1825–56. In D. H. Kaiser and G. Marker (Eds.), *Reinterpreting Russian history. Readings 860-1860s* (pp. 257–262). New York and Oxford: Oxford University Press.

Lindenmeyr, A. (1982). A Russian experiment in voluntarism: the municipal guardianship of the poor, 1894–1904. *Jahrbucher fur Geschichte Osteuropas, 30*(3), 429–451.

Loader, I., and Walker, N. (2001). Policing as a public good. *Theoretical Criminology, 5*(1), 9–35.

Lobachev, D. A. (2006). *Organizatsiya pravookhranitel'noi deyatel'nosti organov vnutrennikh del v usloviyakh mezhetnicheskikh konfliktov [Organization of law enforcement activities of agencies of interior affairs under conditions of multi-ethnic conflicts]*. Saratov Law Institute, Saratov.

Los, M. (2002). Post-communist fear of crime and the commercialization of security. *Theoretical Criminology, 6*(2), 165–188.

Luryi, Y. I. (1986). The use of criminal law by the CPSU in the struggle for the reinforcement of its power and the inner-party struggle. In D. A. Loeber, D. D. Barry, F. J. M. Feldbrugge, and P. B. Maggs (Eds.), *Ruling Communist parties and their status under law* (pp. 91–113). Dordrecht: Martinus Nijhoff Publishers.

Lyubimov, I. L., Pomerantsev, V. A., and Kiselev, I. F. (1928). *Instruktsiya organam militsii o proizvodstve doznanii.[Instruction to the agencies of militia on conducting the preliminary inquiry]*. Moscow: Publisher of the NKViU of USSR.

MacFadyen, D. (2008). *Russian television today*. London and New York: Routledge.

Makarova, M. N. (2011). Osobennosti vospriyatiya organov vnutrennokh delv obschestvennom mnenii regiona [Details of public opinion of police in the region]. *Monitoring of Public Opinion, 1*(101), 64–70.

Makurina, G. A. (2008). Uchastie organov politicheskogo rozyska Sibiri v likvidatsii prestupnykh grabitel'skih grup v 1913 [The participation of the political police in the liquidation of the organized crime groups in Siberia in 1913]. *Bulletin of the Altay State University, 4*(1).

Mamedova, M. A. (2006). Deyatelnost' organov militsii odygei po bor'be s prestupnost'yu i okhrane obschestvennogo porydka v 1920-e gody [The work of police to restore public order and solve crimes in the Republic of Adygeya in 1920s]. *Bulletin of the Adygei State University, 1*, 35–37.

Marshunov, M. N. (2001). *Postateinyi kommentarii k Zakonu RF "O militsii" [Clause-by-clause commentary to the statute of Russian Federation "On Police"]*. St. Petersburg: Publishing house "Gerda."

Martinovitch, I. I., and Pluta, E. F. (1977). *Sud i pravosudie v BSSR [Court and justice in Belarus SSR]*. Minsk: Belarus State University Press.

Masalimov, A. S., and Masalimov, T. S. (2008). Narushenie zakonnosti politsiei Rossiskoi Imperii pri osushestvlenii polnomochii po okhrane obschestvennogo poryadka (1900–1917 gg) [Law of rule violations by the police of the Russian Empire during 1900–1917 years]. *The Bulletin of the East Economic State University, 5*(37), 112–120.

Maslov, A. E. (2010). *Administrativnaya deyatelnost'organov vnutrennikh del [Administrative activities of the agencies of internal affairs]*. Moscow: Schit-M.

Matienko, T. L. (2007). Organizatsionno-structurnye osobennosti sysknoi politsii Rossiksoi Imperii 1908–1917 [Organizational–Structural Features of detective police in Russian Empire (1908–1917)].

Matthews, M. (1989). *Patterns of Deprivation in the Soviet Union under Brezhnev and Gorbachev*. Stanford, CA: Hoover Institution Press.

Matthews, M. (1993). *The passport society. Controlling movement in Russia and the USSR*. Oxford: Westview Press.

Mawby, R. (1990). *Comparative policing issues*. London: Unwin Hyman.

Mawby, R. (1999). The changing face of policing in Central and Eastern Europe. *International Journal of Police Science and Management, 2*(3), 199–216.

Mawby, R. (2001). The impact of transition: A comparison of post-Communist societies with earlier "societies in transition." In A. Kadar (Ed.), *Police in transition* (pp. 19–38). Budapest: Central European University.

Mayurov, N. P. (2005). Sostoyanie i mery po ukrepelniyu distsipliny v organakh militsii v gody velikoi otechestvennoi voiny [Conditions and discipline measures of police during the WWII]. *Bulletin of the St. Petersburg University of MVD, 2*(26), 41–47.

Mazaev, Y. N. (1997). Kak izmenyatsya otnoshenie naseleniya k militsii [How does the public opinion towards the police change?]. *Social Research, 11*, 68–73.

Mazaev, Y. N. (2004). Rol' sredstv massovoi informatsii v formirovanii obschestvennogo mneniya o militsii [The role of mass media in shaping the public opinion about police]. *Social Research, 2*, 106–115.

Mazaev, Y. N., Yakovlev, O. V., and Kamaev, B. G. (2003). *Sostoyanie vzaimootnoshei mezschdu militsiei i naseleniem i perspektivy ih sovershenstvovaniya [The state of relations between the public and police and the perspectives of its improvement]*. Paper presented at the Materials of the Round Table discussion on September 26, 2003, Moscow.

McKean, R. B. (1990). *St. Petersburg between the revolutions. Workers and revolutionaries, June 1907–February 1917*. New Haven and London: Yale University Press.

Medvezhevskyi, A. A., Girin, S. A., and Mizeryi, A. I. (1999). Grazhdane i eksperty o korruptsii [Citizens and experts about corruption]. *Social Research, 12*, 86–94.

Meyr, E. (2001). Russia's police "Black Berets." *Law and Order, 49*(3), 40.

Michael, B. (2010). Issues in anti-corruption law: Drafting implementing regulations for anti-corruption conventions in Central Europe and the former Soviet Union. *Journal of Legislation, 36*.

Milton, J. W. (1976). *Maintaining public order in the Soviet Union: The militia and the MVD in the post-Khruschchev era*. Durham, NC: Duke University.

Ministry of Economic Development. (2011). Sostoyanie bytovoi korrptsiyi v Rossii [The situation with the low level corruption in Russia] Available from http://www.economy.gov.ru/wps/wcm/connect/116f09004739f0c7a2a4eeb4415291f1/doklad_kor.pdf?MOD=AJPERESandCACHEID=116f09004739f0c7a2a4eeb4415291f1.

Mishler, W., and Rose, R. (1998). *Trust in untrustworthy institutions*. Glasgow: Center for the Study of Public Policy. University of Strathclyde.

Mishler, W., and Rose, R. (2005). What are the political consequences of trust? A test of cultural and institutional theories in Russia. *Comparative Political Studies, 38*(9), 1050–1078.

Mitroshenkov, O. A. (2004). Otnoshenie naselenia i gosluzchashih k suschestvuyshemu pravoporyadku [Attitudes of population and government officials towards the existing law and order]. *Social Research, 5*, 113–120.

Mityukova, M. A. (2008). Pravovoe regulirovanie doznaniya v pervye gody sovetskoi vlasti 1917–1921 gg [Legal regulation of inquiry at the first years of Soviets, 1917–1921 years]. *Siberian Law Bulletin, 2*(41), 108–111.

Mizoulina, E. B. (2006a). Khornologiya Sobytii [The chronology of Events]. In E. B. Mizoulina and V. N. Pligin (Eds.), *Uroki reformy ugolovnogo pravosudiia v Rossii [Lessons of reforming criminal justice in Russia]* (pp. 19–34). Moscow: Yurist.

Mizoulina, E. B. (2006b). Rossiya nakanune vvedeniya v deistvie novogo ugolovno protsessual'nogo kodeksa Rossiskoi Federatsii [Russia on the eve of adopting the new Criminal Procedural Code of Russian Federation]. In E. B. Mizoulina and V. N. Pligin (Eds.), *Uroki reformy ugolovnogo pravosudiia v Rossii [Lessons of reforming criminal justice in Russia]* (pp. 783–799). Moscow: Yurist.

Mizoulina, E. B. (2006c). Monitoring kak prognozirovaniya i korrektirovki posledstvii prinyatiya zakonov [Monitoring as a method to forecast and correct the consequences of adopting the laws]. In E. B. Mizoulina and V. N. Pligin (Eds.), *Uroki reformy ugolovnogo pravosudiia v Rossii [Lessons of reforming criminal justice in Russia]* (pp. 87–95). Moscow: Yurist.

Moller, J., and Skaaning, S.-E. (2010). From each according to his need, to each according to his ability: A comparative analysis of post-communist corruption. *Acta Politica, 45*(3), 320–345.

Monas, S. (1961). *The third section. Police and society in Russia under Nicholas I*. Cambridge: Harvard University Press.

Moore, B. (1947). The present purge in the USSR. *The Review of Politics, 9*(1), 65–76.

Morgan, R., and Newburn, T. (1997). *The future of policing*. Oxford: Clarendon Press.

Morn, F., and Sergevnin, V. (1994). Police training in modern Russia. *International Journal of Comparative and Applied Criminal Justice, 18*(1), 118–128.

Morozov, V. M., and Sergevnin, V. A. (1996). Utilization of international experience of the police recruiting, selection, and training in the Russian Federation. In M. Pagon (Ed.), *Policing in Central and Eastern Europe: Comparing firsthand knowledge with experience from the West* (pp. 99–101). Ljubljana, Slovenia: College of Police and Security.

Morukov, Y. N. (2007). *Istoria organov pravoporyadka v tochnykh datakh [History of Russian law enforcement in exact dates]*. Moscow: United Publisher of MVD of Russia.

Moskal'kova, T. N. (2006). Zakon o militsii—pravovaya osnova organizatsionnogo edinistva organov vnutrennikh del Rossiskoi Federatsii [The law "On police"—the legal foundation for organizational unity of the agencies of interior affairs of the Russian Federation]. *Bulletin of Moscow University MVD, 3*, 31–34.

Mulukaev, R. S., Malygin, A. Y., and Epifanov, A. E. (2005). *Istoriya otechestvennykh organov vnutrennikh del [History of agencies of interior affairs]*. Moscow: Nota Bene.

MVD. (1990). *Prestupnost' i pravonarusheniya v SSSR [Crime and delinquency in USSR]*. Moscow: Finansy i statistika.

MVD. (2008a). About MVD. History. 1917-1931. Retrieved from http://www.mvd.ru/about/history/367/.

MVD. (2008b). About MVD. History. 1985-1993. Retrieved from http://www.mvd.ru/about/history/371/.

Naumenko, O. N., and Almukhametova, M. S. (2009). Vliyaniye pravookhranite'noi sistemy na pravosoznaniya gorodskogo obyvatelya zapadnoi sibiri v 19 -nachale 20 vekov [The influence of police on the perception of law among urban population of Western Siberia at the end of 19th, beginning 20th century]. *Bulletin of the Tyumen State University, 2*, 194–199.

Nethercott, F. (2007). *Russian legal culture before and after Communism*. London and New York: Routledge.

Neuberger, J. (1993). *Hooliganism. Crime, culture and power in St. Petersburg, 1900–1914*. Berkley: University of California Press.

Nevirko, D. D., Shenkevitch, V. E., and Gorbach, N. A. (2006). Deyatelnost' militsii v zerkale obschestvennogo mneniya [Police activities in the mirror of public opinion]. *Social Research, 2*, 76–84.

Newcombe, K. (2007). Russia. In C. M. Bradley (Ed.), *Criminal procedure. A worldwide study*. Durham, NC: Carolina Academic Press.

NII MVD. (1993). *Osnovnye tendentsii razvitiya kriminal'noi obstanovki Rossii [Main tendencies in developing the crime conditions in Russia]*. Moscow: Scientific Research Institute of MVD.

Novikova, A. (2005). Social profile of rank and file police officers in the contemporary law enforcement system. In *Reforming law enforcement agencies: Overcoming arbitrary work practices* (pp. 69–74). Moscow: Demos Center.

Novikova, A., and Shepeleva, O. (2005). Principles and directives for reforming of the law enforcement. In *Reforming law enforcement agencies: overcoming arbitrary work practices* (pp. 57–68). Moscow: Demos Center.

Obschestvennaya Palata. (2011a). Doklad ob effektivnosti provodimykh v Rossii anikorruptsionnykh meroproiyati i uchastii institutov grazhdanskogo obschestva v healizatsii antikorruptisonnoi politiki [Report about the effectiveness of current anti-corruption measures and participations of civil society institutes in the implementation of anti-corruption measures] Available from http://www.oprf.ru/files/dokument2011/dokladkorrupciya26012012.pdf.

Obschestvennaya Palata. (2011b). Mezhnatsionalnaya neterpimost' v molodezhnoi gorodskoi srede [Intra-ethnic xenophobia among urban youth] Available from http://www.oprf.ru/files/oprosmolodezh.pdf.

Oda, H. (1989). Law enforcement agencies. In R. M. Buxbaum and K. Hendley (Eds.), *The Soviet sobranie of laws* (pp. 127–139). Berkley, CA: University of California at Berkley.

Oks, S. I. (2010). Otsenka imidga silovukh struktur: natsionalnyi aspekt [Police image assessment: the national aspect]. *Bulletin of Voronezh State University, 1*, 167–172.

Oleinik, A. (2003). *Organized crime, prison and post-Soviet societies.* Aldershot, U.K.: Ashgate.

Oleinik, I. I. (2008). Oranizatsiya i resul'taty yuridicheskoi podgotovki pravookhranitel'nykh organov v sovetskom gosudarstve, 1917–1941 [Organization and results of legal training for police in Soviet state, 1917–1941]. *Bulletin of the Volgograd Law Institute, 2*(7), 259–264.

Ombudsman. (2009). Annual report by Russian Ombudsman. Available from www.ombudsmanrf.org.

Ombudsman. (2010). Annual report by Russian Ombudsman. Available from www.ombudsmanrf.org.

Ombudsman. (2011). Annual report by Russian Ombudsman. Available from www.ombudsmanrf.org.

Orland, L. (2002). A Russian legal revolution: The 2002 criminal procedure code. *Connecticut Journal of International Law, 133*(18).

Orlovsky, D. (1981). *The limits of reform: The Ministry of Internal Affairs in Imperial Russia, 1802–1881.* Cambridge and London: Harvard University Press.

Osakwe, C. (1983). Modern Soviet criminal procedure: A critical analysis. *Tulane Law Review, 439*(57).

Paldam, M., and Svendsen, G. T. (2001). Missing social capital and the transition in Eastern Europe. *Journal for Institutional Innovation, Development and Transition, 5*, 21–34.

Panchenko, P. N. (2010). Obschestvennyi kontrol v sfere pravoporyadka: voprosy formirovaniya sistemy [Public control over law enforcement: issues of system forming]. *Russian Justice, 4*, 50–53.

Paneiakh, V. M. (2003). The political police and the study of history in the USSR. In M. Siefert (Ed.), *Extending the borders of Russian history* (pp. 301–314). Budapest, New York: CEU Press.

Panina, T. V. (2006). *Formirovanie gumannogo otnosheniya k cheloveku u buduschikh sotrudnikov pravookhranitel'nykh organov [Shaping the human attitudes among future law enforcement employees].* Yakutsk State University, Yakutsk.

Panteleev, B. N. (2002). *Administrativnaya deyatel'nost' organov vnutrennikh del [Administrative activities of the agencies of interior affairs].* Yekaterinburg.

Pasechnik, A. F. (2008). Istoricheskii opyt reorganizatsii kamchatskoi militsii na osnove okruzhnogo otdeleniya v 1926-1930-kh godakh [Historical experience of reorganization of Kamchatskaya police during 1926-1930s]. *Power and Administration in Eastern Russia, 1*(42), 115–118.

Pavlov, A. N. (2006). Vzaimodeistvie organov militsii i obschestvennoi organizatsii po okhrane pravoporyadka v period novoi ekonomicheskoi politiki [Interaction of police and non-government organizations during NEP]. *Bulletin of the St. Petersburg University of MVD, 3*(31), 47–53.

Pechnikov, N. P. (2005). *Pravookhranitel'nye organy [Law enforcement agencies].* Tambov: Tambov State Technical University Press.

Pelfrey, W. V. (2005). Perceptions of police style by Russian police administrators. *Journal of Slavic Military Studies, 18*(4), 587–598.

Peregudova, Z. I. (2000). *Politicheskiy sysk [Political policing]*. Moscow: ROSSPEN (Rossiskaya Politicheskaya Entsiklopedia) [РОССПЭН (Russian Political Encyclopedia].

Petrov, A. V. (2004). Problemy organisatsii obschei militsii v Rossiskoi imperii v nachale 20 veka. [Problems of organization of common police in the Russian Empire at the beginning of the 20th century]. *The Bulletin of Omsk State University, 3*, 134–137.

Petrov, A. V. (2006a). Osnovnye napravleniya deyatel'nosti pravookranitel'nykh organov sibirskogo i ural'skogo regionov v period grazhdanskoi voiny v rossii (1918–1919) [Main directions of police activities in Ural and Siberian regions during the civil war in Russia, 1918-1919]. *Siberian Law Bulletin, 1*(28), 19–24.

Petrov, A. V. (2006b). Osnovnye napravleniya deyatel'nosti sovetskoi militsii urala i sibiri (1919–1921gg) [Main directions of activity of Soviet police of Ural and Siberia, 1919–1921]. *Siberian Law Bulletin, 2*(29), 20-26.

Petrov, A. V. (2006c). Systema Sovetskoi militsii: problema razvitiya v 1919–1921 gg [System of Soviet police: problems of development in 1919–1921]. *Bulletin of Omsk State University, 3*, 134–139.

Petrov, D. E. (2011). Politko-resursnye aspekty reformy vnutrennikh del v sovremennoi Rossii [Political and resource aspects of police reform in modern Russia]. *Bulletin of Saratov University, 11*(4), 102–105.

Petrov, N., and Slider, D. (2007). Putin and the regions. In D. R. Herspring (Ed.), *Putin's Russia* (pp. 75–98). New York: Rowman and Littlefield Publishers.

Pino, N., and Wiatrowski, M. (2006). Assessing the obstacles. In N. Pino and M. Wiatrowski (Eds.), *Democratic policing in transitional and developing countries* (pp. 11–42). Burlington, U.K.: Ashgate.

Pinter, W. (1970). The social characteristics of the early nineteenth century Russian bureaucracy. *Slavic Review, 29*(3), 429–443.

Pistor, K. (1996). Supply and demand for contract enforcement in Russia: Courts, arbitration, and private enforcement. *Review of Central and East European Law, 22*(1), 55–87.

Poduzov, S. (2010). Is police reform taking place in Russia. A view from the regions. *Russian Analytical Digest, 84*, 7–9.

Politov, V. E. (2007). Tambovskaya kriminal'noi politsiya v kontse 19 nachale 20 veka [Tombov criminal police at the end of 19th–beginning of the 20th century]. *Bulletin of the Tomsk State University, 1*(45), 123–127.

Popov, A. N. (2005). *Deyatel'nost' organov mestnogo samoupravleniya po obespecheniyu okhrany obschestvennogo poryadka [Activities of the local authorities for purposes of protecting public order]*. Tambov: Tambov State Technical University Press.

Potlachuk, N. V. (2008). Kommunikativnaya kopmpetentnost' sotrudnikov kriminal'noi militsii [Communicative competence of police officers]. *Bulletin of the Russian State Pedagogical University, 49*, 171–174.

Prokhorova, E. (2003). Can the meeting place be changed? Crime and identity discourse in Russian television series of the 1990s. *Slavic Review, 62*(3), 512–524.

Pronyakin, A. D., and Pronyakin, D. A. (2003). *Pravookhranitel'nye organy RF [Law enforcement agencies of Russian Federation]*. Moscow: Moscow International Institute of Econometrics, Informatics, Finaces and Law.

Public Verdict Fund. (2005). Analiticheskyi otchet. Situatsiya v pravookhranitelnoi sisteme Rossii i ee vliyanie na prava is svobody grazhdan [Analytical report. The situation with law enforcement and the rights of citizens] Available from www.publicverdict.org.

Public Verdict Fund. (2008). Otnoshenie naselenia k reforme militsii [Public attitudes about police reform]. Available from www.publicverdict.org.

Public Verdict Fund. (2010). Reforma militisii: otsenki i ozhidaniya grazhdan [Police reform: public expectations and assessment] Available from www.publicverdict.org.

Pukhno, P. S. (2005). *Formirovanie professional'noi identichnosti sotrudnikov MVD [Forming professional identity of police officers personality in MVD].* Southern Russian Technical University, Novocherkassk.

Pustintsev, B. (1996). Russian political police: immortal traditions and eternal threats. *Demokratizatsiya, 4*(4), 531–537.

Pustintsev, B. (2000). Police reform in Russia: Obstacles and opportunities. *Policing and Society, 10*, 79–90.

Pysh'ev, A. N. (2006). Soblyudenie prav i svobod cheloveka i grazhdanina -osnova deyatel'nosti militsii [Protection of the human rights of individual—the basis of police work]. *Bulletin of Moscow University MVD, 3*, 45–46.

Ra'anan, U., and Lukes, I. (1990). *Inside the apparat. Perspectives on the Soviet system from former functionaries.* Lexington, MA, Toronto: Lexington Books.

Radaev, V. V. (1998). Nekotorye institutsionalnye usloviya formirovaniya rossiiskih rynkov. [Some institutional conditions of shaping the Russian markets]. *Sociological Journal, 3/4*, 57–85.

Radchenko, V. I. (2006). *Ugolovnyi protsess* [Criminal procedure]. Moscow: Yustitsinform.

Raef, M. (1983). *The well-ordered police state.* New Haven and London: Yale University Press.

Revin, I. A. (2004). *Vzaimodeistvie organov vnutrennikh del s obschestvennymi formirovaniyami pravookhranitel'noi napravlennosti v obespechenii obschestvennoi bezopasnosti v Svero-Kavkazkom regione [Interaction of agencies of interior affairs with the public organizations of law enforcement purposes in order to maintain public order in the North Caucasian region].* All Russian Scientific Research Institute of MVD Russia, Moscow.

Reynolds, K. M., Semukhina, O. B., and Demidov, N. N. (2008). A longitudinal analysis of public satisfaction with the police in the Volgograd Region of Russia: 1998–2005. *International Criminal Justice Review, 18*(2), 158–189.

Richelson, J. (1985). *Sword and shield. The Soviet intelligence and security apparatus.* Cambridge, MA: Ballinger Publishing Company.

Rigberg, B. (1966). The efficacy of Tsarist censorship operations, 1894–1917. *Jahrbucher fur Geschichte Osteuropas, 14*, 327–346.

Rigberg, B. (1969). Tsarist censorship performance, 1894–1905. *Jahrbucher fur Geschichte Osteuropas, 17*, 59–76.

Rimashevskaya, N. M. (2002). Sotsialnaya zaschita naseleniya [Social protection of population] Available from http://www.gks.ru/dbscripts/Cbsd/DBInet.cgi?pl = 2415003.

Rimskyi, V. L. (2007). Korruptsiya vo vzaimodeistviyakh grazhdan s organami gosudarstvennoi vlasti kak sotstialnoe yavlenie. [Corruption in the relationship between citizens and government agencies as social issue] *Problemy modernizatsii ekonomiki i eknomicheskoi politiki Rossiii [Problems of modernization of economics and economic policy in Russia]* (pp. 1132–1146). Moscow: INDEM.

Rimskyi, V. L. (2008). Korruptsiya vo vzaimodeistviyakh rossiikikh grazhdan s predstavitelyami gosudarstvennykh organov [Corruption in the relationship between Russian citizens and representatives of government agencies]. *Public sciences and modernity, 5*, 59–67.

Robertson, A. (2004). Police reform in Russia. In M. Caparini and O. Marenin (Eds.), *Transforming police in Central and Eastern Europe: Process and progress* (pp. 289–304). Munster, Germany: Lit Verlag.

Rogatchevski, A. (2004). May the [police] force be with you. *Russian Studies in Literature, 40*(3), 79–94.

Romanov, V. I. (2008). Revolutsionnoe pravotvorchestvo na urale v nachalnyi period fevral'skoi revolutsii [Revolutionary legislation in Urals during the February revolution]. *Bulletin of the Chelyabinsk State University, 34*, 68–71.

Romanova, V. V. (2007). *Sluzhba zhenschin v organakh vnutrennikh del [Service of female police officers in MVD]*. MVD Academy of Management, Moscow.

Rose, R., and Mishler, W. (2010). Experience versus perception of corruption: Russia as a test case. *Global Crime, 11*(2), 145–163.

Roudik, P. (2008). Policing the Russian federation. In M. R. Haberfeld and I. Gerrah (Eds.), *Comparative policing* (pp. 139–167). Los Angeles: Sage Publications.

Rousset, D. (1953). *Police-state methods in the Soviet Union*. Boston: The Beacon Press.

Rowney, D. K. (1971). The study of the Imperial Ministry of Internal Affairs in the light of organization theory. In R. E. Kenet (Ed.), *The behavioral revolution and communist studies* (pp. 209–232). New York and London: The Free Press and Collier-Macmillan Limited.

Rowney, D. K. (1972). Higher civil servants in the Russian Ministry of Internal Affairs: Some demographic and career characteristics, 1905–1916. *Slavic Review, 31*(1), 101–110.

Rozin, N. N. (1913). *Ugolovnoe sudoproizvodstvo: posobie po lektsRudinsky, F. M. (2008). Civil human rights in Russia*. New Brunswick and London: Transaction Publishers.

Rutkevitch, M. N. (1998). Protsessy sotsial'noi degradatsii v Rossiiskom obschestve [The processes of social degradation in Russian society]. *Social Research, 6*, 3–12.

Ruud, C. A. (1993). A. A. Lopukhin, Police insubordination, and the rule of law. *Russian History, 20*, 147–162.

Ryan, B. (2011). *Statebuilding and police reform*. London, New York: Routledge.

Rybnikov, V. V., and Aleksushin, G. V. (2008). *Istoriya pravookhranitel'nykh organov otechestva. [History of law enforcement agencies of homeland]*. Moscow: Schit-M.

Ryvkina, R. V. (2000). Tenevizatsiya rossiskogo obschestva: prichiny i posledstviya. [Shadowing of Russian society: reasons and consequences]. *Social Research, 12*, 3–13.

Safronov, A. D. (1997). Problemy riska v deyatel'nsoti MVD [The problems of risk in activity of MVD]. *Sociological Research, 11*, 74–77.

Sajo, A. (1998). Corruption, clientelism, and the future of the constitutional state in Eastern Europe *Eastern European Constitutional Review, 7*(2).

Sakhno, A. V. (2005). *Obraz militsii v rossiskoi kul'ture: konstruktsiya i dekonstruktsiya tipov vospriyatiya [The image of police in Russian culture: construction and de-construction of types of understanding]*. Rostov State Pedagogical University, Rostov-on-Don.

Salagaev, A., Shashkin, A., and Konnov, A. (2008). One hand washes the other: Informal ties among orginized crime groups and law enforcement agencies in Russia. In R. W. Orttung and A. Latta (Eds.), *Russia's battle with crime, corruption, and terrorism* (pp. 76–102). London and New York: Routledge/Taylor and Francis Group.

Savchenko, I. A. (2011). Refroma MVD: vzglyad iz nutri [MVD reform: the internal view]. *Monitoring of Public Opinion, 2*(102), 38–46.

Savel'ev, A. I. (2010). Obschestvennoe mnenie o deyatelnosti milisii v Omskoi oblasti [Public opinion on police in Omsk region]. *Scientific bulletin of Omsk Academy of MVD, 1*, 25–27.

Savitsky, V. M. (1979). Criminal procedure. In Bassiouni (Ed.), *The criminal justice system of the USSR.* Springfield, IL: Charles C. Thomas Publishers.

Schaible, D. S. (2001). Life in Russia's "closed city": Moscow's movement restrictions and the rule of law. *New York University Law Review, 76*, 344–373.

Semenova, Y. V. (2009). Individual'no-psykhologicheskie osobennosti sotrudnikov pravookhranitel'nykh organov [Individual psychological features of police officers]. *Bulletin of the Buryat State University, 5*, 175–181.

Sergeyev, V. M. (1998). *The wild East. Crime and lawlessness in post-Communist Russia.* Armonk, NY; London: M.E. Sharpe.

Serio, J. (1992). *USSR crime statistics and summaries 1989 and 1990.* Chicago: The University of Illinois at Chicago.

Serio, J. (2008). *Investigating the Russian mafia.* Durham, NC: Carolina Academic Press.

Shabel'nikova, N. A. (2009). Militsiya v bor'be s prstupnost'yu na dal'nem vostoke rossii 1920–1930e gody [Militia in prevention of crime in the Russian Far East in the 1920s–1930s (historiographic survey)]. *Humanities research in the Eastern Siberia and Far East, 1*(5), 30–34.

Sheifer, S. A., and Bobrov, A. V. (2006). Protsessual'nye o organizatsionnye problemy sovershenstvovaniya deyatel'nosti sledstvennogo apparatta. [Procedural and organizational issues of improving the activities of investigative apparatus]. *Legal Analytical Journal, 1*(15), 5–13.

Shelepova, M. A. (2004). *Pedagogicheskie usloviya professional'noi adaptatsii buduschikh sledovatelei v vuze MVD Rossii [Pedagogical conditions of professional adaptation of the futher intvestigators in the educational institutions of MVD Russia].* St. Petersburg University of MVD, St. Petersburg.

Shelley, L. (1980). The geography of Soviet criminality. *American Sociological Review, 45*(1), 111–122.

Shelley, L. (1986). Party members and the courts: Exploitation of privilege. In D. A. Loeber, D. D. Barry, F. J. M. Feldbrugge, and P. B. Maggs (Eds.), *Ruling communist parties and their status under law* (pp. 75–90). Dordrecht: Martinus Nijhoff Publishers.

Shelley, L. (1989). Soviet criminal law and justice: Are there or were there secrets? In R. M. Buxbaum and K. Hendley (Eds.), *The Soviet sobranie of laws* (pp. 140–155). Berkley: University of California at Berkley.

Shelley, L. (1991). Crime in the Soviet Union. In A. Jones, W. D. Conno, and D. E. Powell (Eds.), *Soviet social problems* (pp. 227–251). Boulder, CO: Westview Press.

Shelley, L. (1992). The Ministry of Internal Affairs. In E. Huskey (Ed.), *Executive power and Soviet politics. The rise and decline of the Soviet state* (pp. 202–221). Armonk, NY and London: M.E. Sharpe.

Shelley, L. (1994). The sources of Soviet policing. *Police Studies, 17*(2), 49.

Shelley, L. (1995). Privatization and crime: The post-Soviet experience. *Journal of Contemporary Criminal Justice, 11*(4), 244–256.

Shelley, L. (1996). *Policing Soviet society. The evolution of state control*. London and New York: Routledge.

Shelley, L. (1999). Post-Socialist policing: Limitations on institutional change. In R. I. Mawby (Ed.), *Policing across the World. Issues for the twenty-first century* (pp. 75–87). New York: UCL Press/Taylor and Francis Group.

Shelley, L. (2000). Is the Russian state coping with organized crime and corruption? In V. Sperling (Ed.), *Building the Russian state. Institutional crisis and the quest for democratic governance*. Boulder, CO: Westview Press.

Shelley, L. (2002). Post-Soviet organized crime: Implications for economic, social and political development. In M. Galeotti (Ed.), *Russian and post-Soviet organized crime* (pp. 223–240). Dartmouth, U.K.: Ashgate.

Shepeleva, O. (2005a). Arbitrariness in police work: Typical practices, In *Reforming law enforcement agencies: Overcoming arbitrary work practices* (pp. 19–39). Moscow: Demos Center.

Shepeleva, O. (2005b). Reforming law enforcement agencies: Overcoming arbitrary work practices. Introduction. In *Reforming law enforcement agencies: Overcoming arbitrary work practices* (pp. 5–17). Moscow: Demos Center.

Shepeleva, O., and Novikova, A. (2005). The main problems of the contemporary police. *Reforming law enforcement agencies: overcoming arbitrary work practices* (pp. 40–56). Moscow: Demos Center.

Shergina, K. F. (2001). Korruptsiya v Rossi i problemy ugolovno-pravovogo protivodeistviya ei [Corruption in Russia and problems of struggling with it by the means of criminal legal actions] *Investitsionnyi klimat i perspektivy ekonomicheskogo rosta v Rossii [Investment climate and the perspectives of economic growth in Russia]*. Moscow: Moscow State University. High Schools of Economics.

Shikhantsov, G. G. (2009). *Kriminologiya [Criminology]*. Moscow: Izdatel'stvo Grevtsova.

Shishkin, V. S. (2006). Osnovnye prioritety v deyatel'nosti militsii [Main priorities in the police activities]. *Bulletin of Moscow University MVD, 3*, 49–50.

Shtromas, A. (1977). Crime, law and penal practice in the USSR. *Review of Socialist Law, 3*, 297–324.

Shubkin, V. N. (1997). Strahi v Rossii [Fears in Russia]. *Sociological journal, 3*, 62–78.

Sichinskii, E. P. (2002). *Ugolovnyi sysk Rossii v X - nachale XX v.v. [Criminal investigation in Russia in X-XX centuries]*. Chelyabinsk: Chelyabinsk Law Institute of MVD.

Simis, K. M. (1982). *USSR: The corrupt society*. New York: Simon and Shuster.

Simonov, A. (2005). *Osveschenie deyatelnosti pravookhranitelnykh organov v SMI [Coverage of law enforcement agencies by media]*. Paper presented in Moscow at the Naruscheniya prav cheloveka Rossiksimi pravookranitel'nymi organami [Violations of human rights by Russian law enforcement]. Retrieved from http://www.p ublicverdict.o rg/topics/libr ary/DOKLAD _05_06.html.

Skomorokhov, R. V., and Shikhanov, V. N. (2006). Ugolovnaya statistika i problema sotsial'noi deformtasii organov vnutennikh del [Criminal statistics and the problem of professional deformation of the agencies of interior affairs]. *State and Law, 3*, 62–70.

Slusser, R. M. (1959). The budget of the OGPU and the special troops from 1923–1924 to 1928–1929. *Soviet Studies, 10*(4), 375–383.

Solomon, P. H. (1978). *Soviet criminologists and criminal policy*. New York: Columbia University Press.

Solomon, P. H. (1981). Criminalization and decriminalization in Soviet criminal policy, 1917–1941. *Law & Society Review, 16*(1), 9–43.

Solomon, P. H. (1985). Local political power and Soviet criminal justice, 1922–1941. *Soviet Studies, 37*(3), 305–329.

Solomon, P. H. (1987). Soviet criminal justice and the great terror. *Slavic Review, 46*(3/4), 391–413.

Solomon, P. H. (1992). Reforming criminal law under Gorbachev. In D. D. Barry (Ed.), *Toward the "rule of law" in Russia? Political and legal reform in the transition period* (pp. 235–255). Armonk, NY: M.E. Sharpe.

Solomon, P. H. (1996). *Soviet criminal justice under Stalin*. Cambridge: Cambridge University Press.

Solomon, P. H. (2005a). The criminal procedure code of 2001: Will it make Russian justice more fair? In W. A. Pridemore (Ed.), *Ruling Russia: Law, crime, and justice in a changing society*. Lanham, MD: Rowman and Littlefield.

Solomon, P. H. (2005b). The reform of policing in the Russian Federation. *The Australian and New Zealand Journal of Criminology, 38*(2), 230–240.

Squire, P. S. (1968). *The Third Department. The establishment and practices of the political police in the Russia of Nicholas I*. Cambridge: Cambridge University Press.

Starr, S. F. (1972). *Decentralization of self-government in Russia, 1830–1870*. Princeton, NJ: Princeton University.

Stolee, M. K. (1988). Homeless children in the USSR, 1917–1957. *Soviet studies, 40*(1), 64–83.

Stremoukhova, I. V. (2008). Stratifikatsionnyi analiz sovremennogo rossikogo obschestva: polozhenie sotrudnikov pravookhranitel'nykh organov [Stratification analysis of Russian society: position of the law enforcement officers]. *Bulletin of the St. Petersburg University of MVD, 1*(37), 216–220.

Strogovitch, M. S. (1940). *Ugolovnyi protsess [Criminal procedure]*. Moscow: Legal publishers of NKiU of USSR.

Studenikin, V. E. (2004). *Praookhranitel'naya deyatel'nost' vnutrennikh del kak ob'ekt organizatsii [The law enforcement activity as an object of management]*. Academy of Management of MVD, Moscow.

Suchkov, E. N. (2008). Otsenka sostoyania politicheskogo syska rossiskoi imperii v period 1989-1902 i predlozcheniya po ego reformirovaniyu [The assessment of political police of the Russian Empire during 1989–1902]. *Public Administration. E-Journal of Moscow State University, 15*, 1–6.

Swafford, M. (1987). Perception of social status in the USSR. In J. R. Millar (Ed.), *Politics, work and daily life in the USSR* (pp. 279–300). New York: Cambridge University Press.

Sweet, K. (2002). Russian law enforcement under President Putin. *Human Rights Review, 3*(2), 20–33.

Szeftel, M. (1958). Personal inviolability in the legislation of the Russian absolute monarchy. *American Slavic and East European Review, 17*(1), 1–24.

Tagaev, N. M. (2010). Proekt federal'nogo zakona "O Politsii": problemy protivodeistviya prestupnsoti cotrudnikov vnutrennikh del [Draft law "On Police": issues of illegal police activities]. *Lawyer, 6*, 118–121.

Tarasov, T. I. (1910). *Lektsii po politseiskomu (administrativnomu) pravu. Chast' 2 [Lectures on police (administrative) law Part 2]*. Moscow: Pechatnya A.I. Snegiryevoi [Publishing house of A.I. Snegiryeva].

Taubina, N. (2011). Reforma: cto sdelano i chego ne hvataet [Reform: what was done and is missing]. *Bulletin of Fund of Public Verdict, 2*(11), 19–21.

Taylor, B. D. (2006). Law enforcement and civil society in Russia. *Europe-Asia Studies, 58*(2), 193–213.

Terrill, R. J. (1989). The organization of law enforcement in the Soviet Union. *Police Studies, 12*(1), 18.

The Harvard Project on the Soviet Social System. Datasystem. Retrieved on January 3, 2013 from http://hcl.harvard.edu/collections/hpsss.

Thomas, T. L. (1998). Restructuring and reform in Russia's MVD: Good idea, bad timing? *Low Intensity Conflict and Law Enforcement, 7*(2), 96–106.

Thurston, R. W. (1980). Police and people in Moscow, 1906–1914. *Russian Review, 39*(3), 320–338.

Tikhonova, S. S. (2010). Yuridiko-teknicheskyi analiz proekta federalnogo zakona Rossiskoi federatsii "O Politsii" [The legal and technical analysis of the draft law "On Police"]. *Bulletin of Nizhny Novgorod University, 5*(1), 298–304.

Timofeev, V. V. (2006). Bor'ba organov militsii Chuvashii c ukloneniem ot vyplaty denezhnykh povinostei [The struggle of the police of the Republic of Chuvashia against tax evasion crimes]. *Bulletin of the Chuvashkyi University, 6*, 188–192.

Timoshenko, S. (1997). Prospects for reform of the Russia militia. *Policing and Society, 8*, 117–124.

Tomin, V. T. (1976). *Ispol'zovanie sredstv massovoi informatsii v borbe s prestupnost'yu [Using mass media to fight crime]*. Gorkyi: Ministry of Internal Affairs, Gorkovskaya Highest School.

Torke, H.-J. (1971). Continuity and change in the relationship between bureaucracy and society in Russia, 1613–1864. *Canadian Slavic Studies, 5*(4), 457–476.

Treml, V. G. (1991). Drinking and alcohol abuse in the USSR in the 1980s. In A. Jones, W. D. Conno, and D. E. Powell (Eds.), *Soviet social problems* (pp. 119–136). Oxford: Westview Press.

Tudupova, T. T., and Ochirov, V. S. (2009). Etnopsihkologicheskaya podgotovka sotrudnikov pravookhranitel'nykh organov [Ethnopsychological training of law-enforcement agencies' officers]. *Bulletin of the St. Petersburg University of MVD, 3*(43), 226–230.

Uhlin, A. (2006). *Post-Soviet civil society*. London and New York: Routledge.

Uidriks, N., and Reenen, P. V. (2003). *Policing post-Communist societies. Police-public violence, democratic policing and human rights*. Antwerp, Oxford, New York: Intersentia. Open Society Institute.

Uidriks, N., and Reenen, P. V. (2005). *Police reform and human rights*. Antwerp, Oxford, New York: Intersentia. Open Society Institute.

Vagin, O. A., Isichenko, A. P., and Chechetin, A. E. (2009). *Kommentarii k zaknoy ob operativno-rozysknoi deyatelnosti [Commentary to the law "On operative-search activity]*. Moscow: Delovoi mir.

Vasil'ev, A. T. (1933). *The Ochrana, the Russian secret police*. Philadelphia: Lippincott.

Verin, V. P., and Mozyakov, V. V. (2004). *Kommentarii k ugolovno-protsessualnomu kodeksu Rossiskoi Federatsii*. [Commentary to the Criminal Procedural Code of Russia]. Moscow: Yekzamen.

Viktorov, B. A. (1974). The preliminary investigation agencies of the USSR Ministry of Internal Affairs in the struggle against crime. *Soviet Law and Government, 13*, 63–75.

Viktorskyi, S. I. (1912). *Russkiyi ugolovnyi protsess [Russian criminal procedure]*. Moscow: Gorodetz.

Vladimirov, L. E. (1910). *Uchenie ob ugolovnyh dokazatel'stvah [The study about criminal evidence]*. St. Petersburg: Izdanie Knizhnago magazina "Zakonovedenie."

Vladimirtsev, N. I., and Kokurin, A. I. (2008). *NKVD-MVD SSSR v borb'e s banditismom i vooruzhennym natsionalisticheskim podpol'em na Zapadnoi Ukraine, v Zapadnoi Belorussii i Pribaltike (1939–1956) [NKVD-MVD of USSR in the struggle against banditism and nationalism in Western Ukraine, Western Belarus and Baltic States 1939–1956)]*. Moscow: United Publishers of MVD.

Volkov, A. P., and Berkutov, A. S. (2009). Bor'ba s nezakonnymi migratsiyami v SSSR v poslevoennyi period, 1945–1960e gg [The struggle against illegal migration in the USSR in the after-WWII period, 1945–1960s]. *Bulletin of Ekaterina's University, 3*, 33–36.

Volkov, V. (2000). Between economy and the state: Private security and rule enforcement in Russia. *Politics and Society, 28*(4), 483.

Volkov, V. (2002). *Violent entrepreneurs. The use of force in the making of Russian capitalism*. Ithaca: Cornell University Press.

Vorob'ev, A. M. (1992). Sotsial'nyi portret rabotnika organov vnutrennih del [Social image of policemen]. *Social Research, 10*, 107–109.

Voronkov, V., and Gladarev, B. (2011). Militsiya, etnicheskie menshinstva i ksenofobiya [Police, ethnic minorities and xenophobia]. In B. Gladarev, V. Voronkov, and L. Sagitova (Eds.), *Militsiya i ethnicheskie migranty: praktiki vzaimodeistviya [Police and ethnic immigrants: practices of interaction]* (pp. 1–46). St. Petersburg: Aleteya.

Vyshinskyi, A. Y., and Undrevitch, V. S. (1934). *Kurs ugolovnogo protsessa. Sudoustroistvo. [The course of criminal procedure. Court system]*. Moscow: Soviet legislation.

Wade, R. A. (1984). *Red Guards and workers' militias in the Russian Revolution*. Stanford, CA: Stanford University.

Waldron, P. (2007). *Governing Tsarist Russia*. New York: Palgrave Macmillan.

Walkin, J. (1954). Government controls over the press in Russia, 1905–1914. *Russian Review, 13*(3), 203–209.

Walkin, J. (1962). *The rise of democracy in pre-revolutionary Russia*. New York: Frederick A. Praeger.

Waller, J. M. (1994). *Secret empire. The KGB in Russia today*. Boulder, CO: Westview Press.

Waller, J. M. (1995a). The KGB legacy in Russia. *Problems of Post-Communism, 42*(6), 3.

Waller, J. M. (1995b). Russia's great criminal revolution: The role of the security cervices. *Journal of Contemporary Criminal Justice, 11*(4). Retrieved from http://www.demokratizatsiya.org/html/Vol12.html.

Waller, J. M. (1997). Police, secret police, and civil authority. In J. D. Sachs and K. Pistor (Eds.), *The rule of law and economic reform in Russia* (pp. 95–121). Boulder, CO: Westview Press.

Waller, J. M. (2004). Russia: Death and resurrection of the KGB. *Demokratizatsiya, 12*(3). Retrieved from http://www.demokratizatsiya.org/html/Vol12.html.

Waller, J. M., and Yasmann, V. J. (1995). Russua's great criminal revolution: The role of the secret service. *Journal of Contemporary Criminal Justice, 11*(4), 276–297.

Waxmonsky, G. R. (1982). *Police and politics in Soviet society 1921–1929*. Princeton, NJ: Princeton University.

WCIOM. (1998). Blitz-WCIOM 1998-5. Retrieved on November 10, 2011, from http://wciom.ru/.

WCIOM. (2004). Omnibus WCIOM conducted on April 15, 2004. Retrieved on November 25, 2010, from www.wciom.ru.

WCIOM. (2005). Omnibus WCIOM conducted on June 21, 2005. Retrieved on November 25, 2010, from www.wciom.ru.

WCIOM. (2006). Bezopasnost' rossiyan: otsenivaya rabotu militsii, FSB i prokuratury [Safety of Russian citizens: assessing the work of police, FSB and Procuracy]. Retrieved on November 10, 2011, from http://wciom.ru/index.php?id=459&uid=2642.

WCIOM. (2007). Omnibus WCIOM conducted on February 4, 2007. Retrieved on November 25, 2010, from www.wciom.ru.

WCIOM. (2010a). Novyi zakon o militsii: chto on izmenit v rabote MVD [New law "On Police"—what would it change in the work of MVD?]. Retrieved on July 15, 2012, from http://wciom.ru/index.php?id=459&uid=111115.

WCIOM. (2010b). Rabota GIBDD: otsenka rossiyan [The work of traffic police: the assessment of Russians]. Retrieved on November 25, 2010, from http://wciom.ru/index.php?id=268&uid=13883.

WCIOM. (2011a). Doverie politikam [Trust to politicians]. Retrieved January 7, 2011, from http://wciom.ru/index.php?id=169.

WCIOM. (2011b). Politsiya i obschestvo: otnoshenie, doverie, vzaimodesitvie [Police and society: relationships, trust, and cooperation]. Retrieved July 7, 2012, from http://wciom.ru/index.php?id=459&uid=112346.

WCIOM. (2011c). Povyshenie zarplat sotrudnikam MVD i voennym: za i pritv [Increasing wages for employees of MVD and military: for and against]. Retrieved July 7, 2012, from http://wciom.ru/index.php?id=459&uid=111452.

Weber, M. (1948). *From Max Weber: Essays in sociology*. London: RKP.

Webster, W., Borchgrave, A., Peterson, E. R., Burke, G. P., Cilluffo, F. J., and Nelson, T. (2000). *Russian organized crime and corruption*. Washington, D.C.: Center for Strategic and International Studies.

Weiler, J. (2004). *Human rights in Russia. A darker side of reform*. Boulder, CO, and London: Lynne Rienner Publishers.

Weissman, N. (1985). Regular police in Tsarist Russia, 1900-1914. *Russian Review, 44*(1), 45–68.

Weissman, N. (1986). Prohibition and alcohol control in the USSR: The 1920s campaign against illegal spirits. *Soviet Studies, 38*(3), 349–368.

Weissman, N. (1991). Policing the NEP countryside. In S. Fitzpatrick, A. Rabinowitch, and R. Stites (Eds.), *Russia in the era of NEP* (pp. 174–191). Bloomington, Indianapolis: Indiana University Press.

Wilcox, E. H. (1917). The secret police of the old regime. *Fortnightly Review 108*(1), 826–836.

Williams, J. L. (1993). The Russian militia: An organization in transition. *Police Studies, 16*(4), 124.

Wilson, D. G., Kolennikova, O., Kosals, L., Ryvkina, R., and Simagin, Y. (2008). The "economic" activities of Russian police. *The International Journal of Police Science and Management, 10*(1), 65–75.

Wolf, S. (2009). Assessing Eastern Europe's anti-corruption performance: views from the Council of Europe, OECD, and Transparency International. *Global Crime, 11*(2), 99–121.

Wolin, S., and Slusser, R. M. (1957). *The Soviet secret police.* New York: Frederick A. Praeger Publisher.

Worobec, C. D. (1985). Reflections on customary law and post-reform peasant Russia. *Russian Review, 44*(1), 21–25.

Yanbukhtin, R. M. (2005). Lichnost' sotrudnika organov vnutrennikh del kak ob'ekt upravlencheskih otnoshenii [The personality of the employee of the agencies of interior affairs as an object of management relations]. *The Bulletin of Omsk State University, 3*, 193–197.

Yaney, G. L. (1973). *The systematization of Russian government.* Urbana, Chicago: University of Illinois Press.

Zakhartsev, S. N. (2004). *Sovetskoe pravo v gody NEPa [Soviet law during the NEP era].* Tambov: Tambov State Technical University Press.

Zelitch, J. (1931). *Soviet administration of criminal law.* Philadelphia: University of Pennsylvania Press.

Zentsova, Y. A. (2011). O kostseptsii komplektovaniya kadrov politsii Rossiskoi federatsii [About the concept of cadres recruitment of police of Russian Federation]. *Bulletin of Omsk University, 2*(27), 176–183.

Zhukov, I. A. (2004). *Psikhologiya attestatsii rukovodyaschikh kadrov organov vnutrennikh del MVD [Psychology of attestation of MVD leadership].* Moscow MVD University, Moscow.

Zhukova, E. I. (2008). Metodologicheskie aspekty izucheniya korporativnoi kul'tury militsii [Methodological aspects of research on the corporate culture of police]. *Bulletin of the Povolzhskaya Academy of Public Administration, 3*(16), 174–179.

Zimmerman, W. (1987). Mobilized participation and the nature of Soviet dictatorship. In J. R. Millar (Ed.), *Politics, work and daily life in the USSR* (pp. 332–353). New York: Cambridge University Press.

ZIRCON. (2005). Predstavleniya rossiyan o preffesionalnom dolge advokata (Public perceptions of Russians about professional duty of defense counsel). Retrieved on April 9, 2007, from www.zircon.ru.

ZIRCON. (2009). Rossiyane o televidenii i obschestvennom vliyanii na ego soderzhanie [Russians about TV and public influence on its content]. Retrieved on October 1, 2011, from www.zircon.ru.

Zuckerman, F. S. (1992). Political police and revolution: The impact of the 1905 revolution on the tsarist secret police. *Journal of Contemporary History, 27*(2), 279.

Zuckerman, F. S. (1996). *The Tsarist secret police in Russian society, 1880–1917.* London: Macmillan.

Zvekic, U. (1996). Policing and attitudes toward private police in countries in transition. *Policing in Central and Eastern Europe: Comparing firsthand knowledge with experience from the West,* Retrieved on May 10, 2006, from http://www.nc jrs.gov/policin g/contents.html.

References for Survey Studies Cited in Table 6.1 through Table 8.1

FOM. (1996a). Kak vy otsenivaete rabotu militsii po sderzhivaniju prestupnosti v tom meste gde vy zhivete? [Public attitudes toward agencies dealing with crime control and crime prevention]. Retrieved on June 17, 2011, from www.fom.ru.

FOM. (1996b). Moskvitchi chustvuyt sebya nezashischennymi na ulitsakh Moskvy [Residents of Moscow feel unsafe on the streets of their city]. Retrieved on September 10, 2006, from www.fom.ru.

FOM. (1997a). Kak vam kazhetsja,po sravneniju s tem, chto bylo dva goda nazad, sotrudniki GIBDD seichas rabotajut luchshe ili khuzhe? [Public opinion about improvements in the work of the Traffic Police during two previous years]. Retrieved on June 23, 2011, from www.fom.ru.

FOM. (1997b). Reitingi doveria/nedoveriya institutam obschestva [Ratings of trust and distrust of the societal institutions]. Retrieved on May 12, 2006, from www.fom.ru.

FOM. (1998). O doverii militsii, organam vnutrennikh del [About trust of police and institutions of interior affairs]. Retrieved on May 12, 2006, from www.fom.ru.

FOM. (1999). A v kakoi mere lichno vy doveryaete segodnya militsii, organam vnutrennikh del [To what degree do you personally trust police and institutions of interior affairs today?]. Retrieved on May 12, 2006, from www.fom.ru.

FOM. (2001a). Poslednie dva-tri mesjatsa vam prikhodilos' ili ne prikhodilos' imet' delo, obschat'sja s sotrudnikami militsii? Esli da to to kakoe vpechatlenie v tselom u vas slozhilos' ot etogo obschenija - polozhitel'noe ili otritsatel'noe? [Did you have to deal with the Police officers in the last few months?]. Retrieved on June 22, 2011, from www.fom.ru.

FOM. (2001b). Reitingi doveria/nedoveriya institutam obschestva [Ratings of trust and distrust of the societal institutions]. Retrieved on May 12, 2006, from www.fom.ru.

FOM. (2002a). K kakim iz perechislennykh institutov obschestva vy otnosites' otritsatelno, c nedoveriem? Rabotu kakikh iz nikh vy otsenivaete kak plokhuju? [Public attitudes toward other societal institutions]. Retrieved on June 17, 2011, from www.fom.ru.

Fom. (2002b). K kakim iz perechislennykh institutov obschestva vy otnosites' polozhitel'no, s doveriem? Rabotu kakikh iz nikh vy otsenivaete kak khoroshuju? [Public attitudes toward other societal institutions]. Retrieved on June 17, 2011, from www.fom.ru.

FOM. (2002c). Kak po vashej otsenke, segodnja rabotaet MVD - khorosho ili plokho? [To what degree are you personaly satisfied with the work of the Ministry of Interior Affairs?]. Retrieved on June 17, 2011, from www.fom.ru.

FOM. (2002d). Korruptsia v Rossii [Corruption in Russia]. Retrieved on May 12, 2006, from www.fom.ru.

FOM. (2002e). Reitingi doveria/nedoveriya institutam obschestva [Ratings of trust and distrust of the societal institutions]. Retrieved on May 12, 2006, from www.fom.ru.

FOM. (2002). Kak po vashemu mneniju, rabotaet militsija, kak ona spravljetsja so svoimi objazannostjami - otlichno, khorosho, udovletvoritel'no, plokho ili ochen' plokho? [To what degree are you personaly satisfied with the work of the Militia?] Retrieved on June 7, 2011, from www.fom.ru.

FOM. (2003a). Kak po vashemu mneniju, rabotajut segodnja uchastkovye militsionery, kak oni spravljautsja so svoimi objazannostjami -otlichno, khorosho, udovletvoritel'no, plokho ili ochen' plokho? [To what degree are you personaly satisfied with the work of the Divisional officers?]. Retrieved on June 17, 2011, from www.fom.ru.

FOM. (2003b). Skazhite, pozhailusta, kogda v poslednii raz vy videli svoego uchastkovogo militsionera ili obschalis' s nim? [When was the last time you saw your divisional officer?]. Retrieved on June 22, 2011, from www.fom.ru.

FOM. (2003c). Stolichnaja militsia rabotaet plokho? [Public opinion about the work of the Police in Moscow]. Retrieved on June 23, 2011, from www.fom.ru.

FOM. (2004a). Byvaet li, chto, narushiv pravila dorozhnogo dvizhenija, vy daete den'gi sotrudniku GIBDD naprjmuju, bez kvitantsii? Esli byvaet to chasto ili redko? (If you were ever stopped for violating the Traffic rules, did you ever give money directly to a Traffic Police officer, instead of being issued a ticket?). Retrieved on June 22, 2011, from www.fom.ru.

FOM. (2004b). Po vashemu mneniju, kak segodnja rabotaet GIBDD, kak ona spravljaetsja so svoiomi objazannostjami - khorosho, udovletvoritelno ili plokho? [To what degree are you personally satisfied with the work of the Traffic Police?]. Retrieved on June 17, 2011, from www.fom.ru.

FOM. (2004c). Za poslednii god vam prixodilos' ili ne prixodilis' imet' delo s sotrudnikami GIBDD? Esli da to kakoe vpechatlenie v tselom ostalos' u vas ot etogo obshenija - polozhitel'noe ili otritsateljnoe? [Did you recently have to deal with the Traffic Police officers? What impression did the Traffic Police officers make on you?] Retrieved on June 22, 2011, from www.fom.ru.

FOM. (2005). Militsia i ee reputatsiya [Police and its reputation]. Retrieved on May 12, 2006, from www.fom.ru.

FOM. (2006). Vy kogda-nibud' davali ili nikogda ne davali vzjatku dolzhnostnomu litsu? [Did you ever give a bribe to the executive officer?]. Retrieved on June 22, 2011, from www.fom.ru.

FOM. (2007). Novatsii v otnosheniyakh mezhdu GIBDD i voditelyami [The new relationship between the traffic police and the drivers]. Retrieved on May 12, 2006, from www.fom.ru.

FOM. (2008a). Kak po vashemu mneniju, rabotajut segodnja uchastkovye militsionery, kak oni spravljautsja so svoimi objazannostjami otlichno, khorosho, udovletvoritelno, plokho ili ochen' plokho? [To what degree are you personaly satisfied with the work of the Divisional officers?]. Retrieved on June 17, 2011, from www.fom.ru.

FOM. (2008b). Kak vy schitaete, kakoe otnoshenie k rabotnikam militsii segodnja preobladaet sredi naselenija - polozhitelnoe ili otrizatelnoe? [Public attitudes toward the Militia among Russian society]. Retrieved on June 17, 2011, from www.fom.ru.

FOM. (2008c). O militsii i militsionerakh [About police and police officers]. Retrieved on November 24, 2010, from http://bd.fom.ru/report/cat/power/pow_l/d084423.

FOM. (2008d). Skazhite, a vam kogda-nibud' prikhodilosj ili nikogda ne prikhodilos' davat' vzjatku sotrudnikam militsii? I esli prikhodilos' to komu - sotrudnikam avtoinspektsii, sotrudnikam drugikh podrazdelenii militsii ili tem i drugim? [Did you ever give a bribe to a Police officer?]. Retrieved on June 22, 2011, from www.fom.ru.

Fom. (2008e). Vy kogda-nibud' obraschalis' ili nikogda ne obraschalisj v dezhurnuju chast' ili rajonnoe otdelednie militsii? I esli da to kogda eto bylo v poslednii raz? [How frequently the community applies to the Police]. Retrieved on June 22, 2011, from www.fom.ru.

FOM. (2009). Kak vy schitaete, kakoe otnoshenie k rabotnikam militsii segodnja preobladaet sredi naselenija? [Public attitudes toward the Militia among Russian society]. Retrieved on June 17, 2011, from www.fom.ru.

FOM. (2010a). Kak vy otnosites' k idee o pereimenovanie? [Public attitudes toward the renaming of the Militia to the Police]. Retrieved on June 17, 2011, from www.fom.ru.

FOM. (2010b). Kak vy schitaete, segodnja tam, gde vy zhivete, militsija rabotaet khorosho ili plokho? [To what degree are you personally satisfied with the work of the Militia in your neighborhood?]. Retrieved on June 17, 2011, from www.fom.ru.

FOM. (2010c). Osvedomlennost' o podgotovke novogo zakona "O Politsii." [Public awareness about adoption of the federal law "About the Police"]. Retrieved on June 17, 2011, from www.fom.ru.

FOM. (2010d). Po vashemu mneniju, v poslednee vremja tam, gde vi zhivete, militsija rabotaet luchshe ili khuzhe chem prezhde? [Have you noticed recently any improvements in the work of the Police in your neighborhood?]. Retrieved on June 23, 2011, from www.fom.ru.

FOM. (2011a). 1 marta 2011 goda vstupaet v silu zakon o "Politsii". Militsija pereimenovana v politsiju.Vy znaete, chto-to slyshali ili slyshate vpervye? [Public awareness about adoption of the new federal law "About Police". Public attitudes toward the renaming the Militia to the Police]. Retrieved on June 17, 2011, from www.fom.ru.

FOM. (2011b). Gotovit'sja novyj zakon "O Politsii". Znaete chto-to, slyshali o nem ili shlyshate o nem vpervye, chto etot zakonoproekt dostupen dlja obsuzhdenija na spetsialnom saite? [What do you know about adoption of new federal law about "Police"? Have you ever heard that this draft bill is available for public debates via Internet?]. Retrieved on June 17, 2011, from www.fom.ru.

FOM. (2011c). K kakim is perechislennykh institutov obschestva vy otnosites polozhitelno, s doveriem? Rabotu kakikh iz nikh vy otsenivaete kak khoroshuju ili udoletvoritelnuju? [Public satisfaction with the work of societal institutions. The level of trust of societal institutions]. Retrieved on June 17, 2011, from www.fom.ru.

FOM. (2011d). K kakim iz perechislennykh institutov obschestva vy otnosites otritsatelno, s nedoveriem? Rabotu kakikh iz nikh vy otsenivaete kak plokhuju ili neudoletvoritelnuju? [Public satisfaction with work of the societal institutions. The level of distrust of the societal institutions] Retrieved on June 17, 2011, from www.fom.ru.

FOM. (2011e). Kak vy lichno otnosities k militsii - polozhitelno ili otritsatelno? [To what degree are you personally satisfied with the work of the Militia?]. Retrieved on June 17, 2011, from www.fom.ru.

FOM. (2011f). Kak vy schitaete, posle vstuplenija v silu novogo zakona "O Politsii" rabota pravookhranitelnykh organov uluchshitsja, ukhudshitsja ili ne izmenitsja? [Public opinion about the impact of the adoption of the new federal law "About Police" on daily police work.] Retrieved on June 17, 2011, from www.fom.ru.

FOM. (2011g). Vospriyatie urovnya prestupnosti [Perceptions of crime rates]. Retrieved on July 17, 2011, from http://bd.fom.ru/report/cat/power/pow_terr/crim/d111115.

IKSI. (1996). Monitoring IKSI 1996-IV [Institute of Complex Strategic Research]. Retrieved on February 8, 2010, from http://sophist.hse.ru.

IKSI. (1999). Monitoring IKSI 1999-II [Institute of Complex Strategic Research]. Retrieved on February 8, 2010, from http://soph ist.hse.ru.

INDEM. (2001a). Diagnostika rossiiskoi korruptsii [Diagnostics of Russian corruption]. Retrieved on November 25, 2010, from http://soph ist.hse.ru/.

INDEM. (2001b). Raspredelenie (v prozentakh) chastot otvetov respondentov na voprosy (popadali li vy korruptsionnuju situatsiju i davali li v neji vzjatku?) [How often have you been involved in the corruption situation (how did you resolve it)?]. Retrieved on June 22,2011, from www.wciom.ru.

IS_RAN. (1992). Zerkalo mnenii 1992-III [The mirror of opinions]. Retrieved on February 8, 2010, from http://sophist.hse.ru.

IS_RAN. (1995). Zerkalo mnenii 1995-IX [The mirror of opinions]. Retrieved on February 8, 2010, from http://sophist.hse.ru.

LEVADA. (2004a). Kurier 2004-10. Doveryaete li vy pravookhranitel'nym organam [Do you trust law enforcement agencies?]. Retrieved on February 14, 2010, from http://sophist.hse.ru/.

LEVADA. (2004b). Otnoshenie k militsii sredi zhitelei krupnykh gorodov Rossii [Public attitudes of police among residents of large urban cities of Russia]. Retrieved on November 14, 2010, from http://www.levada.ru/milicia04.html.

LEVADA. (2007a). Kak vy otsenivaete rabotu militsii v vashem raione? [Public satisfaction with the work performance of the Militia in the region]. Retrieved on June 17, 2011, from www.levada.ru.

LEVADA. (2007b). Napravleny li usilija militsii seichas v osnovnom "na obespechen. ie tol'ko sobstvennykh interesov"? [Public opinion about "Do the Police mostly concerns themselves with their own interests?"]. Retrieved on June 22, 2011, from www.levada.ru.

LEVADA. (2008). Otnoshenie naseleniya k reforme militsii [Public attitudes of police reform]. Retrieved on July 19, 2011, from http://www.levada.ru/press/2008031901.html.

LEVADA. (2010a). Kak vi dumaete deistvitel'no li budet provedna radical'naja reforma militsii ili vse svedet'sj k dekorativnomu pereimenovaniju i perestanovke nachal'stva? [Public opinion about adoption of the new federal law "About Police." How drastic is the impact supposed to be?]. Retrieved on June 17, 2011, from www.levada.ru.

LEVADA. (2010b). Otnoshenie rossiyan k militsii [Public attitudes of police among Russians]. Retrieved on November 14, 2010, from http://www.levada.ru/press/2010111001.html.

Public_Verdict. (2008). Otnoshenie nasseleniya k reforme militsii [Public attitudes about police reform]. Retrieved on November 25, 2010, from http://www.publicverdict.org/topics/research/reform_police.html.

Robertson, A. (2005). Criminal Justice Policy Transfer to Post-Soviet States: Case of Police Reform in Russia and Ukraine. *European Journal of Criminal Policy and Research*, 11(1), 128.

ROMIR. (2000). Omnibus ROMIR 2000-10. Retrieved on February 8, 2010, from http://sophist.hse.ru.

ROMIR. (2004). Tsyfry I facty: Doverie vlast' [Numbers and Facts: Trust in the government]. Research report. Retrieved on May 4, 2006, from www.romir.ru.

ROMIR. (2005a). Tret' rossiyan doveryayut prezidentu, a tret' - nikomu [One third of Russians trust the President, and one third doesn't trust anyone]. Retrieved on November 25, 2010, from http://www.romir.ru/news/res_results/14.html.

ROMIR. (2005b). Tsyfry I facty: Chto zchelaut grazdane svoei militsii [Numbers and Facts: What Russian citizens wish to their police]. Retrieved on May 4, 2006, from www.romir.ru.

ROMIR. (2006). Tsyfry i facty. Chestnost' vlasti [Numbers and Facts. The honesty of authorities]. Retrieved on May 4, 2006, from www.romir.ru.

ROMIR. (2011a). Tzifry i facty. Kak vy otnosites' k vozmozhnosti o pereimenovanii? [Public attitudes toward the possibility of renaming the Militia the Police]. Retrieved on June 17, 2011, from www.romir.ru.

ROMIR. (2011b). Tzifry i facty. Slyshali li vy chto-to o proekte federal'nogo zakona "O Politsii"? [Public awarness about adoption of the new federal law "About Police"]. Retrieved on June 17, 2011, from www.romir.ru.

WCIOM. (1989). Omnibus WCIOM 1989-20. Retrieved on November 25, 2010, from http://sophist.hse.ru.

WCIOM. (1990). Omnibus WCIOM 1990-3. Retrieved on November 25, 2010, from http://sophist.hse.ru.

WCIOM. (1991a). Fakt 1991-2. Retrieved on August 25, 2011, from http://sophist.hse.ru.

WCIOM. (1991b). Omnibus WCIOM 1991-2. Retrieved on November 25, 2010, from http://sophist.hse.ru.

WCIOM. (1992). Fakt 1992-2. Retrieved on August 25, 2011, from http://sophist.hse.ru.

WCIOM. (1993a). Fakt 1993-5. Retrieved on August 25, 2011, from http://sophist.hse.ru.

WCIOM. (1993b). Monitorign sotsial'no ekonomicheskikh peremen 1993-2 [Monitoring of the social economic changes]. Retrieved on November 25, 2010, from http://sophist.hse.ru.

WCIOM. (1993c). Monitoring sotsialno-ekonomichestkih peremen 1993-5 [Monitoring of socio-economic changes]. Retrieved on August 25, 2011, from http://sophist.hse.ru.

WCIOM. (1994). Monitoring sotsial'no ekonomicheskikh peremen 1994-1 [Monitoring of the social economic changes]. Retrieved on November 25, 2010, from http://sophist.hse.ru.

WCIOM. (1995a). Kurier 1995-12 [Courier]. Retrieved on August 25, 2011, from http://sophist.hse.ru.

WCIOM. (1995b). Monitoring sotsialno-ekonomichestkih peremen 1995-1 [Monitoring of socio-economic changes]. Retrieved on August 25, 2011, from http://sophist.hse.ru.

WCIOM. (1995c). Omnibus WCIOM 1995-4. Retrieved on November 25, 2010, from http://sophist.hse.ru.

WCIOM. (1996). Kurier 1996-1 [Courier]. Retrieved on August 25, 2011, from http://sophist.hse.ru.

WCIOM. (1997). Kurier 1997-1 [Courier]. Retrieved on August 25, 2011, from http://sophist.hse.ru.

WCIOM. (1998). Monitoring sotsialno-ekonomichestkih peremen 1998-7 [Monitoring of socio-economic changes]. Retrieved on August 25, 2011, from http://sophist.hse.ru.

WCIOM. (1999). Monitoring sotsialno-ekonomichestkih peremen 1999-7 [Monitoring of socio-economic changes]. Retrieved on August 25, 2011, from http://sophist.hse.ru.

WCIOM. (2000a). Monitoring sotsialno-ekonomichestkih peremen 2000-1 [Monitoring of socio-economic changes]. Retrieved on August 25, 2011, from http://sophist.hse.ru.

WCIOM. (2000b). Omnibus WCIOM from August 30, 2000. Retrieved on November 25, 2010, from http://wciom.ru/zh/print_q.php?s_id=339&_id=27266&da te=30.08.2000.

WCIOM. (2001a). Monitoring sotsialno-ekonomichestkih peremen 2001-1 [Monitoring of socio-economic changes]. Retrieved on August 25, 2011, from http://sophist.hse.ru.

WCIOM. (2001b). Na skol'ko vy udovletvoreny dejatel'nost'ju militsii v masshtabakh Rossii? [Public satisfaction with the work of the Militia across the country]. Retrieved on June 17, 2011, from www.wciom.ru.

WCIOM. (2001c). Na skol'ko vy udovletvoreny dejatel'nost'ju militsii v tom meste gde vi prozhivaete? [To what degree are you personally satisfied with the work of the Militia in your neighborhood?]. Retrieved on June 17, 2011, from www.wciom.ru.

WCIOM. (2002a). Kak vam kazhetsja, po sravneniju s tem chto bylo dva goda nazad, militsija stala rabotat'.......? [Public opinion about improvements in the work of the Police during two previous years]. Retrieved on June 23, 2011, from www.wciom.ru.

WCIOM. (2002b). Monitoring sotsialno-ekonomichestkih peremen 2002-7 [Monitoring of socio-economic changes]. Retrieved on August 25, 2011, from http://sophist.hse.ru.

WCIOM. (2002c). Naskol'ko vy udovletvoreny dejatel'nost'ju militsii v tselom? [Public satisfaction with the work performance of the Militia]. Retrieved on June 17, 2011, from www.wciom.ru.

WCIOM. (2002d). Naskol'ko vy udovletvorerny dejatel'nost'ju militsii v tom meste gde vy prozhivaete? [To what degree are you personally satisfied with the work of the Militia in your neighborhood?]. Retrieved on June 17, 2011, from www.wciom.ru.

WCIOM. (2002e). Omnibus WCIOM from August 15, 2002. Retrieved on November 25, 2010, from http://wciom.ru/zh/print_q.php?s_id=293&q_id=23372&date=15.08.2002.

WCIOM. (2003a). Kak vam kazhetsja, po sravneniju s tem chto bylo dva goda nazad, militsij stala rabotat'.......? [Public opinion about improvements in the work of the Police during two previous years]. Retrieved on June 23, 2011, from www.wciom.ru.

WCIOM. (2003b). Monitoring sotsialno-ekonomichestkih peremen 2003-1 [Monitoring of socio-economic changes]. Retrieved on August 25, 2011, from http://sWCIOM. (2004a). Kak vam kazhetsja, po sravneniju s tem chto bylo dva goda nazad, militsija stala rabotat'.......? [Public opinion about improvements in the work of the Police during two previous years]. Retrieved on June 23, 2011, from www.wciom.ru.

WCIOM. (2004b). Kak vy otsenivaete rabotu militsii v nashem regione? [To what degree are you satisfied with the work of the Militia in your region?]. Retrieved on June 17, 2011, from www.wciom.ru.

WCIOM. (2004c). Kak vy otsenivaete rabotu militsii? [Public satisfaction with the work performance of the Militia]. Retrieved on June 17, 2011, from www.wciom.ru.

WCIOM. (2004d). Otnoshenie rossiyan k militiss [Attitudes of Russians about police]. Retrieved on November 25, 2010, from http://wciom. ru/index.php?id=268&uid=978.

WCIOM. (2004e). Prihodilos' li vam za poslednij god nabludat' deistvija sotrudnikov organov vnutrennih del, pri kotoryx, na vash vzgljad, dopuskalis' narushenija prav cheloveka? [Did you recently see law enforcement officers ignoring human rights?]. Retrieved on June 13, 2011, from www.wciom.ru.

WCIOM. (2005a). Kak vam kazhetsja, po sravneniju s tem chto bylo dva goda nazad, militsij stala rabotat'.......? [Public opinion about improvements in the work of the Police during two previous years]. Retrieved on June 23, 2011, from www.wciom.ru.

WCIOM. (2005b). Omnibus WCIOM from September 21, 2005. Retrieved on November 25, 2010, from http://wciom.ru/zh/print_q.php?s_id=159&q_id=13300&date=21.09.2005.

WCIOM. (2005c). Prikhodilos' li vam predlagat' den'gi i podarki sotrudnikam pravookhranitel'nykh organov? [Did you ever give a bribe (monetary or non-monetary) to a law-enforcement agency officer?]. Retrieved on June 22, 2011, from www.wciom.ru.

WCIOM. (2005d). Prixodilos' li vam nabludat' deistvija sotrudnikov militsii pri kotoryh narushalis' prava cheloveka? [Have you ever seen The Militia's officers ignoring human rights?]. Retrieved on June 17, 2011, from www.wciom.ru.

WCIOM. (2006a/2006b). Kak by vy otsenili dejatel'nost' organov vnutrennikh del? [Public satisfaction with the work performance of Ministry of Interior Affairs]. Retrieved on June 17, 2011, from www.wciom.ru.

WCIOM. (2006b). Omnibus WCIOM from May 30, 2006. Retrieved on November 25, 2010, from http://wciom.ru/zh/print_q.php?s_id=371&q_id=30025&date=30.05.2006.

WCIOM. (2006c). Omnibus WCIOM from July 7, 2006. Retrieved on November 25, 2010, from http://wciom.ru/zh/print_q.php?s_id=363&q_id=29443&date=07.07.2006.

WCIOM. (2007). Omnibus WCIOM from November 11, 2007. Retrieved on November 25, 2010, from http://wciom.ru/zh/print_q.php?s_id=322&q_id=25929&date=11.11.2007.

WCIOM. (2008). Omnibus WCIOM from September 7, 2008. Retrieved on November 25, 2010, from http://wciom.ru/zh/print_q.php?s_id=569&q_id=40787&date=07.09.2008.

WCIOM. (2009a). Kak vy v tselom otsenivaete rabotu militsii v nashem regione? [Public satisfaction with the work of the Militia in the region] Retrieved on June 17, 2011, from www.wciom.ru.

WCIOM. (2009b). Prikhodilos' li za poslednie 12 mesjatsev vam ili chlenam vashej sem'i imet' delo s sotrudnikami organov vnutrennikh del? Esli da, to kakovy v zelom resultaty? [Did you (or members of your family have to deal with officers of interior affairs in the last twelve months?]. Retrieved on June 22, 2011, from www.wciom.ru.

WCIOM. (2009c). Prikhodilos' li za poslednie 12 mesjatsev vam ili chlenam vashej sem'i imet' delo s sotrudnikami organov vnutrennikh del? Esli da, to kakovy v zelom resultaty [Did you (or members of your family have to deal with officers of interior affairs in the last twelve months? (refers to the citizens of Moscow and St. Petersburg)] Retrieved on June 22, 2011, from www.wciom.ru.

WCIOM. (2009d). Rossiyane o militsii: otsenka, emotsii, otnoshenie [Russians about police: assessment, emotions, attitudes]. Retrieved on November 25, 2010, from http://wciom.ru/index.php?id=268&uid=11972

WCIOM. (2010a). Kak otrazitsj na rabote militsii prinjatie novogo zakona? [Public opinion about the impact of the new federal law on the routine work of the Militia]. Retrieved on June 17, 2011, from www.wciom.ru.

WCIOM. (2010b). Kak vy v tselom otsenivaete rabotu militsiii v nashem regione? [Public satisfaction with the work of the Militia in the region]. Retrieved on June 17, 2011, from www.wciom.ru.

WCIOM. (2010c). Prikhodilos' li za poslednie 12 mesjatsev vam ili chlenam vashej sem'i imet' delo s sotrudnikami organov vnutrennikh del? Esli da, to kakovy v tselom resultaty? [Did you (or members of your family) have to deal with officers of interior affairs in the last twelve months?] Retrieved on June 22, 2011, from www.wciom.ru.

WCIOM. (2010d). Rossiiskaya miltisiya: effektivnost' i doverie grazhdan [Russian police: effectiveness and public trust]. Retrieved on November 25, 2010, from http://wciom.ru/index.php?id=268&uid=13676.

WCIOM. (2011). Odobrjaete li vy dejtel'nost' pravookhranitel'ykh organov? [Public satisfaction with the work of law enforcement agencies]. Retrieved on June 17, 2011, from www.wciom.ru.

Wolf, S. Assessing Eastern Europe's anti-corruption performance: views from the Council of Europe, OECD, and Transparency International. *Global Crime, 11*(2), 99–121.

Wolin, S., & Slusser, R. M. (1957). *The Soviet Secret Police.* New York: Frederick A. Praeger Publisher.

ZIRCON. (2001). Obschestvennoe mnenie ob organakh gosudarstvennoi bezopasnosti [Public opinion about the state security agencies]. Retrieved on April 5, 2006, from www.zircon.ru.

Index

D

R

For Product Safety Concerns and Information please contact our EU
representative GPSR@taylorandfrancis.com
Taylor & Francis Verlag GmbH, Kaufingerstraße 24, 80331 München, Germany

www.ingramcontent.com/pod-product-compliance
Ingram Content Group UK Ltd.
Pitfield, Milton Keynes, MK11 3LW, UK
UKHW022009180926
475701UK00003B/281

* 9 7 8 0 3 6 7 8 7 8 7 9 5 *